THE METHOD OF EARLY ADVAITA VEDĀNTA

The Method of Early Advaita Vedānta

A Study of Gauḍapāda, Śaṅkara, Sureśvara and Padmapāda

MICHAEL COMANS

MOTILAL BANARSIDASS PUBLISHERS
PRIVATE LIMITED • DELHI

First Edition: Delhi, 2000

ISBN: 81-208-1722-2

Also available at:
MOTILAL BANARSIDASS
236, 9th Main III Block, Jayanagar, Bangalore 560 011
41 U.A. Bungalow Road, Jawahar Nagar, Delhi 110 007
8 Mahalaxmi Chamber, Warden Road, Mumbai 400 026
120 Royapettah High Road, Mylapore, Chennai 600 004
Sanas Plaza, 1302 Baji Rao Road, Pune 411 002
8 Camac Street, Calcutta 700 017
Ashok Rajpath, Patna 800 004
Chowk, Varanasi 221 001

Printed in India
BY JAINENDRA PRAKASH JAIN AT SHRI JAINENDRA PRESS,
A-45 NARAINA, PHASE-I, NEW DELHI 110 028
AND PUBLISHED BY NARENDRA PRAKASH JAIN FOR
MOTILAL BANARSIDASS PUBLISHERS PRIVATE LIMITED,
BUNGALOW ROAD, DELHI 110 007

for my parents

Contents

Acknowledgments

There are a number of people who enabled this book to be possible, even though some of them may think they have had no direct connection with it; here I have in mind my co-students in the period 1980-82, and they deserve my thanks. To single out the people whom I would especially like to acknowledge, I refer firstly to my Vedānta *ācārya*, Śrī Swami Dayānanda Saraswatī, without whose teaching none of this work would have been possible. I would then like to thank his student, and my *gurubhai*, Swami Paramārthānanda, of Chennai, who is always willing to discuss with me some obscure matter and make me the beneficiary of his clarity and his kindness. I wish to thank Dr R. Krishnamurthi Śāstrī, Professor of Vedānta, Madras Sanskrit College, under whose able guidance it became possible for me to understand at least a significant portion of the *Pañcapādikā*.

I would like to acknowledge here the great assistance of my wife, Archanā, for her willing support of my interests. I would like to mention the help of my friend, Mr Craig Littler, who took the trouble to read an early draft of some of the chapters, and who gave me his advice as well as assistance in procuring materials. I would also like to acknowledge the staff of the School of Asian Studies and of the School of Religion, at The University of Sydney, who generously assisted me during my time teaching there. Professor J.W. de Jong deserves my thanks, firstly for bringing to my attention the importance of Śaṅkara's commentary on the first *pāda* of the second chapter of the *Brahmasūtra*, when we read that portion in class during the time I was his Ph.D. student. And also for supplying some references to do with my work on Gauḍapāda and Buddhism. I wish also to acknowledge the assistance of Dr Richard V. De Smet, S.J. (1916-97) who kindly sent me a copy of his doctoral thesis. Dr A.J. Alston has been of assistance in loaning me a copy of his doctoral thesis. My thanks, too, to Stephen Cross, for providing me with a copy of Dr Alston's translation of the *Mūlāvidyānirāsa* by Saccidānandendra Sarasvatī, as well as for some editorial assistance. Finally, I would like to acknowledge the contributions of those scholars who commented upon an earlier version of the text.

ये गुणा इह दृश्यन्त उक्तशिष्टगणस्य ते ।
ये त्ववशिष्टदोषास्ते मत्स्था न परतां गताः ॥

Introduction

A number years ago, in Australia, I met an Indian Jesuit priest who lived in India where he taught Zen. As his interest in Zen seemed rather unusual considering his vocation, I asked him whether he ever had the opportunity to study Vedānta. He said that, yes, he had studied some Vedānta, but he could not find a method in it. When I naively asked him to tell me about the method he found in Zen, he smilingly replied: "Just sitting!". This meeting was not the reason I undertook to write this book but it served as a motivation to include some discussion and clarification on the method of Advaita Vedānta.

In this book I try to explain the teachings and the method of Advaita Vedānta as seen in the writings of four early Advaitins: Gauḍapāda, Śaṅkara, and his disciples Sureśvara and Padmapāda. I have not discussed the work of that other great scholar of the period, Maṇḍanamiśra, except to show some differences between his views and those of Śaṅkara and Sureśvara. The topic of method is directly addressed in chapter six, though it underlies some of the issues raised in earlier chapters, particularly in chapters three and four, and it again figures in discussion towards the end of chapters seven and eight. I have summarised my views on the subject in the "Postscript on Method" at the end of this book.

While I have tried to write with as much objectivity as possible, my interest in Advaita is a personal one, and this book is the outcome of study extending over a number of years. I first began a serious investigation of Advaita Vedānta more than twenty years ago, when I had the good fortune to sit at the feet of Swami Dayānanda Saraswatī. For two and a half years I had the opportunity to study the Sanskrit grammar of Pāṇini and to listen to a number of Upaniṣads and other texts, and to study some Upaniṣads, *Kaṭha, Taittirīya* and *Māṇḍūkya*, with the commentary of Śaṅkara. At that time I also studied the *Bhagavadgītā* with Śaṅkara's commentary, as well as his commentary to the *Catussūtrī* (the first four *sūtras)* of the *Brahmasūtra.* Later, staying in Rishikesh, I had the opportunity to listen to Swami Dayānanda teach most of Sureśvara's *Naiṣkarmyasiddhi.* I still cherish the memory of that time, listening twice daily to the *Naiṣkarmyasiddhi,* and coming out from the late afternoon class into the chill evening air to feel the wind as it came down the valley, to hear the sound of the Gaṅgā as it rushed over rocks partially submerged in the middle of its stream, and then the sound of the conch announcing *ārati* at the small temple dedicated to Śiva as Gaṅgādhareśvara.

In preparation for this work I began to study each of these Advaita authors based on their acknowledged writings. As far as possible I have read and tried to explain each author on his own terms and not in the light of the later commentators, though it is not always possible, nor is it advisable, to simply ignore the commentators. For Gauḍapāda there is but a single source work, the *Gauḍapādakārikā.* For the chapters on Śaṅkara my three primary sources are, in order of importance: his commentary on the *Brahmasūtra,* his commentary on the *Bṛhadāraṇyaka* Upaniṣad, and then the *Upadeśasāhasrī* which is probably his only authentic non-commentarial work. I first read the commentary on the *Bṛhadāraṇyaka* in Sanskrit, taking assistance from Swami Mādhavānanda's very readable English translation. Then I carefully read through the full *Brahmasūtrabhāṣya* in Sanskrit, keeping as my companions over many months the fine translations of Swami Gambhīrānanda and George Thibaut. After these three sources, I relied on the commentaries to the *Taittirīya* and some of the other Upaniṣads according to my familiarity with them. I did not use the commentary on the *Māṇḍūkya* Upaniṣad in these chapters on Śaṅkara, for even though it may be an authentic commentary it has some unusual characteristics and frequently does not share the same standard as his other works. I also did not use his commentary on the *Bhagavadgītā* to any great extent. I have not relied at all on any works where there is considerable uncertainty concerning authorship, such the popular, but post-Śaṅkara, *Vivekacūḍāmaṇi.*

With regard to the chapter on Sureśvara, my primary source was the *Naiṣkarmyasiddhi.* I did go through his *Vārtika* on Śaṅkara's commentary to the *Taittirīya* Upaniṣad with the help of the translation of Dr R. Balasubramanian and I also attempted to cross the ocean of the *Vārtika* on the *Bṛhadāraṇyaka Upaniṣadbhāṣya,* but unlike Hanumān, I did not succeed in reaching the further shore. We are perhaps not yet in a position to do full justice to the thought of Sureśvara. The final chapter, on Padmapāda, required my reading, at least cursorily, through the full *Pañcapādikā* and then I concentrated on the important first section which is his commentary upon Śaṅkara's *Adhyāsabhāṣya*. I was fortunate to receive help from Dr R. Krishnamurthi Śāstrī, Professor of Vedānta at Madras Sanskrit College, who discussed this portion of the *Pañcapādikā* with me.

There are a couple of ways a reader can approach this book. The reader is of course welcome to go through the chapters sequentially. However, if one just wishes to gain a generally complete understanding of Śaṅkara, chapters four to six should prove sufficient, and I look upon these as forming the principal chapters of the book. Chapter four, then, might prove a good place to start. The chapter dealing with Sureśvara extends some of the points raised in the chapters on Śaṅkara. The chapter dealing with the work of Padmapāda is still more technical, and is for those who wish to enter into Śaṅkara's famous *Adhyāsabhāṣya* in greater detail. The three chapters on Gauḍapāda stand a little apart from the other chapters. While it is reasonably clear what Śaṅkara and his students are saying, it is not always so clear in the case of Gauḍapāda. I believe that Gauḍapāda was a follower of the Upaniṣadic tradition and that he was neither a Buddhist nor a "concealed Buddhist" and I have argued accordingly. That is not to down-play the numerous references to Buddhist literature in his work, which, it must be said, is something the traditional commentators have often failed to perceive. While there are real continuities between the major teachings of all the four *ācāryas*, and I have tried to note some of these, the connection between Gauḍapāda and his successors is not quite as strong as between Śaṅkara and his disciples and the chapters on Gauḍapāda could be read without reference to the other chapters if one so wished. The first of the three chapters on Gaudapada is especially lengthy and somewhat difficult in places, for it virtually forms a running commentary on most of the kārikās, and so it does not always lend itself to easy reading. The more general reader should feel free to pass over those passages in this chapter, or in any chapter, where the discussion involves more detail than is required. For the committed student of Advaita, however, I would suggest that there is benefit to be gained in proceeding carefully though at least most of the chapters of this book.

This book is based closely upon the source literature. I have tried to keep somewhat abreast of the secondary literature and from time to time I discuss views found in academic publications. With regard to the four Advaita authors whose works form the content of this book, I do not pretend to have addressed and clarified all the terminological and other difficulties that stand in our way of clearly comprehending their meaning. I do believe, however, to have contributed to an accurate understanding of these *ācāryas* through this examination of their teachings as it can be found in their own writings. In the chapters on Śaṅkara I have especially highlighted two issues that have not received sufficient attention in many of the publications dealing with Śaṅkara's thought. These are, firstly, the question about the nature of Īśvara in Śaṅkara's Advaita. This is a topic that has hereto been given a fairly scant treatment (though Rudolf Otto and Paul Hacker have stimulated my discussion on this important matter). Then there is the discussion of method, i.e., exactly how, and to what extent, does Śaṅkara understand the Upaniṣads to be a revelation about Brahman. I hope to have made some contribution to a better understanding of Advaita through my discussion of these two matters in particular. While there are numerous books on Advaita, they are not all reliable in their interpretations. I trust this book will be found reliable and reasonably accessible. I hope it will be of value to people who wish to gain a better understanding of the great tradition that is Advaita Vedānta, in one of its greatest periods.

Detailed Table of Contents

Information Regarding the Texts Cited

The references in the Notes to each chapter refer to the following editions. Unless otherwise stated, the translations are my own.

Gauḍapāda

All references concerning the *Gauḍapādakārikās* are to:
R.D. Karmarkar, (ed. and tr.) *Gauḍapāda-Kārikā.* Poona: Bhandarkar Oriental Research Institute, 1973.

Śaṅkara

Page and line references are to the following editions:

Works of Śaṅkarācārya in Original Sanskrit, vol. 1. *Ten Principal Upaniṣads with Śāṅkarabhāṣya.* Delhi: Motilal Banarsidass, 1978.

Works of Śaṅkarācārya in Original Sanskrit, vol.11. *Bhagavadgītā with Śāṅkarabhāṣya.* Delhi: Motilal Banarsidass, 1978.

Brahmasūtra-Śāṅkarabhāṣyam. Edited by J.L. Shastri. Delhi: Motilal Banarsidass, 1980.

Upadeśasāhasrī of Srī Sankarāchārya: A Thousand Teachings in two parts-prose and poetry. Translated by Swami Jagadānanda. 7th. ed. Madras: Sri Ramakrishna Math, 1984.

In addition to the references to the original works, I have also cited the page reference to a previously published translation, for the additional assistance of the reader. These references are to the following translations:

Swami Mādhavānanda (tr.), *The Bṛhadāraṇyaka Upaniṣad with the commentary of Śaṅkarācārya.* Calcutta: Advaita Ashrama, (5th Ed.) 1975.

Swami Gambhirananda (tr.), *Eight Upaniṣads With the Commentary of Śaṅkarācārya* (Two Vols.). Calcutta: Advaita Ashrama, 1977.

Swami Gambhirananda, (tr.) *Chāndogya Upaniṣad With the Commentary of Śrī Śaṅkarācārya.* Calcutta: Advaita Ashrama (n.d.).

Swami Gambhirananda (tr.), *Brahma-sūtra-bhāṣya of Śrī Śaṅkarācārya.* Calcutta: Advaita Ashrama, 1977.

Swami Gambhirananda (tr.), *Bhagavadgītā With the Commentary of Śaṅkarācārya.* Calcutta: Advaita Ashrama, 1984.

Sureśvara

Regarding the works of Sureśvara, references are to the following editions:

R. Balasubramanian (ed. and tr.), *The Naiṣkarmyasiddhi of Sureśvara.* Madras: Radhakrishnan Institute for Advanced Study in Philosophy, University of Madras, 1988.

R. Balasubramanian (ed. and tr.), *The Taittirīyopaniṣad Bhāṣya-Vārtika of Sureśvara.* Madras: Radhakrishnan Institute for Advanced Study in Philosophy, University of Madras, (revised ed.) 1984.

S. Subrahmanya Shastri (ed.), *Bṛhadāraṇyakopaniṣad Bhāṣyavārtikam (vol. 1), with the Commentary Śāstraprakāśikā of Ācārya Śrī Ānandagiri.* Varanasi: Mahesh Research Institute, 1982.

S. Subrahmanya Shastri (ed.), *Bṛhadāraṇyakopaniṣad Bhāṣyavārtikam (vol. 2), with the Commentary Śāstraprakāśikā of Ācārya Śrī Ānandagiri.* Varanasi: Mahesh Research Institute, 1990.

Padmapāda

References to the *Pañcapādikā* are to the following editions:

S. Srirāma Śāstrī and S.R. Krishnamurthi Śāstrī (ed.), *Pañcapādikā of Śrī Padmapādācārya with the commentaries Prabodhapariśodhinī of Ātmasvarūpa and Tārtparyārthadyotinī of Vijñānātman and Pañcapādikāvivaraṇa of Śrī Prakāśātman with Tātparyadīpikā of Citsukhācārya and Bhāvaprakāśikā of Nṛsimhāśramin Vol.1 comprising 1 and 2 Varṇakas.* Tirupati: Kendriya Sanskrit Vidyapeetha, 1985 (reprint of first two Varṇakas from the Madras Government Oriental Series CLV, 1958.).

S. Subrahmanyaśāstrī (ed.), *Srī Padmapādācārya's Pañcapādikā with the commentaries Vivaraṇa by Śrī Prakāśātmamuni, Tattvadīpana by Śrī Akhaṇḍānandamuni and Ṛjuvivaraṇa by Śrī Viṣṇubhaṭṭopādhyāya.* Varanasi: Mahesh Research Institute, 1992.

In addition, I have also cited the page reference to a previously published translation:

D. Venkataramiah (tr.), *The Pañcapādikā of Padmapāda.* Baroda: (Gaekwad's Oriental Series No. CVII) Oriental Institute, 1948.

Abbreviations

AU	Aitareya Upaniṣad
Bh	bhāṣya
BG	Bhagavadgītā
BU	Bṛhadāraṇyaka Upaniṣad
BS	Brahmasūtra
CU	Chāndogya Upaniṣad
GK	Gauḍapāda Kārikā
KaU	Kaṭha Upaniṣad
KeU	Kena Upaniṣad
MāU	Māṇḍūkya Upaniṣad
Mbh	Mahābhārata
MRI	Mahesh Research Institute Edition
MU	Muṇḍaka Upaniṣad
NS	Naiṣkarmyasiddhi
PP	Pañcapādikā
PU	Praśna Upaniṣad

ŚvU	Śvetāśvatara Upaniṣad
tr	Translation
TU	Taittirīya Upaniṣad
V	Vārttika
US	Upadeśasāhasrī

CHAPTER ONE

A Running Commentary upon Gauḍapāda's Kārikās

The name Gauḍapāda occurs among the lineage of teachers *(paramparā)* that students of Advaita Vedānta traditionally acknowledge when they commence their study of Śaṅkara's *Brahmasūtrabhāṣya:*

> I repeatedly bow down to Nārāyaṇa, to the one born from a lotus [Brahmā], to Vasiṣṭha, Śakti, and his son Parāśara, to Vyāsa, Śuka, to the great Gauḍapāda, to Govinda the best of yogis, then to his student Śrī Śaṅkarācārya, and to his students Padmapāda and Hastāmalaka, Toṭaka and the Vārttikakāra [Sureśvara], and others [up to and including] my own teacher.[1]

This list pays homage to a transmission of teaching that is believed to have commenced with Viṣṇu-Nārāyaṇa Himself, and to have been passed on through a succession of teachers down to present times. It includes divinities, Nārāyaṇa and Brahmā; human beings who figure in the legendary histories, Vasiṣṭha, Śakti, Parāśara, Vyāsa, and Śuka; and historical personages whose writings we possess, Gauḍapāda, Śaṅkara, Padmapāda, Hastāmalaka, Toṭaka and Sureśvara. The list does not say what kind of relationship existed between most of these figures, such as between Śuka and Gauḍapāda or between Gauḍapāda and Govinda, whereas it does mention a teacher-student relationship between some names, such as Govinda and Śaṅkara. In the best known of the traditional accounts of Śaṅkara's life, Mādhava's *Śaṅkaradigvijaya*, the relationships are spelled out more closely and it is said that Vyāsa was the son of Parāśara and

Śuka was the son of Vyāsa and that Gauḍapāda was the student of Śuka and the teacher of Govinda.[2] The historical accuracy of the accounts in the "biographies" of Śaṅkara cannot be determined with any certainty, but whether Gauḍapāda was directly the guru of Śaṅkara's teacher or whether he was a more distant guru, Gauḍapāda is nonetheless accepted by tradition as a figure of great importance in Advaita Vedānta and his collection of kārikās, or verses, are the earliest systematic Advaita treatise we possess.[3] Furthermore, tradition holds the kārikās to have been commented upon by Śaṅkara himself and although there is some uneasiness on this point, even from those within the Advaita tradition, nonetheless the tradition of authorship has been accepted by some modern scholars.[4] For these reasons the study of Gauḍapāda's kārikās forms a natural place to commence our investigation into early Advaita teachings and the method of spiritual liberation that it prescribes.

The *Gauḍapādakārikā* consists of four inter-related treatises, or "chapters".[5] About the relationship between these four I shall have something to say later. The first chapter is directly based upon the *Māṇḍūkya* Upaniṣad while the other three are independent of any specific text. The first chapter is called the "treatise concerning the scriptural text" *(Āgamaprakaraṇa)*, the second is the "treatise concerning unreality" *(Vaitathyaprakaraṇa)*, the third is the "treatise on non-duality" *(Advaitaprakaraṇa)* and the fourth is known as the "treatise on the quelling of the fire-brand" *(Alātaśāntiprakaraṇa)*. On the basis of numerous references to Buddhist writings, particularly in the fourth chapter, some scholars have thought that Gauḍapāda was possibly himself a Buddhist, or at least a *de facto* Buddhist in so far as he was heavily influenced by Mahāyāna Buddhism.[6] This view has been opposed by other scholars who have argued that Gauḍapāda should not be considered a Buddhist just because he showed a considerable familiarity with Buddhist thought.[7] I shall discuss this question in some detail later.

I will begin by offering a short explanation of the *Māṇḍūkya* Upaniṣad, so that we can better understand Gauḍapāda's first chapter which takes this Upaniṣad as its source text.

The *Māṇḍūkya* Upaniṣad

The *Māṇḍūkya* is the smallest of the ten major Upaniṣads. It consists of just twelve brief prose passages and is barely one printed page in length. The purpose of the *Māṇḍūkya* is to reveal that there is a single Absolute Reality which underlies the cosmos, yet is inherently acosmic, and which constitutes the essential "core", or "Self", of all beings. The Upaniṣad calls this Reality by the name Brahman and it explicitly says that Brahman is identical to the Self *(ayam ātmā brahma).* The Upaniṣad proceeds to reveal the true nature of the Self, as Brahman, by means of an investigation of the three states of ordinary human experience: waking, dream and dreamless sleep. The sacred Vedic syllable 'OM' is then used to provide a focus for contemplative insight into this teaching.

As mentioned, the means to reveal the true nature of the Self is the investigation of the states of waking, dream and dreamless sleep. Let us see how the Upaniṣad proceeds. It says that this Self can be conceived as having four "quarters" *(pādas).*

> The first quarter is *Vaiśvānara,* who is associated with the state of waking, whose consciousness is external, who has seven limbs and nineteen mouths, and who experiences gross objects. [MāU 3]

Here, the first quarter of the Self as associated with the waking state. But not only does it comprise the waker, it comprises the waking world as well. This Upaniṣad mantra is not just referring to the individual waker, but it refers to both the individual, the microcosm, and to the macrocosm. This can be seen by the use of the word *Vaiśvānara* which primarily refers to the Lord as identified with the total gross cosmos. The Lord, as so identified, is otherwise called in Vedānta as Viraṭ. The phrase "seven limbs" perhaps refers to the visualisation in the *Chāndogya* Upaniṣad 5.18.2, where it is said of the *Vaiśvānara* (Viraṭ) that heaven is the head, the eye is the sun, the mouth is fire, the vital-energy is wind, the trunk of the body is the sky, the bladder is the ocean and the feet are the earth. The phrase "nineteen mouths" does not refer to *Vaiśvānara,* but to the individual, having the five organs of knowledge (the organs of sight, sound, smell, taste and touch), the five organs of action (the organ of speech, hands, legs, the organ of excretion and the genitals), the five vital-energies (respiration, evacuation, circulation, regurgitation and digestion) and the four aspects of mental life (thought, intellect, memory and ego). Thus the mantra treats the individual, the microcosm, as well as the macrocosm, together, so that the waker can see itself as a part of the total cosmos, as a part to be included within the Whole.

> The second quarter is *Taijasa,* who is associated with the state of dream, whose consciousness is internal, who has seven limbs and nineteen mouths, and who experiences subtle objects. [MāU 4]

Here too, the individual and the total are treated together. Most of the words refer to the individual who is associated with the dream state, though the phrase "seven limbs" would again seem to refer to the macrocosm. So just as in the third mantra, where the microcosm is to be included in the macrocosm, in this mantra too, the individual, called as *taijasa,* is to be included in its macrocosmic counterpart, Hiraṇyagarbha, or the Lord as identified with the total subtle world.

> The state of deep sleep is where the sleeper does not desire any enjoyable object and does not see any dream. The third quarter is *Prājña,* who is associated with the state of sleep, who has become unified, who is just a mass of consciousness, who is full of bliss, who is verily an experiencer of bliss, and who is the doorway to the experience [of waking and dream]. [MāU 5]

This mantra speaks of the Self as associated with the state of deep sleep. Whereas the previous two mantras each treated the microcosm and the macrocosm together, this mantra speaks only of the microcosm while the following mantra speaks of the macrocosmic counterpart:

> This one is the Lord of all, this one is omniscient, this one is the inner-controller, this one is the source of all, the very place of origin and dissolution of all beings. [MāU 6]

This mantra refers to the Lord Itself as the macrocosm that includes the deep sleeper. Thus far the Upaniṣad has spoken of the Absolute Self associated with three conditions, that of the waker, dreamer and sleeper. The Self, in association with these three conditions, is what is known as an individual soul, and the latter is to be related to a corresponding macrocosmic world: the waker is to be included in the Lord as the total manifest physical world, the dreamer is to be included in the Lord as the total subtle world and the unmanifest condition of sleep is to be included in the causal nature of the Lord Itself.

The Upaniṣad then presents its principal mantra, which proceeds to negate all of the above: the state of waking together with the waking world, the state of dream together with the dream world, and the state of deep sleep and the causal world. Thus even the causality of God gets negated in the final revelation of the Absolute who (which) is the invariable Self unrelated to any state:

> They consider that the "fourth" is neither dream consciousness, nor waking consciousness, nor both dream as well as waking consciousness, nor is it a mass of consciousness, neither is it consciousness [i.e. a cognition], nor the absence of consciousness. It is unseen, it is outside the range of empirical dealings, it cannot be grasped [as an object], it is without a distinguishing characteristic [whereby it could be inferred], it is unthinkable, indescribable, it constitutes the essence of the single thought "I". It is where there is the cessation of the phenomenal world, it is peaceful, auspicious and non-dual. That is the Self, That is to be known. [MāU 7]

The term "fourth" *(turīya)* is used only in relation to the three states of waking, dream and deep sleep. It is incorrect to think that the "fourth" is some state of experience that is entirely separate from the three states. The "fourth" is the invariable substrate of the three states: the states of waking, dream and deep sleep are located in the "fourth". Waking, dream and sleep alternate, but the "fourth", the essential Self which is Brahman, does not undergo any change.[8] The essential Self is not the consciousness associated with the waking state *(bahiṣprajña),* nor the consciousness associated with the dream state *(antaḥprajña)*, nor is it the consciousness associated with the deep sleep state *(prajñānaghana)*. The essential Self is consciousness unassociated with any state: it is the pure Awareness (or Consciousness) *through which* the waking state along with the waking world, the dream state together with the dream world, and the unmanifest condition called "deep sleep", all stand revealed. The single positive statement, "it constitutes the essence of the single thought 'I'" *(ekātmapratyayasāra)*, should not be overlooked amidst the series of negations. This is a most important statement, for it directly indicates that the *turīya*, the pure Awareness, is the very core of the ego, and is thus the true Self of all.

If one inquires as to the relation between the three states and the "fourth", the Absolute Self, the answer is that there is no real relation between the three states and the Self because the three states are not truly real. That is why the absolute, the "fourth", is said to be acosmic: "It is where there is the cessation of the phenomenal world" *(prapañcopaśama)*. The Advaita understanding is that the fundamental reality, which is identical to our essential Self, is simple Awareness, in which occurs the waking state along with the entire waking world, the dream state together with the dream world, and the unmanifest condition of sleep. These states change and pass, they are only of apparent reality *(mithyā)*, but the absolute and unconditioned Awareness is ever constant, not altering during any of the states. As it is inherently unaffected by the states, it is said to be "peaceful" *(śānta)*, "auspicious" or "happy" *(śiva)*, and it is also said to be "non-dual" *(advaita)* since the three states do not share the same degree of reality as their pure Awareness substratum. They are appearances on the real, for in Advaita only the changeless is truly real and only Awareness is truly changeless. Gauḍapāda's entire teaching of *ajātivāda* is based upon these passages from the *Māṇḍūkya* Upaniṣad which teach that although the three states of experience do not exist in separation from the Self [A is non-separate from B] the Self is intrinsically unrelated to the states [B is separate from A].[9]

Before we proceed to examine the kārikās of Gauḍapāda, it may be worthwhile to first consider a recent interpretation of the *Māṇḍūkya*. It is an interpretation that has gained some currency in academic circles in recent times, as can be seen by the fact that the respected scholar of Śaṅkara, Richard De Smet, has incorporated it into his remarks on Advaita in the latest edition of the Jesuit publication, *Religious Hinduism.*[10] The author of this interpretation, Thomas Wood, has challenged the traditional Advaita understanding which links mantra six, cited above, ("This one is the Lord of all" etc.) with mantra five describing the state of deep sleep and the *prājña.* According to Wood, mantra six should not be read with mantra five, but mantras six and seven ought to be read together as they *both* refer to the *turīya.*[11] The *turīya* is described in positive terms in mantra six and in the language of negation in mantra seven. Wood argues that mantra five is complete in itself, for it concludes with the words *tṛtīyaḥ pādaḥ* ("the third quarter") just as mantras three and four conclude with *prathamaḥ pādaḥ* ("the first quarter") and *dvitīyaḥ pādaḥ* ("the second quarter") respectively. So the question is how are we to understand mantra six: should it be read along with mantra five, or with mantra seven? I believe Wood has raised a point that is worth considering, for prima facie it does seem that mantra six presents a problem. But I will endeavour to show why Advaitins have read mantras five and six together and have understood mantra seven as alone referring to the *turīya.*

The *Māṇḍūkya,* as Wood and others have noted, is based upon *Bṛhadāraṇyaka* Upaniṣad 4.2.1- 4.4.25. The statement in *Māṇḍūkya* five, referring to deep sleep ("where the sleeper does not desire any enjoyable object and does not see any dream") is a direct quotation from *Bṛhadāraṇyaka* 4.3.19. If we ask why it is that deep sleep seems to be a condition of nothingness, or unconsciousness, the *Bṛhadāraṇyaka* answers this question in 4.3.21 when it says:

> As a man, fully embraced by his beloved wife, does not know anything at all, either external or internal, so does this infinite being (self), fully embraced by the supreme Self *(prājñena-ātmanā),* not know anything at all, either external or internal.[12]

In sleep, the individual soul does not know anything because it is in a condition of oneness with the supreme Self *(prājñenātmanā).* In this passage, the supreme Self is called by the term *prājña-ātman.* Wood significantly does not mention this usage of the term *"prājña",* where it is used to refer to the supreme Self. The word *"prājña"* can therefore be used in two ways: it can refer to the sleeper and it can also refer to the supreme Self, the *prājñātman*, with whom the sleeper has become identified. In mantra five of the *Māṇḍūkya*, the word *"prājña"* describes the sleeper. Mantra six, however, does not refer to the sleeper but, as I mentioned earlier while commenting on that mantra, it refers to the Lord (the *prājñātman)* with whom the sleeper is identified. According to Śaṅkara, in his commentary on the *Brahmasūtra*, the *prājñātman* is none other than the highest Lord *(parameśvara)*.[13] So it is the *prājña*, as the highest Lord, who is being referred to in mantra six of the *Māṇḍūkya*. This is evident from the words of the passage, which mostly consists of quotations from various Upaniṣads describing the Lord: "this one is the Lord of all" (BU 4.4.22), "this one is omniscient" (MU 1.1.9), "this one is the inner-controller" (BU 3.7.1 ff.), "this one is the source of all" (MU 1.1.6).[14] Therefore I believe Wood is right in thinking that mantra six refers to God. But his objection to the Advaita teaching, which he interprets as saying that the Lord would then be identified with the sleeper, is a misconception of that teaching which actually says the reverse: in sleep, the sleeper *(prājña)* has become identified with the highest Lord, the *prājñātman*.

When Śaṅkara discusses the passage, "This one is the Lord of all" (BU 4.4.22), in his commentary on the *Brahmasūtra*, he says that these attributes of Lordship etc. are finally negated by the subsequent statement "not this, not this" (BU 4.4.22) which reveals the absolute Brahman as free from all attributes *(nirguṇa)*.[15] Therefore, according to Śaṅkara, the *prājñātman* is the Lord who is referred to in mantra six, but those attributes whereby Brahman is the cosmic Lord are subsequently negated from Brahman by the sentence "not this, not this" *(neti neti)* which negates all attributes in their entirety. The *turīya* is said to be "outside the range of empirical dealings" *(avyavahāryam)* whereas according to Śaṅkara the attributes of Lordship etc. fall within the sphere of empirical dealings.[16] In his commentary upon the *Bṛhadāraṇyaka*, Śaṅkara has specifically equated the *turīya* and the Self indicated by the terms *"neti neti"*.[17] Therefore we are in a position to understand why mantra six in the *Māṇḍūkya* is read together with mantra five: mantra six refers to the *prājñātman*, the Lord, or "God", with whom the sleeper *(prājña)* has become temporarily identified, or merged, whilst in the unmanifest condition called deep sleep. In mantra six everything has been reduced to the Lord. Mantra seven then negates the phenomenal world in its totality, the effects as well as their Cause, thus it negates even the attributes of Lordship from the Absolute, and then it indicates that the Absolute, the acosmic and unconditioned Brahman *(paraṁ brahman)*, is identical to one's own true Self.

We will have more to say on Śaṅkara's understanding of Brahman, as both the Lord and as the unconditioned Absolute, in chapters four and five.

(1) The *Āgamaprakaraṇa* of the *Gauḍapādakārikā*

Gauḍapāda inserted his first nine kārikās between mantras six and seven of the *Māṇḍūkya*. The first five of these kārikās are based upon mantras three to five, the other kārikās refer to mantra six. Gauḍapāda does not comment upon the first two mantras of the Upaniṣad, presumably considering them to be introductory. In his first kārikā he says:

> The all pervading one *(vibhu)* is *viśva* when its consciousness is external, it is *taijasa* when its consciousness is internal, and when a mass of consciousness it is *prājña*. The same one is thought of in three ways. [1.1]

In this kārikā Gauḍapāda changes the name *vaiśvānara*, occurring in mantra three, to *viśva*. This is significant in so far as he drops the Upaniṣad presentation of microcosm and macrocosm and he discusses only the former, i.e., the waker, dreamer and sleeper. He says that the one all pervasive reality *(vibhu)*, i.e., Brahman-Ātman, is considered to exist in a threefold manner: as the waker *(viśva)* who is characterised as having consciousness externally oriented *(bahiṣprajña)*, as the dreamer *(taijasa)* whose consciousness is internally oriented *(antaḥprajña)*, and as the sleeper *(prājña)* whose consciousness is massed together without distinction *(ghanaprajña)*. He then presents three locations in the body where the Self, as conditioned in this way by the three states, can be conceptually meditated: the *viśva* has its location in the right eye, the *taijasa* is within the mind and the *prājña* is in the space within the heart.

In the following two kārikās (three and four) he speaks of the three types of experience which relate to the Self as it exists in these three ways. He says:

> Know experience to be of three kinds. *Viśva* always experiences what is gross, *taijasa* experiences what is subtle and *prājña* always experiences bliss. [1.3]

There is thus a single all pervasive entity which acquires three different names as a result of being associated with three different states, and can be imagined as having three different locations in the body, and is further presented as having three different types of experience. The main points can be represented thus:

Subject	*Location*	*Object*
viśva (the Self associated with the waking state)	right eye	experiences physical objects
taijasa (the Self associated with the dream state)	mind	experiences subtle objects
prājña (the Self associated with the deep sleep state)	space in the heart	experiences bliss

Gauḍapāda adds a final comment to the above presentation when he says:

> He who knows both of these: what is experienced in the three states and who is said

> as the experiencer, that person, even while
> experiencing, is not tainted. [1.5]

Why is the person who understands the experiencer and the experienced in each of these states not tainted by experience? Gauḍapāda is saying that one and the same Self becomes associated with three different conditions: as the waker it experiences physical objects, as the dreamer it experiences mental objects, and as the sleeper it experiences blissful sleep. Each of these states has a subject and an object, but this relation is restricted to a particular state. There is a subject-object relation between the waker and the waking world, so long as one is awake. There is a subject-object relation between the dreamer and the dream world, so long as there is a dream. And there is a subtle experience of bliss in sleep. There are thus three different states of experience, each having its own subject-object relation. Such a relation holds good from its own standpoint, but not from the standpoint of the other states, because each state is negated when the other state is present. Waking experience is negated by dream, and dream by waking, and both are negated when there is the absence of specific cognition during deep sleep. The one who knows that the experiencer-experienced relation in any state, though valid from its own standpoint, is variable and hence not absolutely real, and who knows that the Self, though the experiencer in relation to each state, is not of itself the waker, dreamer or sleeper, but is the *turīya,* that person, even while experiencing, is not tainted by experience.

As we mentioned, kārikās six to nine form a comment upon mantra six of the *Māṇḍūkya* which refers to the Lord with whom the *prājña* is identified in sleep. Various expressions are used in this mantra to describe the Lord: "the Lord of all", "omniscient", "the inner-controller", "the source of all" and "the place of origin and dissolution of all beings". Among these expressions, the latter two speak of the Lord as the cause of the world and it is only this aspect of the mantra, having to do with the origin of the world, that Gauḍapāda takes up for comment in the four kārikās. In these kārikās he merely presents a number of differing views about the origin of the world. He begins by saying: "that there is an origin for all existing things is very evident" and he then lists a whole variety of opinions. The first resembles Sāṅkhya, if by the word *prāṇa* we can understand that *prakṛti* is meant: *"Prāṇa* creates everything, the *puruṣa* creates the rays of consciousness separately [from one another]". He then lists seven more opinions about creation: some say creation reveals the glory [of the Lord]; others look upon creation as comparable to a dream or magic *(svapnamāyā);* some say that creation is the will of the Lord; others, astrologers perhaps, say that things originate from time; some believe that creation is meant for the enjoyment [of the Lord]; others say it is His play. Others maintain that it is the very nature of the Lord to create, and they argue that it must be so because the Lord can have no unfulfilled desires.

The question arises as to whether Gauḍapāda accepts any of these views. Advaitins tend to see the statement that, "others look upon creation as comparable to a dream or magic" as expressing Gauḍapāda's own view. R.D. Karmarkar, however, is of the opinion that Gauḍapāda is here referring to the views of the Mahāyāna Buddhists, as expressed in the *Laṅkāvatārasūtra,* and he considers all the views to be those of Gauḍapāda's opponents.[18] I suggest that in these kārikās Gauḍapāda is merely presenting a number of opinions, none of which is actually representative of his own position, for in all of them there is the tacit acceptance of the fact of creation *(sṛṣṭi),* whereas Gauḍapāda - speaking, as we will see, from his standpoint of "absolute reality" *(paramārtha)* - is going to deny creation as a fact.

In kārikās ten to eighteen Gauḍapāda comments upon the important seventh mantra of the *Māṇḍūkya:*

> They consider that the "fourth" is neither dream consciousness, nor waking consciousness, nor both dream as well as waking consciousness, nor is it a mass of consciousness, neither is it consciousness [i.e. a cognition], nor the absence of consciousness. It is unseen, it is outside the range of empirical dealings, it cannot be grasped [as an object], it is without a distinguishing characteristic [whereby it could be inferred], it is unthinkable, indescribable, it constitutes the essence of the single thought, "I". It is where there is the cessation of the phenomenal world, it is peaceful, auspicious and non-dual. That is the Self, That is to be known. [MāU 7]

He briefly sums up the Upaniṣad mantra in a single kārikā before proceeding with his own commentary. He refers to one aspect of the *turīya* which was not stated in the Upaniṣad mantra, though it was hinted at by the word "peaceful" *(śānta)*, when he says that the *turīya* is free from all sorrow. The only specific word from the Upaniṣad that he cites here is the word "non-dual" *(advaita)*:

> The all pervading, effulgent one, is considered to be the "fourth": it is the Lord of the cessation of all sorrow, powerful, changeless, the non-dual [reality] of all things. [1.10]

Gauḍapāda now comments upon the teaching of the four "quarters" *(pādas)* of the Self and it is here, in kārikās eleven to fifteen, that he introduces his distinctive terminology and presents his own perspective of the Upaniṣad text. In the first two kārikās he says:

> The waker *(viśva)* and the dreamer *(taijasa)* are considered to be conditioned by cause *(kāraṇa)* and effect *(kārya)*. The sleeper *(prājña)* is conditioned solely by the cause. These two [cause and effect] do not exist in the *turīya*.[19] [1.11]

> The sleeper *(prājña)* does not know anything, it knows neither itself nor others, it knows neither truth nor falsehood. The *turīya* is always all-seeing. [1.12]

In kārikā eleven Gauḍapāda introduces the words "cause" *(kāraṇa)* and "effect" *(kārya)*, but he does not yet tell us what he means by these terms. In kārikā twelve he points out the difference between the sleeper and the *turīya*: the sleeper does not know anything, whereas the *turīya* is the invariable Awareness, the Seeing, for it reveals the states of waking, dream and dreamless sleep. In the first line of kārikā thirteen he indicates the common feature between the sleeper and the *turīya* and in the second line he again makes a distinction between them:

> Non-perception of duality is common to both the sleeper as well as the *turīya.* The sleeper is associated with "sleep that is the seed". But the "sleep that is the seed" does not exist in the *turīya.* [1.13]

The similarity between the sleeper and the *turīya* is that the sleeper does not apprehend duality, and neither is there duality for the *turīya.* The difference between them is that the sleeper is associated with "sleep that is the seed" *(bījanidrā),* whereas the *turīya* has no such intrinsic association. Gauḍapāda has again used an enigmatic term, *bījanidrā,* which he leaves unexplained. However, in the following two kārikās, the meaning of these terms begins to become clear. He says:

> The waker and the dreamer are associated with "dream" *(svapna)* and "sleep" *(nidrā),* whereas the sleeper is associated with "sleep" but not with "dream". Those who know, see neither "sleep" nor "dream" in the *turīya.* [1.14]

Kārikā fourteen speaks of "dream" *(svapna)* and "sleep" *(nidrā).* However kārikā fourteen has the very same meaning as kārikā eleven, it is only using different terms. We can see this when we juxtapose the two kārikās and translate the first quarter of kārikā eleven more literally:

> The waker and the dreamer are considered to be conditioned by "effect" *(kārya)* and "cause" *(kāraṇa).* The sleeper is conditioned by the "cause". These two ["effect" and "cause"] do not exist in the *turya.* [1.11]

> The waker and the dreamer are associated with "dream" and "sleep", whereas the sleeper is associated with "sleep" but not with "dream". Those who know, see neither "sleep" nor "dream" in the *turya.* [1.14]

In kārikā fourteen Gauḍapāda is repeating the same idea as in kārikā eleven, only instead of using the words "cause" and "effect" he sets up a new set of terms, "sleep" *(nidrā)* and "dream" *(svapna)*. Therefore the words "cause" *(kāraṇa)* and "effect" *(kārya)* of kārikā eleven are equivalent in meaning to the words "sleep" *(nidrā)* and "dream" *(svapna)* of kārikā fourteen. These words "sleep" and "dream" do not refer to the states of sleep and dream, what they refer to is some condition that is associated with the three states. He clarifies what that condition is in kārikā fifteen:

> "Dream" *(svapna)* belongs to the one who misapprehends reality. "Sleep" *(nidrā)* belongs to one who does not know reality. When both of those errors are removed, one attains the *turīya*.[20] [1.15]

The first line of kārikā fifteen explains what is meant by the two terms "sleep" and "dream". The word "sleep" *(nidrā)* is being used in a special sense to mean the "ignorance of reality" *(tattva-ajñāna)*. "Dream" has the meaning of "misapprehension of reality" *(anyathāgrahaṇa)*. Therefore we can understand that the words *"kāraṇa"* and *"nidrā"* are used synonymously to refer to the basic ignorance of reality, while *"kārya"* and *"svapna"* are likewise used as synonyms to refer to the misapprehension of reality that is the outcome of that ignorance. Thus we have:

"cause" *(kāraṇa)* = "sleep" *(nidrā)* = "ignorance of reality"
"effect" *(kārya)* = "dream" *(svapna)* = "misapprehension of reality"

What Gauḍapāda says is that the waker, the dreamer and the sleeper are each associated with the condition of ignorance of reality. The waker and dreamer are further associated with the condition of positively misapprehending reality. The sleeper is just ignorant of reality, the non-dual *turīya*, whereas the waker and the dreamer are not only ignorant, but also misapprehend reality in that they see duality where there is really no duality. Ignorance of reality is referred to as the cause *(kāraṇa)* because the ignorance of a thing is the precondition for the subsequent misapprehension of that thing. Ignorance is also called "sleep" *(nidrā)* because it is a condition of not knowing, like sleep. When it is said that the sleeper is associated with "sleep that is the seed" the word "seed" *(bīja)* indicates that this "sleep" is the potential cause for the subsequent misapprehension. Misapprehension is called the "effect" *(kārya)* because misapprehension is the outcome of ignorance. It is also called as "dream" *(svapna)* because it is a condition where things are taken wrongly; for duality, though not real, appears to be real, like it does in dream.[21] Gauḍapāda repeatedly makes the point, in kārikās eleven, thirteen and fourteen, that neither of these two factors, ignorance and misapprehension, intrinsically exist in the *turīya*, the unchanging witness *(sarvadṛk sadā)* of the three states.

To try to interpret this in a straightforward way we can say that the three states, waking, dreaming, and deep sleep, occur when the *turīya* is associated, as it were, with three different conditions of the mind. When the mind is awake, consciousness is externally orientated; when the mind is dreaming, consciousness is internally orientated; and when the mind is in deep sleep consciousness is "massed together". The *turīya*, the pure Awareness, is called *viśva* when the mind is in a waking condition, it is called as *taijasa* when the mind is in a dreaming condition and it is called *prājña* when the mind is in the condition of deep sleep. Though the *turīya* is present in and through each of the three states, it is not inherently the waker, the dreamer, or deep sleeper, for these are three conditions specifically related to the functioning of the mind. The *turīya* is the unchanging pure Awareness, which equally reveals the waking state, the dreaming state and the blankness of deep sleep.

We have just said that the state of deep sleep is associated with ignorance of reality which is the cause or "seed" for the further misapprehension of reality that is associated with the waking and dream states. Does Gauḍapāda look upon this causal ignorance that is present in each state as merely the absence of true metaphysical knowledge, or does he see it as some sort of positive "power", or *śakti*, that is the actual cause of the states themselves? It is hard to know on the basis of the evidence of the text, though the word "cause" *(kāraṇa)*, and especially the word "seed" *(bīja)*, which indicates some sort of transformative potency on the part of ignorance, tends to indicate the latter view. The question of the nature of "ignorance" will be taken up for discussion in chapter five. But whether ignorance is a simple absence of having true knowledge or whether it has a transformative potency, Gauḍapāda nonetheless makes it clear that all three states are "conditioned" *(baddha),* or "associated" *(yuta),* with ignorance, and that means that the *viśva, taijasa* and *prājña* are, in their very nature, conditioned states. But if each state is intrinsically conditioned, enlightenment would seem to be precluded because the *viśva* would always be conditioned by ignorance *(kāraṇabaddha).* The solution would seem to lie in the idea, made explicit in later Advaita, that ignorance, though in some sense persisting, stands negated by knowledge *(bādhitānuvṛtti).* It must be so, because the states of *viśva* etc. are said to continue even after enlightenment. What the *jñānī,* while in the waking state, directly knows, is that the real Self is the *turīya* which is distinct from the states *(viśvataijasaprājñavilakṣaṇa)* and though the three states continue as appearances *(mithyā),* they stand negated by the knowledge: "I am not any of these states, I am the *turīya*".

In the second half of kārikā fifteen Gauḍapāda says: "when both of those errors are removed, one attains the *turīya.*" This means that when the twofold error, consisting of the ignorance of reality and the misapprehension of reality, stand negated by the knowledge or insight into one's real nature, one "attains" the non-dual *turīya.* The word "attains" is metaphorical, for there can be no attainment of one's own Self.[22] The idea is that such a person, the *jñānī,* sees that his (or her) own essential nature, here called the *turīya,* is not the sleeper, who is associated with ignorance, nor the waker and dreamer, who are associated with both ignorance and misapprehension. Due to ignorance we erroneously take ourselves to be the three states: we are the sleeper, the dreamer, or the waker, and in the latter two states we have the misapprehension of being real subjects over and against real objects. The truth is that we are not the sleeper, the dreamer, or the waker: we are unchanging Awareness, or "Seeing", which neither sleeps, dreams nor wakes up, which illumines the waker together with the waking world *(jāgratprapañca),* the dreamer and the dream world *(svapnaprapañca)* and the state of deep sleep where nothing is objectively experienced. In short, the *jñāni* knows that the waker, dreamer and sleeper are all apparent *(mithyā)* and that the pure Awareness-Self is untouched by the three states even while the latter do not exist apart from It.

Gauḍapāda sums up with a verse that is often quoted by later Advaita authors:

> When the individual self *(jīva),* asleep due to beginningless *māyā,* awakens, it knows the *[turīya]* which is unborn, in which there is neither "sleep" nor "dream", and which is non-dual.[23] [1.16]

By the expression, "in which there is neither 'sleep' nor 'dream'" *(anidra asvapna),* we could perhaps understand that the *turīya* is simply distinct from the states of sleep and dream, which would be perfectly correct. But we have seen that Gauḍapāda also uses the words "sleep" and "dream" as technical expressions to refer to the ignorance of reality and to the misapprehension of reality respectively, and it is this meaning that we should understand here. Incidentally, this expression *anidram asvapnam,* which as we have just seen has its own technical meaning that can be understood only by reading kārikā fifteen of the *Āgamaprakaraṇa,* provides an argument as to why the *Gauḍapādakārikā* is a unitary work and why the four treatises can be read in the order in which they traditionally appear. The identical expression, *anidram asvapnam,* occurs in the *Advaitaprakaraṇa* , in kārikā thirty-six, and it also occurs in the *Alātaśāntiprakaraṇa* in kārikā eighty-one. But the usage of the expression in those two treatises cannot be correctly understood if we are unaware of the explanation given here, in kārikā fifteen. Thus there is justification for maintaining that the traditional order of the text does seem to be correct, for the later treatises presuppose a knowledge of the *Āgamaprakaraṇa.*

Concerning the interrelationship between the four treatises, or chapters, Vidhushekhara Bhattacharya, in the introduction to his work *The Āgamaśāstra of Gauḍapāda,* has argued that: "the treatise consisting of the kārikās of Book 1 has no relationship to any of the Books that follow."[24] We have just shown that this view is not justified. His conclusion on the interrelationship of the four treatises is that: "these four Books are four independent treatises and are put together in a volume under the title of the *Āgamaśāstra*".[25] However, if the four are independent treatises, we have to account for the numerous instances where the kārikās of book four repeat the kārikās from the other books (4.6=3. 20; 4.7=3. 21; 4. 8=3. 22; 4. 29=3. 21 [the last line of each is identical]; 4. 31=2. 6; 4. 32=2. 7; 4. 34=2.2 [the last line of each is identical]; 4. 61 and 62 are almost identical to 3. 29 and 30; 4. 71=3. 48; 4. 81 is closely related to 1. 16 and 3. 36; 4. 94 refers to 3.1). Bhattacharya accepts there is "rather a close" relationship between book four and the other books, and even though he cites the repetitions that I have just given, he nonetheless argues that book four is an independent treatise on the ground that so much repetition would be unwarranted if book four is related to the other three! But surely it would be simpler, and I believe fundamentally correct, to argue on the basis of the evidence just the reverse, namely that the extent of repetition and the dependence upon the ideas of the earlier kārikās shows that the fourth treatise is interrelated with the other three. The four treatises are undoubtedly interrelated, and because of their close interrelationship they can justifiably be seen as constituting a single work.[26]

To return to the discussion of kārikā sixteen. In this kārikā Gauḍapāda refers to the *turīya* as "unborn" *(aja).* This is the first time Gauḍapāda has used this expression, which does not occur in the *Māṇḍūkya* Upaniṣad, though it does occur in the *Bṛhadāraṇyaka* Upaniṣad, as well as in the *Muṇḍaka* and the *Kaṭha* Upaniṣads, and it also occurs a number of times in the *Bhagavadgītā.*[27] Thus we can see numerous precedent uses of the word in both *śruti* and *smṛti.* In his later kārikās Gauḍapāda draws out the implications of maintaining that the ultimate reality is "unborn". If the *turīya* is unborn, then the *turīya* cannot become the waker and the waking world, or the dreamer and the dream world, or even the sleeper: for if there is any change on the part of the "unborn", in so far as it becomes the waker and the waking world etc., then it would no longer be unborn, because by undergoing the change involved in "becoming" it would be taking birth, so to speak. But if the *turīya* has not transformed into the world, how then, we may ask, does the world come about? How can the many originate from the One, if that One is absolutely changeless? Gauḍapāda, accepting the Upaniṣadic teaching that the ultimate reality is "unborn", proceeds to deductively argue that the world cannot logically originate, and even though the world does appear in all its rich variety and complexity, it nonetheless cannot have truly come into being given that the ultimate reality is the unborn Brahman.

Gauḍapāda does not deny the empirical experience of the world. But the world is accepted only as it empirically presents itself, i.e., as an appearance, not as something laying claim to absolute reality. For since there is no separation in traditional Hindu thought between the efficient and the material cause, how could the "born" world have truly come into being out of the one reality if that reality is said to remain unborn? In short, how can becoming arise out of immutable Being? If Brahman remains untransformed then the world cannot logically arise from Brahman. But if the world appears, and the fact of its appearance is not at issue, then it has to be accepted as an appearance, but not as a reality. Gauḍapāda's reasoning shows some similarity to the pre-Socratic Greek philosopher Parmenides in so far as Greek thought too, at that period, had not separated the efficient cause from the material cause, and so their reasoning is similar in that both conclude that the world is a "seeming", and not a reality, from the premise that the One Being cannot enter into a process of becoming without negating itself as Being. While Parmenides poem is presented as a revelation, it is more likely to be the outcome of his own deductive reasoning. Gauḍapāda's similar conclusion about the seeming nature of the world is also the outcome of deductive reasoning, but from the premise given by the revelation of the Upaniṣads that the ultimate reality, *turīya* (Brahman/Ātman), is unborn *(aja).*

We have seen that in kārikās six to nine Gauḍapāda mentions various views about creation. None of these views represent his own position because they all, explicitly or implicitly, accept that creation *(sṛṣṭi)* is a fact. Gauḍapāda now presents his view in kārikās seventeen and eighteen, where he takes up the meaning of the word "non-dual" *(advaita),* which is mentioned in kārikā sixteen, and which is to be found in the seventh mantra of the Upaniṣad ("[the *turīya]* is where there is the cessation of the phenomenal world *(prapañcopaśama),* it is peaceful, auspicious and non-dual *(advaita)").* In fact, it could even be said that the entire *Māṇḍūkyakārikā* is a commentary upon these two words of the *Māṇḍūkya* Upaniṣad: "non-dual" *(advaita)* and "cessation of the phenomenal world" *(prapañcopaśama).* In kārikā seventeen he says that the appearance of the world does not contradict the teaching that the *turīya* is non-dual:

> If the phenomenal world *(prapañca)* did exist, it should cease to exist, of that there is no doubt. [But] this duality is merely *māyā.*

> From the standpoint of ultimate reality, there is non-duality.[28] [1.17]

If the world is real, then in order for there to be non-duality this world of duality would have to cease to exist. But the world does not need to be removed, because duality is merely a "magical" appearance *(māyā),* like a snake appearing upon a rope, or like some display of magic. If the world has an apparent reality only, then there are not two realities, the *turīya* and the world, there is but a single reality, the *turīya,* the substratum of the appearance, because an unreal appearance does not constitute a second reality. This amounts to saying that the world is *mithyā:* it appears empirically, though it is not truly real. So there is always non-duality, in spite of the appearance of duality, and the consequence of this understanding is that the world need not cease in order for non-duality to exist.

He makes a similar point in kārikā eighteen:

> If [the phenomenal world] is a projection that is conceived by someone, the projection should come to an end. This position is adopted for the purpose of instruction. When [the highest truth] is known, there is no duality. [1. 18]

If this world is the projection of someone, even of the Lord, then it would have to cease in order for there to be non-duality, since the world is still someone's actual creation. But this teaching, which Gauḍapāda himself will adopt in the *Vaitathyaprakaraṇa* (kārikā twelve), is a means to teach the highest truth, it is not itself the highest truth.

So far, I have tried to demonstrate that Gauḍapāda's teachings should be seen in their proper context. That context is provided by the *Māṇḍūkya* Upaniṣad. What Gauḍapāda has done in the *Āgamaprakaraṇa* is to develop the teaching of the *Māṇḍūkya* to its logical conclusion. We have seen that in the *Māṇḍūkya* the *turīya* is neither the waker, nor the dreamer, nor the sleeper, but is the invariable Awareness *(sadā sarvadṛk)* in which the waker together with the waking world, the dreamer along with the dream world, and the unknowing of the deep sleeper, all stand revealed. The *turīya* does not awake, does not dream, and does not sleep; it remains untouched by the presence or absence of the three states. The *Māṇḍūkya* also says that the *turīya* is the ground of "the cessation of the phenomenal world" *(prapañcopaśama)* and "non dual" *(advaita)*. Gauḍapāda makes explicit what is implicit in the words of the *Māṇḍūkya* Upaniṣad itself. Gauḍapāda says that given the fact that the *turīya* is immutable and unborn, the world cannot truly originate out of the *turīya*. Therefore, the world is like a wondrous magical appearance, a *māyā*. Thus Gauḍapāda's teaching of *"ajātivāda"* must be seen to be deductively derived from the principal statements in the Upaniṣads, particularly the *Māṇḍūkya*. The *Māṇḍūkya* Upaniṣad is therefore not peripheral, but is central to his entire teaching.

This conclusion is at variance with the view of scholars such as T. Vetter, who have argued that the *Alātaśāntiprakaraṇa* is the earliest of the four treatises of the *Gauḍapādakārikā*, because the teaching of non-origination presupposes the teaching about the non-arising of *dharmas* as discussed in the fourth *prakaraṇa*.[29] But I do not think that the teaching of non-origination need depend upon the conception of the non-arising of *dharmas* as found in Mahāyāna Buddhism and referred to in the fourth *prakaraṇa*. As I have tried to show, the teaching of non-origination can be "unpacked", so to speak, from some of the words in the seventh mantra of the *Māṇḍūkya* Upaniṣad itself, as well as from the teachings of other Upaniṣads, such as the *Bṛhadāraṇyaka*. Consequently, the traditional order in which the *prakaraṇas* are read need not be overturned.

In the following three chapters: the "treatise on unreality" *(Vaitathyaprakaraṇa)*, the "treatise on non-duality" *(Advaitaprakaraṇa)* and the "treatise on the quelling of the fire-brand" *(Alātaśāntiprakaraṇa)*, Gauḍapāda develops various arguments to advance the position reached here in the "treatise concerning the Vedic text" *(Āgamaprakaraṇa)*. As I have mentioned, the remaining chapters could be seen to form an elaborate commentary upon two expressions occurring in mantra seven, namely, that the *turīya* is "where there is the cessation of the phenomenal world" *(prapañcopaśama)*, and that it is "non-dual" *(advaita)*.

(2) The *Vaitathyaprakaraṇa*

At the beginning of the "treatise on unreality" *(Vaitathyaprakaraṇa)* Gauḍapāda argues that the waking world *(jāgratprapañca)* is unreal. By the word "unreal" I do not mean that the world is a fictitious presentation, existing only subjectively in the imagination; rather I mean that the world is empirically evident, and continues to remain so, even when it is found, upon inquiry, to be "not truly existing".[30] The Sanskrit word to express this idea is *mithyā*, which can be translated as "apparent" or as "seeming", though the English language unfortunately does not possess a single conceptually equivalent term.

That the world is unreal, in the sense just mentioned, is indicated in the Upaniṣad itself by the two expressions: "the cessation of the phenomenal world" *(prapañcopaśama)* and "non-dual" *(advaita)*. If the world is real, it must exist as a reality over and against the reality of the *turīya*, and if such a dualism exists, then the Upaniṣad could not speak of the *turīya* as non-dual. What Gauḍapāda seeks to do in the first six kārikās of the *Vaitathyaprakaraṇa* is to demonstrate the unreality of the world by a process of inference. But in order to prove this inference he requires, in accordance with the convention regarding the formation of inference in Indian thought, an illustration *(dṛṣṭānta)*, the veracity of which cannot be called into question. The illustration that he takes is the unreality of dream. He begins the *Vaitathyaprakaraṇa* by establishing that the dream world is unreal, and once he has shown that his illustration is indisputable, he then presents his inference that the waking world is unreal.

He demonstrates the unreality of dream in the first three kārikās by referring to three means of knowledge: inference *(anumāna)*, perception *(pratyakṣa)* and verbal testimony, in this case the *śruti*. In the first kārikā he argues by inference that things in dream are unreal, because they are internal to the body. The reason is that since they exist in such an enclosed space, they must be unreal. It is impossible for dreamt objects, such as elephants and mountains etc., to exist within the body of the dreamer. In this first kārikā he argues that dream objects are unreal because there is an insufficiency of space. Śaṅkara too has used this argument in his discussion of the unreality of dream in the *Brahmasūtrabhāṣya*. The language he employs is similar to that of Gauḍapāda in that they both use the word "enclosed" *(saṁvṛta)* space.[31]

In the next kārikā Gauḍapāda infers that dream objects are unreal because there is an insufficiency of time for the dream events to actually take place. Śaṅkara too uses this argument in the *Brahmasūtrabhāṣya*, and he utilises it to bolster the first reason when he says that if it is objected that the dream objects are not within the body at all, but the dreamer really travels outside the body to experience those things, then it can be said in reply that it is impossible to travel to those dream locations in a mere instant.[32] Gauḍapāda also argues on the basis of our own perception *(pratyakṣa)* when he says that a person who awakens from a dream does not find himself in the place that was dreamt about. Śaṅkara too uses the same argument.[33] In the third kārikā Gauḍapāda refers to the *Bṛhadāraṇyaka* Upaniṣad 4.3.10 which speaks of the unreality of the dream world. Śaṅkara too cites this *śruti* text.[34]

Gauḍapāda concludes by saying that because of these reasons, based on *śruti, yukti* and *anubhava*, it is evident that the dream world is unreal. In these kārikās Gauḍapāda, like Śaṅkara, has argued that dream is unreal by contrasting it with the waking state which is accepted as real. But it would not be correct to contend that there is the defect of mutual dependence in Gauḍapāda's argument, in that he uses the waking world to prove that dream is unreal, and then he will use dream to prove the unreality of the waking world. There is no mutual dependence because Gauḍapāda does not rely on dream to *prove* the unreality of the waking world. An inferential proof requires a reason *(hetu)* the validity of which depends upon the validity of the relation of invariable concomitance *(vyāpti)* that must exist between the reason and the thing to be proved *(sādhya)*. The illustration is not itself a proof, it is something that is cited to elucidate the reason. Gauḍapāda does not use dream to prove that the waking world is unreal, he cites it to illustrate the reason *(hetu)*, and consequently there is no mutual dependence.

In the fourth kārikā he takes up the issue of inferring the unreality of the waking world. He begins by saying:

> Just as in dream, so too in waking, it is considered that there is [unreality] *(vaitathya)*. However [waking] differs from dream because in dream the objects are within on account of being enclosed.[35] [2.4]

Gauḍapāda says that both the dream world and the waking world are unreal. However the reason that was given for proving the dream world to be unreal, namely that dream objects are enclosed within the body, cannot be the reason for proving that the waking world is unreal. It was said that dream objects, in contrast to the objects of the waking world, lack the appropriate space or time *(ucitadeśakālābhāva)* in which they could really happen. The same cannot be said of things in the waking world, because in the latter the objects are external to the body and hence there is the appropriate space and time *(ucitadeśakāla)* for the events to occur. So another reason has to be given, different from the reasons used to prove the unreality of dream, in order to prove the unreality of the waking world. But before presenting this reason, Gauḍapāda says that though the waking world and the dream world do differ in respect of having or not having the required space and time, they are, nonetheless, equally unreal:

> The wise say that the states of dream and waking are one, because the objects [in both states] are of a similar nature due to a well-known reason. [2.5]

Bhattacharya and Karmarkar understand "being within" the body *(antaḥsthāna)* as the reason for the unreality of the waking world, and recent scholars, generally following Bhattacharya, adopt the same perplexing interpretation.[36] But this interpretation cannot be correct, because in the previous kārikā [2.4] Gauḍapāda did not conflate dream and waking, he actually made a distinction between them, in that the former is within the body whereas the latter is external to the body.

What, then, is this "well-known reason"? Gauḍapāda provides the reason in his next kārikā:

> What does not exist at the beginning and at the end, likewise [does not exist] even in the present. The things that are appearing are equivalent to unreal things, [yet] they are looked upon as though they are real. [2.6]

Having created an expectation as to the reason in kārikā five, it is appropriate that he provides the reason in kārikā six.[37] Things are unreal, *vitatha* or *mithyā*, because they are impermanent. The above reason articulates a major philosophical presupposition which is present in much of Indian thought (and, judging from the writings of Plato, can be found in Greek philosophy as well): to be fully real means to be free from all change.[38] This idea is expressed, for example, in the *Bhagavadgītā*, which says: "The real does not cease to be" *(nābhāvo vidyate sataḥ)*.[39] Reality is equivalent to persisting in being. The corollary of that proposition is that anything that changes cannot be fully real. Change is a proof of unreality, because as a thing changes it becomes different from what it already is; it becomes, in fact, what it is not. In order for change to occur, the present condition of a thing must cease; otherwise change would be impossible. So in "becoming", a thing ceases to be what it is, and becomes what it is not. How can a changing object be thought of as "truly real" when the act of change calls for its non-existence?

Gauḍapāda thus takes impermanence *(anityatva)*, or the deviation *(vyabhicāritva)* from being, as proof of unreality. When it is said that objects are "unreal" what is meant is that they are *mithyā*. The word that Gauḍapāda uses, *"vaitathya"*, conveys the same idea as the word *"mithyā"* which is the more commonly used term in later Advaita texts. As mentioned earlier, *mithyā* is an important technical term in Advaita to describe what is empirically evident, and continues to remain so, even when it is found, upon inquiry, to be "not truly existing". According to Advaita, if something is truly real *(sat, satya)* it must be changeless. If something is entirely imaginary, like a barren woman's son or a square circle, it is absolutely unreal, or non-existent *(asat)*. But suppose something is empirically evident, though it is (a) transient, which is the argument that Gauḍapāda uses, or (b) it exists in a state of ontological dependence upon something else, then such a thing cannot be designated as truly, or absolutely real. But neither is it absolutely unreal, i.e., simply non-existent, since it *does* appear. Such an object is designated as *"mithyā"*; a word that can be translated as "unreal", or as only "apparently real", though in the precise understanding of the term it refers to something that is empirically evident but which, when investigated, is found to be indeterminable as either absolutely real or as absolutely unreal.[40] Though there is a difference between the waking world *(jāgratprapañca)* and the dream world *(svapnaprapañca)*, in that the former is external to the body whereas the latter is within the body, according to the understanding of Gauḍapāda both are equally *mithyā*.

Therefore we have arrived at the following inference:

pratijñā (the proposition to be proved):
"The waking world is unreal" *(jāgratprapañco mithyā)*.
hetu (reason):
"Because it has a beginning and an end" *(anityatvāt/ vyabhicāritvāt)*.
udāharaṇa (statement of invariable concomitance *(vyāpti)*, with an appropriate illustration):
"Whatever has a beginning and an end is unreal, like a dream" *(svapnavat)*.

Arguments put forward to establish the unreality of the world have not proved uncontroversial. Rāmānuja, for example, who attempted to uphold a common-sense view of the world, argued against Advaita that impermanence does not prove unreality.[41] It is natural, then, that Gauḍapāda might wish to defend his argument, and he does so in the next three kārikās. An objection is raised that dream and waking cannot have the same ontological status, as *mithyā*, because the waking world has a practical utility unlike the dream world. So even though dream is unreal we cannot say that the waking world is unreal. To such an objection Gauḍapāda gives the reply:

> The utility of those [things in the waking state] is contradicted in dream. Therefore, they are considered just to be *mithyā* on account of their having a beginning and an end.[42] [2.7]

Gauḍapāda says that the utility of objects in the waking state is relevant only to the waking state. The food that satisfies hunger in the waking world cannot satisfy hunger in a dream, nor can the food that satisfies the dreamer be used to satisfy the waker. The waking world has utility for the waker, but not for the dreamer, and vice versa. Thus the waking state is empirically real from the standpoint of the waker, but it is not absolutely real, because its claim to reality is negated by dream which is empirically real from the standpoint of the dreamer. So Gauḍapāda says that the argument that the utility of waking objects proves that the waking world is real is not valid, and he repeats his reason that waking objects are *mithyā* because they have a beginning and an end.

The next objection calls into question the illustration of dream. The objection is that the illustration is not proved *(dṛṣṭāntāsiddhi).* It is not right, the objector says, to say that dream is unreal; on the contrary, it can be argued that dream is real because of the novelty of what is seen in dream. Since dream is not a mere copy of the waking state, but it has its own novel *(apūrva)* features which are not seen in waking, we are not entitled to say that dream is unreal. In reply, Gauḍapāda says that novelty is not a criterion for reality:

> The novelty is an attribute of the one who is in that state, just as it is for those who dwell in heaven. This person [i.e. the dreamer, *sthānī]* sees those novel things when he goes there. Just as here, a well educated person sees novel things when he goes [to a new place]. [2.8]

The idea is that the novelty belongs to the person who is in that state *(sthanī),* the novelty does not belong to the state itself *(sthāna).* In other words, the novelty is purely subjective, and so novelty cannot be used to prove that something is real. Gauḍapāda gives the example of a scholar. When, in olden days, an educated person travelled to a different country to pursue further studies, he might find the customs of that place to be strange, but the strangeness is the experience of the traveller, for the inhabitants of the place do not find their customs strange. So too, if one went to dwell in heaven one might find everything there highly unusual, but that is not to say it is unusual, it just seems so to the one who goes there. The feeling of novelty or strangeness of dream is only from the standpoint of the person who dreams and later on reflects upon the experience when awake. Since novelty is subjective it cannot be used as an argument to prove that dream is real.

The third objection is that waking world *(jāgratprapañca)* is real because it is has an objective existence. We know that dream is unreal because it is a subjective experience within our own mind, but the waking world is different because it is experienced as external to ourselves. So, in accord with our common-sense understanding, the world must be real. Gauḍapāda replies:

> Even in the case of the dream state, what is imagined within by the mind is unreal, whereas what is experienced externally by the mind is real. But it is evident that both are unreal. [2.9]
>
> So also in the case of the waking state, what is imagined within by the mind is unreal, whereas what is experienced externally by the mind is real. It is logically correct that both are unreal. [2.10]

Arguing by way of analogy with dream, Gauḍapāda says that even the distinction of internal and external does not prove that the waking world is real. Suppose a dreamer, while seeing a dream world as something external and real, has some internal musing on the basis of what is seen, and then thinks that the inner-imagination is unreal in comparison to the perception of the external dream world. But upon waking, the person sees that both experiences, the internal dream musing, as well as the objective, external dream world, are equally unreal. Likewise, Gauḍapāda says, in the waking world we make a distinction between inner-imagination which is unreal and external experience which is real. But the experience of an external world does not prove that such a world is real. It is logically feasible that the objective waking world is unreal, just as the dream world that the dreamer experiences as something external and real. If we object that Gauḍapāda is able to prove that the dream world is unreal because it is seen to be so when we wake up, but there is no standpoint by which we can sublate the waking world to prove that it is unreal, Gauḍapāda would presumably reply that the experience of dream sublates the waking world (which we can know by reflection once we wake up). Or, he might argue that the reality of the waking world is sublated from the standpoint of pure Awareness. However Gauḍapāda does not carry the argument further, as his point is only to show that the experience of the waking world as something external does not prove that it is real. The reality of the world is an assumption that we make in accordance with our "common sense" understanding, but such an assumption does not itself constitute a poof. Gauḍapāda's own proof of unreality *(mithyātva)* is impermanence, as we have seen in kārikā six.

At this point he introduces a question:

> If the things in both states [dream and waking] are unreal, who cognises them? Who projects them? [2.11]

The *vaitathya,* the unreality of things, does not mean they are non-existent, for then they could not even be experienced. The unreal things, whether in dream or in the waking state, do appear, and given that fact, a question is raised: who experiences these objects in the waking and dream states? Who creates, or projects them? Gauḍapāda addresses both questions in the following verse, taking the second question first.

> The Self, the effulgent one, apparently creates Itself through Itself due to its own *māyā.* It is just the Self who knows the objects. Such is the conclusive teaching of Vedānta. [2.12]

In this verse, the Self *(ātman)* is used in apposition with the word "effulgent" *(deva)* which was previously seen in apposition with the word *turīya* in 1.10 ("The all pervading, effulgent one is considered to be the 'fourth'"), therefore we can understand that the Self here means the *turīya.* It is the absolute Self, the *turīya,* pure Awareness, that projects, or apparently creates *(kalpayati)*, the waking and dream worlds. An act of creation, however, requires a number of components: apart from the Creator, or efficient cause *(kartṛ),* there is the need for the appropriate means to bring about a creation, i.e., an instrumental cause *(karaṇa),* and there is also the important requirement of some material which becomes the object of the creative process, i.e., the material cause. In Upaniṣadic thought there is no conception of *creatio ex nihilo,* the doctrine of creation that developed in Christian theology towards the end of the second century C.E., and which teaches that God made the world out of sheer nothing, i.e., there is no material cause. In Vedānta, as we can see expressed in the *Brahmasūtra,* the Creator is both the efficient and the material cause.[43] So Gauḍapāda says that the Ātman is the Creator which Itself becomes the created world: "The Self apparently creates *(kalpayati)* Itself *(ātmānam)."* He also says that no separate instrumental cause is required apart from the Ātman, for the apparent creation happens "through Itself" *(ātmanā).*

But how could the *turīya-* Ātman, unchanging and therefore absolutely real, undergo the change that would be required for it to "manifest" as the world? If the Self undergoes any change whatsoever it would become impermanent, and therefore *mithyā.* Gauḍapāda says that no change actually took place. The act of creation has occurred through *māyā,* a "wondrous power" belonging to the changeless *turīya,* Ātman-Brahman *(svasya māyā).* Since Brahman is by definition changeless, there is no possibility for a creation to occur without postulating some power belonging to Brahman. Brahman, in association with this power, is the Creator, the cosmic Lord, who creates through Itself the objects which are not other than Itself. This power, moreover, as the name *māyā* itself implies, does not have the same ontological status as Brahman, its substratum. So *māyā* too is *mithyā.* Since the created world, the effect, is apparent *(mithyā),* the power by which Brahman is the cause should have the same ontological status as its effect, i.e., that power should also be *mithyā,* and as a consequence the changelessness and the non-duality of Brahman remain untouched. We shall have the opportunity to discuss this very important point in more detail later when we come to Śaṅkara.

It is evident that Gauḍapāda is teaching from two standpoints: from the perspective of ultimate truth *(paramārtha),* as well as at the level of empirical truth *(vyavahāra).* Advaita cannot be correctly understood without an appreciation of these two "levels" of truth and, as we shall later see, Śaṅkara repeatedly takes his stand on these "two truths" when he refers to the nature of the unconditioned Brahman *vis-a vis* the nature of the cosmic Lord *(Īśvara).* From the standpoint of ultimate truth *(paramārtha),* the world cannot logically come into being given that

Brahman is pure Consciousness which is identical to Being itself, and Being, by definition, does not *become*. Yet, from the standpoint of empirical truth, or everyday life *(vyavahāra)*, the appearance of the world is an undeniable fact. From this empirical standpoint Brahman must be the Creator of the world. But when we see that the empirical world is *mithyā*, we pass from the "level" of empirical truth to that of absolute truth, and it is from this latter perspective that the power postulated of Brahman, by which Brahman is the Creator, must also be ultimately unreal, it too is *mithyā*.

It is from the empirical perspective that Gauḍapāda answers the first question of kārikā eleven, when he says that: "it is just the Self who knows the objects". It is the Self, pure Awareness, that is the individual epistemological subject *(pramātā)*, the *jīva*, when the Self is in association with an individual body-mind complex.[44] Gauḍapāda concludes kārikā twelve saying: "Such is the conclusive teaching of Vedānta". Gauḍapāda relies upon argument to establish the unreality of the world, but when he comes to speak of the true nature of things we see that he explicitly refers to the Upaniṣads.

Gauḍapāda continues to discuss the *mithyā* nature of the creation, and in doing so he makes a clear distinction between the waking and dream states. He says:

> [The Self] creates the things which reside in the mind when it is internal, as well as other, constant things, which are present in the mind when it is external. Thus does the Lord apparently create.[45] [2.13]

Here, the reference to the mind as being either "external" or "internal" is reminiscent of the statement in *Māṇḍūkya* Upaniṣad 3 and 4, where the waker is spoken of as one "whose consciousness is external" *(bahiṣprajña)* and the dreamer as one "whose consciousness is internal" *(antaḥprajña)*. Gauḍapāda is saying that the Lord creates the things of the dream world and the things of the waking world. He then says:

> The things that are internal only exist in mental time, whereas the things that are

> external exist in a twofold time. They are all apparently created [by the Self]. The distinction [between dream and waking] does not rest upon any other reason. [2.14]

Here, Gauḍapāda makes a distinction between the waking world and the dream world. The dream world is subjective, it lasts as long as the thought persists. The waking world, however, is objective, because it exists in a twofold time. In the waking world there is subjective time, such as when we feel that time is passing quickly or slowly, and there is also objective time which is measured by apparent solar time, or by a clock. Scholars who believe that Gauḍapāda simply conflates the waking and dream states, or that he is a subjective idealist, have misunderstood his point. What he says is that although there is a distinction between dream and waking in so far as dream has a subjective reality whereas waking has an objective reality, both states are ontologically the same, for both are transient and therefore both are equally *mithyā*. But the fact that they are both classed as *mithyā* does not mean that there is no secondary distinction (an *avāntarabheda*) within that classification. Gauḍapāda clearly says that there is such a distinction. He makes this point again in the following verse:

> Whereas the things that are internal are indistinct, the things that are external are clearly evident. They are all apparently created [by the Self]. The distinction is due to the difference in the sense-organs. [2.15]

In dream there is the operation only of the mind, whereas in waking there is the mind functioning together with the various sense-organs. Looking at dream and waking experiences from the standpoint of the waking state, Gauḍapāda distinguishes between them while maintaining that both are ontologically *mithyā*.

He then provides more details about the process of creation, a topic that began with kārikā eleven.

> Firstly, [the Ātmā] apparently creates the individual soul *(jīva)*, then the objects of different types, those that are external as well as those that are internal. As [the *jīva]* knows, so it thinks. [2.16]

The idea behind this remark, "As [the *jīva]* knows, so it thinks", would seem to be explained in the subsequent verses where Gauḍapāda says that the *jīva*, being ignorant of its own true nature, the Ātman that is its basis *(adhiṣṭhāna)*, then proceeds to develop any number of mistaken views of reality. Gauḍapāda first gives the famous example of the rope and the snake and then goes on to list all sorts of possible misconceptions of reality.

> Just as a rope, when not ascertained, in the darkness, to be a rope, is mistaken for various things such as a snake, or a streak of water etc., likewise is the Self mistaken [by the *jīva]*. [2.17]

> Just as, when the rope is ascertained as a rope, the mistaken notion ceases and there is the non-dual knowledge: "the rope alone is", likewise is the ascertainment of the Self. [2.18]

> The Self is mistaken [by the *jīva]* to be these countless things beginning with the life-energy *(prāṇa)*. This is the *māyā* of that effulgent one [the Self] by which He himself has become deluded! [2.19]

Gauḍapāda then spends nine verses describing various mistaken views. He concludes by saying:

> Whatever thing [the teacher] would point out to him, he sees it [i.e. comes to have that

> conception]. That idea, by becoming one with him, protects him. Attachment to that view possesses him. [2.29]
>
> This [Self] is held to be different owing to these things which are not different [from the Self]. The one who knows this to be a fact may imagine [the Self in various ways] without hesitation! [2.30]

What, according to Gauḍapāda, constitutes the correct understanding *(saṁyagdarśana)?* In the next four kārikās he presents his *siddhānta*, the conclusive teaching. In the first two kārikās he speaks of the unreality, i.e., the "apparent reality" *(mithyātva)*, of the world. He says:

> Like a dream and a magic are seen, and just as a mirage city is seen in the sky, so is this universe seen by those who are well-versed in the Vedānta [i.e. Upaniṣads]. [2.31]
>
> There is no cessation, there is no origination, no one is bound and no one strives [to be free], no one desires liberation, nor is anyone liberated. This is the ultimate truth. [2.32]

Kārikās 31 and 32 present Gauḍapāda's famous teaching of "non-origination" *(ajātivāda)*. These kārikās exhibit a very close resemblance to some portions of Mahāyāna Buddhist literature. The expressions "mirage city" *(gandharvanagara)* and "dream" *(svapna)* are found a number of times in the *Mūlamadhyamakakārikā* of Nāgārjuna. In 7.34 of this work Nāgārjuna says:

> Like a magic *(māyā)*, like a dream *(svapna)*, and just like a mirage city seen in the sky *(gandharvanagara)*, so have been described origination, duration and cessation. [MK 7.34][46]

It is widely accepted that Nāgārjuna lived in the second or third centuries CE and it is thought that Gauḍapāda lived *circa* 500 CE.[47] There is a clear resemblance between the language of kārikā 31 and the verse of Nāgārjuna just quoted. There is also a resemblance between kārikā 32, where Gauḍapāda says: "There is no cessation *(na nirodha)*, there is no origination *(na ca-utpatti)*", and the two introductory verses of the *Mūlamadhyamakakārikā* where Nāgārjuna uses the same expressions: *anirodha anutpāda.* There is also some resemblance between this kārikā and *Sāṅkhyakārikā* 62 of Īśvarakṛṣṇa (c. 350-450).[48] These resemblances strongly suggest that Gauḍapāda was drawing upon such verses in the composition of these two kārikās.

Though Gauḍapāda's language here is undeniably similar to that of Nāgārjuna and to Mahāyāna Buddhism in general, the similarity ends at this point, for Gauḍapāda's perspective is quite different. Gauḍapāda's perspective is based upon the teaching contained in the *Māṇḍūkya* Upaniṣad. This Upaniṣad teaches the existence and the nature of an absolute reality called either as Brahman, *ātman*, or *turīya*. Since it is axiomatic for Gauḍapāda that reality cannot undergo alteration, it follows that the phenomenal world cannot logically arise from Brahman. If the world cannot logically arise, yet if the world is an empirical fact, then the world has ultimately to be an unreal appearance of Brahman, analogous to a magical creation *(māyā)* etc. This is the meaning of verse thirty one. If the phenomenal world is an unreal appearance, then there is no real origination or real destruction, there can only be an apparent origination and an apparent destruction. Accordingly, there is no one who is really bound etc. From the level of ultimate truth *(paramārthatā)*, and it is important to remember that this is his standpoint, the whole world is a phenomenal appearance, akin to a magic display. This is the essential meaning of verse thirty two.

In the third of these four *siddhānta* verses, and in an altogether too cryptic way, Gauḍapāda dismisses even the concept of "non-dual" from the absolute standpoint. But in the second line of the verse he makes an important point that clearly differentiates Advaita Vedānta from most Buddhist teachings, and the point is that an unreal appearance is always the appearance *of* something real *as* something else that is unreal. An unreal appearance must be grounded in the real, for there can be no unreal appearance without a real substratum.

> This [Self] is falsely imagined to be the unreal things, and the Self is falsely imagined to be non-dual. Those things, moreover, exist just through the non-dual. Therefore non-duality is auspicious.[49] [2.33]

The idea seems to be that the word "non-dual" is relative to the idea of duality, and once duality is negated, the Self cannot be designated even as "non dual". It is the same with other words commonly used to describe Brahman, such as "substratum" *(adhiṣṭhāna)*, because an *adhiṣṭhāna* is relative to what is supported *(adhiṣṭheya)*. Even the words Brahman ("expansion"), *ātman* (Self) and *turīya* (Fourth) acquire their meanings in relation to what is finite, what is not-Self, or in the case of *turīya*, to the three conditions, i.e., the waker, dreamer and sleeper. Therefore Brahman, as it is, is without name and is neither dual nor non-dual *(dvaitādvaitavilakṣaṇa)*. If the verse is interpreted in this way, the idea that is expressed here is reminiscent of Nāgārjuna who argues that all concepts can be shown to be interdependent and are therefore "empty" of any inherent nature. But Gauḍapāda is saying something different from Nāgārjuna, for he says that it is the absolute reality, the *ātman* (referred to by the pronoun *"ayam"* in the kārikā), that is being falsely imagined in these various ways. It is important to remember that Vedānta never says that things are merely apparent *(mithyā)*, without also pointing out what is real *(satya)*. In the second line of the kārikā Gauḍapāda says that things exist "just through the non-dual" *(advayena-eva)*, meaning that there can be no appearance of the world without a substratum. From the empirical perspective of the world there is the experience that things exist, and they can only do so because they have no separate existence from Brahman, which is Being Itself. Therefore, from the empirical perspective, the understanding of non-duality is auspicious and not any other understanding.

In the last of these four verses, Gauḍapāda refers to the relationship between the world and Brahman:

> This plurality does not exist as identical to the Self, nor even does it somehow exist of its own accord. Those who know reality,

> know that nothing exists different [from the Self] or as identical [to the Self]. [2.34]

This phenomenal world does not exist as identical to the Self *(ātman)*, pure Awareness, for in that case no world would even be present to be experienced as something "other". Nor does the world have an inherent existence of its own, because in that case the world would be real, it would be self-existent. But the world is not a self-existent reality, its being is reducible to the Being that is Brahman. Those who know the truth know that: "nothing exists different *(pṛthak)* [from the Self] or as identical *(apṛthak)* [to the Self]."

The above statement, that nothing exists different from the Self or as identical to the Self, could help clarify a phrase frequently used by Śaṅkara in his *Brahmasūtrabhāṣya*, as well as elsewhere.[50] The phrase to which I am referring is: *tattvānyatvābhyām anirvacanīya [nāmarūpa]* which can be literally rendered as: "[the name-and-form] is indeterminable as 'that' or as something else." Later Advaitins regularly use the expression *sadasadbhyām anirvacanīya* to describe the causal, cosmic "Ignorance" *(ajñāna/avidyā)*, in which case this expression means that *avidyā* is indeterminable as to whether it truly exists *(sat)*, or simply does not exist *(asat)*.[51] This amounts to saying that *avidyā* is indefinable as either identical to Brahman or as not identical to Brahman, since Brahman is Being Itself *(sat)*. Now if we follow the teaching of Gauḍapāda here, that the world is not different from the Self, nor is it identical to the Self, then it is highly likely that Śaṅkara is saying the same thing when he uses the somewhat formulaic expression *"tattvānyatvābhyām anirvacanīya"*. Here, the word *"tattva"* would ultimately refer to Brahman and the statement would mean that the name-and-form, i.e., the "stuff" of the world, is indeterminable, or indefinable, as either identical with Brahman or as something other than Brahman. This meaning is possible if we interpret Śaṅkara in the light of Gauḍapāda. It is also possible to understand the phrase in this way just from Śaṅkara's own works and we will refer to this point in considerably more detail in chapter five.

The well known illustration of the rope-snake, which Gauḍapāda mentioned in 2. 17 and 18, can help to elucidate all the points in the above four verses. We should bear in mind that the rope-snake analogy is attempting to depict the relation between Brahman and the world at the level of ultimate reality. The rope should be understood as equivalent to the Brahman-Ātman and the snake-appearance as equivalent to the world. The rope is real, i.e., changeless, it is "unborn" for it has not changed into the snake through any transformation on its part. The rope therefore is not the snake. Yet the snake does appear, and it appears exactly where the rope is. The snake therefore has the rope as its substratum. Is the snake-appearance different from the rope, or is it identical to the rope? It is not different, because it has no independent existence of its own. Then it must be identical? It is not entirely identical either, for in that case there would only be the rope and no snake-appearance. Similarly (and we must keep in mind that the perspective here is that of ultimate truth) the Ātman is changeless and "unborn", for it has not changed into the world through any transformation. But the world does appear, so the world-appearance exists: "As a dream and a magic are seen..." (2.31). And therefore, from this perspective of ultimate reality: "There is no cessation, there is no origination" etc. (2.32), for since the universe has no real origin it can have no real destruction either. The statement: "just through the non-dual" (2.33) indicates that the empirically evident, *mithyā* universe, is grounded in the Ātman. This world is not different from the Ātman, because in that case it would have an independent ontological status, nor is it entirely identical to the Ātman, since there is the empirical experience of a world (2. 34).

(3) The *Advaitaprakaraṇa*

Gauḍapāda introduces his third treatise with two cryptic verses which require some discussion. Firstly, he says:

> A doctrine (dharma) based upon a conceptual meditation occurs when Brahman is born. [That doctrine is]: "prior to origination, everything is unborn." Therefore, that doctrine is considered as pitiable. [3.1]

The chief difficulty in this verse is the word dharma. Śaṅkara, who is traditionally held to be the author of the commentary upon the *Māṇḍūkya* Upaniṣad and the *Gauḍapādakārikā*, interprets the word dharma as the "seeker" *(sādhaka)*, meaning the individual soul *(jīva)*.[52] But why should the word dharma have this unprecedented meaning? To this question, Advaitins answer that there is a precedent, for in the *Kaṭha* Upaniṣad the word dharma is twice found in the sense of soul. In *Kaṭha* 1.1.21, we read *"aṇur eṣa dharmaḥ"* and here Śaṅkara says, "this dharma called the Self".[53] In 2.1.14 the statement *"evaṁ dharmān pṛthak paśyan"* occurs, where Śaṅkara understands the word *dharmān* to be the individual selves *(ātmanaḥ)*.[54] The fact that the word dharma is interpreted as "self" by the author of the commentary on the *Māṇḍūkyakārikā*, consistent with the commentary upon *Kaṭha* Upaniṣad 2.1.14, lends incidental support to the view that the commentary on the *Gauḍapādakārikā* is an authentic work of Śaṅkara. But the question still remains, why should the word dharma mean Self, or selves, in the *Kaṭha* Upaniṣad when it is not used in that way in any of the other major Upaniṣads, such as the *Bṛhadāraṇyaka* or the *Chāndogya?*

The peculiarity of the meaning of dharma in *Kaṭha* Upaniṣad 2.1.14 was noticed long ago by Theodore Stcherbatsky who suggested that this passage, in referring to *pṛthag-dharmān*, might be indicating the existence of a pre-Buddhistic *anātma-dharma* theory. He saw in *Kaṭha* Upaniṣad 2.1.14 a refutation of those who uphold the existence of separate elements *(pṛthag-dharmān)*.[55] Hajime Nakamura, on the other hand, asserted that the word dharma in this passage is undoubtedly of Buddhist usage.[56] In Buddhism the word dharma traverses a range of meanings starting with law or doctrine and ending up including all the things that have been taught by the doctrine, whereby all things are reduced to a number of discrete elements which are called dharmas.[57] The distinctive meaning of the word dharma in Buddhism, in the sense of an "element, or "factor of existence", perhaps developed from an older use of the word dharma in the sense of a "quality" or an "essential property". We can see the usage of the word dharma in the sense of a "quality" in *Chāndogya* Upaniṣad 2.1.4 *(sādhavo dharmāḥ)*. And in the *Bṛhadāraṇyaka* Upaniṣad 4.5.14 we find the word dharma used in the sense of an "essential property", for when Yājñavalkya says to Maitreyī that the Self has the property, or nature, of being indestructible, he uses the word dharma: "This Self is of an indestructible nature" *(ayam ātmā anucchittidharmā)*. But when Buddhism repudiated the concept of substance, the idea of dharma as a "quality" of a thing, or as its "essential property", developed into the idea of a quality without the support of a substance, or a property without reference to a substance; it became an "independent quality", and was seen as an ultimate, unique component, bearing its own specific characteristic *(svalakṣaṇa)*.[58]

In Kaṭha Upaniṣad 1.1.21, the statement *"aṇur eṣa dharmaḥ"* could be understood as "this is a subtle teaching (a subtle matter)". Nakamura suggests "law or creed".[59] Such a meaning could have a precedent in the use of the word dharma in *Bṛhadāraṇyaka* Upaniṣad 1.5.23, and the *Kaṭha* Upaniṣad seems to refer to this passage at one place.[60] Śaṅkara is not wrong in understanding the word dharma in *Kaṭha* 1.1.21 to mean the Self, for the Self is the subject under discussion from the previous verse. Perhaps, rather than saying as he does, "this dharma called the Self" *(eṣa ātmākhyo dharmaḥ)*, it would be preferable to understand dharma as a "teaching", or "subject matter", about the Self *(eṣa ātmaviṣayo dharmaḥ, arthaḥ)*. The word *dharmān* in *Kaṭha* 2.1.14 could also be understood as "teachings" or "doctrines", or perhaps, as "thing". The explanation of dharma as soul *(dehasya dhāraṇād dharmaḥ, jīvaḥ)* in both the commentary to the *Kaṭha* Upaniṣad and to the *Gauḍapādakārikā* is somewhat forced, and it would be better to understand the word dharma in kārikā 3.1 along the lines of "teaching" or "doctrine".

In the next kārikā Gauḍapāda says:

> Therefore I will tell that which is not
> pitiable, which is without birth and uniform.
> [So that one understands]: nothing is born,
> even while things are born all around. [3.2]

A difficulty with this kārikā lies in the reading: "which is without birth and uniform" *(ajāti samatāṁ gatam)*. Christian Lindtner, a scholar of Buddhism, has argued that the expression *"ajāti samatām"* in this verse (and also the identical expression in 3. 38) should be read as an appositional *(karmadhāraya)* compound, *ajātisamatāṁ gatam*, and the meaning would then be, literally: "unborn-sameness".[61] This may seem a mere grammatical quibble, but it is more than that because what is at stake here is not just the arrangement of the words but the whole meaning of the text. Lindtner suggests that the various editors have been misled by following the commentary of Śaṅkara. I do not know why they should be so misled, especially Vidhushekhara Bhattacharya, who on occasion chooses to amend the text simply because he finds the reading incompatible with his own understanding.[62] Lindtner gives two reasons why this expression should be read as a compound. Firstly, he suggests that the Mādhyamika author Bhāvaviveka (c.490-570) refers to the *Gauḍapādakārikā* when he writes *ajātisamatā* in the eighth chapter (dealing with Vedānta) of his *Madhyamakahṛdaya-Kārikā.* Secondly, Lindtner proposes that Gauḍapāda himself understands "unborn" *(aja)* to be an adjective to "sameness" *(sāmya)* in verses 93, 95 and 100 of the fourth chapter. On this basis, he concludes that there is sufficient evidence to accept that Gauḍapāda's intended phrase was indeed *ajātisamatāṁ gatam.* I wish to defend the reading as it appears in the printed editions and I believe that the interpretation given in the *bhāṣya* is correct.

The traditional explanation is that the object of the verb "I will tell" is *akārpaṇyam* ("not pitiable"), which refers to Brahman, and that the word *ajāti* is a *bahuvrīhi* compound *(nañbahuvrīhi)* describing Brahman *(jāti na vidyate yasya tad brahma, ajāti).* In other words, *ajāti* does not mean simply "no-birth", as it does in Mahāyāna Buddhism, but it means "that which *has* no birth", and it refers to the *akārpaṇyam* Brahman. This is a perfectly plausible explanation of the term *ajāti* and it is entirely in keeping with Gauḍapāda's exposition as we have seen it so far. There is no need to adjust the text to conform to the reading of Bhāvaviveka, who may or may not have been referring to these kārikās, and if he was, he may have misinterpreted them. In any case, the printed text of the *Gauḍapādakārikā* is based on the support of many manuscripts, whereas the state of the printed text of the *Madhyamakahṛdaya* is less certain, being based upon Tibetan translations which were compared with a single available Sanskrit manuscript.[63]

With regard to the instances Lindtner has cited from the fourth chapter (vv. 93, 95 and 100), where he says that *sāmya* is a substantive predicated by the adjective *aja,* we should, however, firstly see 4. 80 where *aja* and *sāmya* are both adjectives describing the word *tat* (referring to the *citta).* In 4. 93 and 95 there is greater difficulty in determining the relationship of the two words, but in 93 both Karmarkar and Bhattacharya understand *aja* and *sāmya* as adjectives describing an unexpressed subject (Karmarkar: "The highest"; Bhattacharya: "The absolute") and I suggest the same is the case in verse 95. In verse 100 *aja* and *sāmya* are adjectives to the word *pada* ("state" i.e. reality). Karmarkar and Bhattacharya understand this to be the case. In verses 80 and 100 *aja* and *sāmya* are both used adjectively, and I think that *sāmya* is not used substantively in any of these verses . Therefore *ajāti* in 3.2 (and also in 3.38) should not be compounded in apposition with *samatā*. The word *ajāti* is a *bahuvrīhi* compound meaning "the unborn" and it is descriptive of Brahman. The word *sāmya* itself occurs in the *Bhagavadgītā* 5.19 where it refers to Brahman.

In the following kārikās Gauḍapāda proceeds to show how "nothing is born, even while things are born all around". Using the analogy of space and something which seems to delimit space, such as a pot, Gauḍapāda says that Brahman has never actually "taken birth", i.e., Brahman never really became a *jīva*, an individual soul, but Brahman is said to be the *jīva* from the standpoint of the conditioning provided by the limiting adjuncts *(upādhi)* of the body-mind complex. Gauḍapāda's analogy of space and pots has been frequently used in later Advaita. He first presents the analogy and then draws forth its implications. He says:

> The Self *[ātman]* seems *[iva]* to have become the individual souls, just as space seems to have become the "pot-spaces". And [the Self] seems to have become the aggregates [body, sense organs etc.] which are comparable to the pot etc. This is the illustration concerning origination. [3.3]

The particle *"iva"*, "as though/seems" indicates that the whole discourse concerning creation is from the standpoint of *māyā*. The verse says that the Self does not undergo a process of change to appear as the individual soul *(jīva)*, any more than space undergoes change to become the space limited by a physical form such as a pot etc. The individual soul is not something other than the Self itself, just as the pot-space is not other than space itself. The pot-space, however, is differentiated from unconditioned space when it is considered from the standpoint of the pot. Similarly, individuality is brought about by the body-mind complex. Individuality is a construction depending upon the body-mind and in the absence of the body-mind there is no "individual soul" as such, just as in the absence of the pot, there is no "pot-space". Implicit in this verse is the idea of *upādhi* or "limiting adjunct" which is central to Śaṅkara's own explanation of the nature of the individual soul, as we shall see later. In Gauḍapāda's illustration, the pot is the *upādhi;* it is the limiting adjunct which seems to create the individuality of pot-space. In the same way, the body-mind complex is the *upādhi* which seems to give rise to an individual soul. It may be noted here that the Self not only appears as the individual soul, but the Self also appears as the matter as well, the body-mind complex, as we see in the second sentence *(ghaṭādivat-ca saṅghātaiḥ).*

Gauḍapāda then draws a number of conclusions from his model. He says:

> Just as when the pots etc. are destroyed, the pot-spaces etc. are merged in space, likewise, the individual souls are merged here in the Self. [3.4]

He says that just as the individual pot-space merges into total space when the pot is destroyed, so too the individual souls resolve into the Self upon the destruction of the limiting adjuncts. Thus origination and destruction are only with reference to the *upādhi*. The loss of "individuality" is therefore not the destruction of what is intrinsically real, but it is the cessation of something produced by the *upādhi*. This verse is suggestive of the *Bṛhadāraṇyaka* passage 4.4.6 (and 7) where it is said of the liberated person: "...his organs do not depart; being nothing but Brahman, he is merged in Brahman."

In the next verse Gauḍapāda uses the illustration to account for the variety of individual experiences, given the teaching that there is just one Self in all bodies. He says:

> Just as when a single pot-space is associated with dust and smoke etc. all [pot-spaces] do not come into association with the dust etc., likewise, all the individual souls are not associated with happiness and so forth. [3.5]

Here he says that just as when the space associated with one pot is affected by smoke etc. it does not mean that every pot-space is similarly affected, so too when one individual soul experiences happiness or suffering all souls do not partake of that same experience, because the experience is confined to a particular limiting adjunct. The first line of this kārikā is almost identical to a line contained in the (pre-Śaṅkara) Vedānta chapter of the *Madhyamakahṛdaya-Kārikā* of Bhāvaviveka (c.490-570).[64] Altogether it would seem that Bhāvaviveka made two other direct references to the *Gauḍapādakārikā*. The first, which we have already seen, is where he uses the expression *ajātisamatā*. The other is a verse that is identical to 2.38 of *Gauḍapādakārikā*.[65] From these references it would appear that Bhāvaviveka was at least familiar with the second and third books of the *Gauḍapādakārikā*, though apart from making these references he has not discussed the teachings of Gauḍapāda in any detail.

It could be objected that there must be a real plurality of individual souls since there are differences among them due to name, form and function.[66] Gauḍapāda says that such differences pertain only to the limiting adjuncts, and therefore a difference in name, form and function cannot be used to infer a real difference among souls. He says:

> The form, the function and the name differ in each case, but space does not differ. The conclusion is the same with regard to the individual souls. [3.6]

He then negates the idea that the individual soul could be considered as a part of Brahman, or as a modification of Brahman.[67] He says:

> As the pot-space is neither a modification nor a part of space, likewise, the individual soul is never either a modification nor a part of the Self. [3.7]

He makes the point that the Self is innately pure:

> Just as, according to children, space becomes polluted with dirt, so too to the unenlightened the Self becomes polluted by impurities. [3.8]

He sums up:

> In death and in birth, in going or coming, and in being present in all bodies, [the Self] is just like space. [3.9]

Just as in the illustration the space does not really arise, dissolve, move etc., and its origination and so forth are only with reference to the limiting adjunct, so too the Self is not born, does not die, and neither does it move etc. Birth, death, motion and the multiplicity of selves are brought about by the limiting adjuncts.

He then makes a point with reference to kārikā 3, where he had said: "And [the Self] seems *(iva)* to have become the aggregates [body, sense organs etc.] which are comparable to the pot etc." Not only does the Self seem to have become the individual souls on account of the limiting adjuncts, but the Self seems to have become the limiting adjuncts as well. Thus there is nothing separate from the Self. Gauḍapāda now explicitly states what was only implied in kārikā 3 by his use of the word "seems" *(iva)* when he says that all talk of "becoming" is only from the standpoint of *māyā*. He says:

> All the aggregates have been created out of the *māyā* of the Self, analogous to a dream. There is no logical possibility here concerning either their superiority or their equality. [3.10]

The second sentence probably contains an oblique reference to an unidentified Mahāyāna text. Presumably the idea is that as all forms are creations of *māyā*, they are ultimately just appearances, and so there is no reason to determine the superiority or the equality among unreal forms.

He now seeks to show that what he said in the above verses harmonises with the teachings of the Upaniṣads. He refers [kārikā 11] to the teaching of the five sheaths *(kośa)* in the *Taittirīya* Upaniṣad (2. 1-5) and he says that such an analysis reveals that the self of all the *kośas* is none other than the supreme soul who is analogous to space.[68] He says [12] that the supreme Brahman is revealed by the various pairs spoken of in the *Madhubrāhmaṇa* portion of the *Bṛhadāraṇyaka* Upaniṣad (2.5), just like a single space is shown to be delimited by two sets of limiting adjuncts, such as the earth *(adhidaiva)* and one's own belly *(adhyātma)*. He then says [13] that the Upaniṣads praise the identity without distinction of the individual soul and the Self and they censure statements of plurality. He says that such a view can be seen to be intelligible in the light of the presentation given in kārikās 3-10.

He then defends this view. Suppose it is argued that there is a real difference between the individual soul and Brahman, because in the Upaniṣads we hear statements such as the following from the *Chāndogya* Upaniṣad: "having entered these three gods along with (as) the individual soul" (6.3.2). In reply, Gauḍapāda says [14] that these statements are not to be taken literally; they are merely figurative expressions referring to the state of things to come after creation. He then states his own view about creation in a verse that is often cited by later Vedāntins. He says:

> Creation has been presented in different ways [in the Upaniṣads], by using [illustrations of] clay, iron, sparks etc. This is a means to lead to [the truth]. There is no difference whatsoever [between the *jīva* and the Ātman]. [3.15]

Śaṅkara quotes this kārikā in his commentary upon *Brahmasūtra* 1.4.14 and so does Sureśvara in his *vārtika* to Śaṅkara's commentary on the *Bṛhadāraṇyaka* Upaniṣad.[69] Why does the *śruti* adopt such a means *(upāya)?* Gauḍapāda says [16] it is because people are at different stages of understanding, and for such people (presumably he is referring to those who are at the lower and middling stages), the *śruti*, in its compassion, teaches this type of conceptual meditation based upon ideas of creation and duality.[70] He says [17] that while the dualists are firmly convinced of their own conclusions, they contradict each other since their conclusions are discrepant. However this teaching of non-difference does not contend with them. He says [18] that for us, non-duality is the highest truth, while duality is said to be the product of that non-duality. Whereas for the dualists there is duality as the highest truth, as well as in appearance. So, since we also accept the appearance of duality, this teaching of non-difference does not conflict with the dualists.

Gauḍapāda then puts forward his own position regarding creation:

> This unborn [non-dual, *turīya-ātman]* becomes different just through *māyā*, not otherwise. For if it is altered in reality, the immortal would become mortal. [3.19]
>
> The disputants consider that an unborn thing takes birth. How, indeed, will an unborn [and thereby] immortal thing become mortal? [3.20. 4.6]
>
> The immortal does not become mortal, nor does the mortal become immortal. In no way will an intrinsic nature change. [3.21, 4.7]
>
> If someone is of the view that an intrinsically immortal thing can become mortal, how can he continue to maintain that this artificially immortal thing will remain changeless? [3.22, 4.8]

We shall discuss some of these verses in the following chapter when we look at the relation between Gauḍapāda and Nāgārjuna. Such verses as the above are just a further articulation of Gauḍapāda's fundamental reasoning. If a thing can be defined as having an intrinsic nature *(svabhāva)* "A", and if that thing undergoes an actual alteration, then it is no longer identical to itself as "A", for it has altered to become, say, "A-B". But in becoming "A-B" and in abandoning its intrinsic nature as "A" the very idea of an intrinsic nature is nullified. Impermanence is the consequence of accepting that an intrinsic nature can alter, because in the very process of becoming "A-B" an initial change has occurred, and further change, leading to destruction, cannot logically be ruled out. Gauḍapāda says that if you first accept that something is immortal, and then you also accept that it changes, that thing would necessarily become mortal, i.e., impermanent. If the unborn Brahman really *becomes* the world, then Brahman would have undergone alteration in the process, and it could not be changeless and immortal. Gauḍapāda's view is especially expressed in kārikā 19: the unborn *turīya* (Brahman-Ātman) appears in the form of the world just because of *māyā*, for if it actually undergoes alteration the immortal would become impermanent.

Gauḍapāda now takes up, in the light of the Upaniṣad texts, this issue about the reality of the origination of the world. He firstly says [23] that the *śruti* seems equivocal about whether creation is an ultimately real fact *(bhūtataḥ)* or not.[71] He says that we should only accept what is (a) ascertained to be the true meaning of the *śruti*, and (b) which proves to be reasonable. Taking up the first point, he cites [24] two *śruti* texts: "there is no difference whatsoever in it [in Brahman]" and "Indra [becomes manifold] through wondrous powers *(māyābhiḥ)*", and he also refers obliquely to a third *śruti* text, the *Puruṣasūkta* of the *Taittirīyāraṇyaka*, in his conclusion that the Ātman, "while remaining unborn", is born "in various ways" due to *māyā*.[72] There are [25] other *śruti* texts too which deny a real creation, such as the denial of "coming into being" *(saṁbhūti)* in the *Īśa* Upaniṣad, and the statement in the *Bṛhadāraṇyaka* which denies a cause for the origination of the *jīva*: "who indeed would produce him?".[73] Furthermore, he says [26] that in the *Bṛhadāraṇyaka* the passage: "This [Self] is 'not this, not this'" denies everything that had been previously stated. The Upaniṣad proceeds in this way because the Self is not an object, and by teaching in this manner the unborn Self *(aja)* is revealed.[74]

He then takes up the second point, namely that the meaning of the *śruti* must also be reasonable. To this end he presents the following two verses:

> The birth of what exists *(sat)* is reasonable
> *(yujyate)* only through *māyā*, not in reality.
> If someone thinks that what exists is born in

> reality, he would have to accept that what is born is born! [3.27]
>
> The birth of what does not exist *(asat)* is certainly not reasonable- whether it is through *māyā* or in reality. The son of a barren woman is not born in reality, nor even through *māyā*. [3.28]

These verses utilise the principle of logical contradiction employed by the Madhyamaka. If something already exists, it cannot be said to come into being, for the simple reason that it exists. Conversely, if something is totally fictitious, like the son of a woman who has never given birth, there is no way that such a product of the imagination could even appear. As Brahman already exists, how could Brahman be said to "take birth" as the world except by *māyā?* Therefore the expressions in the Upaniṣads which speak of Brahman becoming "born" as the world, such as when the *Taittirīya* and the *Chāndogya* Upaniṣads say: "I shall become many. I shall be born" *(bahu syāṁ prajāyeya)*, must be seen as speaking at the level of *māyā*.[75] Kārikā 27 essentially repeats a Madhyamaka argument, as we can see it in the *Madhyamakakārikā*, where Nāgārjuna upholds that it is not logically tenable to speak of the origination of something that already exists. Nāgārjuna says, for example, while restating a previously argued position:

> The origination of what exists *(sat)* as well as the origination of what does not exist *(asat)* [are both] not reasonable *(na yujyate)*. [MK 7.20, first line]

And Candrakīrti remarks on another occasion when this is discussed: "the supposition of a cause for something that already exists, i.e., for what has already been 'born' *(labdhajanma)*, is futile."[76] Gauḍapāda's pun on the word "born": "he would have to accept that what is born *(jātam)* is born *(jāyate)*" is presumably also derived from a Madhyamaka text, possibly the *Catuḥśataka* of Āyadeva, the disciple of Nāgārjuna, as Vidhushekhara Bhattacharya points out that Āyadeva also used such a pun on the word "birth".[77] Candrakīrti too, in his *Madhyamakāvatāra*, quoted in the *Prasannapadā*, has used the same type of expression.[78] So we can see that Gauḍapāda is here drawing upon an argument used by the Madhyamaka. He does so when it suits his purpose, and that is to argue that Brahman cannot really have "taken birth" as the world.

At this point we will leave the remainder of the third *prakaraṇa* in order to follow other arguments raised by Gauḍapāda in the fourth *prakaraṇa* . The two verses that follow those just cited are mentioned in almost identical form in the fourth *prakaraṇa* and we shall refer to them in the next chapter. The remaining eighteen kārikās, which have to do with *sādhana*, will be discussed in chapter three.

(4) The *Alātaśāntiprakaraṇa*

In chapter four, from kārikās three to five, Gauḍapāda refers to the doctrine of origination espoused by the followers of Sāṅkhya and the followers of Nyāya-Vaiśeṣika. He says their teachings are mutually contradictory, and this contradiction only serves to demonstrate that their attempt to uphold real origination is fraught with difficulty:

> Some disputants [followers of Sāṅkhya] consider that there is the origination of a thing that already exists. Other intelligent people [the Vaiśeṣikas] maintain there is origination of what is non-existent - thus do they carry on a dispute with one another. [4.3]

The followers of Sāṅkhya uphold the doctrine of the "origination of the existent effect" *(satkāryavāda)*. Their view is that the material cause contains the effect as a potentiality. The clay, for example, is the material cause of the clay pot which is the effect *(kārya)* . The effect exists in the clay in a potential condition, and due to the operation of instrumental factors like the potter's wheel, the clay transforms into the pot. The effect is nothing in addition to what was already potential within the material cause.[79] The material cause and the effect are the one substance, but the effect is nonetheless considered to be a real entity in its own right. In regard to the origination of the world, the followers of Sāṅkhya believe that the material cause *(prakṛti)* of the world is uncreated and the entire material creation exists potentially within *prakṛti* and then becomes manifest through the transformation of *prakṛti.*

The followers of Nyāyā-Vaiśeṣika uphold the doctrine called *asatkāryavāda,* the doctrine of the "origination of the non-existent effect". They have the opposite view to Sāṅkhya, for they maintain that the effect is an entirely new production in its material cause. In the making of the clay pot, the pot did not come *out of* the clay, as the Sāṅkhya would argue, but the pot is an entirely new creation that comes to inhere *in* the clay through a special relation called "inherence" *(samavāya).* According to this doctrine, the pot and the clay are two different things, each having its own essence. The pot inheres in the clay through this relation called "inherence". The doctrine of *asatkāryavāda* amounts to accepting that something comes from nothing, because from where did the pot come if the pot is a substance in its own right, distinct from the substance of the clay? The Sāṅkhya and the Nyāyā-Vaiśeṣika thus have opposing views about the relation of the effect to its material cause, but they both believe there is a real production and that the effect is a real entity.

> Disputing in this way: "nothing that is already existent originates!", "nothing non-existent can ever originate!", those dualists serve to proclaim non-origination![80] [4.4]

> We applaud the non-origination that they proclaim. We do not dispute with them. Now listen to what is beyond dispute. [4.5]

He then tells what is beyond dispute. In the next three verses he restates what he had said earlier, namely the idea: "In no way will an intrinsic nature change" [4.7, 3.21].[81] If the material cause of the Sāṅkhya is inherently uncreated and eternal, how could it enter into a real process of becoming, with the consequence of impermanence, and yet still be believed to be eternal? Gauḍapāda then puns on the meaning of the word *prakṛti,* which in Sāṅkhya philosophy has the specific meaning of the original material cause of the world; but the word *prakṛti* also has the general meaning of a "natural condition", i.e., an "intrinsic nature". He says:

> *Prakṛti* is to be known as that which is self-existent, inherent, natural, not artificial, and which does not abandon its own nature.[82] [4.9]

Gauḍapāda continues his critique of *satkāryavāda* up to kārikā twenty-three. In kārikā eleven he calls into question the Sāṅkhya conception of *prakṛti* as "unborn". According to Sāṅkhya, *prakṛti*, the material cause, is "unborn", by which they mean it is without origin. But even if that is so, Gauḍapāda says that the Sāṅkhya cannot legitimately call *prakṛti* as "unborn" once it has become the effect. He says if the Sāṅkhya hold that the material cause has become the effect, it would amount to saying that the material cause is born as the effect. But if the material cause is born as the effect, how could it be called "unborn"? And when it has undergone such an alteration, how could it be eternal? In the next verse he shows that there is an unacceptable outcome for the Sāṅkhya in which ever way the Sāṅkhya wishes to state their view. If the Sāṅkhya maintain that the effect is not other than (i.e. not separate from) the material cause (the unborn *prakṛti*), Gauḍapāda says the consequence is that the effect too is unborn! If the Sāṅkhya state their doctrine the other way, that the material cause is not other than the effect that originates, then Gauḍapāda asks (like in verse eleven), how could the followers of Sāṅkhya hold the view that the cause is eternal?

In the next kārikā he says:

> He who accepts that [the effect] originates from the unborn [material cause] is not able to give an example. And an infinite regress would result [if you accept that the effect] originates from [a cause] that is born. [4.13]

The follower of Sāṅkhya can provide no illustration of an unoriginated material cause giving rise to an effect. If, however, it is said that an effect arises from a material cause that is itself a product, then an infinite regress would result.

The follower of Sāṅkhya, wishing to avoid the two defects just mentioned, might take refuge in the argument that cause and effect constitute a beginningless *(anādi)* series, like the seed and the sprout. If cause and effect are beginningless there is no need to discuss the first cause and this would obviate the objections raised in verse thirteen. Gauḍapāda's response is to question this defence of "beginninglessness". He says:

> There are those who say that the effect is the origin of the cause and the cause is the origin of the effect. How can they say that the cause and the effect are without a beginning? [4.14]

Gauḍapāda takes the opponent to task over the inappropriate use of the word "beginningless". He says that the opponent is not correct to call a series "beginningless" when the opponent himself acknowledges a beginning. For when the opponent accepts that each individual seed and sprout has a beginning, he is not then justified to call the whole series "beginningless". Gauḍapāda next says [15] there can be no "beginningless" relation of cause and effect between the binary members of a series, because that would result in mutual dependence: the cause would produce an effect which, in its turn, would produce its own cause, and "birth would be like the birth of the father from his son!".[83]

If the opponent wishes to maintain that there is a "beginningless" relation of cause and effect between the members of a series, Gauḍapāda says [16] that the opponent needs to specify the order as to which is the cause and which is the effect between the individual members of the series. If the opponent says that cause and effect arise simultaneously, Gauḍapāda replies that in that case there would be no connection at all between cause and effect, and he says there would be as much relationship between cause and effect as there is between the two horns of a cow! V. Bhattacharya points out three propositions regarding the order of cause and effect: (i) the cause produces the effect; (ii) the effect produces its cause; and (iii) the cause and its effect mutually produce each other.[84]

Gauḍapāda argues [17] that (ii) is by definition untenable. Regarding (iii) he says:

> If the cause comes into being from the effect and the effect comes into being from the cause, which of the two is produced earlier, depending on which, [the other one] can come into being? [4.18]

As before [in 15], he argues that cause and effect cannot be established between the binary members of a series, on account of their interdependence. Bhattacharya shows that Gauḍapāda is here drawing upon an argument of Nāgārjuna.[85] In fact, Gauḍapāda does not conceal his borrowing, he often provides us with a literary clue about his sources by citing words from the original. But it is important to note, as we will see in more detail later, that Gauḍapāda takes only as much of the Buddhist argument as suits his purpose, and the fact that he finds inspiration in some of the works of the Mahāyāna does not mean that he is committed either to the premises or to the overall philosophical view(s) of the Mahāyāna.

If there is a beginningless series, then the logical position is (i) the cause produces the effect. But Gauḍapāda says, in a difficult verse [19], that the cause has no capability *(aśakti)* to give rise either to an effect that exists prior to its origination *(satkārya)*, or to an effect that does not exist prior to its production *(asatkārya)*.[86] Nor is it possible to determine, in a beginningless series, which actually is the cause and which is the effect and such an inability leads to a violation of the order of cause and effect. However, the opponent could well reply that Gauḍapāda is merely exhibiting his (borrowed) sophistry, for we all know that the seed and the sprout provide an example of a beginningless series. Gauḍapāda replies to this possible objection, by saying [20] that the illustration of the seed and the sprout cannot be used as an example of a beginningless series, because we do not know whether the relation between seed and sprout is in fact beginningless. Gauḍapāda's criticism of the illustration of seed and sprout would presumably put him at odds with Śaṅkara. For Śaṅkara has used this illustration in his *Brahmasūtrabhāṣya* when he attempts to avoid accepting a mutually dependent relation between the performance of karma and the production of a physical body: for there is no possibility of having a physical body without first producing karma, but there can be no production of karma without first having a physical body. Śaṅkara says such faults do not arise since there is the logical possibility of accepting that creation is beginningless, on the analogy of the seed and spout.[87] This contradiction between Gauḍapāda and Śaṅkara can be reconciled, if we bear in mind that Gauḍapāda is seeking to establish what to him is the "ultimate truth" *(paramārthatā)*, namely that no world can really originate from the unborn Brahman, while Śaṅkara is following the argument put forward by the author of the *Brahmasūtra*. Śaṅkara, as we shall see, does not deny this view of Gauḍapāda, but his commentarial works are for the most part written at the level of transactional life *(vyavahāra)*, and his discussions are largely defined by the issues in the texts upon which he comments.

Gauḍapāda concludes this discussion with the following two verses. The first verse refers to the teachings of the Sāṅkhya and the Vaiśeṣika:

> No thing is born either from itself, or from something else. Whether [the effect is said to be] existent [in the material cause], non-existent [in the material cause], or both existent and non-existent [in the material cause] - nothing whatsoever is born.[88] [4.22]

An effect cannot arise out of itself. If the effect already exists within its material cause then it amounts to saying that the effect is born from itself. If the effect is different from the material cause, then anything could originate from anything. In the second sentence he says that all explanations of how a real effect arises out of its material cause are flawed. There are difficulties with the explanation of *satkāryavāda*, that the effect is unmanifest in its cause, and there are even greater difficulties with the *asatkāryavāda*, that the effect is an entirely new creation. If both these explanations are defective, a composite explanation, that the effect is both existent and non-existent in its material case, will not shed more light on the situation. Therefore the doctrines of the Sāṅkhya and the Vaiśeṣika cannot explain how a real effect can arise from the material cause. This argument, as noted by Bhattacharya and others, is also stated by Nāgārjuna in nearly the same way:

> An existing thing does not arise from itself, nor from something else, nor from both. How then does it arise?[89] [MK 21.13]

Lastly, Gauḍapāda says about this defence of "beginninglessness":

> Neither a cause nor an effect arise from what is inherently beginningless. That which *has no beginning*, is beginningless. [4.23]

In 4.14 Gauḍapāda took the opponent to task over the inappropriate use of the word "beginningless". In the above kārikā he specifies what the word "beginningless" should mean: it means that which is without any origin. The word "beginningless" should not be allowed to abandon this literal meaning and acquire instead the meaning that something does have an origin, but that origin is indeterminate. Gauḍapāda's own position was stated earlier, in the second *prakaraṇa*, in verses thirty-one and thirty-two, as well as in the third *prakaraṇa*, in verse nineteen. These verses have been cited above.

Having dismissed the *satkāryavāda* and the *asatkāryavāda* with help from the Madhyamaka, Gauḍapāda now takes up Buddhist thought for discussion. He introduces the Yogācāra, and then raises an objection against it in order to present his own view. It seems that in verse twenty-four he presents the Yogācāra position: we have to admit the empirical existence of the "other-dependent nature" *(paratantrasvabhāva)*, i.e., that there exists a dependently originated *(pratītyasamutpanna)* flow of consciousness, otherwise we cannot account satisfactorily for our various dualistic experiences, as well as for the existence of mental defilements such as passion, hatred and delusion etc. The verse reads:

> A conventional designation has an objective cause, otherwise there would be the disappearance of duality. And as there is the experience of defilements, the existence of the

> "other-dependent" *(paratantra)* has to be accepted. [4. 24]

A "conventional designation" *(prajñapti)*, that "this is such and such", requires an objective cause *(nimitta)*. A conventional designation, as for instance the word "tree", must have an objective cause, i.e., there should be some sense-data because of which we have the conventional designation "this is a tree". If there was no objective basis for our conceptions then there would be no duality, but as there is the experience of the duality of the perceiver and the perceived, some objective basis must exist. It is also a fact that we experience mental defilements such as passion and hatred etc., and these must have a cause. Hence the Yogācāra says that a dependently originated flow of consciousness does exist.

The teaching of the Yogācāra has a different orientation from the Madhyamaka. According to the Madhyamaka, existential statements referring to an object, such as X "is", or X "is not", are characteristic of the two extreme doctrines of eternalism *(śāśvatavāda)* and annihilation *(ucchedavāda)*, both of which the Buddha avoided. The "middle path", according to the Madhyamaka, lies between the two extremes of "is" or "is not", of absolute being or absolute non-being. The Madhyamaka views everything as originating in dependence upon something else, and as a consequence, everything lacks an intrinsic nature of its own. The existence that anything has is due only to its relation to something else upon which it depends: like left exists only in relation to right and vice versa. As all things are dependently originated, all things are necessarily empty of having any inherent nature *(svabhāvaśūnya)* of their own, and so it is illegitimate to use the language of eternalism, to say that a thing has real and independent being, i.e., it "is", when it acquires its existence only through a relation of dependence upon something else. When the applicability of characterising a thing as "is" is found inadmissible, the applicability of "is not" is automatically denied, for once something cannot be characterised by "is", how could it be characterised at some later time by "is not"? According to the Madhyamaka, both being and non-being are relational terms.

The Yogācāra has a somewhat different perspective from that of the Madhyamaka and they do not try to deconstruct the concept of "being" in the same way as the Madhyamaka. We shall try to elucidate their general perspective at the beginning of the following chapter, but suffice to say here that the Yogācāra were prepared to say that things exist, though not in the way that ignorant people imagine them to exist! According to the Yogācāra, the dependently originated flow of consciousness really exists, but the duality of subject and object does not really exist in that dependently originated flow of consciousness.[90] The later followers of the Madhyamaka, Bhāvaviveka and Candrakīrti, considered that the Yogācāra had hypostatised the concept of an "other-dependent" *(paratantra)* nature and criticised the Yogācāra doctrines accordingly.[91]

Christian Lindtner has shown that *Gauḍapādakārikā* 4.24 is almost identical to a verse cited by Bhāvaviveka (c.490-570) in his *Madhyamakahṛdaya-Kārikā,* where in chapter five he discusses the Yogācāra.[92] Richard King, following upon Lindtner's observations, has argued that since Bhāvaviveka in his *Madhyamakahṛdaya-Kārikā* appears to have cited *Gauḍapādakārikā* 3. 5 almost verbatim [supra], as well as referred to *Gauḍapādakārikā* 3.2 (also 3.38) in his expression *ajātisamatā* [supra], it is likely that in these instances Bhāvaviveka is citing the *Gauḍapādakārikā.* But in 4. 24 the situation is reversed, for Gauḍapāda seems to be citing Bhāvaviveka's *Madhyamakahṛdaya-Kārikā,* and so the possibility exists that the *Gauḍapādakārikā* is a work of multiple authorship. King suggests that as the chapters of the *Gauḍapādakārikā* (he refers to chapters 11, 111 and IV) clearly uphold the same general philosophical position, the *Gauḍapādakārikā* probably originated among the members of the same, pre-Śaṅkara, Advaita school, possibly established in Bengal.[93] This is a plausible interpretation. However, the possibility also exists that both Gauḍapāda and Bhāvaviveka are quoting from a common source, or perhaps the verse in question was present in more than one work. There is the possibility of a common source, for Lindtner says that Bhāvaviveka probably quoted this verse from a voluminous Yogācāra work that he used as a resource for his knowledge of the Yogācāra; this text is ascribed to Asaṅga, but is now extant only in a Chinese version (c. 310-390).[94] Although Lindtner finds it unlikely that Gauḍapāda would be using such a work, the possibility nonetheless remains, as does the possibility that this verse appeared in other Yogācāra literature. I think that given the considerable interrelationship among the four chapters of the *Gauḍapādakārikā,* as I pointed out earlier, and given the still tentative nature of the hypothesis of multiple authorship, we are entitled to assume a single authorship for the entire *Gauḍapādakārikā* until more conclusive evidence becomes available.

In the next kārikā Gauḍapāda replies to the Yogācāra view put forward in kārikā 24, and in the following two kārikās he gives his reason for rejecting it. He says:

> From a logical point of view it is accepted that a conventional designation has an objective cause. But in fact, it is maintained that the objective cause *(nimitta)* is no cause *(nimitta).* [4.25]
>
> Consciousness does not come into contact with an object, nor with the appearance of an object. For the object does not exist, and the appearance of the object is not separate from that [object]. [4.26]
>
> At no time does consciousness come into contact with an objective cause. How will consciousness have a causeless error *(viparyāsa)*? [4.27]

He asks the follower of Yogācāra to explain how the error of an externally existing world could ever arise in consciousness, given that, according to the Yogācāra, there is no external object to consciousness. In the Yogācāra works of Asaṅga (c.310-390) and Vasubandhu (c.320-400) the concept of a "store-consciousness" *(ālayavijñāna)* became an established doctrine. The *ālayavijñāna* is the basic causal condition of the other seven types of consciousness (i.e. the five sense perceptions, non-sensory cognition or *manovijñāna*, and the subtle feeling of "I" called *kliṣṭamanas). Ālayavijñāna* consists of the impressions *(vāsanā)*, or "seeds" *(bīja)*, of all past experience, and the maturation of those seeds is what accounts for all experience. The seeds of each individual *ālayavijñāna* evolve into the dependently originated flow of consciousness which then erroneously bifurcates into a subject *(grāhaka)* over against an object *(grāhya)*. Thus the subject of experience, as well as the world experienced in space and time, are both the outcome of the evolution of the seeds of the *ālayavijñāna*.[95] Though Gauḍapāda does not use the term *ālayavijñāna*, we can assume that it is implicit in his argument because kārikās twenty-five to twenty-seven are easily explainable given the context of the Yogācāra teaching of *ālayavijñāna*.

In kārikā twenty-five Gauḍapāda plays upon two meanings of the word "cause" *(nimitta)*. In the first sentence, he says that according to the Yogācāra the dependently originated flow of consciousness *(paratantrasvabhāva)* is the objective cause *(nimitta)* for the error of imputed subject-object duality. In the second sentence, he says that this objective cause *(nimittasya)* is no cause *(animittatvam)*. In this last usage, where he says "no cause", he puns, referring both to the technical Yogācāra meaning and to its common understanding of cause in a general sense. He says that since your *nimitta*, in the Yogācāra sense of an objective cause, i.e., sense-objects, does not exist, it cannot be considered to be a cause *(nimitta)* for error. He explains this point in kārikā twenty-six when he says that "consciousness does not come into contact with an object" *(cittam arthaṁ na saṁspṛśati)*, and he shows in the following kārikā that he understands *artha* and the Yogācāra usage of *nimitta* to mean the same thing when he says: "At no time does consciousness come into contact with an objective cause" *(cittaṁ nimittaṁ na saṁspṛśati)*. In the second sentence of this kārikā he uses the word *nimitta* in the same *double entendre* as he did in kārikā twenty-five, and he says: "How will consciousness have a causeless error?" Gauḍapāda here seems to be saying that the Yogācāra cannot explain how error can arise in consciousness given that, according to the Yogācāra, there is nothing external to consciousness about which there could be an error. There can be an error about something (X) which is erroneously taken as something else (Y), but if there is no *objective cause* then there is *no cause* for an error to arise in consciousness.

It is well known that Buddhism is essentially a teaching about conditions and causes and that the idea of causality is implicit in Buddhism from its earliest recorded teachings.[96] The central conception of Buddhism, "dependent origination" *(pratītyasamutpāda)*, provides the link between the first noble truth, that of the universality of suffering, and the second noble truth as to how suffering arises. We read how the famous

Buddhist monk, Śāriputra, initially became a follower of the Buddha when, upon inquiring about the content of the Buddha's teaching, he was told: "The Tathāgata has explained the origin of those things which proceed from a cause. Their cessation too he has explained. This is the doctrine of the great Śramaṇa."[97] From this we can see that a central concern of Buddhist thought is causality, or "conditionality", i.e., things arise in a state of dependence upon causes and conditions *(hetu-pratyaya)* and cease upon the cessation of those causal factors. It is this idea of causality that Gauḍapāda is targeting in his criticism of the Yogācāra. The Yogācāra teaching is situated within the Buddhist framework of causal operations, but according to Gauḍapāda the causal model of the Yogācāra does not work, for the Yogācāra cannot satisfactorily explain how the error of an unreal subject-object dichotomy, leading to the perception of an external world, can actually arise in the non-dual flow of consciousness without an object.

Since the causality of the Yogācāra is flawed, Gauḍapāda says the truth of the matter is that consciousness does not actually arise, though it seems to do so.

> Therefore, consciousness is not born. The object of consciousness is not born. Those [followers of Yogācāra] who perceive the origination of consciousness, see the footprints [of birds] in the sky! [4.28]

He says that [29] since consciousness is actually unborn, non-origination is its natural state, and he once again repeats the principle, also used by Nāgārjuna: "In no way will an intrinsic nature change".[98] He then says [30] that the Yogācāra cannot take refuge in the defence of the beginninglessness of *saṁsāra,* because it cannot be demonstrated how a beginningless *saṁsāra* can come to an end, and even if that can be shown, the consequence would be that liberation is impermanent, since liberation would have a beginning.

In the next six kārikās, Gauḍapāda reiterates many of the statements that he had presented at the beginning of the second *prakaraṇa.* He repeats verbatim [31] the earlier kārikā [2.6], the first line of which contains his reason *(hetu)* for the *mithyātva* of the waking world: "what does not exist at the beginning and at the end, likewise [does not exist] even in the present. The things that are appearing are equivalent to unreal things, [yet] they are looked upon as though they are real." He then cites [32] the same objection that he had presented earlier [2.7] against the validity of this inference and the use of the illustration of dream. The following four kārikās argue that dream is unreal and the arguments are substantially identical to those given earlier in 2.1-3.[99] The jumbled fashion in which these arguments are presented here in chapter four has congruity only if they are seen to be serving as a reminder of what had already been argued at the beginning of chapter two. If the fourth chapter is an entirely independent treatise, this sequence of verses would hardly make sense.

In the last of these six kārikās [36], Gauḍapāda briefly argues, through analogy with dream, that just as the things seen in dream are unreal, so too "every object of consciousness is unreal". The expression that he uses here, *sarvaṁ cittadṛśyam avastukam,* is reminiscent of the *Laṅkāvatārasūtra,* where the expression *cittadṛśya* regularly occurs.[100] There are obvious external similarities between the teachings of Gauḍapāda and those found in the *Laṅkāvatārasūtra,* but it should not be thought that they are identical teachings; the resemblance is somewhat superficial, for the Vedānta and Buddhist teachings of "non-origination" are governed by a very different internal logic.[101] This has already been indicated, and we hope to make the distinction clearer in the following chapter.

When Gauḍapāda says [36] that just as dream objects are found to be unreal, so too "every object of consciousness is unreal", he is arguing that the experience of objects in the waking world is ontologically equivalent to the experience of objects in the dream world. He now raises an objection against this view:

> Because the apprehension [in dream] is like that of the waking state, dream is considered to be caused by the waking state. Since dream just has the waking state as its cause, the waking state is considered to be real.[102] [4.37]

The objector says that the similarity between dream objects and waking objects, in so far as both are equally objects of consciousness, does not prove that the waking world is unreal. The objects seen in dream are invariably based upon the data given in the waking world; so although dream is unreal, it has the real waking state as its cause. Gauḍapāda replies to this objection by saying that even if dream has the waking state as its cause, it does not follow that the waking state is real. He says [39][103] that when something unreal is experienced in the waking state, a person may, on account of that experience leaving a strong impression in the mind, see that unreal object in dream. However, when something unreal is seen in dream, the person does not find it in the waking state. For example, in the waking world we can watch some gruesome horror movie, which is something unreal, and then have nightmares about it in dream, but upon waking we do not see any of those frightening things. Here, Gauḍapāda accepts the empirical evidence that the waking state exerts a causal influence on dream, but he is also saying that since we can experience unreal things from the waking state during dream, we cannot therefore conclude that our dream experience is based upon a real waking experience. Gauḍapāda's view is that waking and dream are both ontologically unreal (though, as we have pointed out earlier, he also accepts a practical distinction between the two states).

Gauḍapāda further answers this objection by denying the logical possibility of a real causal relation between waking and dream. He says [38] that it has already been argued that everything is unborn because we have not been able to establish how a real origination takes place [from Brahman]. Then, referring to the situation under discussion, concerning the objection about the unreal dream world having its cause in the real waking world, he says that there can be no origination of what is unreal from what is real. Taking the help of the logic of Nāgārjuna, Gauḍapāda says:

> (a) A non-existent *(asat)* [effect] does not arise from a non-existent cause. (b) Nor does an existent [effect] arise from a non-existent cause. (c) And an existent [effect] does not arise from an existent cause. (d) How can a

> non-existent [effect] arise from an existent cause? [4.40]

A similar verse of Nāgārjuna reads:

> (c) An existing thing does not arise from what exists. (b) An existing thing does not arise from what does not exist *(abhāva).* (a) What does not exist does not arise from what does not exist. (d) What does not exist does not arise from what does exist. [MK 21.12][104]

We may note here that Gauḍapāda seems to be using the word *asat* differently in kārikā 39 and 40. In the former kārikā, *asat* means "unreal" *(mithyā)*, i.e., something that appears, but is "not truly existing", whereas in kārikā 40 he uses it in the sense of complete non-existence, following the sense of the word *abhāva* in the above verse of Nāgārjuna. What Gauḍapāda says in this kārikā is that (a) a non-existent effect does not arise from a non-existent material cause because neither exist and so there can be no question of a cause-effect relation. (b) A real effect cannot arise from a non-existent material cause for the simple reason that the latter does not exist. (c) A real effect does not arise from a real material cause for the reason that it cannot be determined how the real effect could originate according to either the explanation of *satkāryavāda*, where the effect is somehow already implicit in the cause, or the explanation of *asatkāryavāda* according to which the effect is an entirely new creation which was previously non-existent in the cause. (d) [refers to the point under discussion, i.e., the unreal *(asat)* - and ultimately non-existent *(asat)* - dream world cannot arise from the real waking world] Nor can a non-existent effect arise from a real material cause, for something real should give rise to something of the same type, i.e., real, but not to something that is of a different order of reality to itself. Candrakīrti remarks in this context that non-existence is opposed to existence, so how could non-existence arise from existence? If it could arise, then darkness could arise from light![105] Taking the support of the Madhyamaka critique of causal relations that are predicated upon ideas of being and non-being, Gauḍapāda uses this argument just to refute the proposition that the unreal dream world can arise from a real waking world.

Gauḍapāda then argues, in verses forty-two through forty-four, that the teaching of "non-origination" *(ajātivāda)* is not contradicted by the perception of duality. He says [42] that the wise people teach a doctrine of origination to people who believe that objects are real because they perceive the objects and because of the ordinary dealings of transactional life. Gauḍapāda says that such people are deceived by perception into concluding that the world is real, and then he says [44] that just as something conjured up by magic, such as a phantom elephant *(māyāhastī)*, could appear to be real and may even function as if it were real, so too the world of existing things appears to be real according to our perception and our ordinary dealings, though it is as unreal as a magical creation.[106] Here, Gauḍapāda makes it clear that non-duality does not mean the absence of perceptual duality, but it is the knowledge that this empirically presented duality is unreal in an absolute sense. We may recall what he said earlier, in a memorable verse: "Like a dream and a magic are seen, and just as a mirage city is seen in the sky, so is this universe seen by those who are well-versed in the Vedānta [i.e. Upaniṣads]." [2.31]. Ultimately *(paramārthataḥ)*, according to Vedānta, there are not two realities: Brahman existing over and against a real universe. In the final analysis, the universe is an appearance *(māyayā)* of Brahman; it is an appearance in and of pure Awareness itself, and since the real and its appearance do not constitute two realities, the truth is therefore non-duality *(advaita)*. There is more to be said on this topic, and we shall take it up for further discussion in chapter four.

In the remaining sixty verses of the fourth chapter *(alātaśāntiprakaraṇa)* the language and arguments of Gauḍapāda are redolent with the vocabulary and thought of the Mahāyāna. We will see more of this portion in the following chapter, when we discuss the question of the influence of Buddhist thought on Gauḍapāda.

---

1 Muralidhara Pandeya, *Śrī Śaṅkarātprāgadvaitavādaḥ*. Delhi: Bharatiya Vidya Prakasan, 1986, p.304. R.D. Karmarkar (ed. and tr.), *Gauḍapāda-Kārikā*. Poona: Bhandarkar Oriental Research Institute, 1973 (1st ed. 1953), p.xxiii.

2 *Śrīmat-Śaṅkaradigvijaya*. Srirangam: Sri Vani Vilas, 1972, v.105, p.60. Also, Swami Tapasyananda (tr.), *Sankara-Dig-Vijaya: The Traditional Life of Sri Sankaracharya by Madhava-Vidyaranya*. Madras: Sri Ramakrishna Math, 1978, p.50.

3 Karmarkar, op.cit., p. xlvii. T.M.P. Mahadevan, *Gauḍapāda: a study in Early Advaita*. Madras: Univ. of Madras, 1960 (3rd Ed.), p.233.

4 I recall that, some years ago, while hearing the exposition of the *bhāṣya* on the *Māṇḍūkya* Upaniṣad and the *Kārikās*, from Swami Dayānanda Saraswati, how he would sometimes pause and express his reservation on the matter of the authorship of the *bhāṣya*, although he taught the *bhāṣya* as if it was the composition of Śaṅkara. Karmarkar, op.cit., seems to be quite ambivalent on the question of authorship, and on a number of occasions he queries whether this commentary could have been authored by Śaṅkara, eg., pp.94f., 97. With regard to a notable opinion of modern scholarship concerning Śaṅkara's authorship of this *bhāṣya*, cf. S. Mayeda, "On the Author of the Māṇḍūkya Upaniṣad and the Gauḍapādīyabhāṣya", *The Adyar Library Bulletin*, Dr V. Raghavan Felicitation Volume, Vols. XXXI-XXXII, 1967-68, p.73-94. I believe that there are some grounds for accepting the commentary as a work of Śaṅkara, but it is not my intention to develop this point here. The suggestion that it might have been Śaṅkara's first commentary is plausible and helps to reconcile the traditional view of authorship with the difficulties encountered in the text.

---

5 Thibaut translates the word *"prakaraṇa"* as "chapter" in his *Vedānta-Sūtras with the commentary by Śaṅkarācārya*, cf. 4.3.1. (Part 11), p.383.

6 S. N. Dasgupta in his, *A History of Indian Philosophy*, Vol 1, Delhi: Motilal Banarsidass, 1975, p.423, says "...I believe that there is sufficient evidence in his kārikās for thinking that he was possibly himself a Buddhist, and considered that the teachings of the Upaniṣads tallied with those of the Buddha."

7 Mahadevan, op.cit., p. 213ff. B.K. Matilal, "Gauḍapāda" in M. Eliade (ed.), *Encyclopedia of Religion*, Macmillan and Free Press, 1987. Karmarkar, op.cit., p.xxvi, makes the valid point that Gauḍapāda's *ajātivāda* is "far removed from the main tenets of Buddhist philosophers, viz. (1) Momentariness *(kṣaṇikatva)* and (2) Dependent origination *(pratītyasamutpāda)* which all schools of Buddhist philosophy accept." And he says (p. xl): "The Ajātivāda of Gauḍapāda has thus nothing in common with the Śūnyavāda of the Buddhists. Gauḍapāda believes in a permanent, unchangeable Principle which cannot be proved to be originated."

8 Andrew Fort says that according to Gauḍapāda and Śaṅkara the *turīya* is considered to be the invariable basis of the three states; whereas in some of the Yoga Upaniṣads, and such texts as the *Yogavāsiṣṭha*, the *turīya* is not so much thought of as an invariable substratum, but as something to be gained through the cultivation of an exalted state of meditation. This difference in understanding the nature of *turīya* is reflected in present day teachings about *turīya*. Cf. Andrew O. Fort, *The Self and Its States*. Delhi: Motilal Banarsidass, 1990, chapters VI and VII. Andrew Fort further differentiates the type of Advaita taught by Śaṅkara from the "Yogic Advaita" of such texts as the *Yogavāsiṣṭha* and the *Jīvanmuktiviveka* in a useful discussion in

---

his book, *Jīvanmukti in Transformation: Embodied Liberation in Advaita and Neo-Vedānta.* State Univ. of New York Press, 1998.

9 Most of the propositions advanced by Gauḍapāda in his kārikās, especially in the first three books, though also in the fourth, consist in making explicit what is already implicit in the *Māṇḍūkya* Upaniṣad, which itself draws upon other Upaniṣadic teachings, most notably BU 4.2.1-4.4.25.

10 R. De Smet and J. Neuner (eds.), *Religious Hinduism* (fourth revised edition). Bombay: St Pauls, 1997, p.89.

11 Thomas Wood, *The Māṇḍūkya Upaniṣad and the Āgama Śāstra: an investigation into the meaning of the Vedānta.* Delhi: Motilal Banarsidass, 1992, (first published Univ. of Hawaii Press, 1990), p.2ff. Wood has his own interpretation of the Upaniṣads, according to which the world is a real transformation of the power of Brahman. He evidently would disagree with such writers on the Upaniṣads as A.E. Gough and Paul Deussen whose views - in spite of the intense cultural chauvinism and tendency to read the Upaniṣads in the light of later Vedānta exhibited by Gough, and the Kantian presuppositions displayed by Deussen - are not without value especially those of Deussen. Gough is of the opinion that: "the unreality of the world...is part and parcel of the philosophy of the Upaniṣads" (p.237). He further says: "The tenant of Māyā is ...no modern invention. The thought, if not the word, is everywhere present in the Upaniṣads, as an inseparable element of the philosophy" (p.248). Gough and Deussen both refer to the use of the particle *iva* ("as it were") and on this point Deussen makes the noteworthy comment: "Strictly speaking, such an 'as it were' or *iva* should be supplied to every page and every line in which the Upanishads are concerned with something other than the ātman." (p.158. Also p.228ff.). Cf. A.E. Gough, *The Philosophy of the Upanishads and Ancient Indian Metaphysics.* London: Kegan Paul, Trench, Trubner and

Co., 1891. Paul Deussen, *The Philosophy of the Upanishads.* New York: Dover, 1966 (first published 1906).

12 The translation is here by Swami Mādhavānanda. Swami Mādhavānanda (tr.), *The Bṛhadāraṇyaka Upaniṣad with the commentary of Śaṅkarācārya.* Calcutta: Advaita Ashrama, 1975, p.460.

13 BSBh 1.3.42, p.288, line 8f., *prājñaḥ parameśvaraḥ, sarvajñatvalakṣaṇayā prajñayā nityam aviyogāt.* (tr) p. 240. Also, line 11. Also 1.3.43, p.289f., (tr) p.242. Also, cf. J. Gonda, "The Īśvara Idea", in his *Change and Continuity in Indian Religion.* Delhi: Munshiram Manoharlal, 1985, p.137.

14 The phrase *prabhavāpyayau hi bhūtānām* in MāU 6 resembles the statement in the *Bhagavadgītā* (11.2), *bhavāpyayau hi bhūtānām.*

15 BSBh 3.3.39, p.745, line 16f., (tr) p.717. Also, BSBh 2.1.14, p.383, line 3f., (tr) p.335.

16 BSBh 2.1.14, p.382f., line 14f., (tr) p.334f. *evaṁ paramārthāvasthāyāṁ sarvavyavahārābhāvaṁ vadanti sarve. ...vyavahārāvasthāyāṁ tu-uktaḥ śrutau apīśvarādivyavahāraḥ "eṣa sarveśvara eṣa bhūtādhipatir eṣa bhūtapāla eṣa setur vidharaṇa eṣāṁ lokānām asambhedāya"* (BU 4.4.22) *iti.*

17 BUBh 4.2.4, p.859f., line 27f., *"neti netyātmānam turīyaṁ pratipadyate".* (tr) p.414.

18 Karmarkar, op.cit., p. 60f.

19 The word *turya* is used in the kārikā, I have replaced it here and in the following kārikās with the more familiar word *turīya*, both words mean "fourth". I also added the word "solely" for emphasis.

---

20 The commentary ascribed to Śaṅkara takes *viparyāsa* to refer to the non apprehension and misapprehension. It understands *"tayoḥ"* to refer to the three states: the waker and dreamer making a single group in that they both have misapprehension in common, and the sleeper making up the second group. Ānandagiri says: "How can the dual *"tayoḥ"* refer to the three, the waker etc? He [Śaṅkara] says that the waker and dreamer constitute one group and the sleeper makes a second group, hence the dual case in the verse is not contradicted." *Upaniṣadbhāṣyam* (vol 1) p.243. This explanation of *tayoḥ* is quite acceptable in terms of the overall meaning, but I hesitate to see why the dual *tayoḥ* should be understood to refer to the three states in the absence of Gauḍapāda giving some indication for us to understand the dual case in that way.

21 Though Gauḍapāda does not use the word "Ignorance" *(avidyā)* here, these passages can be seen to contain the foundation for the teaching that developed in later Advaita, that *avidyā* or *māyā* is a twofold power which both conceals *(āvaraṇa)* the real and projects *(vikṣepa)* the unreal.

22 Śaṅkara says that attaining means, "as he does not see the twofold bondage there [in the *turīyātman]*, he has certain knowledge of the *turīya*. MāUBh 1.15, p.190, line 6f., (tr.) p.216f.

23 This kārikā is cited by Śaṅkara in BSBh 2.1.9. It is clearly evident from the context that the verse can only refer to the *turīya* even though that word is not mentioned.

24 Vidhushekhara Bhattacharya, *The Āgamaśāstra of Gauḍapāda.* Delhi: Motilal Banarsidass, 1989 (1st ed. 1943), p. li.

25 Ibid., p.lvii. Against this view, Karmarkar argued that the four books are inter-related and constitute a "single and complete

treatise propounding the Upaniṣadic philosophy". R.D. Karmarkar (ed. and tr.), *Gauḍapāda-Kārikā*. Poona. Bhandarkar Oriental Research Institute, 1973 (1st ed. 1953), p. xli. My own view is in agreement with Karmarkar.

26 The other argument that Bhattacharya puts forward (p.lv-lvi) in favour of viewing the fourth *prakaraṇa* as an independent work is that it contains invocatory verses *(maṅgalācaraṇa)* at the beginning, as well as an invocatory verse at the conclusion, and this seems to suggest that the fourth book is a separate work from the other three. However, we can see in the verse portion of the *Upadeśasāhasrī* of Śaṅkara that there is an invocatory verse at the beginning of chapter one and there are also invocatory verses at the beginning and at the end of chapters seventeen and eighteen. So the presence of the *maṅgalaślokas* does not preclude the chapters forming a single work with a single authorship. It is admitted that the verse chapters of the *Upadeśasāhasrī* are separate treatises collected into a single work, but the *prakaraṇas* of the *Gauḍapādakārikā* have a closer relationship with one another than do the *prakaraṇas* of the *Upadeśasāhasrī* because, as was shown above, there is considerable interrelationship among the verses and consequently an interrelationship must exist among the ideas as well. Richard King, in a recent article: "Early Advaita Vedānta : The Date and Authorship of the *Gauḍapādīyakārikā", Indo-Iranian Journal,* Vol 38, No. 4, 1995, suggests that the *Gauḍapādīyakārikā* is a composite work written by members of the same, pre-Śaṅkara, Advaita *sampradāya,* possibly in Bengal. He argues that this is so because the fourth *prakaraṇa,* while related to the others, especially to the second and the third, is a later composition than the others. His conclusion appears reasonable on the evidence presented. But perhaps we are not yet entitled to draw such a conclusion from evidence which is still too tentative. King places importance on the separate *maṅgalācaraṇa* in the fourth prakaraṇa. But that proves nothing,

as we have seen from its presence in the *Upadeśasāhasrī*. More importantly, King says that the Buddhist Bhāvaviveka, who is placed sometime in the sixth century CE, cites the fifth kārikā of the *Advaitaprakaraṇa* and showed considerable familiarity with that *prakaraṇa*. King then points out that the twenty-fourth kārikā of the *Alātaśāntiprakaraṇa* quotes a verse that is found in Bhāvaviveka's *Madhyamakahṛdayakārikā* (V.6). In addition, Gauḍapāda's refutation of the Yogācāra teaching in the following kārikā (4.25) is in agreement with the argument of Bhāvaviveka. King argues that since the fourth *prakaraṇa* is likely to be quoting Bhāvaviveka, the fourth *prakaraṇa* is later that the third *prakaraṇa* which Bhāvaviveka himself cites. The weak point in the argument is in demonstrating that Gauḍapāda is in fact quoting from Bhāvaviveka, since the verse in question is also found in a work ascribed to Asaṅga, the *Vikhyāpana* (King, ibid., p.339f.), which is itself, according to H. Nakamura *(Indian Buddhism: a Survey with Bibliographical Notes.* Delhi: Motilal Banarsidass, 1987, p.266f.) substantially based upon the *Yogācārabhūmi*. It is possible that Gauḍapāda did not depend upon Bhāvaviveka as the source for this verse. Christian Lindtner, on whose work King relies for the tracing of kārikā twenty-four, says that: "I am, however, far from suggesting that this observation in itself is strong enough to make us assume that the GK is dependent upon MHK" (Christian Lindtner, "Remarks on the Gauḍapādīya-Kārikās (GK)", *Indo-Iranian Journal,* 28 (1985) p.275-279.). It would seem that King is arguing more than what is warranted and he is not justified in making this point a foundation upon which to construct a sound hypothesis of chronology. Given that Gauḍapāda shows familiarity with the work of Maitreya/Asaṅga, in so far as kārikā seventy- five of the fourth *prakaraṇa* refers to the first verse of the *Madhyāntavibhāga* of Maitreya/Asaṅga, it is quite possible that Gauḍapāda cites the verse in question from a source other than Bhāvaviveka's *Madhyamakahṛdayakārikā*. Thus King's conclusion needs further evidence before it can be confidently accepted and while such evidence is lacking we shall continue to maintain, given the considerable interrelationship among the kārikās, the single authorship of the entire *Gauḍapādakārikā.*

27 BU 4.4.20; 4.4.22, 24, 25. MU 2.1.2. KaU 1. 2.18; 2.2.1. BG 2.21; 4.6; 7.25; 10.3, 12.

28 The word *"prapañca"*, which occurs in MāU 7 and 12, is used in Vedānta in the sense of "phenomenal world", or just as "world". In Buddhist literature the word *prapañca* has a somewhat different sense and it is sometimes translated as "conceptual differentiation", for it conveys more of the idea that the reality of the world is something that is conceptually "constructed" by the use of language.

29 Vetter's views are discussed in the article by King, op.cit., p.333.

30 "Unreal", in the sense that I am using the term, corresponds to the meaning of *asatya* as explained by Paul Hacker in his article, "The Theory of Degrees of Reality in Advaita Vedānta", in Wilhelm Halbfass (ed.). *Philology and Confrontation: Paul Hacker on Traditional and Modern Vedānta.* Albany: State University of New York Press, 1995, p.139f.

31 Gauḍapāda says: "since objects are within [the body] for the reason that they are enclosed." Śaṅkara, too, says: "For chariots and the like cannot find room within the enclosed space of the body." BSBh 3.2.3. p.624, line 8.

32 Ibid., p.624, line 8f., (tr) p.591.

33 Ibid., p.625, line 1f., (tr) p.591.

34 Ibid., p.626, line 6, (tr) p.592.

---

35 The syntax of this kārikā is particularly difficult to determine. Both Karmarkar and Bhattacharya have trouble here and Bhattacharya op.cit., p.17f., chooses to amend the text without manuscript support. I tentatively suggest the following *anvaya: yathā tatra svapne tathā jāgarite (vaitathyaṁ) smṛtam. antaḥsthānāt tu bhedānāṁ saṁvṛtatvena, tasmāt (svapnāt) (jāgaritaṁ) bhidyate.*

36 See the previous note. F. Whaling, "Śaṅkara and Buddhism", *Journal of Indian Philosophy*, 1979, 7, p.24. S. Kaplan, "A Critique of an Ontological Approach to Gauḍapāda's Māṇḍūkya Kārikās", *Journal of Indian Philosophy*, 1983, 11, p.343f. Richard King, *Early Advaita Vedānta and Buddhism: The Mahāyāna Context of the Gauḍapāda-kārikā.* Albany: State Univ. of New York Press, 1995, p.170.

37 Bhattacharya, op.cit., p.19. Karmarkar, op.cit., p.73. The author of the Sanskrit commentary, whom we provisionally accept as Śaṅkara and this commentary as his first, understands kārikā six to supply an additional reason. It seems that Śaṅkara gives the reason of *dṛśyatva* to explain the *"prasiddhenaiva hetunā"* in kārikā five. This is unnecessary, for we should expect that Gauḍapāda, having so carefully proved the unreality of dream, would not fail to tell us the *hetu* for proving the unreality of the waking world. And Gauḍapāda does give the *hetu* in kārikā six.

38 This presupposition is accepted by the Advaitins and by the Mādhyamika Buddhists. I do not think we need say that Gauḍapāda learnt this from Nāgārjuna, rather both were articulating a commonly accepted idea.

39 BG 2. 16. Śaṅkara defines *satya* and *mithyā (anṛta)* on the basis of changelessness and change, cf. TUBh 2.1., p.283, line 8f. (tr.) p.291, "...a thing is said to be *satya*, true, when it does not

change the nature that is ascertained to be its own; and a thing is said to be unreal when it changes the nature that is ascertained to be its own. Hence a mutable thing is unreal...".

40 See Hacker's clear exposition in, "The Theory of Degrees of Reality in Advaita Vedānta" in W. Halbfass (ed.), *Philology and Confrontation: Paul Hacker on Traditional and Modern Vedānta,* op.cit., p.137-145. On p. 143 he says: "...'indeterminable' is a synonym of 'not truly existing'."

41 Rāmānuja argued that if two cognitions have the same object, but are found to contradict each other, then the cognition produced by a valid means of knowledge will negate the erroneous cognition and the object of the erroneous cognition can be accepted as unreal, such as when the cognition of the rope negates the cognition of the superimposed snake, which is then admitted to be unreal. But when no such contradiction occurs between cognitions there is no occasion for unreality. Change does not involve a contradiction of cognitions and so, he says, the fact that something is not eternal does not mean it is unreal. Cf. R.D. Karmarkar (ed. and tr.), *Śrībhāṣya of Rāmānuja,* (Three Parts), Poona: University of Poona Sanskrit and Prakrit Series Volume 1, 1959-64. Part 1, para 31, p.52f. Also, Michael Comans, "Later Vedānta", B. Carr and I. Mahalingam (ed.), *Companion Encyclopedia of Asian Philosophy,* London: Routledge, 1997, p.219f.

42 V. Bhattacharya, op.cit., p.19, has again chosen to amend the text and he misunderstands the verse.

43 BS 1.4.23.

44 We also read in the *Bṛhadāraṇyaka* Upaniṣad that: "There is no other witness but This, no other hearer but This, no other thinker

but This, no other knower but This." BU 3.8.11, translation by Swami Mādhavānanda. Also, cf. 3.7.23.

45 I read *"bahiścitte"* in the third *pāda*, following Bhattacharya, op.cit., p.23. Śaṅkara understands *"bahiścittaḥ"*. The former reading gives a more straightforward meaning.

46 MK 7.34; 17.33 and 23.8. Bhattacharya notes that the phrase "dream and magic" *(svapnamāyā)* can be found a number of times in the *Laṅkāvatārasūtra*. Bhattacharya, ibid, p.38. According to A.K. Warder, the *Laṅkāvatārasūtra* is a composite work. A.K. Warder, *Indian Buddhism*. Delhi: Motilal Banarsidass: 1991 (2nd ed.), p.433. H. Nakamura lists various opinions about the date of composition of the *Laṅkāvatārasūtra* but the consensus seems to be that it was composed around 400 CE. Cf. H. Nakamura, *Indian Buddhism: a Survey with Bibliographical Notes.* Delhi: Motilal Banarsidass, 1987, p.231.

47 H. Nakamura places Nāgārjuna c. 150-250 AD. Cf. Nakamura, ibid, p.235. C. Lindtner also places him in the second or third centuries AD. Christian Lindtner, "Nāgārjuna", in B. Carr and I. Mahalingam (ed.), *Companion Encyclopedia of Asian Philosophy,* op.cit., p.350. Christian Lindtner, in his Foreword to V. Bhattacharya's work, *The Āgamaśāstra of Gauḍapāda,* suggests ca. 500 AD as the period of the composition of the *Gauḍapādakārikā* (p.vic). This is the time proposed by Bhattacharya also, p.lxxvi. Karmarkar is of the opinion that Gauḍapāda cannot have lived later than c. 500 AD. R.D. Karmarkar, *Gauḍapāda-Kārikā,* op.cit., p.iv.

48 *Sāṅkhyakārikā* 62 reads: *tasmān na badhyate 'ddhā na mucyate nāpi saṁsarati kaścit, saṁsarati badhyate mucyate ca nānāśrayā prakṛtiḥ.*

---

49 The placement of the particle "and" *(ca)* makes this verse somewhat difficult to understand. The difficulty lies in whether *ca* is merely conjunctive, in which case we can understand: *ayam asadbhir bhāvair eva-advayena ca kalpitaḥ*. Or whether, as Karmarkar suggests, it means "further", so that the idea could be: "this Self, moreover *(ca)*, is imagined to be the unreal things through the non-dual." Bhattacharya takes it to be a conjunction, but linked with *bhāvā api* in the second line. I originally followed Karmarkar's interpretation, but in the text I have translated and explained the kārikā according to the explanation given by Swami Paramārthānanda of Chennai (Madras).

50 BSBh 1.1.5, p.106, line 5, (tr) p.50; 1.4.3, p.298, line 1, (tr), p.249; 2.1.14, p.382, line 3, (tr) p.334; 2.1.27, p.401, line 8, (tr) p.356. BUBh 2.4.10, p.763, line 15ff., (tr) p. 252.

51 For example, S. Nikhilananda (tr.), *Vedāntasāra: or the Essence of Vedānta of Sadānanda Yogīndra*. Calcutta: Advaita Ashrama, 1974, p.21. Also, similar ideas are expressed in the *Vivekacūḍāmaṇi*, which I believe to be a work composed at a much later period than that of Śaṅkara. For example, cf. v.109.

52 MāUBh 3.1, p.208, line 14, (tr) p, 269.

53 KaUBh 1.1.21, p.66, line 2.

54 KaUBh 2.1.14, p.90, line 16.

55 Th. Stcherbatsky, *The Central Conception of Buddhism and the Meaning of the word "Dharma"*. First published 1923 by the Royal Asiatic Society. Reprinted, Delhi: Motilal Banarsidass, 1970, p.68.

---

56 H. Nakamura, *A History of Early Vedānta Philosophy.* (Translated into English by T. Leggett, S. Mayeda, T. Unno and others). Delhi: Motilal Banarsidass, 1983, p.20f.

57 See Stcherbatsky, *The Central Conception of Buddhism and the Meaning of the word "Dharma"*, op.cit. A.K. Warder preferred the term "principle" to "element". Cf. A.K. Warder, "Dharmas and Data", *Journal of Indian Philosophy,* vol.1, 1971, p.272-295.

58 Cf. Stcherbatsky, ibid, p.44.

59 Nakamura, op.cit., n.17, p.32.

60 In BU 1.5.23 the word dharma could mean "law". The KaU 2.1.9 seems to refer to BU 1.5.23.

61 Chr. Lindtner, "Remarks on the Gauḍapādīya-kārikās". *Indo-Iranian Journal,* vol. 28, 1985, p.275-279.

62 Eg., Bhattacharya, op.cit., p.128 in his note to kārikā 4.23.

63 Nakamura, *A History of Early Vedānta Philosophy,* op.cit., p.184f. In the case of the passages that Lindtner cites there is no Tibetan text to corroborate the Sanskrit reading, cf. Nakamura, ibid, p.200.

64 V.V. Gokhale, "The Vedānta-Philosophy Described by Bhavya in his *Madhyamakahṛdaya.*" *Indo-Iranian Journal,* vol.2, no.3, 1958, p.175. Nakamura, *A History of Early Vedānta Philosophy,* op.cit., p.185.

65 Nakamura, ibid., p.201 (GK 2.38, not 3.38 as given on p.201).

66 A similar type of prima facie argument, which relies on name, form and function, in order to prove difference, is raised by Toṭaka, who tradition accepts as one of the principal pupils of Śaṅkara, in his *Śrutisārasamuddharaṇam*. Cf. Michael Comans (tr.), *Extracting the Essence of the Śruti: the Śrutisārasamuddharaṇam of Toṭakācārya*. Delhi: Motilal Banarsidass, 1996, vv.137-138, p.91.

67 This point is discussed in the *Śrutisārasamuddharaṇam*, ibid, vv.40-41, p.31.

68 I presume that the word "ātman" in the verse means '"self", in just the general sense of something "interior", in the same way as it is used in the expressions referring to the *kośas* in TU (2.2-5) which repeatedly speak of *"anyo'ntara ātmā"* as a way of negating identification with each *kośa*. The word *"para"* would then qualify *jīva*, which is a somewhat unusual usage, perhaps it has some precedent in the *parā prakṛti* of Īśvara as *jīvabhūtā* in BG 7.5. V. Bhattacharya reads *para* along with *ātman*. Bhattacharya also reads *"sa yathā"* instead of *khaṁ yathā*, but the latter is a better reading because space is used as the illustration of the nature of the ātman in verses 3-9 and it is fitting that he would say that the Upaniṣads reveal the Self to be like space. He uses the illustration of space again in the following verse.

69 BUBhV 2.1. 387

70 Śaṅkara makes a similar statement in BUBh 4.4.25, p.938, line 25f., (tr.) p.534.

71 The usage of the word *bhūta* as meaning "really existing" can be seen in MK 23.v.24: *yadi bhūtāḥ svabhāvena kleśāḥ keciddhi kasyacit; kathaṁ nāma prahīyeran kaḥ svabhāvaṁ prahāsyati.*

---

72 Cf. *neha nānā-iti* BU 4.4.19, KaU 4.11. *Indro māyābhir iti* Rgveda 6.47.18; BU 2.5.19. *ajāyamāno bahudhā* cf. *Taittirīyāraṇyaka* 3.13.1 *(ajāyamāno bahudhā vijāyate),* is a very well known hymn forming part of the *Puruṣasūkta* in the Yajur Veda.

73 Following Deussen, *The Philosophy of the Upanishads,* op.cit., p.155, I have understood *saṁbhūti* to mean "coming into being". The Upaniṣad passages referred to are *Īśa* 12 and BU 3.9.28.7.

74 BU 2.3.6, 3.9.26, 4.2.4, 4.4.22, 4.5.15.

75 TU 2.6.1 and the identical expression in CU 6.2.3.

76 P.L. Vaidya (ed.), *Madhyamakaśāstra of Nāgārjuna with the commentary Prasannapadā by Candrakīrti.* Buddhist Sanskrit Texts no. 10. Darbhanga: The Mithila Institute of Post-Graduate Studies and Research, 1960, 1.8, p.28.

77 Bhattacharya, op.cit., p.66. *"sato yadi bhavej janma jātasyāpi bhaved bhavaḥ".*

78 P.L. Vaidya (ed.), *Madhyamakaśāstra of Nāgārjuna with the commentary Prasannapadā by Candrakīrti,* op.cit, p.5, *"jātasya janma punar eva ca naiva yuktam."*

79 It should be noted that: "even according to the Sāṁkhya, a cloth as such [i.e. an effect] does not exist before its origination; only its essence or substance-stuff exists in the form of the threads." D. N. Shastri, *The Philosophy of Nyāya Vaiśeṣika and its Conflict with The Buddhist Dignāga School.* Delhi: Bharatiya Vidya Prakashan, 1976, p.237.

---

80 I read "dualists" *(dvayāḥ)*, following the edition of Karmarkar, and I am in agreement with his opinion (p.111) that the word *dvayāḥ* spoken of in kārikā 4 refers just to the followers of the two views mentioned in the previous kārikā. Some texts read *"advayā"*, as does V. Bhattacharya, whose views on this kārikā are criticised by Karmarkar (p.111).

81 In kārikās 4.6-8 he restates what was said in 3.20-22.

82 The word *sāṁsiddhika* occurs in *Sāṅkhyakārikā* 43.

83 GK 4.15.

84 Bhattacharya, op.cit., p.119.

85 Ibid., p.120. Nāgārjuna's verse refers to the interdependent relation between things, using the illustration of fire and fuel: *yadīndhanam apekṣyāgnir apekṣyāgniṁ yadīndhanam, katarat pūrvaniṣpannaṁ yadapekṣyāgnir indhanam.* [MK 10.8]

86 I have followed Bhattacharya's explanation of the term *aśakti*. Ibid., p.121f.

87 BSBh 2.1.36, p.409, line 8f., (tr) p.365.

88 For a further explanation of this argument in reference to *"sadasatsadasat"* cf. Michael Comans (tr.), *Extracting the Essence of the Śruti: the Śrutisārasamuddharaṇam of Toṭakācārya*, op.cit, verses 141-150.

89 *na svato jāyate bhāvaḥ parato naiva jāyate, na svataḥ parataścaiva jāyate jāyate kutaḥ.*

---

90 For the Yogācāra perspective on the existence of emptiness and the existence of the "unreal imagination" in emptiness, cf. "What Remains in Śūnyatā: A Yogācāra Interpretation of Emptiness" in Gadjin M. Nagao, *Mādhyamika and Yogācāra.* Edited and translated by L.S. Kawamura. Delhi: Sri Satguru Publications, 1991 [reprint].

91 Bhāvaviveka discusses the Yogācāra in ch.5 of his *Madhyamakahṛdaya-Kārikā.* Candrakīrti (c.650) criticises the Yogācāra in his *Madhyamakāvatāra.* Cf. C.W. Huntington, *The Emptiness of Emptiness.* Honolulu: Univ. of Hawaii Press, 1989. Candrakīrti also says, in his commentary *Prasannapadā* upon the MK 15.11: "The [follower of the Yogācāra] who accepts the 'other-dependent' *(paratantra)* nature of consciousness and its formations, avoids [the extreme] of eternalism since he says that the 'imagined nature' *(parikalpitasvabhāva)* does not exist in the other-dependent nature. He also avoids [the extreme] of annihilation, since he accepts that the 'other-dependent' nature exists, as it is associated with the defilements and their purification. [Candrakīrti's refutation:] Since [the follower of Yogācāra] says that the 'imagined nature' does not exist, and the 'other-dependent' nature does exist, he therefore ends up holding *both* the views, eternalism as well as annihilation. How can he avoid both extremes? His explanation does not make sense, because [we have] demonstrated that it is not logically correct to maintain that the ["other-dependent" nature], which is produced out of causes and conditions, can have an inherently existing nature. Thus it is only in the Madhyamaka view that there is freedom from the consequences of the two views of eternalism and annihilation, but not in such doctrines as those of the Vijñānavādin." Vaidya (ed.), op.cit., *Prasannapadā* on MK 15.11, p.120, line 13f. Candrakīrti also refers to the Vijñānavāda teachings as *neyārtha,* i.e., taught by the Buddha as a provisional

teaching, to assist those who could not yet understand the final teaching *(nītārtha)*, ibid, line 23f.

92 The verse in the *Madhyamakahṛdaya-Kārikā*, ch.5.v.6, reads: *prajñapteḥ sanimittatvād anyathā dvayanāśataḥ, saṁkleśasyopalabdheśca paratantrāstitā matā.* Cf. Chr. Lindtner, "Remarks on the Gauḍapādīya-kārikās". *Indo-Iranian Journal,* vol. 28, 1985, p.275-279. Lindtner says that Bhāvaviveka has also quoted the same verse in the appendix to chapter 25 of his commentary, *Prajñāpradīpa,* on the *Madhyamakakārikā,* while criticising the Yogācāra concept of *paratantrasvabhāva.*

93 Richard King, *Early Advaita Vedānta and Buddhism: The Mahāyāna Context of the Gauḍapādīya-kārikā.* Op.cit., 1995, p.235. This matter has also been discussed in note 26 *supra.*

94 Ibid. p.277. Lindtner refers to its reconstructed name as *"Vikhyāpana"* (Nagao refers to it as *Āryadeśanā-vikhyāpana,* cf., *Mādhyamika and Yogācāra,* op.cit., p.56). Cf. H. Nakamura, *Indian Buddhism,* op.cit., p.266f. Nakamura says that this work is "substantially based upon Maitreyanātha's *Yogācārabhūmi.*" Lindtner also suggests that on the basis of readings of the verse as found in the *Madhyamakahṛdaya-Kārikā* (ch.5.v.6) and in the **Vikhyāpana,* the word *sanimittatvam* in GK 4. 24 should be amended to *sanimittatvāt,* which he says, makes good sense as well as good syntax. However, when Gauḍapāda quotes a verse from some source he generally makes an alteration to it, so *sanimittatvam* need not be changed to *sanimittatvāt.* The syntax of the verse as it stands is satisfactory; if anything it seems a slight improvement over the original. Lindtner (p.277) also takes Śaṅkara to task for misunderstanding the expression *"paratantra",* which refers, as he has shown, to the Yogācāra thought and not as Śaṅkara says to "other systems". I think that Śaṅkara (provisionally accepting that this is his earliest commentarial work) has, on the whole, given a good account of Gauḍapāda's

teachings. It has to be accepted, however, that Śaṅkara's commentary is deficient in failing to inform us of the context of some of Gauḍapāda's kārikās, as well as for its occasional misinterpretations on account of not being aware of that context. The study of Śaṅkara's *bhāṣya* on this text needs to be supplemented and amended at certain places in the light of what we know of Gauḍạpāda's considerable knowledge of the Mahāyāna, for this is not adequately brought out in the *bhāṣya*.

95 Cf. Nagao, *Mādhyamika and Yogācāra*, op.cit., p.126, "time and space are produced on the basis of the evolving cognition (viz., on the basis of the evolution of the *ālaya-vijñāna*). Also, p.143, "...both sentient beings and the world as a container are found, ultimately and truly, only in the *ālaya-vijñāna*." Also cf. Lambert Schmithausen, *Ālayavijñāna -On the Origin and the Early Development of a Central Concept of Yogācāra Philosophy* (Two vols.). Tokyo: The International Institute for Buddhist Studies, 1987. In the course of a highly detailed exploration of the term *ālayavijñāna*, Schmithausen remarks, p.100, that: "In the *Mahāyānasaṃgraha* and also...in the *Abhidharmasamuccaya* [two main works of Asaṅga], ālayavijñāna is primarily conceived of as a container or even hypostasis of Seeds *(bīja)*. This function of ālayavijñāna is, of course, extremely important in a mind-only system in which even the content of perceptions and cognitions cannot be derived from an external world but only from a mental source." Nakamura, *Indian Buddhism*, op.cit., p.255, states in summary that: "Buddhist Idealism teaches that all phenomena are nothing but the manifestations *(pratibhāsa)* out of the 'seeds' of the phenomena and that all the seeds constitute the Ālayavijñāna. No object can exist apart from the function of cognition by the subject."

96 See, for example, A.K. Warder, *Indian Buddhism*. Delhi: Motilal Banarsidass (2nd. Ed.) 1980, p.107.

---

97 Bhikshu Sangharakshita, "Buddhism", in A.L. Basham (ed.) *A Cultural History of India.* Oxford: Oxford University Press, 1975, p.85.

98 In 4.29 he repeats the reason given earlier in 3.21 and again in 4.7. See MK 15.8.

99 4.33 is identical in meaning to 2.1. 4.34 is identical in meaning to 2.2 (the last line of each is the same).

100 Eg., 1., p.5, line 3; 3.v.75 p.75; 10. vv.362, 363, 594, 651. P.L. Vaidya (ed.), *Saddharmalaṅkāvatārasūtram.* Buddhist Sanskrit Texts no. 3. Dharbanga: The Mithila Institute, 1963.

101 Regarding the teaching of "non-origination" *(anutpāda)* in the *Laṅkāvatāra,* cf. D.T. Suzuki, *Studies in the Lankavatara Sutra.* London: Routledge and Kegan Paul, 1957 (reprint) p.122f.

102 I am reading *tasya* in the third *pāda* to refer to dream mentioned in the second *pāda* , i.e., "Since dream just has waking as its cause". The understanding of *tasya* as *svapnadṛśaḥ* seems to make the meaning unnecessarily complex.

103 V. Bhattacharya, op.cit., p. 146, considers that kārikās 38 and 40 should be read together as they are logically connected, as are kārikās 39 and 41. He says, p.146, "I think the logical order of the following four kārikās, viz., 38-41 should be as follows: 39, 41, 38 and 40. For the kārikās 39 and 41 with 32-37 form the same subject of discussion, i.e., the equality of the states of dream and wakefulness, while the kārikās 38 and 40 are meant for showing the impossibility of origination directly." That does have a certain merit, though I am hesitant to link 41 with 39.

---

104 This verse was noticed by Bhattacharya, p. 148. The verse reads: *na bhāvājjāyate bhāvo, bhāvo 'bhāvānna jāyate; nābhāvājjāyate 'bhāvo, abhāvo bhāvānna jāyate.*

105 P.L. Vaidya (ed.). *Madhyamakaśāstra of Nāgārjuna with the commentary Prasannapadā by Candrakīrti*, op.cit., cf. 21. 12, p.182.

106 The word *māyāhastī* occurs, as noted by V. Bhattacharya, p.152, in the *Laṅkāvatārasūtra*, 10. 126. It does not, however, seem to be a frequently used expression in the *Laṅkāvatāra*.

CHAPTER TWO

Gauḍapāda's Teachings in relation to Buddhist Thought

It is not a matter for dispute whether Gauḍapāda was familiar with Buddhist thought. It is clear from the third chapter of his work, and especially so from the fourth, that he was familiar with Buddhism in considerable detail. This is not in itself so extraordinary, considering that during the period in which he lived (c.500 CE) Buddhism was in a position of intellectual dominance in India, through the development of the Madhyamaka and the Yogācāra schools. However Gauḍapāda's teaching should not be mistaken as Buddhist even though he utilised some arguments from notable Buddhist authors and made reference to their works, for even as he did so, he distanced his teachings from Buddhism. I will try to show in what way his teaching differs from Buddhist thought, but firstly it may be useful to describe briefly the central themes of the two main schools of Mahāyāna Buddhist philosophy, the Madhyamaka and the Yogācāra, so that we are in a better position to see the difference between Gauḍapāda and Buddhism.

The logical foundation of Buddhism is the teaching of "dependent origination" *(pratītyasamutpāda)* about which the Buddha is said to have remarked: "Whoever understands it understands the Dharma and whoever understands the Dharma understands it."[1] This teaching can be expressed by the formula: "This being, that is; from the arising of this, that arises"; and in reverse: "This not being, that is not; on the cessation of this, that ceases."[2] In saying that "dependent origination" stands squarely at the centre of Buddhist thought, I am not referring just to its specific exemplification in the form of well-known "twelve links" *(nidāna)* of the cycle of existence, but to the general principle that all phenomena arise in dependence upon causes and conditions, i.e., everything comes into being only in a relation of dependence upon something else. The teaching of "dependent origination" is said to avoid two extreme views, the extreme position that there is something permanent *(śāśvatavāda)* and the other extreme that there is nothing that endures *(ucchedavāda)*. The Buddha's view is a middle way between these two extreme positions, for he taught that while all things do have continuity, it is the continuity that belongs to a changing series. Each member of the series is impermanent; a member of the series arises in a condition of dependence upon the previous member and, in turn, provides the condition for the arising of the next member of the series. Buddhism thus teaches the "middle way" between the extremes of Being and non-Being.

The Madhyamaka school was founded, or consolidated, by Nāgārjuna (c. 150-250 CE) who criticised the realistic pluralism of the Buddhist Sarvāstivādins who held that the elements of existence *(dharmas)*, although transitory, were yet real entities *(dravya)* having an essential nature *(svabhāva)*. Nāgārjuna took his stand on the principle of dependent origination and developed it to its logical conclusion.[3] He argued that if some thing is said to have an essential nature it would mean that the thing could exist independently in its own right. But according to Buddhism all things originate only in dependence upon other things; when 'A' depends for its existence upon the existence of 'B', how can 'A' be said to have an independent nature of its own? To be dependently originated is to have no essential nature; and since everything is dependently originated, everything is without an essential nature *(nissvabhāva)*, i.e., everything is *empty* of an essential nature *(svabhāvaśūnya)*. Therefore everything is empty *(śūnya)*. "Emptiness" is the equivalent of *nissvabhāva*, which is the outcome of the understanding of dependent origination. Thus we can see how Nāgārjuna has used the central teaching of early Buddhism to prove the "emptiness" *(śūnyatā)* of all phenomena. The followers of Madhyamaka said that this teaching of *śūnyatā* is the correct understanding of the "middle way", because it avoids the two extremes of permanence and of annihilation. For if a thing has no real existence *(bhāva)*, then its real non-existence *(abhāva)* too cannot be established. Thus all concepts such as being and non-being, *saṁsāra* and *nirvāṇa* etc. are found to be only relational, like "left" is relative to "right" and vice versa.

The other great tradition of Mahāyāna Buddhism, the Yogācāra (Vijñānavāda), accepted the Madhyamaka teaching of the emptiness of all phenomena. The followers of Yogācāra, however, considered the Madhyamaka too abstract and not sufficiently focused upon the fundamental psychological experience of consciousness. According to the Yogācāra, consciousness *(vijñāna)* exists as a series of momentary states, one consciousness-state arising in dependence upon the previous consciousness-state. Consciousness is thus a flow of momentary states, each of which is dependently originated. In consciousness there is neither a subject *(grāhaka)* nor an object *(grāhya)*, there is just a flow of consciousness, and it is this stream of consciousness which is erroneously divided into a personal subject and an objective world. The truth about consciousness is that it is dependently originated and is intrinsically free from the dichotomy of subject and object. The Yogācārins call this dependently-originated stream of consciousness the "other-dependent nature" *(paratantrasvabhāva)* of consciousness. This stream of consciousness, however, is erroneously imagined to be divided into subject and object and this is called the "imagined nature" *(parikalpitasvabhāva)*, and this is the basis for all *saṁsāra*. This error has to be removed by the practice *(ācāra)* of meditation *(yoga)*, and when the practitioner is able to remove the imaginary subject-object division in consciousness, consciousness becomes known for what it really is: a dependently originated flow, empty of the division of subject and object. This is called the "perfected nature" *(pariniṣpannasvabhāva)*.[4]

Thus while the followers of Yogācāra accepted the earlier teaching of emptiness *(śūnyatā)*, they were not content merely to deconstruct the world in the manner of the Madhyamaka. The Madhyamaka were concerned to demolish the notion that things have an inherent existence, whereas the focus of the Yogācāra was instead on the dichotomy of subject *(grāhaka)* and object *(grāhya)*, and in apprehending meditatively the absence of such duality. As a result of meditative practices the school of Yogācāra developed their fundamental and distinctive teaching of the "three natures" of consciousness outlined above: the "imagined nature" *(parikalpita-svabhāva)*, the "other-dependent nature" *(paratantra-svabhāva)* and the "perfected nature" *(pariniṣpanna-svabhāva)*. The "other-dependent nature" is individual to each person; it is said to be dependent because it arises from the transformation of the seeds of past impressions *(vāsanā)* that have been deposited in the "store-consciousness" *(ālayavijñāna)* and, in turn, it replenishes the "store-consciousness" with new impressions. It is this "other-dependent nature" of consciousness that is the basis of both *saṁsāra* and enlightenment: for when the erroneous subject-object division is removed from the "other-dependent nature", the latter is seen for what it really is, a non-dual flow of consciousness, and it is then called the "perfected nature". The Yogācāra differed from the Madhyamaka not only in their emphasis on consciousness and its processes, but also because the Yogācāra were prepared to grant the flow of dependently-originated consciousness a more positive ontological status than the Madhyamaka, leading to debates between these two traditions.[5]

When we examine the kārikās in the fourth book we find a good deal of Buddhist terminology, especially that of the Yogācāra, and a seeming agreement with Buddhist thought. Yet there is a fundamental difference between the thought of Gauḍapāda and that of Buddhism and it lies in this: Buddhism has its philosophical basis in the doctrine of "dependent origination". Yet Gauḍapāda nowhere refers to the doctrine of "dependent origination", nor does he even presuppose that doctrine in the formation of any of his arguments. Gauḍapāda ought not to be considered a Buddhist since he does not at all rely upon this central teaching of Buddhism. Though this argument may seem distinctly reductionist, I nonetheless believe that it is fundamentally correct. The Madhyamaka teaching regarding emptiness *(śūnyatā)* is the outcome of reasoning based upon the principle of "dependent origination". The Yogācāra philosophy is centred around the concept of the "three natures" *(trisvabhāva)* where the "other-dependent" *(paratantra)* nature refers to what is "dependently originated". Gauḍapāda's *"ajātivāda"*, on the other hand, is the outcome of reasoning applied to the teaching of the Upaniṣads that there is a reality that is unborn, changeless and non-dual. Arguing from the premise that the real must be changeless, for impermanence would be the consequence if it enters into becoming, he concludes that the changeless Brahman has not actually become the world, and therefore the world can only be an unreal appearance of Brahman. Although Gauḍapāda may have been initially inspired by the teachings of the Mahāyāna, his whole approach is fundamentally different from that of Buddhism, and that remains true even though there are some noticeable similarities in the method of reasoning, as well as in the conclusions that follow from that reasoning.

(1) Gauḍapāda and Nāgārjuna

I shall clarify the last sentence of the above paragraph by taking up the comparison of Gauḍapāda and Nāgārjuna. Nāgārjuna states that if a thing has an essential, i.e., an inherently existing nature *(svabhāva)*, that thing could not change, because an essential nature cannot undergo any kind of alteration. Nāgārjuna says:

> The arising of an essential nature *(svabhāva)* through causes and conditions is not intelligible. An essential nature that arises out of causes and conditions would be artificial. [MK 15.1]
>
> But how can an essential nature be artificial? An essential nature is not created and it does not depend upon something else. [15.2]
>
> If something exists in its own right, it cannot not exist. For the change of an intrinsic nature is in no way logically possible *(prakṛter anyathābhāvo na hi jatūpapadyate)*.[6] [15. 8]

Nāgārjuna further says that if a thing has an essential nature, the consequence would be that it would neither arise nor cease *(aniruddham anutpannam aśūnyaṁ tad bhaviṣyati)* [20.17]. At 24.38, Nāgārjuna says:

> If there is a *svabhāva*, the world would be devoid of diverse states, it will be unborn, without cessation, immutable.[7]

Gauḍapāda accepts Nāgārjuna's axiomatic statement that if something does have an intrinsic nature it cannot become different, and he also accepts the consequence that Nāgārjuna says entails from holding such a view. It is clearly evident that he accepts the axiom put forward by Nāgārjuna, that an essential nature does not change, for we see that he employs the very same definition of *svabhāva*. Gauḍapāda quotes Nāgārjuna almost verbatim in the second sentence of the following verse:

> The immortal does not become mortal, nor does the mortal become immortal. In no way will an intrinsic nature change *(prakṛter anyathābhāvo na kathaṁcid bhaviṣyati)*. [3.21, 4.7, 29 second line]

> An intrinsic nature *(prakṛti)* is to be known as that which is self-existent, inherent, natural, not artificial, and which does not abandon its own nature. [4.9]

It is at this point, however, that Gauḍapāda parts company with Nāgārjuna; for in opposition to Nāgārjuna, Gauḍapāda holds that there *is* one thing that has a *svabhāva*.[8] On the basis of the Upaniṣads - and Gauḍapāda has cited a number of Upaniṣads apart from the *Māṇḍūkya* which formed the basis of the *Āgamaprakaraṇa* - he asserts that there is a Reality *(sat)* that is unborn *(aja)* and is, therefore, free from becoming. Gauḍapāda says:

> This unborn [non-dual, *turīya-ātman]* becomes different just through *māyā*, not otherwise. For if it is altered in reality, the immortal would become mortal. [3.19]

And in the following verse he asks: "how indeed will an unborn [and thereby] immortal entity become mortal?". Gauḍapāda says that there is such a Reality, that is specifically spoken of in the Upaniṣads as unborn: "That great, birthless Self, undecaying, undying, immortal, and fearless is Brahman".[9] If the unborn Ātman-Brahman were to undergo an intrinsic change by becoming the world, it would cease to be unborn, for it would have taken "birth" by undergoing an alteration, and thereby it would enter into "becoming". If the Ātman enters into "becoming" it would become mortal, i.e., impermanent. But Gauḍapāda says this is not possible, because as we have seen, he accepts that a thing does not change its own, inherent, nature.

Gauḍapāda not only accepts Nāgārjuna's axiom about the changelessness of a *svabhāva,* he also accepts the consequence *(prasaṅga)* that Nāgārjuna says would result from upholding such a view. The consequence is that nothing would arise and nothing would cease. For Nāgārjuna that is an absurd conclusion, because it would contradict all ordinary relations *(vyavahāra)* of cause and effect and so on. But Gauḍapāda's intention is very different from that of Nāgārjuna who is analysing phenomena to show that they are *nissvabhāva,* i.e., *śūnya.* Gauḍapāda is not interested in the ontology of the phenomena of the world; his ontology is cosmological in its perspective: he is dismissing the world, *in toto,* from the standpoint of Brahman, by applying the logic of *svabhāva* to Brahman. Gauḍapāda would perhaps agree with Nāgārjuna's analysis of the world and its interdependent relationships, but that is not his concern. His concern is to show that Brahman does not actually become the world given that Brahman has the *svabhāva* of being "unborn". Since the world has not originated by way of a transformation of Brahman, but given the fact that there is an empirical world, the world must have originated through *māyā.* Therefore Gauḍapāda says that from the level of ultimate truth the world is a cosmic illusion (but not a subjective hallucination). His position therefore is:

> Like a dream and a magic are seen, and just as a mirage city is seen in the sky, so is this universe seen by those who are well-versed in the Vedānta [i.e. Upaniṣads]. [2.31]
>
> There is no cessation, there is no origination, no one is bound and no one strives [to be free], no one desires liberation, nor is any one liberated. This is the ultimate truth. [2.32]

This conclusion about the ontological status of the world seems identical to the understanding of Nāgārjuna and other Mahāyāna Buddhists who follow in the wake of the *Prajñāpāramitā* literature. Yet there is one important difference that must not be overlooked. The Madhyamaka arrived at their conclusion about the unreality of the world from the application of the central teaching of Dependent Origination (things are dependently originated, therefore they are without an inherent nature, *nissvabhāva*, i.e., *śūnya*, and therefore there is neither real origination nor real destruction). Gauḍapāda arrived at the same conclusion about the nature of the world, namely that it is only apparently real, by applying Nāgārjuna's own reasoning about *svabhāva* to the unborn Brahman. But though the Madhyamaka and Gauḍapāda have the same, or at least a very similar, understanding about the ontological nature of the world, they have diametrically opposite starting points, and as a result, their final "world-view" remains very different. Nāgārjuna's central teaching is Dependent Origination, whereas the central teaching for Gauḍapāda is the changelessness of Brahman, Being itself. Therefore although the Buddhist and the Vedāntin seem here to be similar, there is a very significant difference between them, because the Vedāntin unequivocally affirms that there is a permanent substratum underlying the world of appearance, whereas for the Buddhist there is no such thing, there is only the dependently originated, appearance itself.[10]

It has long been thought that Gauḍapāda simply plagiarised the Buddhist teachings, because of the close similarity that exists between Gauḍapāda and Mahāyāna Buddhism concerning the nature of the phenomenal world. Indeed, the Buddhist scholar Śāntarakṣita (ca. 725-788 CE) cited *Gauḍapādakārikā* 2.31 and 32, mentioned just above, as well as 2. 35, in his *Madhyamakālaṅkāravṛtti*, and he wrote, perhaps with some indignation: "What they state has already been said by the Tathāgata!".[11] Leaving aside the controversial question of whether the historical Buddha did in fact teach such a doctrine, Śāntarakṣita's objection is still misplaced, because Gauḍapāda's teaching only resembles the Mahāyāna since Gauḍapāda nowhere abandons the Upaniṣadic ontology of the changelessness of Being, whereas Nāgārjuna arrives at non-origination by rigorously cutting a "middle path" between what he sees as the extremes of Being and non-Being.

Gauḍapāda may have been inspired to formulate his teachings in the way that he did under the influence of reading Nāgārjuna's own clear presentation of what it means to have a *svabhāva*. The question may then arise as to whether Nāgārjuna himself initiated this axiom that a *svabhāva* must be independently existent, and would consequently be eternal, or whether he simply took over an idea already accepted at the time. It is not impossible that the latter is the case, for we know from E.H. Johnston that Aśvagoṣa (c.50 BCE -100 CE) drew upon some portions of the *Rāmāyaṇa* in the composition of his poem about the life of the Buddha, the *Buddhacarita*.[12] E. Lamotte has noted the possible influence of Vaiṣṇava theology on the development of the Mahāyāna.[13] R.H. Robinson has remarked that the structure of Nāgārjuna's verses confirms a statement in the Chinese biography of Nāgārjuna, that he adopted methods of formal reasoning from the Tīrthikas and utilised them to expound the Dharma.[14] We can see in the first line of the well-known verse of the *Bhagavadgītā* (2.16), "The unreal has no being; the real has no non-being *(nāśato vidyate bhāvo nābhāvo vidyate sataḥ)*" a teaching that is identical to the axiom of Nāgārjuna, namely that if something really exists, it should not change. I am not suggesting that Nāgārjuna knew the text of the *Bhagavadgītā*, but I suggest that the *Gītā*, a work most scholars accept was composed before the beginning of the Christian era, is here articulating a general principle that was current among some significant sections of the non-Buddhist traditions and that Nāgārjuna may have been familiar with the idea of the inalterability of a *svabhāva* from non-Buddhist sources. And so we should be wary of saying that Gauḍapāda simply borrowed the idea of the changelessness of *svabhāva* from Nāgārjuna who developed it *ab initio*.

The same could perhaps be said for another notable similarity between Gauḍapāda and Nāgārjuna, namely the teaching of the two levels of truth. Though Gauḍapāda does not speak about a level of conventional or everyday truth *(lokasaṁvṛti /vyavahāra)*, it is necessarily implied by his statement in 2. 32 about the nature of the "ultimate truth" *(paramārthatā)*. The idea that there are two levels of truth, or reality, is not a Buddhist innovation since this teaching is also explicitly stated in the *Muṇḍaka* Upaniṣad (1.1.4-5.) where it is said: "The knowers of Brahman say that there are two kinds of knowledge which are to be known, the higher and the lower. The lower comprises the *Ṛg* Veda...[etc.]. Then there is the higher knowledge, by which the Immutable is attained." So while Gauḍapāda's own presentation about the nature of ultimate truth, as stated in 2. 31-32, may well have been inspired by what he found in Mahāyāna literature, the idea that there are two "levels" of reality would not itself have been a new idea to Gauḍapāda.

I will leave the intriguing question about Gauḍapāda's own attitude towards Buddhism till the end of the chapter. Before concluding our discussion of Gauḍapāda and Nāgārjuna there is a further resemblance which should be remarked upon, and that is between some expressions of Nāgārjuna and the *Māṇḍūkya* Upaniṣad itself. In the two introductory verses of the *Mūlamadhyamakakārikā* Nāgārjuna characterises Dependent Origination as "the cessation of phenomena" *(prapañcopaśama)* and as "auspicious" *(śiva).* In *Māṇḍūkya* Upaniṣad 7, the *turīya*- Ātman is also referred to in the very same words: "The fourth is....where there is the cessation of the phenomenal world *(prapañcopaśama),* it is peaceful, auspicious *(śiva)* and non-dual." I am just drawing attention to this remarkable similarity of expression, which seems too close to be entirely coincidental. Perhaps the *Māṇḍūkya* is here influenced by the Mahāyāna, or could it be that Nāgārjuna is influenced by the *Māṇḍūkya,* or are they both drawing upon a set of common ideas?[15] I have no evidence to say that Nāgārjuna was aware of the *Māṇḍūkya* Upaniṣad. Paul Deussen classifies the *Māṇḍūkya* in the third or latest grouping of the major Upaniṣads and while he expresses the view that the *Māṇḍūkya* appears to have belonged, along with the *Muṇḍaka* and the *Praśna,* "from the beginning to the Atharvaveda", he nonetheless expresses some hesitation on the question of the age of the *Māṇḍūkya,* since it is not referred to in either the *Brahmasūtra* or in Śaṅkara's commentary on that work.[16]

Hajime Nakamura is of the opinion that the *Māṇḍūkya* Upaniṣad seems to have been influenced by "the thought of *Śūnyatā* of Mahāyāna Buddhism" and he estimates the composition of the *Māṇḍūkya* as between the beginning of the common era and 200 CE.[17] Vidhushekhara Bhattacharya says that the expression *prapañcopaśama* does not occur in pre-Buddhist Brahmanic works, but unlike Nakamura he does not draw the conclusion that it has been borrowed from the Mahāyāna.[18] Nakamura's further discussion of this point remains in Japanese and is unavailable to me, but his view is that while it is not possible to say that the *Māṇḍūkya* has taken the expression directly from Nāgārjuna, there can be no doubt that it has been taken over from Mahāyāna literature.[19] This is, of course, a possibility, but it remains no more than that, and the issue cannot be determined with certainty. In any case, as I am writing principally about the ideas of Gauḍapāda, Śaṅkara and two of his principal followers, I do not propose to enter into a discussion about the possible "dating" of Upaniṣads which, according to the belief of the four personages mentioned in this book, have the status of being a revelation without human (or divine) authorship *(apauruṣeyapramāṇa).* But even if we were to provisionally accept Nakamura's speculation about the age of the *Māṇḍūkya,* it is difficult to follow him when he says: "the concept of the fourth realm *(caturtha)* was perhaps influenced by the *Śūnyatā* of the Mahāyāna Buddhism."[20] It is impossible to see how the unequivocal teaching of a permanent, underlying reality, which is explicitly called the "Self", could show early Mahāyāna influence. Professor Nakamura himself has shown that the Upaniṣadic teaching of a permanent underlying reality has influenced later Mahāyāna *Sūtras,* such as the *Laṅkāvatārasūtra,* which he says: "were composed while struggling against and rejecting, yet at times coming under the influence and persuasion of Vedānta thought."[21] In the case of the doctrine of the *Tathāgatagarbha,* as presented in the *Ratnagotravibhāga,* Nakamura says that it is likely that the doctrine of *Tathāgatagarbha* was "formed under the influence of the Upaniṣadic thought" and he also points out the near identity between verse 52 of the *Ratnagotravibhāga* and 13.32 of the *Bhagavadgītā.*"[22] Even if we were to accept that there is some influence of the early *Mahāyānasūtras* in the formation of the *Māṇḍūkya,* that influence would be limited to the two words *prapañcopaśama* and *śiva,* for there can be no suggestion that the teaching about the underlying Self as contained in the *Māṇḍūkya* shows any trace of Buddhist thought, as this teaching can be traced to the pre-Buddhist *Bṛhadāraṇyaka* Upaniṣad.

(2) Gauḍapāda and the Yogācāra

We shall now discuss a number of instances in the fourth book where Gauḍapāda's ideas so resemble those of Yogācāra that it could be believed that Gauḍapāda was a follower of that tradition. It is undeniable that Gauḍapāda uses the terminology of the Yogācāra, and at times he argues in a very similar manner when he says that there is nothing external to consciousness. But there is a major distinction between Yogācāra and Gauḍapāda. The Yogācāra, as we have noted, accept that consciousness is momentary, continually arising and perishing in accord with the principle of Dependent Origination. For Gauḍapāda, however, Consciousness is non-dual, motionless, and neither arises nor perishes. Since pure Consciousness is the non-dual reality, the world cannot exist as something separate from Consciousness; Gauḍapāda utilises ideas from the Yogācāra to show that the world is an appearance of Consciousness and is not something that exists apart from Consciousness, but he is also careful to point out, as we shall see, that he does not share all aspects of the Yogācāra understanding of consciousness.

In Buddhist thought, the terms "consciousness" *(vijñāna)* and "mind" *(citta* or *manas)* are used interchangeably.[23] Gauḍapāda also uses these words as synonyms, but he invests them with his own meaning, and he distinguishes his view from Yogācāra. This is clear from the following verses where he says:

> Consciousness *(vijñāna)* is calm and non-dual, it is unborn, motionless, and is not an object. It has the appearance *(ābhāsa)* of birth, the appearance of moving and the appearance of being an object. [4. 45]

> Thus Consciousness *(citta,)* is not born. So too, things *(dharmas)* are considered to be unborn. Those who know in this way do not fall into error. [4. 46]

It is evident that Gauḍapāda is here distinguishing his teaching from Yogācāra, in spite of a certain similarity of expression, such as can be seen in the use of the word *ābhāsa.* The Yogācāra do not accept that Consciousness is "unborn" or "motionless", but Gauḍapāda explicitly says that this is how Consciousness really is. Consciousness only appears to have origination etc.[24] This idea is identical to what has been expressed in earlier verses, such as: "This unborn [non-dual, *turīya-ātman]* becomes different just through *māyā,* not otherwise" [3.19]. The Yogācāra accept that consciousness actually has the false division of subject and object etc. which must be removed through yogic practice. Gauḍapāda says that Consciousness does not really have such divisions; these are unreal appearances in Consciousness which is by nature "calm, non-dual, unborn, motionless, and not an object." "Those who know in this way" do not fall into the error, as the follower of Yogācāra does, of thinking that Consciousness *actually* arises, and *actually* acquires the erroneous subject-object division which must, therefore, *actually* be removed.

Gauḍapāda then introduces the famous analogy of the fire-brand [47-52]. This example is known in Mahāyāna literature, but Gauḍapāda is using it here to explicate his own view.[25] He says that just as when a fire-brand is whirling it appears in various patterns, in a similar way, Consciousness seemingly vibrates as the perceiver *(grāhaka)* and the perception of the object *(grahaṇa)*. When the fire-brand stops moving the appearance of the patterns ceases, so too when Consciousness stops moving the appearance of subject and object also ceases. When the fire-brand moves, the patterns do not come out of something other than the fire-brand, nor, when the fire-brand stops moving, do the patterns merge into something other than the fire-brand. The patterns do not exist apart from the fire-brand, because the various appearances cannot exist independently as they are not substances in their own right. The whole idea is that the appearance of the patterns is nothing other than the movement of the fire-brand, and the appearance of the patterns has no reality other than that of the fire-brand itself. In a similar way, the appearance of subject and object is nothing but the seeming movement of Consciousness.

It is just possible that Gauḍapāda uses the illustration of the fire-brand to criticise the concept of causal relations that is so central to most of Buddhist thought. He says [52] that no cause-effect relation can be established between Consciousness *(vijñāna)* and its appearances, because the appearances are not other than consciousness itself. A relation of cause and effect cannot be established without making a distinction between the cause and the effect. The appearances, he says, are incomprehensible *(acintya)*.[26] So the Buddhist concern with cause and effect is not correct:

> A substance can be the cause of a substance, and something other can be the cause of something other, but things *(dharmas)* cannot possibly be substances, nor can they be

> something other [than Consciousness]. [4. 53]
>
> Thus the things *(dharmas)* do not arise from Consciousness *(citta),* nor does Consciousness arise from the things *(dharmas).* Thus the wise arrive at the non-origination of cause and effect. [4. 54]

And he concludes by saying that it is this very concern with the reality of the cause-effect relation that keeps one in *saṁsāra:*

> As long as there is the fixation with cause and effect, so long will *saṁsāra* be protracted. When the fixation with cause and effect is destroyed, one does not find *saṁsāra.* [4. 56][27]

Gauḍapāda then proceeds to reorientate the Buddhist teaching of the "middle way", so as to bring it into line with his own position. He says:

> Everything is born from the perspective of empirical existence, therefore nothing is permanent *(śāśvata).* In reality, everything is unborn, therefore there is no annihilation *(uccheda).* [4. 57]

If Gauḍapāda was a Buddhist, this would be a peculiar way of expressing the characteristic Buddhist doctrine of the "middle path", the way that lies between the two extremes of either eternalism *(śāśvatavāda)* and annihilation *(ucchedavāda).* The Madhyamaka interpretation of the "middle way" would be that because everything is dependently-originated there is the avoidance of the extreme view of annihilationism, and because everything is empty *(śūnya)* there is the avoidance of the extreme of eternalism. However Gauḍapāda restates the doctrine in his own way, and he reverses the two terms. He says that according to the perspective of everyday life, where things are born and die, there can be nothing eternal *(śāśvata),* but as everything is really unborn, there can be no actual annihilation *(uccheda)* of anything.

Gauḍapāda's perspective is that: (a) it is revealed in the Upaniṣads that Brahman -which/who is both the efficient and the material cause together - is the sole cause of the world. And it is further revealed that Brahman has the essential nature of being "unborn". (b) Since it is not tenable that the essential nature of a thing could alter without the consequence of impermanence, the world cannot actually have arisen from Brahman without Brahman becoming born as the world, and thereby becoming impermanent. Therefore, from the (ultimate) standpoint of Brahman itself, there is no real origination of the world from Brahman.[28] (c) The appearance of the world is, of course, undeniable, and so, (d) the world arises from Brahman in a way that is comparable to a magical appearance *(māyā).* This does not amount to a denial of the law of contradiction that a thing cannot both exist and not exist at the same time and in the same respect, because appearance and reality are considered from two standpoints. From the standpoint of empirical truth *(vyavahāra),* things exist as they do according to common-sense realism. From the standpoint of absolute truth *(paramārtha),* things -though they appear to exist - do not truly exist, for only the unborn (and unaltered) Brahman exists. Since the phenomenal world is ultimately akin to a magical appearance, the Buddhist analysis concerning the avoidance of the extremes of permanence and total annihilation is not applicable, for that is only relevant from an empirical perspective, when phenomena are thought to be real. This can be seen from the following kārikās, where Gauḍapāda, speaking as usual from the absolute perspective *(paramārtha),* says:

> The things *(dharmas)* that are said to be born, are born, but in reality they are not born. Their birth is comparable to a magical appearance *(māyā),* and that magical appearance does not exist! [4.58][29]

> Just as from a seed that is a magical appearance a sprout originates that is equally a magical appearance. That sprout is not

> permanent, nor does it undergo annihilation. The same is applicable to all things. [4. 59]
>
> When all things are unborn, the word "permanent" or "impermanent" is not [applicable]. Where words do not operate, a discrimination cannot be stated. [4. 60]

It is understandable that later Advaita authors do not seem to have quoted from the fourth chapter of Gauḍapāda's work. As we can see, parts of it are far too closely interwoven with a variety of Mahāyāna Buddhist ideas - and this is especially so towards the end of the chapter - to be appreciated by the Advaitins of later times who did not possess Gauḍapāda's degree of familiarity with Buddhist thought, and for whom Buddhism had less relevance as it declined in India. Though Gauḍapāda repeatedly distinguishes his teaching from Buddhism, there are occasions when he seems to come close to the Yogācāra explanation of consciousness. But even in those instances, Gauḍapāda usually makes it clear, as he does in 4.45 (above), that Consciousness is really changeless. Or else he adds the term *māyā* to indicate that Consciousness does not actually undergo change, as the followers of Yogācāra believe, but only appears to arise and undergo change. He says, for example, while comparing the states of dream and waking:

> Just as in dream, Consciousness *(citta)* moves having a twofold appearance [as subject and object] due to *māyā*, so too in the waking state Consciousness moves having a twofold appearance due to *māyā*. [4. 61][30]

There are other instances, in addition to the teaching of the "middle way" referred to above, where Gauḍapāda refers to Buddhist ideas and reorients them to his own perspective. We shall see two such instances. In verses seventy-three to seventy-five of the fourth chapter Gauḍapāda refers to the Yogācāra, and a part of verse seventy-five is taken from the first verse of the *Madhyāntavibhāga* of Maitreya/Asaṅga. The important first and second verse of the *Madhyāntavibhāga* read:

> The imagination of the unreal exists *(abhūtaparikalpo'sti).* Duality does not exist in it *(dvayaṁ tatra na vidyate).* Emptiness, however, exists in it, and that [imagination of the unreal] also exists in emptiness.[31]
>
> Therefore it is stated that everything is neither empty nor not empty, because of existence, because of non-existence, and again because of existence; and this is the Middle Path.

G.M. Nagao considers that these two verses together represent the fundamental point of view of the Yogācāra school.[32] We shall try to explain these, altogether too cryptic verses, in the light of some of Nagao's comments on them. The expression "imagination of the unreal" *(abhūtaparikalpa)* refers to the "other-dependent" nature *(paratantrasvabhāva).*[33] The word "unreal" indicates the fact that the cognitive functioning or thought of ordinary people is always stained by ignorance.[34] Thus it seems that the expression "imagination of the unreal" refers to the other-dependent aspect of consciousness, as tainted by unreal notions.[35] The unreal notions are the "duality" that is referred to, meaning the duality of subject and object. In this dependently-arising, "everyday consciousness", the duality of subject and object does not really exist. "Emptiness" means the absence of the subject-object dichotomy; such an emptiness does exist in the dependently-originated flow of consciousness. The statement that the "imagination of the unreal exists in emptiness" is a reaffirmation of the fact that even though the flow of consciousness is empty of the subject-object relation, it should not be thought that the dependently-originated flow of consciousness is non-existent.

The second verse sums up what has just been said. The statement "because of existence" refers to the existence of (a) the dependently-originated flow of consciousness. "Because of non-existence" refers to the non-existence of (b) duality. The reaffirmation, "because of existence", states that (c) emptiness, i.e., the emptiness of duality, exists, and also that (a) the flow of consciousness exists. So, "everything is neither empty" because "c" exists, and "a" exists as "c". Nor is everything "not empty" since there is the non-existence of "b". The Yogācāra go on to define emptiness as: "the non-being of subject and object and the being of that non-being".[36] This is an attempt to provide an experiential corrective to the overly negative tendency in the reasoning of the Madhyamaka, though by "being" I do not think the Yogācāra school is articulating an ontologically absolute reality, as in the Vedānta.

The above comments may not have succeeded very far in elucidating the Yogācāra, but perhaps they may help to differentiate Gauḍapāda's teachings from the Yogācāra. The three pertinent kārikās of Gauḍapāda are:

> What exists according to the empirical truth which is imagined *(kalpita),* does not exist in reality. It can exist from the outlook of the other-dependent, empirical truth, but not in reality. [4. 73][37]
>
> What is unborn according to the empirical truth that is imagined, is, in reality, not actually unborn. It is born from the outlook of empirical truth, i.e., as arising out of the other-dependent. [4. 74]
>
> A strong adherence to the unreal exists *(abhūtābhiniveśo'sti).* Duality is not present in it *(dvayaṁ tatra na vidyate).* As soon as one knows the absence of duality, one is not born, being without a cause [for birth].[38] [4. 75]

In the first two verses Gauḍapāda seems to be expressing a different view from Yogācāra when he says that whatever exists from the perspective of *abhūtaparikalpa,* i.e., the other-dependent *(paratantra),* does not exist from the standpoint of absolute truth. For we have seen that according to Yogācāra the dependently-originated flow of consciousness exists, and in their theory of the "three natures" there is no reference to an ultimate state in which the "other-dependent" nature does not exist. Unlike the theory of the "three natures", Gauḍapāda is here speaking - and adopting the discourse of the Madhyamaka - from two levels: the empirical *(saṁvṛti)* and the absolute *(paramārtha)*. According to Gauḍapāda, things do exist empirically, but they do not so exist from the perspective of ultimate truth.

In the third verse, which refers to and rephrases the first line from the first of the two verses of the *Madhyāntavibhāga* cited above, the "unreal" presumably means the unreal subject-object relation, as it does in the Yogācāra text. Gauḍapāda says there is a "strong adherence" to the idea that there is a real subject confronting a world of real objects. Then, following the Yogācāra text, he says "duality is not present in it" meaning that the subject-object relation is actually unreal. In the last line of the verse he completely discards the details of Yogācāra philosophy concerning the existence of emptiness and the existence of the "imagination of the unreal" in emptiness. He adds his own conclusion which is: as soon as a person knows that the duality of subject-object is unreal, a person is liberated from repeated birth as there is no longer any cause for rebirth. Thus we can see that in those instances where Gauḍapāda uses Buddhist texts and terminology, he does not use them from a Buddhist perspective, rather he only adopts the terminology and adapts the ideas as far as it suits his purpose, and he does not subscribe to the philosophical conclusions of the texts he cites.

The other instance where Gauḍapāda distinctly refers to Buddhist thought and reorients it for his own purpose can be seen in verses eighty-seven to eighty-nine. These verses read:

> The dual [knowledge] consisting of an object together with the perception [of the object] is considered to be "mundane" *(laukika)*. Whereas the [knowledge] consisting of the perception, but without an object, is considered to be "pure mundane" *(śuddha laukika)*. [4. 87]

> The [knowledge] which is without either an object or the perception is regarded as "supra-mundane" *(lokottara)*. The wise always tell

> about the knowledge, the knowable, and that which is to be clearly known *(vijñeya).* [4.88]
>
> When the threefold knowledge and the threefold object of knowledge are known in due order, the person of great intelligence becomes naturally all-knowing everywhere. [4.89]

The terms "mundane" *(laukika),* "pure mundane" *(śuddhalaukika)* and "supra-mundane" *(lokottara)* are found as part of the technical vocabulary of the Yogācāra school. The word "knowledge", i.e., consciousness, or cognition, is taken to be the implied subject of these verses since the Buddhist literature generally uses the terms *laukika, śuddhalaukika* and *lokottara* along with the noun *"jñāna"*. In Yogācāra, the "mundane" knowledge refers to ordinary, dualistic perceptions, involving subject and object. "Supra-mundane" refers to the knowledge when it is without an apprehending subject or an apprehended object. It is a non-dual and non-discriminative *(nirvikalpa)* knowledge, acquired through long meditative practice, and it represents the ultimate enlightenment in the Yogācāra tradition.[39] The "pure mundane" knowledge refers to the enlightened knowledge that follows from the *nirvikalpa* "supra mundane" knowledge.[40] Such knowledge is also known as *"pṛṣṭhalabdha-jñāna"*, or "knowledge acquired subsequently"; it is a discriminative *(savikalpa)* knowledge, but it is a pure form of knowledge because it flows out of the non-discriminative knowledge.[41]

It is evident that Gauḍapāda is directly using this Buddhist terminology, but it is not so evident that he is expounding a Buddhist meaning. Gauḍapāda makes the sequence of the three knowledges different from the Yogācāra, for he places the *lokottara* after the *śuddhalaukika,* whereas in the Yogācāra understanding the *śuddhalaukika-jñāna* is a knowledge that arises out of the *lokottara-jñāna.* Once again Gauḍapāda can be seen to be reorienting the terminology of Buddhism to his own perspective. Śaṅkara, in his commentary on these verses, considers that the three terms are used in the sense of the three states of experience: waking *(laukika),* dream *(śuddhalaukika)* and deep sleep *(lokottara).*[42]

This is plausible, since dream is a state where the perception of an object exists without a real object, and sleep is a state where there is neither an object nor the perception of an object. The word *vijñeya* could also, as Śaṅkara understands, refer to the *turīyātman* since the latter is spoken of in *Māṇḍūkya* 7 as: "That is the Self, That is to be known" *(sa ātmā sa vijñeyaḥ).*

It is well-known that the fourth chapter is replete with references to Buddhist thought; and that is increasingly the case from verse twenty-four onwards. This makes the interpretation of some of the verses difficult, especially these later ones, for Gauḍapāda traverses a wide range of literature. For instance, verse ninety-two contains these two statements: "all things *(sarve dharmāḥ)* are ascertained as inherently enlightened from the very beginning" *(ādibuddhāḥ);* and the person who thus remains undisturbed is "fit for immortality" *(sa amṛtatvāya kalpate).* It is possible that the expression *"ādibuddha"* is modelled on statements from the *Prajñāpāramitā* literature where it is said many times that: "the elements of existence *(dharmas)* are by nature perfectly pure" *(sarvadharmā evaṁ prakṛtipariśuddhāḥ).*[43] Whereas the statement: "fit for immortality" is taken from the *Bhagavadgītā* 2.15. In the following verse, too, the expressions are likely to be from the *Prajñāpāramitā* literature, as Bhattacharya has noted. However, in spite of the similarity between the teaching of Gauḍapāda and the teachings of the *Prajñāpāramitā,* they are not identical teachings, and we should not be misled by the extreme similarity in their final positions about the non-origination of anything. According to the *Prajñāpāramitā,* as with the Madhyamaka, though things appear to be born etc. they are not really born, because everything is without own-being. For Gauḍapāda, on the other hand, there is no-birth etc. because the underlying absolute reality *(turīya-Ātman)* has undergone no alteration of its changeless Being.

Near the conclusion of the fourth chapter, Gauḍapāda presents the following kārikā:

> It is maintained that the unborn Consciousness is unrelated to the unborn objects *(dharmas).* Since Consciousness does not enter into relation, it is therefore said to be relationless *(asaṅga).* [4. 96]

And he conclSudes the teaching by saying:

> The Consciousness of the Buddha, who instructs the way known to him *(tāyin)*, is not related to the objects *(dharmas)*. So too, all the objects *(dharmas)* are not related to Consciousness. This was not said by the Buddha. [4.99]

According to Gauḍapāda, Consciousness [pure Awareness] is changeless and therefore real, while the objects that appear in Consciousness do not constitute a second reality to Consciousness since they are ontologically unreal *(mithyā)* and are analogous to a magical appearance *(māyā)*. Since Consciousness does not come into contact with a second reality, Consciousness is inherently relationless. The Buddhist teaching, however, is centred around the analysis of causes and conditions, i.e., things arise depending upon other things ("This being, that is; from the arising of this, that arises"; and in reverse: "This not being, that is not; on the cessation of this, that ceases.").[44] So while the objects *(dharmas)* do not inherently exist, they are nonetheless related to the constructive activity belonging to Consciousness itself, and thus for the Buddhists Consciousness is not relationless. R.D. Karmarkar expressed this point, in his characteristically direct manner, when he said: "Buddha no doubt denied the existence of *bāhyārtha* [external objects] and admitted the *vijñānavāda*, but he ....could not get out of the idea of causal relation and origination. To that extent Buddha's philosophy is defective -this seems to be the meaning of this Kārikā."[45] Gauḍapāda says here, as he has said in 4.54, that Consciousness does not enter into relation with the unreal objects, nor do they enter into relation with Consciousness. And he says that this teaching, about the inherently relationless nature of Consciousness, was not told by the Buddha.

The statement: "This was not said by the Buddha" *(nà-etad buddhena bhāṣitam)*, has evoked different interpretations, depending on the extent to which a particular writer believes Gauḍapāda's teachings correspond with those of Buddhism. V. Bhattacharya considers that this statement should be understood only in its implied sense. According to him the statement means that the highest truth cannot be conveyed by instruction through language, and it implies the transcendental nature of the Budda's teaching. Recent authors, such as Thomas Wood and Richard King, have essentially agreed with Bhattacharya's interpretation.[46] I have tried to show that Gauḍapāda's teaching - based as it is upon the Upaniṣads - differs from the teachings of Buddhism in some fundamental aspects; and so I think it more likely that Gauḍapāda is here explicitly differentiating his teaching from that of the Buddha. We need not search for a meaning through implication *(lakṣaṇā)* when the literal meaning *(vācyārtha)* can be accepted, and there are a number of statements in Buddhist texts which refer to the Buddha's speech *(buddhabhāṣita).* For instance, in the *Laṅkāvatārasūtra,* we find the expression: "this was told, is told, and will be told by the Buddhas."[47] And in the *Madhyamakahṛdaya* of Bhāvaviveka we find the statement: "Whatever is well said in the Vedānta is all taught by the Buddha."[48] Such statements as these are quite possibly scattered through a variety of texts.[49] So when there are explicit statements referring to teachings as "spoken by the Buddha" *(buddhabhāṣita),* and given that the teachings of Gauḍapāda do differ from Buddhist teachings, it is correct to adopt only the literal meaning here: "This was not said by the Buddha".[50]

Some notable scholars, such as S.N. Dasgupta, believed that the kārikās contained sufficient evidence to support the conjecture that Gauḍapāda was: "possibly himself a Buddhist, and considered that the teachings of the Upaniṣads tallied with those of Buddha."[51] T.R.V. Murti expressed the same view, but restricted it to the *Alātaśāntiprakaraṇa,* the fourth chapter of the *Gauḍapādakārikā.*[52] B.K. Matilal has, I believe, placed the issue in a better perspective when he wrote: "But while the influence of Buddhist doctrines and arguments upon Gauḍapāda is undeniable, it would be wrong to conclude that he was a Buddhist."[53] More recently, some scholars have begun noticing important discrepancies between the teachings of Gauḍapāda and those of Nāgārjuna.[54]

Vidhushekhara Bhattacharya, in his influential and scholarly work, *The Āgamaśāstra of Gauḍapāda,* has demonstrated that there exists a close relationship between various kārikās of the *Gauḍapādakārikā* and a variety of Mahāyāna texts. But perhaps Bhattacharya overstated his case, for while he has certainly shown a number of textual correspondences, he also finds correspondences that are quite tenuous, and he fails to see that there could be differences between the ideas expressed in the *Gauḍapādakārikā* and the various Buddhist texts. As an instance of Bhattacharya being too ready to see a convergence of ideas, let us examine his following argument. Towards the end of his lengthy introduction, he notes (p.cxxxii) that Gauḍapāda, "though much influenced by the Buddhist thoughts, maintains his position as a Vedāntist". He believes, however, (p.cxlii) that for Gauḍapāda, Brahman and the *citta* of the *vijñaptimātratā* of the Yogācāra are, "in fact the same thing"; and he says (p.cxliv) that is the reason why Gauḍapāda took support from the Buddhists in book four of his work. Bhattacharya himself raises the question (p.cxxxviii) as to how Brahman and the *citta* in the *vijñaptimātratā* of the Yogācāra could be the same when the followers of Vedānta maintain that Brahman is eternal *(nitya)* whereas, according to the followers of Yogācāra, consciousness is momentary *(kṣaṇika)*. He answers this objection by saying (p.cxl ff.) that for the Vedāntists, Consciousness is *nitya*, i.e., without any change, whereas for the Yogācāra consciousness is *druva*, i.e., enduring while undergoing change in an uninterrupted stream *(santati)*. His opinion is that (p.cxlii): "Brahman and the *citta* in *vijñaptimātratā* of the Yogācāras are in fact the same thing with the only one difference that while the former is *nitya* the latter is *druva*.".[55]

I believe that Bhattacharya has accurately presented the major difference between the Advaita Vedānta and the Yogācāra understanding of Consciousness, but it is impossible to concur with the way he glosses over this very substantial distinction to reach his conclusion that Gauḍapāda would have considered the Brahman of the Vedānta and the *citta* of the Yogācāra to be the same. The dispute about whether Consciousness is really changeless, and therefore eternal *(nitya)*, or whether it is actually a momentarily changing series *(kṣaṇika)*, lies at the very centre of the difference between Vedāntins and Buddhists. The Vedāntins and the Buddhists share a great deal in common, but the philosophical difference between them ultimately comes down to this important point: for the Vedāntins, Consciousness is changeless and is not to be confused with the changing cognitions; whereas in the history of Indian Buddhism the dominant view is that Consciousness, like everything else, is subject to dependent origination, it is momentary and thereby impermanent. T.R.V. Murti has accurately depicted the divide between the Vedānta and the Buddhist traditions when he says that the former is a "substance-view" in that it maintains that there is a real underlying Self that is unchanging Consciousness, whereas the Buddhists have traditionally taken the opposite position.[56] This different understanding about the nature of Consciousness is, in the final analysis, the principal philosophical difference between the two traditions, and it is highly unlikely that Gauḍapāda, who was keenly aware of the intricacies of both the Upaniṣads and Buddhist thought, could have ignored this fundamental difference in the way that Bhattacharya has glossed over it.

Parts of the *Gauḍapādakārikā* are certainly enigmatic, especially the latter part of the fourth chapter, and it is not surprising that while Gauḍapāda was revered, he was only selectively quoted by later Advaitins. Concerning the fourth chapter, Professor Hajime Nakamura maintains:

> the fourth chapter accepts the non-self theory and abandons the traditional *ātman* theory of the orthodox *Vedānta* school. The fourth chapter does not refer to Brahman or Ātman at all. Here, non-self, emptiness and the non-differentiated Consciousness-only constitute the basic doctrines.[57]

His first sentence, however, is incorrect because when Gauḍapāda uses the words *citta* (mind or consciousness), or *vijñāna* (consciousness) - which are no doubt frequently employed in the Buddhist texts - he often invests these words with a Vedāntic meaning, as in 4.45 [supra] when he says: "Consciousness *(vijñāna)* is calm and non-dual, it is unborn, motionless, and is not an object. It has the appearance *(ābhāsa)* of birth, the appearance of moving and the appearance of being an object." Here the word "motionless" as a description of *vijñāna* is not in keeping with the Buddhist understanding of consciousness, but it is in keeping with the Vedāntic understanding of Consciousness. Nakamura's second statement is too sweeping, for in 4. 85 Gauḍapāda refers to the highest reality as *brāhmaṇyaṁ padam*, "the state pertaining to Brahman". And his conclusion, too, is hasty. If Gauḍapāda is teaching emptiness etc., then we should expect to find these key Buddhist terms employed in the fourth chapter. However there is no mention of the words "empty" *(śūnya)* or "emptiness" *(śūnyatā)*. There is no mention of Dependent Origination *(pratītyasamutpāda)*, nor of a "store-consciousness" *(ālayavijñāna)*. The absence of such terms, especially any reference to Dependent Origination, and the total absence of the paradigm of Dependent Origination which is so central to Buddhist thought, coupled with his acceptance of the idea of *svabhāva*, only lends further weight to the view that Gauḍapāda is teaching something other than Buddhism. In the fourth chapter, especially, though occasionally in the other chapters as well, Gauḍapāda presents Advaita Vedānta using Buddhist terms, but he uses them in such a way that they can conform to the fundamental Vedāntic understanding of Consciousness.

The question naturally arises as to why Gauḍapāda is doing this. T. G. Mainkar suggests that in Gauḍapāda: "...we have a philosopher with opposing tensions on his mind and trying to resolve them into a harmonious whole by trying to give a Vedic base to the new and more satisfying metaphysical theories."[58] But if there was such a "tension" in Gauḍapāda's thought we would expect it to be evident in the kārikās themselves, in the effort of trying to fuse the Vedānta with the Mahāyāna. But there is no sign of any such tension, for Gauḍapāda skilfully adopts Buddhist argument only as far as it suits his purpose. We have seen, for example, with regard to Nāgārjuna's statements about an "essential nature" *(svabhāva)*, that while Gauḍapāda follows Nāgārjuna's presentation, he actually takes a stand that is diametrically opposite to Nāgārjuna, because he accepts the idea of *svabhāva* while Nāgārjuna does not. I believe that there are other instances too, which I have tried to note, when Gauḍapāda has adapted ideas from Buddhism to suit his own perspective.

T.R.V. Murti has offered the opinion that: "Gauḍapāda appears to us as the Brāhmanical thinker boldly reformulating the Upaniṣadic ideal in the light of the Mādhyamika and Vijñānavāda dialectic. But there was more borrowing of techniques than of tenets."[59] The word "reformulating" suggests that a discrepancy exists between the Upaniṣadic teachings and the ideas of Gauḍapāda, though some Western interpreters of the Upaniṣads, such as A.E. Gough, and more notably Paul Deussen, view the teaching of *māyā* and the unreality of the world as part and parcel of the Upaniṣadic world-view.[60] Murti is willing to entertain the hypothesis, based partly on Śaṅkara's reference to Gauḍapāda as one "knowing the tradition" *(sampradāyavit)*, that there was an Advaitic school of Vedānta already in existence which exerted its influence on the

Madhyamaka and which in time became the dominant Vedāntic school due to the efforts of Gauḍapāda and Śaṅkara.[61]

The hypothesis of Murti is possible, but we do not really know enough to decide on such an issue. Rather than say that Gauḍapāda "reformulated" the Upaniṣadic teachings, I would prefer to say simply that Gauḍapāda "stated" the Upaniṣadic teachings under the inspiration of some of the ideas of the Madhyamaka and the Yogācāra. That he should be stimulated by these ideas is not at all so extraordinary when we consider the dominant influence of Buddhism in India in the early centuries of the Common Era: with its numerous monastic institutions, its large and famous centres of learning, such as Nālandā, its extensive literature and, especially in the case of the Mahāyāna, its teachers of renown such as Nāgārjuna, Ārya Deva, Asaṅga and Vasubandhu, to name only the most prominent in those early centuries. Gauḍapāda was presumably stimulated by the Mahāyāna and his adoption, especially in the fourth chapter, of expressions from Mahāyāna literature closely associate him with Buddhist views. Nonetheless, he only accepts as much of Buddhism as suits his purpose, and he does distinguish his own teaching from Buddhism. He takes his stand on the *Māṇḍūkya* Upaniṣad, and it is there that we find the ultimate source of his inspiration, in the teaching of the absolute Self as pure Awareness, the invariable substratum of experience, free from all relations: "It is where there is the cessation of the phenomenal world *(prapañcopaśama)*, it is peaceful *(śānta)*, auspicious *(śiva)* and non-dual *(advaita)*. That is the Self, That is to be known."

---

1 Cited in E. Lamotte, *History of Indian Buddhism from the origins to the Śaka era.* S Webb-Boin (tr.), Louvain: Peeters Press, 1988, p. 40. Lamotte calls the teaching of dependent origination, "the corner stone of the Buddhist doctrine" (p.36, p.40). Also, cf. the article by Bhikshu Sangharakshita, "Buddhism" in A.L. Basham (ed.), *A Cultural History of India.* Oxford: Oxford Univ. Press, 1975, p.85. G.M. Nagao cites this statement, from the *Majjhima-nikāya* (Sutta 28): "Those who see 'dependent origination' *(pratītya-samutpāda)* will see the dharma; those who see the dharma will see 'dependent origination'."; and Nagao repeatedly refers to the foundational importance of the doctrine of dependent origination. He says: "Dependent co-arising is the basic truth of Buddhism; it is the substance of Gautama Buddha's awakening." Cf. L.S. Kawamura (tr.), *Mādhyamika and Yogācāra: A study of Mahāyāna Philosophies. Collected Papers of G.M. Nagao.* Delhi: Sri Satguru Publications, 1992, p.212. Also cf. his similar remarks about the importance of the *pratītyasamutpāda*, pp.64, 134, 148, 174, 183.

2 Lamotte, ibid., p.36.

3 Cf. the well-known verse in MK 24.18, *yaḥ pratītyasamutpādaḥ śūnyatām tāṁ pracakṣmahe, sā prajñaptir upādāya pratipat saiva madhyamā.* Also, K. Bhattacharya, E. H. Johnston and A. Kunst, *The Dialectical Method of Nāgārjuna: Vigrahavyāvartanī.* Delhi: Motilal Bansaridass, (2nd.ed) 1986, p.11, *iha hi yaḥ pratītyabhāvo bhāvānāṁ sā śūnyatā, kasmāt, niḥsvabhāvatvāt.* Also, G. Nagao, *The Foundational Standpoint of Mādhyamika Philosophy* (J.P. Keenan tr.), Delhi: Satguru Publications, 1989, p.4ff. Also cf. the mention of dependent-origination in the *Prajñāpāramitā* literature: "In this manner the Bodhisattva surveys conditioned co production in such a way that he avoids the duality of the extremes. He surveys it without seeing any beginning, end or middle. To survey conditioned co production in

such a manner, that is the special dharma of the Bodhisattva who is seated on the terrace of enlightenment." Edward Conze (tr), *The Perfection of Wisdom in Eight Thousand Lines and Its Verse Summary*. Berkeley: The Four Seasons Foundation, 1973, p.271.

4 G.M. Nagao, *Mādhyamika and Yogācāra*, op.cit., p.70, gives a free translation from the *Triṁśikā* of Vasubandhu (vv.21, pāda c and d.): "When the other-dependent nature obtains a state absolutely free of the imagined nature, it is then the consummated nature". Also cf., P. Williams, *Mahāyāna Buddhism: The Doctrinal Foundations*. London: Routledge, 1989, p.85.

5 Nagao, *Mādhyamika and Yogācāra*, op.cit., see the discussion regarding "Emptiness", p.214f. Also Williams, *Mahāyāna Buddhism*, op.cit., p.86f. Cf. *Madhyāntavibhāga*, 1.13.

6 For more of Nāgārjuna's statements about the unchanging nature of a *svabhāva*, and the consequences of holding such a view, see for example MK 23. v.24. 24. vv.20-24, 26, 28, 32, 33.

7 Cf. also, 25.2.

8 Thomas Wood, op.cit., p.74f., deserves the credit for noticing and clearly bringing out the fundamental difference between Gauḍapāda and Nāgārjuna on this important point regarding *svabhāva*.

9 BU 4.4.25.

10 There is a clear presentation of the Madhyamaka position in the article by G.C. Nayak, "Does Śaṅkara Advocate Enlightenment Through Analysis?: A Reappraisal of the Vedantic Conception of Enlightenment vis-a-vis the Mādhyamika" (cf. especially pp. 24-31), in S.S. Rama Rao Pappu (ed.). *Perspectives on Vedānta: Essays in Honor of Professor P.T. Raju*. Leiden: E.J. Brill, 1988.

11 Chr. Lindtner, *Nagarjuniana: Studies in the Writings and Philosophy of Nāgārjuna.* Delhi: Motilal Banarsidass, 1990 (reprint), p.280f.

12 E.H. Johnston, *The Buddhacarita or, Acts of the Buddha.* New Delhi: Oriental Books Reprint, 1972 [originally published 1936], p.xlviii.

13 E. Lamotte, *History of Indian Buddhism from the origins to the Śaka era,* op.cit., p.392-398.

14 Richard H. Robinson, *Early Mādhyamika in India and China.* Delhi: Motilal Banarsidass, 1978 (reprint), p.50.

15 Candrakīrti, in his commentary upon MK 5.8, glosses the word *nirvāṇa* as: *ajara* and *amara* (as well as *śūnyatāsvabhāva).* The particular expression *"ajara amara"* can be traced to the BU 4.4.25, which is accepted as a pre-Buddhist Upaniṣad, where the Ātman is said to be: *"ajara, amara"* etc. This is probably an instance of Candrakīrti using a well known "floating expression" rather than a case of direct borrowing from the BU, though it points towards that text. Again, in MK 23.1, Nāgārjuna says: *"saṅkalpaprabhavo rāgaḥ..."* Candrakīrti links this statement to a verse occurring in the *Mahāvastu* (a Vinaya text of the Lokottara branch of the Mahāsaṅghikas). A almost identical expression to MK 23.1 occurs in the *Bhagavadgītā* 6.24, *"saṅkalpaprabhavān kāmān..."* In BG 6.4 Śaṅkara links the word *saṅkalpa* to the Mbh (Śānti Parva) 177.25, where the verse is almost identical to that of the *Mahāvastu* quoted by Candrakīrti. This is perhaps another "floating expression", but this time perhaps pointing in the Buddhist direction.

16 P. Deussen, *The Philosophy of the Upanishads,* op.cit., p.25. Maurice Winternitz expressed the view that the *Māṇḍūkya* Upaniṣad is probably post-Buddhist; however he does not discuss

the matter in any detail. He repeats what Deussen has said, i.e., that Śaṅkara did not cite this Upaniṣad in his BSBh, and he is perhaps influenced by the view of V. Bhattacharya that the MāU is later than the kārikās. M. Winternitz, *A History of Indian Literature, vol.1.* New Delhi: Oriental Books Reprint, 1972 [first published 1927], p.238f.

17 H. Nakamura, *A History of Early Vedānta Philosophy,* Delhi: Motilal Banarsidass, 1983, p.30 and 42.

18 Bhattacharya, op.cit., p.43.

19 I am grateful to Professor J.W. de Jong for providing this information from the third volume of Professor Nakamura's *History of Early Vedānta* (Tokyo, 1955), p.298.

20 Ibid, p.34, note 37.

21 Ibid.. p.157.

22 Ibid., p.182.

23 Lamotte, op.cit, p.596. Candrakīrti says that *citta, manas, vijñāna* and *cetas* are synonyms. Cf. P.L. Vaidya (ed), *Madhyamakaśāstram,* op.cit., p.132, line 13.

24 Bhattacharya, op.cit., p.153, n.2., admits that this description of *vijñāna* as "unborn" *(aja)* does not accord with Buddhist thought.

25 D.T. Suzuki, *Studies in the Lankavatara Sutra.* London: Routledge and Kegan Paul, 1930 (1957 reprint), p.96. Also, A.K. Chatterjee, *The Yogācāra Idealism.* Delhi: Motilal Banarsidass, 1975, p.28. The simile of the firebrand *(alātacakra)* occurs regularly in the *Laṅkāvatārasūtra.* Cf., for example, P.L. Vaidya (ed.), *Saddharmalaṅkāvatārasūtram.* Buddhist Sanskrit Texts no. 3. Dharbanga: The Mithila Institute, 1963, p.38, line

26; p.40, v.155. The simile of the *alātacakra* is also found in the *Rāmāyaṇa* (Critical Edition, Baroda), vol. 4., 45.12.

26 The word *acintya* here in GK 4. 52 seems to convey the same idea as the word *anirvacanīya* used by later writers.

27 Bhattacharya reads *saṁsāro nopapadyate.*

28 Cf. the discussion on kārikā 2.32 ff. in chapter one, section (2) "The *Vaitathyaprakaraṇa*".

29 Bhattacharya reads *saṁvṛtyā* in pāda b (rather than *jāyante).*

30 Kārikās 4. 61, 62 are substantially the same as 3. 29, 30.

31 *abhūtaparikalpo'sti, dvayaṁ tatra na vidyate/ śūnyatā vidyate tv atra, tasyām api sa vidyate//* 1.1. *na śūnyaṁ nāpi cāśūnyaṁ tasmāt sarvaṁ vidhīyate/ sattvād asattvāt sattvāc ca, madhyamā pratipac ca sā//* 1.2. *Madhyāntavibhāga.* G.M. Nagao, in his *Mādhyamika and Yogācāra*, op.cit., p.195, translates these two verses as follows:

> There exists unreal imagination; duality does not exist therein
> Emptiness, however, exists in it, and also the former exists in the latter. (1.1)
> Therefore it is stated that all entities are neither empty nor non-empty
> Because of existence, because of non-existence, and again because of existence.
> And this is the Middle Path. (1.2)

It is said to be the "middle path", Sthiramati says, because: "...otherwise it would lead to the extremes of that which is absolutely empty on the one hand; and that which is not empty on the other." R. Stanley, *A Study of the Madhyāntavibhāga-*

bhāṣya-ṭīkā, unpublished Ph.D. thesis, Australian National University, 1988, p.17.

32 G.M. Nagao, *Mādhyamika and Yogācāra*, op.cit., p.196.

33 Ibid., p.80, 137, 195, 197. Stanley, op.cit., p.26.

34 Nagao, ibid., p.195.

35 Williams, *Mahāyāna Buddhism*, op.cit., p.87.

36 Nagao, op.cit, p.215. *Madhyāntavibhāga*, 1. 13 in Stanley, op.cit., p.57.

37 Bhattacharya chooses to read *paratantro* in pāda c of verses 73 and 74. We read *paratantrābhisaṁvṛtyā* (73) and *paratantrābhiniṣpattyā* (74), following the edition by Karmarkar.

38 *abhūtābhiniveśo' sti, dvayaṁ tatra na vidyate/ dvayābhāvaṁ sa buddhvaiva nirnimitto na jāyate //*

39 Nagao, op.cit., p.204.

40 B.P. Tripathi (general Ed.), *Vijñaptimātratāsiddhi of Ācārya Vasubandhu (Viṁśatikā with autocommentary and Triṁśikā with the commentary of Sthiramati)*, Gaṅgānāthajhā-Granthamālā, vol.V, Varanasi: 1972. *Triṁśikā* v.29, p. 83. Also cf. Vasubandhu on *Viṁśatikā* v.17. The *śuddhalaukika* follows from the *lokottara*, cf. the commentary on *Viṁśatikā* v.17. Also, R. Stanley, *A Translation of the Vijñaptimātratāsiddhi of Vasubandhu: including Vasubandhu's Viṃśatikā (and vṛtti) and Triṃśika and Sthiramati's Triṃśikabhāṣya.* Unpublished Honours Thesis, Australian National University, 1983, p.16.

41 Nagao, op.cit., p.204, 223.

---

42 GKBh 4.87ff., p.252f., line 5f., (tr) p.391f.

43 P.L. Vaidya (ed.), *Aṣṭasāhasrikā Prajñāpāramitā.* Buddhist Sanskrit Texts No. 4. Darbhanga: The Mithila Institute, 1960, p.211, line 25. Edward Conze (tr), *The Perfection of Wisdom in Eight Thousand Lines and Its Verse Summary,* op.cit., p.250. There is also the expression in the *Aṣṭasāhasrikā Prajñāpāramitā* (p.235, line 24): *bodhiḥ sarvadharmā buddhajñānāvabodhanatayā-iti prajñāpāramitā anugantavyā.* "In the conviction that 'all dharmas are essentially enlightenment, because they are all equally understood by the Buddha-cognition'." (Conze, p.274).

44 Lamotte, *History of Indian Buddhism,* op.cit., p.36.

45 Karmarkar, *Gauḍapāda-Kārikā,* op.cit., p.146.

46 Bhattacharya, op.cit., p.213f. Thomas Wood, *The Māṇḍūkya Upaniṣad and the Āgama Śāstra,* op.cit., p.76f. Richard King, *Early Advaita Vedānta and Buddhism,* op.cit., p.191.

47 The translation follows D.T Suzuki (tr), *The Lankavatara Sutra: A Mahayana Text.* London: Routledge, 1932, p.186. P.L. Vaidya (ed.), *Saddharmalaṅkāvatārasūtram.* Buddhist Sanskrit Texts no. 3. Dharbanga: The Mithila Institute, 1963, p.87, line 20, *etad-hi bhāṣitaṁ buddhair bhāṣante bhāṣayanti ca.*

48 V.V. Gokhale, "The Vedānta Philosophy Described by Bhavya in his *Madhyamakahṛdaya*", op.cit., p.179, *Vedānte ca hi yat sūktaṁ tat sarvaṁ buddhabhāṣitam.*

49 Cf. Williams, *Mahāyāna Buddhism,* op.cit., p.31, where he refers to a *sūtra* that is cited by Śāntideva; the *sūtra* says: "Whatever is well spoken *[subhāṣita],* all that is the word of the Buddha *[buddhabhāṣita].*"

50 Much has been made of the statement of salutation in 4.1, as to whether the words *dvipadām̐ varam [vande]* are an epithet of the Buddha. While the expression *dvipadām̐ vara* is used to refer to the Buddha, it is also found in the *Rāmāyaṇa,* (Baroda, critical ed.) 2.76.15, where it refers to Viṣṇu, and it is also to be found in the Nala story (cf. Lanman's *Sanskrit Reader,* p.16, line 2), as well as other places in the Mbh as noted by Karmarkar and Bhattacharya. So, in accord with the *Rāmāyaṇa* passage just referred to, it could well be a statement of homage to Viṣṇu.

51 S. N. Dasgupta, *A History of Indian Philosophy,* Vol 1, Delhi: Motilal Banarsidass, 1975 [reprint], p.423.

52 T.R.V. Murti, *The Central Philosophy of Buddhism.* London: Allen and Unwin 1974 [reprint], p.115: "On internal evidence alone, we may treat the *Alātā* [sic] *Śānti Prakaraṇa* of the *Māṇḍūkya Kārikās* as an independent work, written most probably by a Buddhist."

53 Cf. the entry by B.N.K. Matilal on "Gauḍapāda", in M. Eliade (ed.), *Encyclopedia of Religion,* Macmillan and Free Press, 1987.

54 Notably Thomas Wood, *The Māṇḍūkya Upaniṣad and the Āgama Śāstra,* op.cit., p.74f. See the discussion earlier in this chapter: Gauḍapāda and Nāgārjuna.

55 This juxtaposition of the terms *nitya* and *druva* is quite artificial, for we find that the word *druva* is used in the *Bṛhadāraṇyaka* Upaniṣad (4.4.20) as a description of Brahman, where it obviously has the sense of "eternal" *(nitya).*

56 Murti, op.cit., p.10f. While essentially agreeing with Murti on this matter, I think we should treat his Absolutistic interpretations of the Madhyamaka with considerable caution.

57 H. Nakamura, "The Vijñānavāda Theory as Presented in the Fourth Chapter of the Māṇḍūkyakārikā", in V. Raghavan (ed.), *Proceedings of the First International Sanskrit Conference, March 26-31, 1972.* Delhi: Ministry of Education and Social Welfare, 1981, Vol.4, p.196.

58 T.G. Mainkar, *The Making of the Vedānta.* Delhi: Ajanta Publications, 1980, p.110. Mainkar, in his informative chapter on Gauḍapāda, adopts a middle position between the two "extreme" views represented by V. Bhattacharya, "who thinks that Gauḍapāda merely reproduces Buddhist philosophical ideas in his work", and R.D. Karmarkar, who tries to disprove Buddhist influence as far as possible.

59 T.R.V. Murti, *The Central Philosophy of Buddhism,* op.cit., p.13.

60 (To repeat what was mentioned in a footnote in the previous chapter:) Gough is of the opinion that: "the unreality of the world...is part and parcel of the philosophy of the Upaniṣads" (p.237). He further says: "The tenant of Māyā is ...no modern invention. The thought, if not the word, is everywhere present in the Upaniṣads, as an inseparable element of the philosophy" (p.248). Gough and Deussen both refer to the use of the particle *iva* ("as it were") and on this point Deussen makes the noteworthy comment: "Strictly speaking, such an 'as it were' or *iva* should be supplied to every page and every line in which the Upanishads are concerned with something other than the ātman." (p.158. Also p.228ff.). Cf. A.E. Gough, *The Philosophy of the Upanishads and Ancient Indian Metaphysics.* London: Kegan Paul, Trench, Trubner and Co., 1891. Paul Deussen. *The Philosophy of the Upanishads.* New York: Dover, 1966 (first published 1906).

---

61 T.R.V. Murti, *The Central Philosophy of Buddhism*, op.cit., p.113.

CHAPTER THREE

Gauḍapāda on Liberation and the Means to Liberation

(1) Contemplation based upon the syllable "OM"

In addition to providing insight into the real nature of the Self though the analysis of the three states of experience *(avasthātrayavicāra)*, the *Māṇḍūkya* Upaniṣad also provides a means to assimilate this same truth through contemplation using the syllable OM. We shall briefly indicate how this is done. In the eighth mantra, which begins this topic, the Upaniṣad makes the statement that the Self is to be equated with the syllable OM, and that the letters constituting this syllable, "A", "U" and "M", are to be equated with the "quarters" of the Self.[1] The first quarter, *vaiśvānara*, i.e., the waker together with the waking world, is to be identified with the letter "A"; the second quarter, *taijasa*, i.e., the dreamer and the dream world, is to be identified with the letter "U"; and the third quarter, *prājña*, i.e., the sleeper and the causal world, is to be identified with the letter "M". The Upaniṣad presents some reasons for relating each particular letter with each particular quarter, and it also gives various results that can accrue from performing a contemplative practice *(upāsana)* wherein the contemplator gives predominance to one or the other letters of the syllable OM, but these matters need not concern us. Gauḍapāda's comments to these passages, in kārikās nineteen through to twenty-three, do not add much to what has been given in the Upaniṣad. Kārikā twenty-two, however, is reminiscent of kārikā five which praised (as *phalaśruti)* the knowledge of the three states, but here the praise is directed towards the "great sage" who understands the equation of the three states and the three letters.

In the following kārikā he says:

> The letter "A" leads [the contemplator] to the waker *(viśva)*, the letter "U" leads to the dreamer *(taijasa)*, and the letter "M" to the sleeper *(prājña)*. There is no reaching That which has no letter *(amātra)*. [1.23]

This kārikā introduces the twelfth mantra, the final passage of the Upaniṣad, which says that the "Fourth" *(caturtha)* "has no letter" *(amātra)*. Here the Upaniṣad once again describes the Fourth as: "outside the range of empirical dealings, the cessation of the phenomenal world and non-dual". Thus the three letters of OM are to be equated with the three states of experience. The "non-letter" of the OM is the silence from which the sound "OM" emerges, by which that sound is sustained, and into which the sound resolves; and that awareful silence is to be directly equated with the Fourth "quarter" of the Self, i.e., the Self in its real nature. So we have:

(1) the letter "A" represents the first "quarter" of the Self, i.e., the waker together with the waking world *(virāṭ)*.

(2) the letter "U" represents the second "quarter" of the Self, i.e., the dreamer together with the dream world *(hiraṇyagarbha)*.

(3) the letter "M" represents the third "quarter" of the Self, i.e., the sleeper together with the subtle causal condition *(īśvara)*.

(4) the silence is the fourth "quarter" of the Self, the Absolute Self, the *turīya*.

The Upaniṣad teaches that the contemplation upon OM, when understood in the manner outlined, is a means *(prakiyā)* for enlightenment. When the syllable OM is uttered, the contemplator sees how the sound "OM" arises, persists and disappears into the silence, the *amātrā*, leaving the silence intrinsically undisturbed. In the same way, the contemplator should appreciate that what is represented by the letters, i.e., the three cosmic states, arise, persist and disappear in the acosmic *(niṣprapañca) turīya:* the underlying awareful silence, the pure Awareness, which remains ever untouched by phenomena. In the words of Toṭaka, the disciple of Śaṅkara, the contemplator should come to the direct understanding: "The three states do not belong to Me. I am always the Fourth *(turīya).*"[2]

Thus the contemplation using the syllable OM as a support *(ālambana)* is a means to become imbued with the understanding of Advaita. The method on which this contemplation is based is "superimposition and subsequent negation" *(adhyāropāpavāda).*[3] It is not possible to proceed directly to the unknown without taking the help of the known. Accordingly, the Upaniṣad first identifies the three states and their corresponding macrocosms with the Self; then in mantra seven, and again in mantra twelve, it negates the three microcosms along with their macrocosms in order to reveal the absolute and untouched nature of the Self. All states, comprising waker, dreamer and sleeper, together with their corresponding macrocosms, are finally to be seen as superimpositions upon the unconditioned Self. The states are therefore the Self, for what is superimposed does not exist apart from its substratum. The states are the apparently limiting conditions *(upādhi)* of the Self. The Self as such, however, is intrinsically distinct, or "untouched", by the states, since what is superimposed does not affect the locus of the superimposition. The Self as such is intrinsically free from the superimposed limiting conditions *(nirupādhika).* So in Advaita, enlightenment consists in the apprehension the real *(satya)* and the negation of the unreal. Such negation does not involve the physical destruction of the unreal, but it is the appreciation of the apparent nature of things; it is akin to the knowledge that the blueness of the sky is unreal, i.e., it is apparent, but not truly existing *(mithyā).* "Enlightenment" in Advaita is the direct and existential understanding (or insight) of what is real *(satya)* and what is *mithyā.* It does not depend upon a trance-like condition involving the suspension of awareness, such as the *nirvikalpasamādhi (asamprajñātasamādhi)* spoken of in Patañjali's *Yogasūtra.*[4] Nor is the real something to be reached *(prāpya),* for since it is real, it is already present *(nityasiddha);* it is therefore something to be understood as it is. As Gauḍapāda says: "There is no reaching That which has no letter *(amātra).*"

The contemplation upon OM as presented in the *Māṇḍūkya* and the Kārikā does not simply involve the repetition of the syllable OM. Nor is it a meditation in the yogic sense of requiring the total suspension of cognition *(cittavṛttinirodha).* It is rather a contemplation that is imbued throughout with understanding, for the contemplator has the knowledge of the equivalence of the three letters of OM and the three states of experience, and knows too the identity between the silence of the *amātrā* and the *turīya.* Such a contemplation functions as a means to assist in the direct apprehension, or the direct understanding that: "I am the *turīya*". This is evident from the way the Upaniṣad concludes: "Thus OM is indeed the Self. The one who knows thus, enters the Self by himself."[5]

Gauḍapāda concludes his first chapter with six verses prescribing and praising meditation upon OM. He says:

> One should know OM in relation to the quarters [of the Self]. There is no doubt that the quarters are the letters. Having known OM in terms of each of the quarters, one should not think of anything [else]. [1.24]

The statement, "one should not think of anything [else]", is a quotation from the *Bhagavadgītā,* in the sixth chapter where meditation is taught. There it is said: "having centred the mind on the Self, one should not think of anything [else]" (6.25).

Gauḍapāda further speaks of contemplation based upon the syllable OM:

> Fix your mind upon *Praṇava* [the syllable OM]. *Praṇava* is Brahman, in which there is no fear. There is no fear anywhere for one who is ever focused on *Praṇava.* [1.25]

The expression "fix your mind" *(yuñjīta)* is also likely to have been taken from the sixth chapter of the *Bhagavadgītā,* where it is said: "The yogī should constantly concentrate *(yuñjīta)* himself (i.e. the mind)" (6.10). Similarly, the expression "ever focused" *(nityayukta)* occurs regularly in the *Gītā.*[6] The expression that Brahman is "without fear" *(nirbhaya)* echoes the *Taittirīya* Upaniṣad where it is said: "Whenever one is fearlessly established in this [Brahman] which is unperceivable, incorporeal, inexpressible and without support, then he becomes fearless" (2.7.1); as well as the *Bṛhadāraṇyaka* Upaniṣad where Yājñavalkya says to Janaka: "You have attained That which is free from fear" (4.2.4).

> *Praṇava* [OM] is indeed the lower Brahman and *Praṇava* is considered to be the higher Brahman. *Praṇava* is without prior, without interior or exterior, without posterior, changeless. [1.26]

The syllable OM stands for the "lower Brahman" *(aparabrahman)* as well as the "higher Brahman" *(parabrahman)*.[7] The "lower" Brahman is represented by the manifest sound of OM, while the "higher", or unconditioned Brahman, is revealed as the silence of the *amātrā*. The *āmātrā*, the silence that is pure Awareness, is none other than the *turīya*, and it is the *amātrā* "part" of OM that Gauḍapāda refers to in the second line of the kārikā when he says that OM is: "without prior, without interior or exterior, without posterior, changeless". This statement is a quotation from the *Bṛhadāraṇyaka* Upaniṣad: "Brahman is without prior or posterior, without interior or exterior" (2.5.19). Śaṅkara, in commenting upon this passage of the *Bṛhadāraṇyaka*, says that the words "without prior or posterior" mean that Brahman is without either a cause or an effect.[8] The word "changeless" *(avyaya)* occurs fairly frequently in the Upaniṣads, as well as in the *Bhagavadgītā*, in the context of describing the nature of Brahman or Ātman.[9]

Gauḍapāda says that *Praṇava* is the "beginning, middle and the end of everything" [1.27]. He then says:

> One should know *Praṇava* to be the Lord who is present in the heart of all. Having understood the all pervading OM, a wise person does not grieve. [1.28]

In these two kārikās, it would seem that Gauḍapāda is referring to Īśvara, the *aparabrahman* referred to in kārikā twenty-six, who is to be identified with the manifest sound of OM. Gauḍapāda's expression, "the Lord who is present in the heart of all" is an adaptation of the statement in the *Bhagavadgītā* where Kṛṣṇa says, "I am seated in the heart of all" (15.15). The expression, "Having known...a wise person does not grieve" occurs a number of times in the *Kaṭha* Upaniṣad.[10] Lastly, referring to the *parabrahman*, the *amātrā* of the OM, he says:

> The person who knows that OM is without letter [sound], yet has infinite letters [sounds], that it is the cessation of duality and auspicious, such a person is a sage and no one else. [1.29]

Here he repeats the teaching of the twelfth mantra, combining the two expressions of that mantra: "the cessation of the phenomenal world" *(prapañcopaśama)* and "non-dual" *(advaita)*, into a single statement: "cessation of duality" *(dvaitasyopaśama)*.

(2) Asparśa yoga - the yoga of "no-contact"

There are two principal occasions in the remaining kārikās where Gauḍapāda discusses the nature of liberation and its means. The first occurs at the close of the second chapter, where Gauḍapāda briefly refers to this topic from verses thirty-five to thirty-eight. The next is at the end of the third chapter, and here Gauḍapāda treats the topic more extensively, from verses thirty-one to forty-eight. After discussing the verses from the second chapter, we shall proceed to examine those from the third chapter where we will also observe how the commentators have understand these particular verses.

Introducing the topic of the required discipline *(sādhana)* for the knowledge of the Self, Gauḍapāda says:

> This [turīya-Self], which is non-dual, free from all division *(nirvikalpa)*, where there is the cessation of the phenomenal world, is seen by sages who are free from attachment, fear

> and anger, and who have a thorough knowledge of the Veda. [2.35]

The subject of this verse is the pronoun "this" *(ayam),* which is also used in some of the immediately preceding verses, and it refers in all these instances to the *turīya* -Self. V. Bhattacharya takes the subject of the verse to be *prapañcopaśama* and he translates: "This cessation of the expansion of the universe"[11]; but such a translation is not correct, because the expression *prapañcopaśama* is used in the *Māṇḍūkya* (in mantras 7 and 12) as a *bahuvrīhi* compound describing the *turīya.* So the proper subject of the verse is *ayam,* which refers to Ātman, and *prapañcopaśama* ("where there is the cessation of the phenomenal world") is a *bahuvrīhi* compound describing this pronominal subject.[12]

It may be noted that the adjectives describing the *turīya* -Self: "non-dual" *(advaya),* "free from all division" *(nirvikalpa)* and the ground of the "cessation of the phenomenal world" *(prapañcopaśama),* show that the *turīya* -Self is inherently all of the above. The *turīya,* by its very nature, is *advaya, nirvikalpa* and *prapañcopaśama,* and it does not become non-dual etc. through the performance of any action on the part of the seeker. That is why knowledge is emphasised in traditional Advaita; and what is meant by "knowledge" is the direct and immediate apprehension *(aparokṣajñāna)* that one's essential nature is the pure Awareness, *turīya*-Self. Such a knowledge, or insight, is indicated by the word "seen", a word that is reminiscent of the well-known statement of Yājñavalkya to Maitreyī: "The Self has to be seen; it has to be heard of, reflected on and contemplated upon."[13] In the above verse Gauḍapāda gives two qualifications for this knowledge, the first refers to the seeker's mental and emotional fitness, and it consists of freedom from "attachment, fear and anger". This expression, "free from attachment, fear and anger" *(vītarāgabhayakrodha),* is found twice in the *Bhagavadgītā* (2.56 and 4. 10) and it is obvious that Gauḍapāda is citing the *Gītā* here.[14] Gauḍapāda's second qualification has to do with traditional learning. The expression, "a thorough knowledge of the Veda" *(vedapāraga),* which can also be found in the *Manusmṛti,*[15] is a clear statement of the centrality of the Veda to Gauḍapāda's thinking. To have "a thorough knowledge of the Veda" (literally to have "gone to the further shore" of the Veda) would entail a knowledge of the Upaniṣads which are (mostly) located at the end of their respective Veda.[16]

The next verse deals more specifically with the practice of contemplation:

> Therefore, having known this [Self] to be thus, one should fix one's attention on non-duality. Having become established in non-duality, one should behave among people as if a fool. [2.36]

The expression, "Therefore, having known this [Self] to be thus", occurs in the *Bhagavadgītā* (2.25). And the expression, "one should behave among people as if a fool", can be seen in *Manusmṛti:* "...let a wise man, though he knows [the answer], behave among men as [if he were] an idiot."[17]

The above kārikā contains two injunctions, the first is an injunction to contemplation, "fix one's attention on non-duality", and the second is an injunction about conduct, "one should behave... as if a fool." What is the necessity of the first of these injunctions? The function of the gerund "having known" is to indicate that something has occurred prior to the action of the main verb, which here contains the injunction about fixing the attention.[18] So if the Self is already known, what is the need of the injunction concerning fixing the attention? Though the commentary ascribed to Śaṅkara does not clarify this issue, the sub-commentators explain that verse thirty-six is addressed to those people who have understood the purport of the Vedānta, i.e., the Upaniṣads, and who may even be scholars, but who do not have a firm conviction about non-duality because of the strength of mental impressions pertaining to erroneous knowledge *(mithyājñāna)*. These people, who have some kind of mental impressions which are working counter to the Upaniṣadic teaching and their own reflection upon it, are advised to fix their attention upon non-duality, i.e., to contemplate upon non-duality, in order to make firm their understanding of non-duality.[19] Thus the sub-commentators see this verse as providing an advice on how to remove obstructions to Advaitic understanding, and they say that the injunctions have a restrictive function.[20] An injunction is said to be restrictive *(niyamavidhi)* when it limits a person to one thing when an alternative is available.[21] The first injunction is restrictive in that it enjoins the person to fix the attention on non-duality rather than upon something else, namely duality, and the purpose of so doing is to counteract the habitual, but erroneous notions *(viparītabhāvanā)* of duality; and thereby over time to become firmly grounded (to gain *niṣṭhā)* in the direct understanding of the non-dual Self. The second injunction is also restrictive, in so far as it ordains one way of behaviour when an alternative could also be possible; the idea is that such people ought not make a display of their wisdom, learning, virtue etc.[22]

The next verse gives a further injunction concerning the behaviour of such a person *(jñānī):*

> The ascetic, disassociated from praise and salutation, disassociated from rites with regard to the ancestors, having an unfixed abode, should depend entirely upon circumstances. [2.37]

This verse also occurs in the *Nāradaparivrājaka* Upaniṣad.[23] Evidently Gauḍapāda thinks that such a person would already be, or would become, an ascetic *(yati):* free from ritual obligations and depending upon circumstances as they unfold according to one's *prārabdhakarma*. The commentary ascribed to Śaṅkara gives an unusual, but interesting, explanation of the compound *"calācalaniketa"* which would normally mean "having no fixed abode". Śaṅkara interprets the phrase as, "having the body and the Self as the support", and explains that *cala* refers to the body which is constantly undergoing change while *acala* refers to the changeless Ātman. He says:

> "whenever, under the influence of ordinary activities such as eating etc., he forgets his own support, i.e., his essential nature, the reality of the Self which is unchanging *(acala)* like space, and thinks of himself as "I", then he has the changing *(cala)* body as his support. Thus the knower of the truth has both the changing and the unchanging as his

support, whereas [the person who does not know] has only external objects as support."[24]

Gauḍapāda concludes the second chapter with a verse describing the liberated person *(jīvanmukta)* and he gives a final advice to such a person never to lose sight of the truth:

> Having seen the Reality within and seeing the Reality externally, becoming identified with Reality and finding delight in it, one should not fall away from Reality. [2.38]

As mentioned, there are a number of verses at the end of the third book which discuss the nature of liberation and *sādhana*. Introducing the topic Gauḍapāda firstly presents two kārikās [3. 29, 30] which occur in virtually identical form in the fourth chapter [4. 61, 62] as well; these verses resemble Yogācāra in the way they equate the relation between subject *(grāhaka)* and object *(grāhya)* to the functioning of the mind, on analogy with the way the mind constructs an unreal subject-object relation in dream. Having thus equated duality with the functioning of the mind, Gauḍapāda proceeds to speak about non-duality and the nature of liberation. Commencing the topic, he says:

> This duality - comprising whatever is moving or stationary - is seen by the mind. When the mind becomes "no mind" duality is not perceived.[25] [3.31]

What are we to understand by the enigmatic expression "no-mind"? Gauḍapāda makes this clearer in the next verse:

> When, as a consequence of the knowledge of the reality that is the Self, [the mind] does not conceptually create [the distinction of subject and object], [the mind] then goes to the state

> of being "no-mind". In the absence of [an object] to be perceived, it does not perceive [an object]. [3.32]

The first thing to be noticed here, and in the seven verses that follow, is that Gauḍapāda is not prescribing a spiritual practice *(sādhana)* intended to take the practitioner to enlightenment. What is described in these verses is the "state" of the *jñānī,* the state of enlightenment itself. This is so, because everything follows from the initial statement: "as a consequence of the knowledge of the reality that is the Self" *(ātmasatyānubodhena).* Everything to be told is *subsequent* to this knowledge, not prior to it.[26] Therefore the "mind" of the *jñānī* is the topic elaborated in kārikās 32-39, but not a practice for enlightenment.

As a result of the knowledge of the reality that is the Self the mind does not "conceptually create" *(na saṅkalpayate).* What is meant by the expression that it does not "conceptually create"? What seems to be meant here is that the mind does not create a factual distinction of "I" and "this". Ānandagiri explains that *saṅkalpa* means the "transactional nature of the mind", and this is interpreted to be the everyday mind.[27] In other words, in the ordinary functioning of the mind there is the construction of an ego subject, the transactional "self", which stands in a dualistic relationship to whatever it perceives. So *saṅkalpa* can be understood as the mind's construction of the ego-subject and the resulting division between the subject *(grāhaka)* and the object of cognition *(grāhya).* According to Advaita, the mind has two modes of operation: the first is the subject of transactional life, called *ahaṁvṛtti* (the "I"-thought), and the second is the cognition that represents any external object of perception to the subject, this second type of cognitive act is called as *idaṁvṛtti* (literally, "this"-thought); both types of cognitive activity are illumined by the invariable Self that is pure Awareness.[28] Therefore, both the notion of the ego "I", and the consequent idea of "not-I", are the construction of the mind and do not belong to the illumining Awareness as such. Gauḍapāda says that when there is the knowledge of the *turīya* -Self, the pure Awareness, and as a result the mind does not construct the ego-based *grāhaka-grāhya* relationship, the mind becomes "no-mind". Putting it another way, in language more recognisable to later Advaita discourse, we can say that when the pure Awareness-Self is known, the transactional subject-object relation, which is due to the operation of the mind, is seen as *mithyā* only; while the "substratum" of the mind, the pure Awareness, is recognised as the single reality underlying the transactional subject-object relation.[29]

In the last quarter of the verse Gauḍapāda says: "In the absence of [an object] to be perceived, it does not perceive [an object]." This part of the verse is almost identical to a part of a verse from the *Triṁśikā* of Vasubandhu.[30] Gauḍapāda appears to be saying something akin to the Yogācāra, but we can see that the resemblance is rather superficial, for once again, as Gauḍapāda reveals his detailed knowledge of the Mahāyāna and brings Vedānta into the philosophical milieu dominated at his time by Mahāyāna thought, he still unmistakably differentiates Vedānta from Buddhism when he says: "as a consequence of the knowledge of the reality that is the Self". In making it clear that non-duality is because of the knowledge of the Self, Gauḍapāda shows that he is in the Upaniṣadic tradition and that his teaching of non-duality is not to be construed as the same as Yogācāra. Nonetheless, when he makes use of a variety of quotations from the Buddhist texts, and we can see evidence of one such reference in the above verse, I suspect that the Advaita commentators from Śaṅkara onwards were a little nonplussed. They did not have the same close familiarity with Buddhist literature as did Gauḍapāda, and they possibly failed to recognise in the kārikā before them the oblique quotation from a Mahāyāna text. This accounts for their difficulty in explaining such passages, as well as for the reticence of later Advaitins to quote these kārikās. The final statement of the kārikā: "In the absence of [an object] to be perceived, it does not perceive [an object]" is an elaboration of the preceding word "no-mind". The idea seems to be that when, through Self-knowledge, the whole subject-object operation of the mind is known to be *mithyā* and pure Awareness is known to be the reality of everything, since nothing exists as "other" to Awareness, the mind stops grasping at things as "other".[31]

Gauḍapāda next says that the pure Awareness, the substratum of mind, should be recognised as Brahman:

> They say that the Awareness that is without conceptual constructions, unborn, is not different from that which is to be known.

> Brahman, unborn and eternal, is what is to be known. One knows the unborn through the unborn.[32] [3. 33.]

Gauḍapāda refers to the pure Awareness *(jñāna)* that is, by its very nature, free from the conceptual thought constructions of subject and object, as "unborn" *(aja)*.[33] Gauḍapāda previously used the word "unborn" in the context of the *turīya,* in 1.16, and it would be correct to understand the same meaning expressed here. He then says that this essential Awareness is: "not different from that which is to be known" *(jñeyābhinna)*.[34] The expectation as to what is to be known is satisfied in the second sentence when he says that Brahman is what is to be known.[35] This expression, that Brahman is "to be known" *(jñeya),* occurs also in the *Bhagavadgītā* (13.12) and that is the likely source of its usage here.[36] What Gauḍapāda says is that one's essential Awareness-nature is inherently free from thought constructions *(nirvikalpa)* and unborn and is none other than Brahman.

The last sentence, "One knows the unborn through the unborn", is in reply to an unstated question: "how is Brahman known?" The answer is that Brahman is self-revealing. The reference to Brahman as "to be known" *(jñeya)* must be a metaphorical usage, for otherwise Brahman would become an object, and if Brahman, the ultimate subject, the pure Awareness in whose light everything stands revealed, itself becomes an object, then the question may be asked: to whom would it be an object? Gauḍapāda says that as Brahman is Awareness by its very nature, Brahman does not require another Awareness in order to be revealed, any more than the sun requires another light for its illumination. Śaṅkara's comment makes the Advaita perspective on this matter clear: "the idea is that because [Brahman-Ātman] is ever a mass of uniform [or simple] Awareness, it does not depend upon another Awareness [in order to be revealed]."[37]

Having said that the Awareness, the substratum of the mind, is Brahman, Gauḍapāda now distinguishes between the mind that has become "no-mind" and the condition of a person in the state of deep sleep, where the division of subject and object is temporarily annulled:

> The condition of the mind which is restrained, free from conceptual constructions, awareful, has to be understood. The [condition of the mind] in sleep is different, it is not the same as that [restrained mind free from conceptual constructions, etc.]. [3. 34]

After asserting this difference, Gauḍapāda explains the point further in the next kārikā. Before we proceed, we may pause to consider what Gauḍapāda means by the word "restrained" *(nigṛhīta).* He has just said, in verse thirty-two, that the mind becomes "no-mind" through the knowledge of the reality that is the Self, while in the present verse he refers to the mind being "restrained", which seems to imply control in a yogic sense (i.e. *cittavṛttinirodha).* However the control of the mind about which Gauḍapāda speaks is not brought about *though* suppression of the mind, as it is in Patañjali's system of yoga, but it takes place when, as a *result* of the Self-knowledge spoken of in verse thirty-two, the mind does not create the false division of subject and object, and in the absence of the notion of a real object the mind becomes peaceful and restrained.[38] The word "restrained" does, nonetheless, convey the idea that there is some discipline involved, that there is the deliberate cultivation of a certain type of "mind" subsequent to knowledge. Perhaps we can see an exemplification of such a mind, restrained through Self-knowledge, in the recent example of the life of Ramaṇa Maharṣi (1879-1950) of Aruṇācala (Tiruvannamalai) who wrote, in the last verse of his Sanskrit work *Upadeśasāra:* "The shining forth of one's inherent nature, without the thought of the ego "I": this is the great austerity *(tapas).* This is the word of Ramaṇa."[39]

In the following verse Gauḍapāda gives the reason for the difference between the enlightened mind and the mind resolved in sleep:

> For in deep sleep the mind disappears. The restrained mind does not disappear. That [restrained] mind is indeed Brahman which is free from fear and which has the light of Awareness all around.[40] [3. 35]

In kārikā 1.13 (discussed in section one of chapter one) Gauḍapāda stated that while the non-perception of duality is common to both the sleeper and the Ātman, they differ in that the sleeper is connected to the non-apprehension of reality, or ignorance, which is the "seed" of the other two states, while the Ātman has no connection to either non-apprehension or to misapprehension. The state of deep sleep and the Ātman also differ in that the sleeper does not know anything at all whereas "the *turya* is always all-seeing" (1.12). This means that the *turīya* is present during all three states, illumining equally the presence of cognitive states in waking and dream, as well as their absence in deep sleep. Although the Self does not vary in any state, during sleep the mind "disappears" *(līyate)* and is therefore unable to reflect the Self. In the waking state the mind is present, and when the errors of non-apprehension and misapprehension of reality are removed by Self-knowledge, the waking mind then reveals Brahman without any obstruction.

In the following three verses Gauḍapāda further describes Brahman, as it is revealed in the restrained mind of the *jñānī*. He says:

> It is unborn, in which there is neither "sleep" nor "dream", it is without name or form, ever-effulgent, omniscient - there is no figurative expression here at all. [3. 36]

In 1.16 Gauḍapāda referred to the *turīya* as: "unborn, in which there is neither 'sleep' nor 'dream'" *(ajam anidram asvapnam)*, and these words convey the same sense here as well: the word "sleep" is a metaphor for the non-apprehension of reality, while "dream" is a metaphor for the misapprehension of reality.[41] Gauḍapāda then further describes Brahman as revealed in the restrained mind of the *jñānī*. He says that Brahman is:

> Samādhi, beyond all expression, above all thought, completely calm, ever-effulgent, motionless, without fear.[42] [3. 37]

Regarding the word *samādhi*, Śaṅkara provides two explanations, he says: "*samādhi*, because [Brahman] can be known from the understanding arising out of *samādhi.*" Alternatively, he says: "*samādhi* is that in which one is resolved".[43] The first explanation is somewhat more "yogic" in its orientation, as it says that Brahman can be known through an understanding arising out of *samādhi.* The second explanation is, I believe, more in keeping with the verse, which describes Brahman as *samādhi* itself, not as something to be gained from a particular condition of the mind called "*samādhi*".

These alternative explanations of the word "*samādhi*" are an indication that there probably existed different views on the subject of the attainment of the knowledge of Brahman well before the time of Maṇḍanamiśra and Śaṅkara. I will take this opportunity to make a few remarks on the concept of *samādhi* and spiritual experience. The view of Maṇḍana -which Vācaspatimiśra, in his celebrated commentary on the *Brahmasūtrabhāṣya* of Śaṅkara, *Bhāmatī*, adopted, popularised and explicitly syncretised with Pātañjalayoga- is essentially that Brahman knowledge arises only out of a long and sustained process of meditation.[44] This would accord in general with the first definition given above and it is this view that has become more or less dominant in Advaita circles, especially in the last hundred years.[45] While it is difficult to objectively describe what "*samādhi*" actually is, as it is a personal and necessarily "private" experience, there are a number of difficulties about the concept itself. One difficulty is with the way the term has been adopted, from a yogic or Tantra-yogic milieu, and invested with a new meaning in Advaita Vedānta. Certainly the word *samādhi,* as it is used in some Advaita circles at the present time, is given an entirely different meaning from what it has in the *Yogasūtras* of Patañjali.[46] In the former, it is seen to be the means to gain the realisation of the non-dual Self, while in the dualistic system of Pātañjalayoga it is the way to "burn up" the subliminal seeds of erroneous knowledge, so that the individual *puruṣa* can remain in its true condition, free from contact with *prakṛti.* Although *samādhi* in Advaita Vedānta and Pātañjalayoga are interpreted in such different ways, the practice of meditation with the aim of reaching *samādhi,* as espoused by not a few teachers of Advaita, is basically equivalent to the cultivation of *samādhi* in the yoga tradition. Yet how can the very same practice be accepted as having such different goals?

There is also the problem that the word *samādhi* has been reified to the extent that it embodies a "mystical" state of consciousness which is seen to be the goal of all spiritual practice, as it forms the necessary condition for the realisation of Brahman. In the literature extolling the importance *samādhi* the word is frequently translated as "super-consciousness", a meaning that has nothing to do with the etymology of the word *samādhi.* Such translations succeed only in further conditioning the seeker by fostering an imagination as to what Self-knowledge is like, and what is its precondition. The problem with this whole enterprise is that the seeker then assiduously tries to cultivate a particular type of experience, the nature of which is in the imagination, and this is done at the cost of neglecting the Self that, according to the Advaita of Śaṅkara, is simply Awareness itself. In short, the whole search for a "mystical" *samādhi* experience can be a mistaken adventure, in that it can amount to an ignorant denial of the Self, for in searching for an experience of the Self the searcher overlooks the fact - and the teaching of this fact is made explicit in such Upaniṣads as *Bṛhadāraṇyaka* and *Kena* - that Brahman, the ultimate subject, pure Awareness, cannot be experienced objectively like a sense object, because it is Experience itself.

According to the second explanation in the commentary, i.e., "*samādhi* is that in which one is resolved", Gauḍapāda is using the word *samādhi* as a description of the nature of Brahman, rather than the idea that Brahman is to be gained through a *samādhi* experience. In this interpretation, which seems to be the one the commentator prefers judging from his introduction to the following verse ("Since it was said that Brahman itself is *samādhi,* motionless, without fear..."), Brahman is said to be *samādhi* itself, just as the *turīya* -Self was described earlier as "free from all division" *(nirvikalpa)* (2.35). According to this understanding, the *turīya* -Self is inherently *nirvikalpa* and as such it is "*samādhi*" by nature. What this means is that the *turīya* -Self, as pure Awareness, is Experience *per se (anubhūtisvarūpa),* or in the words of the *Bṛhadāraṇyaka* Upaniṣad: "This Self, the experiencer of everything *(sarvānubhūḥ),* is Brahman" (2.5.19). In this statement of the Upaniṣad the Self is presented as Experience itself. Thus there are two views in Advaita, and at a certain level they are quite divergent: the first, more "yogic" view, advocates realisation through the cultivation of a *samādhi* experience; the second takes its stand on the Self as self-revealing Awareness, as Experience *per se,* and while it does not deny the value of meditation, it looks somewhat critically upon the *samādhi* -oriented search for a special experience of the Self. I believe that the latter view accords more closely with the teachings of Śaṅkara and his disciples. In the following chapters there will be further occasion to refer to this issue.

The next verse completes this topic, which began at verse thirty-two and which describes Brahman as revealed in the restrained mind of the *jñānī*. This verse says:

> Where there is no thought, there is neither getting, nor giving up. Then Awareness rests in Itself, it is without birth and uniform. [3. 38]

The word "where", in the phrase "Where there is no thought", refers to Brahman, for Brahman was described in the preceding verse as "above all thought".[47] So in Brahman, the Awareness that is "interior" to thought, there is no movement toward anything nor away from anything, for such movement is the result of thought. Brahman is the changeless Awareness that illumines the movement of the mind and, as the final subject, is free from all distinctions. Śaṅkara glosses the words "getting" (or "grasping") *(graha)* and "giving up" *(utsarga)* by the terms "acquiring" *(upādāna)* and "abandoning" *(hāna);* these terms are regularly found in his other works and they are a fairly standard expression about the nature of the Ātman in the works of his disciples as well. The expression that the Self can be neither "acquired nor abandoned" is yet a further indication that according to Gauḍapāda, Śaṅkara and other Advaita authors, the nature of the Self is not something to be "gained", but rather it should be recognised as the constant luminous substratum in all particular experience. Through Self-knowledge, Awareness is "seen", or " directly known" to be resting in Itself *(ātmasaṁstham),* i.e., resting in its own inherent nature. The phrase "rests in Itself" *(ātmasaṁstham)* is an echo of the same phrase from the *Bhagavadgītā* (6.25).[48] The last words of the verse, "it is without birth and uniform" *(ajāti samatāṁ gatam),* recall the proposition put forward at the beginning of the third chapter ("Therefore I will tell that which is not pitiable, which is without birth and uniform. [So that one understands]: nothing is born, even while things are born all around." 3.2) and these words indicate, according to Śaṅkara and his sub-commentators, that the topic dealing with the knowledge of the reality that is the Self is now brought to a close.

Gauḍapāda refers to what has been spoken of in these verses (32-38) as *Asparśayoga*, "the yoga of no-contact". He says:

> [This], called "*Asparśayoga*", is difficult for all the yogis to understand. Indeed, yogis are afraid of it, seeing fear where there is no fear. [3. 39]

What does Gauḍapāda mean by the expression "*Asparśayoga*", and how does it differ from the practice of yoga as generally understood? Śaṅkara says that the emphatic particle "*vai*", occurring alongside the other particle *nāma* in the verse, indicates that *Asparśayoga* is something "well-known" in the Upaniṣads.[49] However he does not say where in the Upaniṣads such an expression can be found. The absence of finding such an expression in the Upaniṣads has led some writers to doubt that this commentary is one of Śaṅkara's authentic works.[50] Although the term *asparśa* (non-contact) may not be very evident in the Upaniṣads, the word "*asaṅga*" (unattached) is highly prominent in the *Bṛhadāraṇyaka* Upaniṣad. The term *asparśa*, which Śaṅkara understands to refer to the absence of any "relation" *(sambandha)*, essentially conveys the same idea as the word *asaṅga*. Therefore I do not think that the term *asparśa* is as mysterious as some would make out, and the commentator quite possibly thought that the meaning of *asparśa*, as a synonym for *asaṅga*, would be evident to those who are well-versed in the Upaniṣads.[51] The word *asparśa*, like the word *asaṅga*, is therefore a description of the very nature of the Self. In the fourth chapter, Gauḍapāda uses the term "*asaṅga*" a number of times as a description of the nature of Consciousness.[52]

V. Bhattacharya, in a long note to the only other occurrence of the word *Asparśayoga* in the *Gauḍapādakārikā* (at 4.2), considers the possibility that it refers to the *asamprajñāta samādhi* of the *Yogasūtra*, and he points out that Vidyāraṇya (c. 1296-1386 CE) in the *Pañcadaśī* (2.28) equates it with *nirvikalpa samādhi*. His own suggestion, however, is that it refers to the last of the nine stages of meditation taught in some Buddhist texts.[53] Thus he equates it with a type of yogic practice in which there is suppression of all mental properties. T.M.P. Mahadevan also believes that it means a yogic practice, equivalent to what is taught in the *Yogasūtra* of Patañjali.[54] Nonetheless, and even in spite of Vidyāraṇya's equating it with *nirvikalpa samādhi*, I believe that *Asparśayoga* is not the same as the discipline of the "suppression of the modifications of the mind" *(cittavṛttinirodha)* taught by Patañjali. The so called *Asparśayoga* is not a practice for "enlightenment" because, as mentioned earlier, the *Asparśayoga* follows *from* Self-knowledge, whereas yoga is understood to be the means *for* Self-knowledge. That *Asparśayoga* also has a dimension of "practice" is evident from verse thirty-four (supra) where Gauḍapāda speaks of the "condition of the mind which is restrained *(nigṛhīta)*, free from conceptual constructions *(nirvikalpa)*." But that it is not the same as what is generally understood as *nirvikalpa samādhi* is also evident from his use in that verse of the word "awareful" *(dhīmat)*, which indicates that the mental modifications are not completely suppressed, as they are in *nirvikalpa samādhi*.[55] *Asparśayoga* is to abide in the knowledge of the non-dual Self *(jñānaniṣṭhā)*; it is a practice in so far as it consists in holding the mind in the knowledge of one's true non-dual nature. *Asparśayoga* is the author's nomenclature for all that was spoken of in verses 32-38, and these verses are mostly a description of Brahman, as revealed in the restrained mind of the *jñānī*. The commentator too understands *Asparśayoga* as referring to the very nature of Brahman itself.[56]

The second line of the verse: "Indeed, yogis are afraid of it, seeing fear where there is no fear" is an introduction to the remaining verses of the chapter. This statement serves to distinguish the above teaching from ordinary yoga. Gauḍapāda does not say outright why yogis are afraid of it, but it would seem that dualists are referred to here, and Śaṅkara says that they fear this yoga because they see in it the destruction of their individuality.[57] Having thus differentiated his teaching from ordinary yoga, he then clearly brings forth the distinction by describing the practice of these yogis. He says:

> For all yogis, freedom from fear depends upon restraining the mind, as does destruction of sorrow, spiritual awakening, and everlasting peace. [3. 40]

Gauḍapāda says the practice of yoga is concerned with controlling the mind. But this is not what Gauḍapāda has been teaching in the above verses, where the mind has become "no-mind" as a consequence of the "knowledge of the reality that is the Self" *(ātmasatyānubodha)*. In elucidating this point, Śaṅkara makes an interesting statement which brings out clearly his understanding of the difference between the Vedāntic *jñānī* and the ordinary Yogin. He says:

> There are those who [understand] that the mind and senses and so forth, being merely superimposed [on Brahman], analogous to how a snake is superimposed upon a rope, do not exist in reality as something separate from their essential nature that is Brahman. For such people - for whom Brahman is their essential nature - fearlessness and the everlasting peace known as liberation are established just of their own accord and are not dependent upon something else [i.e. control of the mind]....But the yogis who are different from that, who follow a path, and whose outlook is either low or average, think that the mind is something other, i.e., it is separate from the Self and in association with the Self. For all those yogis, who do not have the knowledge of the reality that is the Self, freedom from fear depends upon the control of the mind. As does the destruction of sorrow. Such people, lacking in discrimination, [erroneously] think that there is no destruction of sorrow so long as the mind, which is something associated with the Self, continues to be active.[58]

The two sub-commentators, Ānandagiri and Anubhūtisvarūpācārya, confirm what I said earlier when they summarise the discussion by saying that for aspirants of the highest qualification, "control of the mind" *(manonirodha)* is the result of the immediate knowledge of the non-dual Self; whereas in the case of aspirants of low or average ability, the immediate knowledge of the Self is made to depend upon control of the mind.[59]

Gauḍapāda then describes how difficult it can be for the yogi to gain control of the mind:

> As the sea can be dried up with a tip of *kuśa* grass that carries a single drop of water, so can the mind be brought under control through unflagging effort. [3. 41]

Even so, Gauḍapāda says there are helpful techniques for bringing the mind under control:

> By employing a method one should restrain [the mind] when it is distracted in desire and sense-enjoyment, and also when it is at ease in sleep, for sleep is [an obstruction] as much as desire. [3. 42]

In the following three verses he mentions four obstacles to meditation and the way to combat them. But firstly he tells a remedy for the situation mentioned in the preceding verse, when the mind is distracted in desire and sense-enjoyments:

> One should turn [the mind] away from desire and sense-enjoyment by repeatedly remembering that everything contains sorrow. And by repeatedly remembering that everything is unborn, one does not see the born [duality].[60] [3. 43]

This kārikā calls to mind a verse in the *Bhagavadgītā*, where Kṛṣṇa, responding to Arjuna's concern about the difficulty in controlling the mind, says: "Without doubt...the mind is difficult to control and it is restless, but it is controlled through practice and non-attachment" (6.35). Śaṅkara says that the first line of the kārikā refers to the attitude of non-attachment *(vairāgya)*, and Ānandagiri adds that the second line refers to the repetition of knowledge *(jñānābhyāsa)*.[61]

Gauḍapāda mentioned two obstacles to meditation in kārikā 42: distraction *(vikṣepa)* and sleep *(laya)*. In kārikā 43 he spoke of non-attachment and the repetition of knowledge as the twofold remedy for the first obstacle. In the next verse, he briefly refers to these two obstacles, as well as to the third obstacle, and in the verse that follows it he mentions the fourth obstacle:

> One should wake up the mind when it goes to sleep. When it is distracted, make it quiet again. Understand when it is under the influence of past impressions. When it is without distinctions, do not disturb it. [3. 44]

> One should not enjoy the happiness there [in that state free from distinctions] but one should be unattached on account of discernment. Through effort one should unify the motionless mind [when it] goes out [towards objects]. [3. 45]

In these verses Gauḍapāda mentions the four obstacles to the control of the mind: distraction *(vikṣepa)*, sleep *(laya)*, the rising of impressions from past experiences *(kaṣāya)* and the desire to enjoy the happiness of the mind when it is established in a state free from distinctions *(rasāsvāda)*. We have seen his remedy for the first obstacle. In dealing with the second, the drowsiness associated with sleep, Gauḍapāda merely says that one should "wake up the mind".[62] Concerning the third obstacle, the sudden arising from the sub-conscious of the memory of earlier experiences in this life, Gauḍapāda advises that "one should understand" when the mind is under the influence of these past impressions, i.e., one should just recognise that this situation is occurring.[63] The fourth obstacle is the enjoyment of the happiness that is present in a mind in a state of evenness, or freedom from distinctions. Gauḍapāda says: "One should not enjoy the happiness there [in that state free from distinctions] but one should be unattached on account of discernment", for absorption in that happiness constitutes yet another, subtle, form of distraction. Gauḍapāda adds that when the mind is motionless, but again moves toward sense objects, one should exert oneself to unify the mind [in the Self].[64]

In the next verse Gauḍapāda acknowledges that such control of the mind is a means to "become" Brahman:

> When the mind does not resolve [into sleep] and does not become distracted any more, then the mind, being motionless and without mental images, becomes Brahman. [3. 46]

Here Gauḍapāda accepts that the path of yogic control of the mind, which he described as long and arduous in verse forty-one, can come to fruition in the realisation of Brahman. However it has to be kept in view that in kārikās thirty-nine and forty Gauḍapāda distinguishes the superior *Asparśayoga*, based upon knowledge of the Self, from the ordinary yoga which depends upon control of the mind. We saw that Śaṅkara also makes a distinction between the *jñānī* and the yogis: "who are different from that, who follow a path, and whose outlook is either low or average, who think that the mind is something other, i.e., it is separate from the Self and in association with the Self."[65] But he too, in a terse comment upon the sentence of the kārikā: "then the mind...becomes Brahman", accepts the outcome proposed by Gauḍapāda.[66] Ānandagiri, the principal commentator on Śaṅkara's works, likewise says that yogic practice, in which apprehension of the Self is made to depend upon the control of the mind, is for those of average *(manda)* ability.[67] But whereas Śaṅkara makes no reference to the Pātañjalayoga, Ānandagiri gives it a significant role in this context. Ānandagiri introduces the cultivation of *samprajñāta* and *asamprajñāta samādhi,* which are central to Patañjali's treatment of Yoga, as a remedy for the removal of the third obstacle, i.e., *kṣāya,* or the influence of past impressions.[68] He also goes further when he makes an explicit equation between Brahman and the state of *asamprajñātasamādhi.* For instance, when Śaṅkara (summing up the statement: "Through effort one should unify the motionless mind when it goes out" 3.45) says: "The idea is that one should bring it just to the condition of pure Being, to the nature of Awareness itself", the comment of Ānandagiri is: "the idea is that one should make it attain the limitless Brahman that is associated with *asamprajñātasamādhi*".[69] So we can see that Ānandagiri (c. 1260-1320), coming at least five centuries after Śaṅkara, and while closely following the themes of Śaṅkara, is more ready than Śaṅkara to make a direct and specific inclusion of the *samādhi* yoga of Patañjali within Advaita, though, as we have just seen, Gauḍapāda has made room for it already.

Just as Gauḍapāda had earlier described Brahman as revealed in the mind of the *jñānī* in the verses referring to *Asparśayoga* (32-38), he now brings his discussion of the practice of yoga to completion by describing Brahman as revealed in the mind of the *yogī* who is in a state of meditative absorption *(samādhi)*. Most of the expressions found here are similar to those used earlier (32-38).[70]

> They say that it [the mind absorbed in pure Awareness] rests in Itself, is calm, liberated, inexpressible, the highest happiness, unborn, [identical] with the unborn knowable [Brahman], omniscient. [3. 47]

The expression "the highest happiness" *(sukham uttamam)* is quite possibly derived from the *Bhagavadgītā* 6. 27, where the context is also that of meditation. Thus the yogin, following the long and difficult path of control of the mind (see verse forty-one), can come to the realisation of the "*Asparśayogī*", the *jñānī*.

The topic is concluded, yet there is one more kārikā, and here Gauḍapāda returns to his perspective of ultimate reality. Introducing this verse, Śaṅkara says:

> All this control of the mind etc., as well as creation using the examples of clay, iron etc. (3.15), and the conceptual understandings [based upon the acceptance of a creation], are stated as a method in order to understand the highest truth, but they themselves are not the highest truth. The highest truth is:

No individual soul *(jīva)* is born, its birth
does not occur. This is the highest truth,
where nothing whatsoever is born. [3. 48][71]

---

1 According to the rules governing the combination of vowels in Sanskrit, the single substitute for the letters "A" and "U" is "O". Therefore the syllable is always pronounced OM, never as AUM.

2 Michael Comans, *Extracting the Essence of the Śruti: The Śrutisārasamuddharaṇa of Toṭakācārya.* Delhi: Motilal Banarsidass, 1996, v.113, p.76.

3 Later I will suggest that the revelation of the real depends upon the use of language functioning by way of implication *(lakṣaṇā).* I have not discussed this matter here, though the following important words in mantra 7: "[the *turīya]* constitutes the essence of the single thought 'I' *(ekātmapratyayasāra)"* do provide an instance of such revelation through *lakṣaṇā.*

4 Cf. Michael Comans, "The Question of the Importance of *Samādhi* in Modern and Classical Advaita Vedānta", *Philosophy East and West,* vol 43, no.1, 1993, p.19ff.

5 MāU 12.

6 Francis X. D'Sa, *Word-Index to the Bhagavadgītā.* Pune: Institute for the Study of Religion, 1985, p.36. The expression occurs in chapter 7. 17; 8. 14; 9. 14 and 12. 2.

7 Cf. PU 5.2.

8 BUBh 2.5.19, p.781, line 3f., (tr) p.281. The explanation of these two words is the same in the *bhāṣya* on kārikā 1.26.

9 Eg. KaU 3.15. MU 1.1.6; 3.2.7. BG 2.17; 2.21.

---

10 KaU 1.2.22, 2.1.4, 2.3.6.

11 V. Bhattacharya, *The Āgamaśāstra of Gauḍapāda,* op.cit., p.42.

12 The commentary, traditionally ascribed to Śaṅkara, explains the compound *prapañcopaśama* thus: *prapañcopaśamaḥ prapañco dvaitabhedavistāraḥ tasyopaśamo 'bhāvo yasmin sa ātmā prapañcopaśamaḥ.* GKBh 2.35, p.206.

13 BU 2.4.5; 4.5.6.

14 BG 2. 56 and 4. 10. It is difficult to understand how Richard King, in his *Early Advaita Vedānta and Buddhism,* op.cit., p. 86, could arrive at the view that "there is no evidence of a direct relationship between the GK and the *Bhagavadgītā.*"

15 *Manusmṛti* 2.148.

16 Śaṅkara's comment with reference to *vedapāraga,* "those who are intent upon the meaning of the Vedānta" *(vedāntārthatatpara)* indicates that he takes the expression to refer to the Upaniṣadic knowledge. GKBh 2.35, p.206, line 15, (tr.) p.263.

17 Cf. *Manusmṛti* 2.110. Georg Buhler (tr.), *The Laws of Manu.* New York: Dover, 1969 (reprint), p.50. Wendy Doniger with Brian K. Smith (tr.), *The Laws of Manu.* New Delhi: Penguin Books, 1991, p.29.

18 Cf. Pāṇini, *Aṣṭādhyāyī,* 3.4.21, *samānakartṛkayoḥ pūrvakāle.*

19 Ānandagiri, in S. Subrahmanyashastri (ed.),*Upaniṣadbhāṣyam Vol. 1.* Varanasi: Mahesh Research Institute, 1979, p.277, line 32ff. Also cf. Anubhūtisvarūpācārya, who mostly follows Ānandagiri, ibid., p.277, line 13f. Also cf.

Svayamprakāśānanda Sarasvatī, *Mitākṣarā, A Gloss on Śrī Gaudapāda Āchārya's Māndūkya Kārikas.* Benares: Haridas Sanskrit Series No. 1, Chowkhamba Sanskrit Book Depot, 1910, p.27. The gloss of Svayamprakāśānanda is a skilful amalgam of Śaṅkara's commentary and Ānandagiri's sub-commentary, rather than an independent work. Svāmī Viṣṇudevānānda, in his gloss *Govindaprasādinī*, explains *smṛtim* as *nididhyāsanarūpām*. Cf. *Māṇḍūkyopaniṣad with the commentary of Śaṅkarācarya and the ṭīkā of Ānandagiri along with the ṭippiṇī Govindaprasādinī by Swami Viṣṇudevānanda and the Hindi gloss Vidyānandīmitākṣarā by Swami Vidyānanda Giri.* Rishikesh: Kailāsa Āśram, (no common era date), p.121, n.1.

20 Ānandagiri, ibid., p.278, line 19. Anubhūtisvarūpācārya, p.277, line 13f.

21 Cf. A.B. Gajendragadkar and R.D. Karmarkar, *The Arthasaṁgraha of Laugākṣi Bhāskara.* Delhi: Motilal Banarsidass, 1984, p.215f.

22 Cf. the discussion on the word *"bālya"* in BSBh 3.4.50.

23 *Nāradaparivrājakopaniṣad* VI. 38. K. Narayanasvami Aiyer (tr.), *Minor Upanishads: Second Series, with Sanskrit Text and English translation,* Madras: Sri Sringeri Jagadguru Santana Dharma Vidya Samiti, 1967, p.301 (text) and (tr) p.338. A similar expression: *"nirnamaskāram, astutim..."* occurs in the Mbh also: XII. cclxix. 34. This Mbh verse is cited twice by Śaṅkara in BUBh, at 3.5.1 and 4.4.9, cf. Mādhavānanda (tr), p.340, 511.

24 GKBh 2.37, p.207, line 6f., (tr) p.265. The word *"aniketa"* also occurs in the BG 12.19, where Śaṅkara glosses it as "having no fixed abode".

---

25 An almost identical verse can be found in the *Haṭhayogapradīpikā* of Svātmārāma. Cf. *The Haṭhayogapradīpikā of Svātmārāma with the commentary Jyotsnā of Brahmānanda and English translation.* Madras: The Adyar Library and Research Centre, 1984 [reprint]. 4.61, p.160.

26 The compound *ātmasatyānubodha* is most often translated as a genitive *tatpuruṣa*, "the knowledge of the truth of [i.e. about] ātman", eg., Bhattacharya, op.cit., p.67; Wood, op.cit., p.23; King, op.cit., p.150. In the commentary ascribed to Śaṅkara, it is taken as a *karmadhāraya* compound, "the knowledge of the truth [i.e. reality] that is the ātman", GKBh 3.32, p.221, line 21f., *ātmaiva satyam, ātmasatyam...tasya...avabodhaḥ.* While both interpretations of the compound are acceptable, perhaps the interpretation as a *karmadhāraya* is to be preferred in so far as it has the advantage of clearly bringing out the central focus of Gauḍapāda which should not be missed, namely that in keeping with the teaching of the *Māṇḍūkya* Upaniṣad, liberation follows from the knowledge of the Self *(ātmā)*, and that Self is the ontological reality *(satya)* of everything.

27 *saṅkalpo hi manaso vyāvahārikaṁ rūpam. Upaniṣadbhāṣyam*, op.cit., p.307, line 23. Anubhūtisvarūpa repeats this explanation. Svāmī Viṣṇudevānanda, in his gloss on the *bhāṣya* and the *ṭīkā*, says that *vyāvahārikaṁ* means *vyavahārasiddham.* Cf. *Māṇḍūkyopaniṣad with the commentary of Śaṅkara, the subcommentary of Ānandagiri and the ṭippaṇī of Viṣṇudevānanda Giri*, op.cit., p.176.

28 Cf. The *Śrutisārasamuddharaṇam* of Toṭaka vv.14-15, 34. Michael Comans, *Extracting the Essence of the Śruti*, op.cit., p.15f., and p.26.

---

29 Ānandagiri says that the knowledge of reality is the ascertainment that there is nothing "other" than the Self, for he glosses the word *"tena"* in the *bhāṣya* as: *tena = tattvajñānena, ātmātiriktārthābhāve niścite. Upaniṣadbhāṣyam*, op.cit., p.307, line 28.

30 The verse in question reads: *yadā tv ālambanaṁ jñānaṁ naivopalabhyate tadā/ sthitaṁ vijñānamātratve grāhyābhāve tadagrahāt//* v. 28. B.P. Tripathi (general Ed.), *Vijñaptimātratāsiddhi of Ācārya Vasubandhu*, op.cit, p. 83. The last *pāda* of this verse resembles the final *pāda* of GK 3. 32, *grāhyābhāve tad agraham*. The idea of the Yogācāra seems to be: "...perceiving the truth of cognition-only, the non-being of outer things is perceived, and when an outer object is not perceived, the perceiving subject likewise is not perceived", G.M. Nagao, *Mādhyamika and Yogācāra*, op.cit, p.261, n.16., also cf. p.147. The same idea occurs in the *Madhyāntavibhāga*, 1.3.

31 Svayamprakāśānanda Sarasvatī, in his gloss *Mitākṣarā*, op.cit., p. 40, explains the phrase *grāhyābhāve tadagraham* as: *vācārambhaṇaṁ vikāro nāmadheyaṁ mṛttiketyeva satyam ity ātmajñāne pṛthaktvābhāvād ityarthaḥ.*

32 I am reading *vibudhyate* in the active voice, like *budhyate* in 1.16. Śaṅkara understands *vibudhyate* as active voice as he glosses it by the word *avagacchati*, GKBh 3.33, p.222, line 9.

33 Here the word *jñāna* would mean *jñapti iti jñānam*, i.e., pure Awareness, in the way Śaṅkara and other Advaitins interpret the word in the phrase *satyaṁ jñānam anantaṁ brahma* in TU 2.1.1.

34 Sureśvara uses this expression *"jñeyābhinnam"*, identical to GK 3.33, in NS 4.54.

---

35 In the third *pāda* of the verse Śaṅkara interprets *"brahma jñeyam"*, not as two words: "Brahman is That which is to be known", but as a *bahuvrīhi* compound describing *jñānam* in the first *pāda*. GKBh 3.33, p.222, line 7, (tr) p.308. Bhattacharya and Karmarkar give the words separately in their editions and their interpretation has been followed here. While there is no substantial change in meaning either way, I believe the latter to be preferable, as Karmarkar says (p101): "The first line says *jñāna* is *jñeyābhinna*, naturally the *ākāṅkṣā* is what is *jñeya?* This *ākāṅkṣā* is satisfied by the statement *jñeya* is *brahma, ajaṁ nityam.*" Also, if it is understood in this way, the word *ajam* in *brahma ajaṁ nityam* would not be redundant since it would refer to Brahman in the second line and not once again to *jñāna*.

36 *jñeyaṁ yat tat pravakṣyāmi... anādimat paraṁ brahma.* BG 13. 12.

37 GKBh 3.33, p.222, line 8f., (tr) p.308, *nityavijñānaikarasaghanatvād, na jñānāntaram apekṣate ityarthaḥ.*

38 In his introduction to verse thirty-four Śaṅkara comments upon the idea of the "restraint" that was referred to when he says: "It was said that through the knowledge of the truth that is the Self the mind does not create subject-object duality *(saṅkalpa)*, and in the absence of external objects it becomes pacified, like fire without fuel, and restrained, i.e., restricted. And that is why it was said that there is no duality when the mind becomes "no-mind". The condition of the mind which has been restrained, i.e., restricted, in this way....has to be understood." Ibid., 3.34, p.222, line 13f., (tr) p.309.

---

39 *ahamapetakaṁ nijavibhānakam, mahad idaṁ tapo ramaṇavāg iyam* (30) [free translation]. *Upadeśasāraḥ, with the bhāṣya of Vāsiṣṭhagaṇapatimuni.* Tiruvannamalai: Sri Ramana Ashram, 1982.

40 Śaṅkara understands the compound *jñānālokam* as a *bahuvrīhi,* but comprised of a *karmadhāraya,* rather than a genitive *tatpuruṣa* as one might expect. He says: *jñaptir jñānam,* i.e., *ātmasvabhāvacaitanyaṁ, tad eva jñānam ālokaḥ prakāśaḥ yasya tad brahma jñānālokam.* Bhattacharya, op cit., 70, has noted this interpretation of the compound.

41 Śaṅkara describes *nidrā* as: "beginningless *māyā* which is characterised by ignorance *(avidyā)" (avidyālakṣaṇānādimāyā...),* GKBh, 3.36, p, 223, line 12, (tr) p.312. He glosses *sakṛdvibhātam* as: *sadaiva vibhātam, sadā bhārūpam,* line 15f., i.e., as ever effulgent pure Awareness. He explains the compound *sarvajñam* rather unusually as: *sarvaṁ ca tajjñaptisvarūpaṁ ceti sarvajñam,* line 18f, i.e., it is everything and it is of the nature of Awareness. Śaṅkara understands the word *upacāra* too in a unusual way; not as meaning "figurative expression", but to mean "further practice" and he comments that once Brahman is known there is no further practice that needs to be performed. He says: "With regard to Brahman having the characteristics [just mentioned] there is no further practice to be done, as for others there is the practice of concentration etc. as something different from the nature of the Self. The idea is that since Brahman is by nature eternally pure, awake and free, there is no possibility at all of anything to be done after the destruction of ignorance." line 19f, (tr) p.313.

42 We understand the subject of the verse to be *"samādhi"* and the other words in the verse to be in grammatical apposition with it. If *samādhi* is the subject of the verse then we can easily account

for the use of the masculine gender throughout the verse. Śaṅkara seems to understand the verse in this way since he introduces the following verse with the words, *"yasmād brahmaiva samādhir acalo'bhāya ity uktam"*, ibid., 3.38, p.224, line 8, (tr) p.314. The commentator Ānandagiri says that the masculine gender is used in the verse because it is accepted that the one who knows Brahman becomes Brahman and so Brahman is described using the masculine gender. *Upaniṣadbhāṣyam*, p. 310, line 29. Anubhūtisvarūpācārya repeats this explanation and adds an alternative explanation that the masculine gender has been used because Brahman really has no gender and so there is no fixed rule regarding which gender to use. Ibid., p.310, line 26.

43 *samādhiḥ, samādhinimittaprajñāvagamyatvāt. samādhīyate 'smin iti vā samādhiḥ.* GKBh 3.37, p. 224, line 3f., (tr) p.314. Ānandagiri comments on Śaṅkara's second explanation: "the *jīva* and its limiting adjunct are resolved in whom, i.e., in the supreme Self. Thus *samādhi* means the supreme Self." *Upaniṣadbhāṣyam*, p.311 line 19ff. Anubhūtisvarūpācārya also says that *samādhi* means Brahman. Ibid., p.310, line 17.

44 For a further discussion of this issue cf. Michael Comans, "Śaṅkara and the Prasaṅkhyānavāda", *Journal of Indian Philosophy*, 24, 1996, pp.49-71.

45 For a discussion of *samādhi* in Advaita Vedānta, cf. Michael Comans, "The Question of the Importance of Samādhi in Modern and Classical Advaita Vedānta", *Philosophy East and West*, vol.43, no.1, 1993, pp.19-38. For a wide ranging and valuable discussion of the concept of "experience" in Indian thought, especially in the Vedānta, by its modern as well as its classical interpreters, see the chapter on: "The Concept of Experience in the Encounter Between India and the West" in W. Halbfass, *India and Europe*. Albany: State Univ. of New York Press, 1988. Also, see chapter Six of the present work: (2) Immediate and

mediate knowledge of Brahman and the question of experience. Also, Andrew. O. Fort, *Jīvanmukti in Transformation: Embodied Liberation in Advaita and Neo-Vedānta.* State Univ. of New York Prc , 1998.

46 For example, Swami Gambhīrānanda, of the Rāmakrishna Mission, in his important and commendable translation of a number of Śaṅkara's commentaries, translates the word *samādhi* in GK 3.37 (p.313) as: "divine absorption". Such an unwarranted translation clearly shows that the learned translator is bringing some major pre-suppositions to bear on this word.

47 Śaṅkara understands the *yatra* and *tatra* as referring to Brahman, GKBh 3.38, p.224, line 8f., (tr) p.314.

48 *ātmasaṁsthaṁ manaḥ kṛtvā;* "having centred the mind in itself (i.e. in its substratum, the Self)." BG 6.25.

49 GKBh 3.39, p.224, line 22f., (tr) p.315f.

50 As noted by King, op.cit., p.152.

51 The word *asparśa* occurs in KaU 3.15. The word *asaṅga* is an important term in the BU, eg. 3.8.8, 3.9.26, 4.2.4, 4.3.15, 4.4.22, 4.5.15. S. Subrahmanyashastri, the editor of the *Upaniṣadbhāṣyam*, op.cit., p.311, in a note on the word *Asparśayoga,* links up the term *asparśa* with the passage in the BU *"asaṅgo hy ayaṁ puruṣaḥ".* He says: *asparśayogaḥ - sparśaḥ sambandhaḥ, tadrahito yogaḥ brahmaṇi ekībhāvaḥ, "asaṅgo hy ayaṁ puruṣa" ity ukteḥ brahmabhāvaṁ prāptasya sarvasambandhābhāvasiddhiḥ.*

52 Cf. 4.72, 96, also 97.

53 V. Bhattacharya, op.cit., p.94f.

---

54 "The purpose for which this yoga is resorted to is the same as that which is set forth in the *Pātañjalasūtra* as the goal of yoga, viz. to stem the tide of the surging psychoses of mind and gradually attain thereby a state of mindlessness." T.M.P. Mahadevan, *Gauḍapāda: A Study in Early Advaita.* Madras: Univ. of Madras, (3rd ed.) 1960, p.181.

55 Śaṅkara glosses *dhīmataḥ* as *vivekavataḥ,* GKBh 3.34, p.222, line 15. V. Bhattacharya, op.cit., p.69, understands the word as referring, not to the mind, but to the wise man: "That state of the mind of a wise man...".

56 *asparśayogo brahmasvabhāva eva.* GKBh 4.2, p.228, line 18, (tr) p.326.

57 Gauḍapāda referred to different types of aspirants in 3.16, and in the following kārikā he spoke of dualists, so he possibly has such *(hīnamadhyama)* people in mind. Śaṅkara says: *bhayanimittātmanāśadarśanaśīlā avivekina ityarthaḥ.* GKBh 3.39, 225, line 1f., (tr) p.316.

58 GKBh 3.40, p.225, line 5f., (tr) p.316f.

59 *Upaniṣadbhāṣyam,* op.cit., p.312, lines 18 and 28. Anubhūtisvarūpācārya, following Ānandagiri, states succinctly: *uttamabuddhīnām advaitātmadarśanaphalaṁ manonirodham abhidhāya, mandadṛṣṭīnāṁ manonirodhāyattam ātmadarśanam.*

60 Regarding the word "born" *(jāta)* in the fourth *pāda* of the verse, Śaṅkara supplies the word *"dvaita"* and interprets *jāta* as if it were at the end of a compound, so that it would mean: "the whole aggregate of duality" *(dvaitajāta).* GKBh 3.43, p.226, line 4.

61 *Upaniṣadbhāṣyam,* op.cit., p.313, line 27f.

---

62 Śaṅkara also connects the method of *jñānābhyāsa* and *vairāgya* as the way to wake up the mind, GKBh 3.44, p.226, line 7, (tr) p.320; but it would seem more likely that this twofold means is the remedy for *vikṣepa* alone.

63 Śaṅkara adds: "When a person repeatedly practises, and his mind has been awakened from sleep and turned away from sense objects and even then does not become established in sameness, but remains in an intermediate state, one should understand that the mind has *kaṣāya*, that it possesses the seeds of desires. By effort one should bring the mind from that state into a condition free from distinctions." GKBh 3.44, p.226, line 9f., (tr) p.320. Ānandagiri includes the two types of meditative absorption [or enstasis] *(samādhi)*, which occupy a central place in the *Yogasūtras* of Patañjali, in the scheme of methods to remove *kaṣāya.* He says: "When the mind has been turned away from sleep and distraction by the repetition of knowledge and by dispassion, but remains obstructed on account of [subtle] desires, then it has to be turned away from that obstruction also through the meditative absorption called *samprajñātasamādhi* which is engendered by the repetition of listening to the teaching, reflecting and contemplating upon it until there is the meditative absorption called *asamprajñātasamādhi." Upaniṣadbhāṣyam*, p.314, line 16f.

64 Śaṅkara adds that the mind is to be restrained in the Self: "But when the mind, which is in a motionless condition as it has withdrawn from the subtle desire for happiness, goes outwards, then restraining it from that object, one should through effort unify it in the Self alone using the previously mentioned methods. The idea is that one should bring it just to the condition of pure Being, to the nature of Awareness itself." GKBh 3.45, p.226, line 18f., (tr) p.321.

---

65 GKBh 3.40, p.225, line 5f., (tr) p.316.

66 *brahmasvarūpeṇa niṣpannaṁ cittaṁ bhavati- ityarthaḥ.* GKBh 3.46, p.226, line 25f., (tr) p, 322.

67 *Upaniṣadbhāṣyam*, op.cit, comment to 3.40 p.312, line 28. Cf. the similar comment by Anubhūtisvarūpācārya in fn.56, supra.

68 *Upaniṣadbhāṣyam*, comment to 3.44, p. p.314, line 16f.

69 *Upaniṣadbhāṣyam*, p. 314, line 37f., *prayatnataḥ* (in the kārikā)= *samprajñātasamādhivaśād ekīkuryāt.* Then he says: *asamprajñātasamādhiyuktaṁ paripūrṇaṁ brahmaiva-āpādayed ityarthaḥ.* He also says that *sāmyaṁ=asamprajñātasamādhim ityarthaḥ*, ibid., 3. 44, p. 314, line 24.

70 *svastham* is equivalent to *ātmasaṁstham* in 3. 38; *śāntam* is equivalent to *supraśāntaḥ* in 3. 37; *sanirvāṇam* would be equivalent (according to Bhattacharya p. 82) to the *amanībhāva* in 3. 31; *akathyam* would be equivalent to *sarvābhilāpavigataḥ* in 3. 37; *ajena jñeyena* refers to Brahman: *brahma jñeyam ajam*, in 3. 33; *sarvajñam* is equivalent to *sarvajñam* in 3. 36.

71 This verse is repeated in 4. 71.

CHAPTER FOUR

Śaṅkarācārya

(1) Śaṅkara and Gauḍapāda

The traditional accounts of the life of Śaṅkara unanimously mention the episode of Śaṅkara meeting his guru Govindapāda.[1] Tradition, moreover, explicitly identifies Govindapāda as the student of Gauḍapāda.[2] In his *Brahmasūtrabhāṣya,* Śaṅkara cites the *Gauḍapādakārikā* on two occasions, and he also makes one other allusion to it. In 1.4. 14 and 2.1.9 of his commentary he quotes kārikās 3.15 and 1.16 respectively, and in 2.1.9 he obliquely refers to kārikā 1.17.[3] He cites these kārikās with obvious respect, for he introduces 1.16 with the words: "Here is what the *ācārya* who knows the traditional teaching of the Vedānta has said...." Similarly, before citing 3.15, he says: "This is what those who know the traditional teaching say..." The question arises, then, as to why Śaṅkara does not refer more frequently to the guru of his own guru. Given the vital importance of the link between guru and disciple *(paramparā)* in the transmission of the tradition of teachings *(saṁpradāya),* one would expect to see Gauḍapāda quoted far more frequently in Śaṅkara's writings.

These relatively few references to the *Gauḍapādakārikā* suggests that perhaps Gauḍapāda was a more distant teacher of Advaita than the traditional accounts indicate. Modern scholarship tends to see Gauḍapāda as belonging to the early part of the sixth century CE and places Śaṅkara in the earlier part of the eighth century CE (c.700-750), which is a revision of the well known dates, 788-820 CE, proposed by earlier generations of scholars.[4] If this is correct, the philosophical conditions when the two men lived were different, and so their concerns as teachers of Advaita were naturally not the same. At the time of Gauḍapāda, early in the sixth century C.E., Buddhism had reached the limit of its influence in India, and this influence is reflected in many of his kārikās where, as we have seen, he displayed a close acquaintance with the prevalent Buddhist thought of his time. By the time of Śaṅkara, in the early part of the eighth century, Buddhism had declined in importance. Śaṅkara perhaps did not have the same intimate knowledge of Buddhism as did Gauḍapāda, but Buddhism was not Śaṅkara's major concern. He saw the Mīmāṁsakas as his principal opponents, and one of his main tasks was to establish against the followers of Mīmāṁsā that the Upaniṣads constitute an independent means of knowledge; that they teach the liberating knowledge of the non-dual Self; and that the knowledge they generate is entirely independent of the performance of rites. Another of his chief concerns was to establish, against the views of others who accepted the Upaniṣads as an independent means of knowledge, that this knowledge of the true nature of the Self does not require to be supplemented by the continued performance of rites. As we proceed to look at the teachings of Śaṅkara, we shall occasionally refer to the question of whether his teachings and those of Gauḍapāda are in complete harmony or whether they show any significant differences.

But before we commence our study of Saṅkara proper, we will point out a few of the more obvious instances of agreement between Śaṅkara and Gauḍapāda, and also some occasions where the language of Śaṅkara is remarkably similar to that found in the *Gauḍapādakārikā*. Both these points suggest that Śaṅkara was following Gauḍapāda more closely than might be supposed if we did no more than count the number of references to Gauḍapāda in the *Brahmasūtrabhāṣya*.

Firstly, Śaṅkara frequently uses the analogy of space, comparing the space within a pot and that outside it with the apparent difference and the ultimate non-difference between the individual soul and Brahman.[5] We have seen in chapter one (section three) how Gauḍapāda elaborated this analogy to bring out various aspects of the nature of the individual soul and its "relation" to the absolute Self.[6] Saṅkara also occasionally uses the analogy of the rope and the snake, which we again see in the kārikās of Gauḍapāda, and he seems to have the *Gauḍapādakārikā* in mind when he employs this illustration in the context of citing kārikā 1.16 in the *Brahmasūtrabhāṣya*.[7]

Secondly, Śaṅkara explicitly says that the states of waking, dream and deep sleep are unreal *(mithyā)*, and in these statements he exhibits a unanimity of view with Gauḍapāda. In *Brahmasūtrabhāṣya* 2.1.9, before he refers to kārikā 1.16, he says:

> ...The single, invariable, Witness of the three states is not touched by the three states which are variable [in relation to one another].[8]

And he goes on to say:

> For, this is a mere *māyā* that the supreme Self appears as the self of the three states. It is comparable to a rope appearing as a snake etc.[9]

In the *Upadeśasāhasrī*, Śaṅkara says:

> One should abandon this triad of waking, dream and their seed called deep sleep which consists of darkness, as non-existent [in the Self] for the reason that they mutually exclude each other.[10]

There are a number of other such instances concerning the unreality *(mithyātva)* of the three states where he shows an identity of perspective to that of Gauḍapāda.[11] The reason which Śaṅkara gives for their unreality, that "they mutually exclude each other" (literally, "they mutually do not exist in each other") relies upon the same fundamental principle that Gauḍapāda relied upon to demonstrate "non-origination", namely that what is truly real must be completely unchanging, it must be invariable, and hence its being must not stand negated, which is what would happen if it underwent any intrinsic alteration.[12] The states of waking, dreaming and deep sleep are variable *(vyabhicāri)*, they "mutually exclude each other" because when one state is present it negates the presence of the others. Changeability is the reason for the unreality of the three states and this is the same reason Gauḍapāda put forward in kārikā 2.6: "What does not exist at the beginning and at the end, likewise [does not exist] even in the present."[13]

With regard to another matter, Śaṅkara's writings corroborate the view expressed in the previous chapter that the *"Asparśayoga"* of Gauḍapāda does not refer to a type of yogic practice but it denotes the immediate knowledge that the Self is nothing other than pure Awareness, and that such Awareness is intrinsically "untouched" by anything that exists as its apparent object. Śaṅkara makes this clear when he says in the *Upadeśasāhasrī:*

> Everything in the intellect, together with the ego-sense, is always [a qualifying attribute] of the Witness. Therefore Awareness illumines everything, while always touching nothing *(kiñcidapi-aspṛśan sadā).*[14]

There are numerous instances where Śaṅkara uses the word *"asparśa"* to refer to the very nature of the Ātman.[15] All these instances serve to strengthen the conclusion that the term *"Asparśayoga"* ought not to be understood as referring to some transic state, like the yogic *nirvikalpa samādhi,* but that it refers to the very nature of Awareness as such.

There are also occasions where the language of Śaṅkara is remarkably similar to that found in the *Gauḍapādakārikā.* Such resemblances can be seen especially in the *Upadeśasāhasrī.* For example, in the *Upadeśasāhasrī* (9.7) Śaṅkara says, "Awareness is constant and without an object" *(nityaṁ nirviṣyaṁ jñānam).* This phrase resembles Gauḍapāda's statement in 4.72, "Consciousness is without an object, constant" *(cittaṁ nirviṣyaṁ nityam).* Śaṅkara uses the expression "ever shining" *(sakṛdvibhāta)* in 10.1 and Gauḍapāda too has used the expression twice, in 3.36 and 4.81. The term itself occurs in the Chāndogya Upaniṣad 8.4.2, "This world that is Brahman is surely ever shining" *(sakṛdvibhāto hi-eva-eṣa brahmalokaḥ).* Śaṅkara says in 10.4, "I am the Fourth, the continuous Seeing, non-dual" *(turīya eva-asmi sadādṛg advayaḥ)* which resembles Gauḍapāda's expression in 1.12, "the Fourth is always all Seeing" *(turyaṁ tat sarvadṛk sadā).* Śaṅkara too uses the expression "all seeing" *(sarvadṛk)* on three occasions, in 17.1, 55 and 59. In 15.40 Śaṅkara uses the expression, "having as its nature the light of Awareness" *(jñānālokasvabhāvataḥ),* which is reminiscent of Gauḍapāda's expression in 3.35, "having the light of Awareness all around" *(jñānālokaṁ samantaḥ).* Śaṅkara uses the expression "the cessation of the phenomenal world, non-dual" *(prapañcopaśamo' dvayaḥ)* in 17.71 and Gauḍapāda uses the same expression in 2.35.

Apart from these similarities of expression, indicating as they do an agreement of thought, there are other broad agreements, some of which were referred to above. There is also, of course, the shared importance of the *śruti* as the means of knowledge *(pramāṇa)* about Brahman. And it is to this topic that we will now turn, to examine Śaṅkara's attitude to the *śruti* as a means of knowledge, and from there to discuss the nature of Brahman itself.

(2) The *śruti* as the means of knowledge for Brahman

In order to know something we require the appropriate means of knowledge *(pramāṇa)*, by means of which, the thing can be known.[16] A means .of knowledge can only acquire the status of a means of knowledge when it reveals something which cannot be known though another means of knowledge.[17] The two principal means of knowledge in ordinary life are perception and inference: perception is the means to reveal a thing that can be directly objectified by our senses; while inference is the means to reveal the existence of a thing (X) that is not in direct contact with our senses, by relying upon the presence of something (Y) that is in sense-contact and is also known to be invariably connected to the former thing (X). In addition to these two means of knowledge, Śaṅkara also mentions comparison, presumption and verbal testimony as other means of knowledge.[18] The followers of the Pūrva Mīmāṁsā and the followers of the Uttara Mīmāṁsā, i.e., the followers of the Vedānta, both agree that the Veda is a means of knowledge as it is a form of verbal testimony. They consider that the Veda is the sole means by which we can know about metaphysical and ethical matters which cannot be determined through perception or by any of the other means of knowledge, such as inference, which themselves depend upon perception. The Mīmāṁsakas and the Vedāntins are at one in so far as they both consider that the Veda is the single means to know about those things which are beyond the scope of sense perception. Śaṅkara says:

> The entire Veda aims at revealing the means to gain what is beneficial and to avoid what is harmful when such means are not known through perception or inference....In matters coming within the scope of what is visible, there is no need for an investigation by means of scripture, since the knowledge of the means to gain what is beneficial and to avoid what is harmful is available just through perception and inference.[19]

The question may be asked as to how the Mīmāṁsakas and Vedāntins justify their doctrine that the Veda is the sole means of knowledge in matters beyond the scope of perception and inference. The Mīmāṁsakas maintain that the Veda is a valid means of knowledge because it provides a knowledge that is eternal, for the knowledge that the Veda reveals has no known author, it is a knowledge that has simply always existed along with the world itself which, according to the Mīmāṁsakas, has always been in existence since no one can testify that it had a beginning. On this basis the Mīmāṁsakas argue that the authorless Vedic knowledge can have no possibility of any defect, whether of omission or of commission, which might arise from authorship.[20] The Veda is thus an inherently valid means of knowledge within the restricted definition of matters that do not form the domain of perception or of the other means of knowledge that depend upon perception.

Śaṅkara shares this general outlook of the Mīmāṁsakas:

> The manifestation of the already arranged and existing Veda takes place like that of a person breathing out; the Veda is not preceded by any human thought or effort. Hence it is a valid means of knowledge about its own meaning which is arrived at without depending [upon another means of knowledge] *(ataḥ pramāṇaṁ nirapekṣa eva svārthe).*[21]

For Śaṅkara, the Veda is an eternally existent body of knowledge that is meant only for revealing supersensuous matters.[22] Though within this specific sphere of operation the authority of the Veda is intrinsic, Śaṅkara does offer a supporting argument in favour of its validity when he says:

> A great proof of the validity of the Upaniṣad statements is that they present a uniformity of view that a sentient Being is the cause of the world, just like our eyes give us a uniform knowledge about colour etc.[23]

Thus Śaṅkara, in company with all Vedāntins, sees the Veda as inherently rational, in that the various texts have a single fundamental teaching, though they may differ over some of the details as, for example, whether there are a series of three or five elements, since the *Taittirīya* Upaniṣad refers to the creation of five elements whereas the *Chāndogya* Upaniṣad mentions just three. These are minor details, and much of the *Brahmasūtra* is directed to this purpose of harmonising the Upaniṣadic texts. But the validity of the Upaniṣads could not be rationally maintained without the supposition that the Upaniṣads do, in fact, contain a teaching that is self-consistent, at least as far as its broader picture is concerned. Thus the rational law of non-contradiction applies as much to the Vedic revelation as it applies to other types of mundane knowledge. The tremendous exegesis of Śaṅkara in his commentaries on the Upaniṣads and the *Brahmasūtra* is substantially directed to demonstrating the consistent theme of all the Upaniṣads, a theme which Śaṅkara believes to be already contained in the texts and which he is merely elucidating.

While Śaṅkara shares the Mīmāṁsaka view concerning the inherent validity of the Veda, he does not share their view about the eternity of the world, nor does he share their generally atheistic outlook, for he considers that the Veda has issued forth from Brahman, as effortlessly as a person may exhale. According to the Vedāntin, the Veda is not composed by anyone, not even by God (Īśvara), it is an eternal knowledge which is revealed by Īśvara at the commencement of creation and passed on to the Seers *(ṛṣi)* in exactly the same form as it had existed in the previous cycle of creation *(yuga)*.[24]

The Mīmāṁsakas maintain that the Veda has a twofold division, *Mantra* and *Brāhmaṇa*, and they consider that the purpose of the entire Veda is to instruct about ethics, otherwise called religious duty *(dharma)*, which is expressed as the object of an injunction to act in a certain way, as in the example: "he who desires heaven should perform the sacrifice".[25] Here, the metaphysical existence of heaven and the enjoined religious duty of sacrifice are both revealed by the Vedic text. If they were not so revealed, we would have no way of knowing that a place such as heaven does exist, and even if we knew of its existence, we would not know how we could reach it. According to the Mīmāṁsakas, the entire Veda is ultimately about *dharma*, and *dharma* is characterised by an injunction to do something or to refrain from doing it.[26]

Śaṅkara argues repeatedly against their position. He does agree that the majority of the Veda is concerned with *dharma* and concerns injunctions to do or to refrain from doing certain types of specified activity, but against the Mīmāṁsakas he strenuously upholds that the Upaniṣad portion of the Veda is distinct from the rest of the Veda in so far as the Upaniṣads aim to teach Self-knowledge,[27] and through this they alone can fulfil the ultimate human-goal, liberation from the sorrows of transmigratory existence *(saṁsāra)*.[28] Śaṅkara says, for example:

> So it is reasonable that just as the scripture instructs the person who is desirous of heaven etc. about the true means such as the *agnihotra* and so forth, so does the scripture instruct the seeker of liberation about the true nature of the Self: "That is the Self, you are That, Śvetaketu."[29]

Śaṅkara also maintains that the Veda has a twofold division, but for him the division is between the bulk of the Veda that largely deals with religious duties centred around rituals and the injunctions concerning them *(vidhiśāstra* or *karmakāṇḍa)*, and that part which consists of the Upaniṣads, the *jñānakāṇḍa*, dealing primarily with liberating, metaphysical knowledge. According to Śaṅkara, the knowledge of Brahman itself is called Upaniṣad, and he finds in the etymology of the word "Upaniṣad" (the verbal root *sad* preceded by the two prefixes *upa* and *ni)* the meaning that such knowledge completely eradicates transmigratory existence *(saṁsāra)* along with its root which is ignorance, or, such knowledge is called Upaniṣad because the knowledge causes the seeker to attain Brahman.[30] The texts are also called Upaniṣads because they have the same purpose: to eradicate *saṁsāra* and to take the qualified seeker to Brahman. So the word Upaniṣad primarily means the knowledge of Brahman and it secondarily refers to the texts which reveal that knowledge.[31]

Śaṅkara sees the ceremonial portion of the Veda *(karmakāṇḍa)*, though valid, as remaining within the sphere of *saṁsāra*, because this part of the Veda only addresses people who desire worldly prosperity and heavenly felicity, who identify with a particular social class *(varṇa)* and stage of life *(āśrama)*, and who think of themselves as agents of actions and as experiencers of the results. He says that the ceremonial portion does not call into question such attitudes, it merely presupposes them, and proceeds to teach people how to gain what is beneficial according to their own desires.[32] The Upaniṣad portion, on the other hand, addresses a different type of person, it is meant for a person who is averse to the idea that either worldly gain or heavenly bliss constitute the real goal of life.[33] It also has an entirely different subject matter. Śaṅkara says that the Upaniṣads have a twofold function: at some places they determine the nature of the supreme Self and at other places they teach the unity of the individual soul with the supreme Self.[34]

Śaṅkara is definite that the knowledge of reality "cannot even be guessed at"[35] without the Upaniṣads which are the only means of knowledge concerning the existence and the nature of Brahman. To cite just a couple of instances of his remarks along these lines:

> The knowledge of reality is only from the Upaniṣad sentences *(tattvajñānaṁ tu vedāntavākyebhya eva bhavati)*.[36]

Also:

> As for the view that there must be other means of knowledge about Brahman since Brahman is an already existing entity, that is mere fanciful thinking. This thing [Brahman] is not an object of perception, because it is without form etc. Nor is it an object of inference etc., since it has no mark *(liṅga)* etc. from which an inference can be made. But like religious duty, it is to be known solely from the scriptures.[37]

If Brahman is an object, then perception would be the means of knowledge to reveal it. But that is not so, for Brahman is without form.

Since Brahman is not available for perception, Brahman also cannot be inferred, because inference relies on some perceptual data which must be necessarily related to Brahman, but such a relation cannot be established if Brahman is not first a sense object. Even if we could infer the existence of Brahman on the basis of cause and effect, we could only arrive at the knowledge of a Being that is the efficient cause of the world. However the Upaniṣads reveal that Brahman is not only the efficient cause of the world, but Brahman is also its material cause. They further reveal that the essential nature of Brahman is Awareness, and that the essential nature of the individual soul is none other than the Awareness that is Brahman. This point, that the true nature of the Self is pure Awareness that is Brahman itself, certainly requires the Upaniṣadic revelation. Early in his commentary upon the *Brahmasūtra*, Śaṅkara raises the objection that it is not correct to maintain that the true nature of the Self is known only through the Upaniṣads, because the Self is contained in the idea of "I". His answer is that:

> No, [the Self] is the witness of the idea of "I". For neither in the section of the Veda which enjoins religious duty, nor in the tenets of the logicians, does any one come to understand that Being *(puruṣa)* which, as distinct from the agent that is contained in the idea of "I", is the witness of that [I-notion], present in all beings, uniform, one, immutably eternal, the Self of all.[38]

Thus Śaṅkara says the self-understanding that people normally possess, that the self is the self-reflexive subject evident in such acts of reflexive awareness as: "I am such and such" etc., is an error, because the true Self is the absolute subject, it is pure Awareness, the "witness" of the ego and its activities, and it is actually without boundary. We do not spontaneously know this, and left to ourselves we would assume that the ego-consciousness, the "I" in the apperception "I think", is the fundamental subject, and we would not orient our thinking otherwise. The Upaniṣads, however, reveal a different understanding. They reveal that there is a reality behind the cosmos; that the cosmos is a unity and is non-separate from that reality; and that this reality is the true Self of everything. Thus the Upaniṣads constitute a revelation in the complete sense of the word.

If the Upaniṣads are revelation, what is the legitimate scope of human reason in determining the nature of reality? One feels that Śaṅkara had developed more than a little personal animosity towards the "logicians" who engaged in independent, unfettered speculation on the nature of reality. When Śaṅkara refers to them, there is at times more than a touch of scorn in his writing. To cite a few colourful examples from his commentary upon the *Bṛhadāraṇyaka* Upaniṣad:

> Oh! the dexterity in inference shown by these bulls of logicians who lack only a tail and horns!...
> ...this unity of Brahman is a secure fortress impregnable to logicians, those first rate heretics and liars, and inaccessible to persons of shallow understanding and to those who are devoid of the grace of the scriptures and the teacher.[39]

The contempt that he shows toward the "logicians" is because they rely on their own unaided powers of reasoning to fathom reality, much like the philosophers of ancient Greece. Śaṅkara thinks that no finality can be reached through such a method of independent speculation, as he says in some well-known passages:

> And for the following reason, a matter to be known from scripture [Veda] ought not be challenged by mere reasoning. For reasoning that is independent of the Veda and relies solely upon human speculation lacks certainty, because pure speculation has nothing to restrain it. For instance, the speculative reasonings assiduously advanced by some clever people are found to be defective by others who are still more clever, and the speculations of the latter are subsequently found defective by others. So independent reasoning cannot be relied upon to be conclusive, for opinions are diverse.[40]
>
> It is not possible to assemble all the logicians of the past, present and future at one place and time so that their

> opinion about one thing would be unanimous and could be called "right knowledge".[41]

Śaṅkara is not against reasoning *per se*, his opposition is towards reasoning that is not in harmony with what the Upaniṣads reveal. Wilhelm Halbfass puts the matter nicely when he says that for Śaṅkara: "[reason] has its legitimate role under the guidance of and in cooperation with śruti".[42] Śaṅkara frequently makes the point that reason must be in accord with the Vedic revelation, as in his comment that when the *Bṛhadāraṇyaka* Upaniṣad ordains rational reflection *(manana)* in addition to hearing the Upaniṣad *(śravaṇa)*, we should not, under such a pretext, try to find an opportunity here for "dry logic" *(śuṣkatarka)*, i.e., independent ratiocination, and he says: "only reasoning that agrees with the *śruti* is to be accepted, for it assists direct experience *(anubhava)*."[43] Following this statement, Śaṅkara proceeds to give some instances of the type of reasoning that he has in mind. He says:

> (1) Since the states of waking and dream both exclude one another, the Self is not intrinsically connected to them. (2) Because the soul in the state of deep sleep leaves behind the waking world and is unified with the Self whose nature is pure Being, it is itself of the nature of pure Being that is free from the phenomenal world. (3) Since the phenomenal world originates from Brahman, it must be non-different from Brahman according to the logic that the effect is not other than its [material] cause.[44]

To take the first instance. As we have seen in the case of the *Māṇḍūkya*, a number of Upaniṣads refer to the states of waking, dreaming and dreamless sleep. These states alternate, whereas the Upaniṣads reveal the Self to be invariable in all the states. Since that is what the Upaniṣads reveal, we are entitled to draw the conclusion that the Self is not intrinsically the waker, the dreamer or the sleeper, for if it was intrinsically associated with one state it could not exist in the absence of that state. In the second instance, he says the Upaniṣads reveal that in dreamless sleep the individual soul leaves behind the waking world and temporarily merges with the unconditioned Self, pure Being. Since that is the case according to the Upaniṣads, we are entitled to draw the conclusion that pure Being, free from phenomenal experience, is the true nature of the soul. Lastly, the Upaniṣads speak of the world originating from Brahman; that being the case, the world cannot be a second thing in its own right, because we know by observation that the product of the material cause is not a second thing to the material cause itself.

These instances present a mode of reasoning where the conclusion is implied as a necessary presumption. Necessary presumption *(arthāpatti),* which is the postulation of a fact to explain another fact, is accepted by Advaita Vedāntins as a means of valid knowledge *(pramāṇa)* distinct from inference. In the well-known example of presumption, we hear that Devadatta is fat but otherwise healthy and we also hear that he never eats during the day. The only conclusion we can draw from all this is that Devadatta must be eating during the night. If we do not draw this conclusion the known facts about Devadatta will remain unintelligible. Śaṅkara uses the mode of reasoning called *śrutārthāpatti*, or the necessary presumption from what is heard, i.e., what is revealed in the *śruti*, to establish some of his most important teachings. For example, in his commentary on the *Bṛhadāraṇyaka* he raises the following question:

> If you say that ignorance is not logically possible in Brahman, we say: no, because knowledge is enjoined about Brahman. If there was no superimposition of silver on the mother-of-pearl shell, and when it is directly present before the eyes, no one would need make known the fact that it is a shell, by saying: "this is a shell, it is not silver". In the same way, if the superimposition of ignorance upon Brahman did not exist, there would be no need to present the knowledge of oneness regarding Brahman through such statements as: "all this is Being itself", "all this is Brahman", "all this is the Self", "this duality does not exist as something apart from Brahman".[45]

So too he argues that if the performance of rites was the means to immortality the depreciating remarks about wealth that Yājñavalkya makes to Maitreyī would be out of place, since rites require wealth.[46] It would not be correct to imagine that Śaṅkara derives all his teachings by the application of reasoning to what the Upaniṣads reveal, for the Upaniṣads are themselves explicit about many matters, but there are some teachings of Śaṅkara which can be seen as the outcome of a process of presumptive reasoning *(arthāpatti)* based upon the Upaniṣads. Notable among them is the famous teaching about superimposition *(adhyāsa)*, a word that is not present in the Upaniṣads, but which is an idea Śaṅkara finds necessarily implied throughout its teachings.

In the *Brahmasūtrabhāṣya* there are numerous occasions where he argues by necessary presumption. For example, he says that when the Upaniṣads make statements that: "Through which [instruction], what is unknown becomes known" (CU 6.1.3), and "When the Self is seen, when it has been heard about, reflected upon and contemplated, all this becomes known" (BU 4.5.6), they must be saying that nothing really exists as an "other" to Brahman, because:

> If anything is other than Brahman, the declaration that everything is known through knowing one thing would be stultified. The non-difference [of anything from Brahman] is only possible if everything whatsoever originates from the one Brahman. We understand that the proof of the declaration is made by the *śruti* in accordance with the logic of the non-difference of the effects from their material cause.[47]

> What we understand from the presentation of the illustrations of the clay etc. (CU 6.1.4ff.), is that this knowledge of everything can be comprehensible only in this way, through the logic of the [non-difference between the] material cause and its effects.[48]

> Moreover, there is non-contradiction of the declaration [of the knowledge of everything through the knowledge of the One] once we accept that Brahman, while remaining unaltered, is the individual soul.[49]

In these quotations Śaṅkara argues by necessary presumption that this declaration of the *śruti*, i.e., that there is knowledge of everything from the knowledge of the One, can only be upheld if Brahman is the material cause of the entire universe and if Brahman is the essential nature of the individual soul itself, for the declaration would be nullified if anything exists as an "other" to Brahman. So we can see from these instances how Śaṅkara uses logic, often of an *arthāpatti* type, to assist in the proof of some of his characteristic teachings. Wilhelm Halbfass, summarising the relation between reason and the revealed text in Śaṅkara's thought, has expressed the situation well:

> In Śaṅkara's understanding, the Upaniṣads, the "knowledge portion" of the Veda, respond to human reason, appeal to it, provide it with a context, goal and basis. They contain so many hints and implicit patterns of reasoning that they seem to anticipate all merely human intellectual efforts. Thus the Upaniṣads are not a set of dogmas against which human reason would have to revolt or assert itself, but rather a source to which it traces itself and its own legitimacy, a universe of meaning in which it can exercise its potential without having to proclaim its autonomy and to which it can subordinate itself without having to sacrifice itself.[50]

Halbfass mentions that the Veda contains many of its own "implicit patterns of reasoning". This is an important point which he also brings out clearly when he says that the Veda:

> ...employs argumentation and demonstration among its own modes of expression and communication. It uses the language of reason, of "logical" demonstration as a means of explication and persuasion, thus creating the basic patterns of and the openness for legitimate human reasoning. In this manner, reasoning itself is traced back to the Veda, as a dimension of its own impersonal, yet benevolent and skilful manner of speaking to the world.[51]

We can see that this is so from Śaṅkara's own comments cited above. Śaṅkara says that the *śruti* itself proves its declaration, that by the knowledge of the One there is the knowledge of everything, by adducing such illustrations as clay and the clay pots in order to demonstrate that by the knowledge of one thing, the material cause, the clay, all the products of the material cause become known for what they are, i.e., mere "names-and -forms" whose reality is ultimately nothing other than clay. Śaṅkara says that the *śruti* is itself employing reason to demonstrate its declaration: "We understand that the proof of the declaration is made by the *śruti* in accordance with the logic of the non-difference of the effects from their material cause" *(śabdebhyaś ca prakṛtivikārāvyatirekanyāyena-eva pratijñāsiddhir avagamyate).* So when Śaṅkara says legitimate reasoning is that which conforms to the *śruti*, we should not think that the *śruti* contains no reasoning of its own. Śaṅkara sees his task as making explicit the reasoning that is often already implicit in the *śruti*. He does, however, have some presuppositions with which he approaches the text. There is, of course, the initial presupposition that the Upaniṣads teach a uniform truth and are "rational", or self-consistent, in their overall purport. There is also the strictly philosophical presupposition that he shares with Gauḍapāda who, as we have seen, shared it with Nāgārjuna and doubtless many others, and that is: to be real is to be changeless. We shall refer again to this important point later.

There are two more issues which ought to be at least briefly addressed. The first is this: if the Upaniṣads reveal that there is non-duality, but our perception reveals only duality, then the Upaniṣads and perception stand opposed to each other. If the Upaniṣads and perception mutually conflict, how can they both be considered to be means of valid knowledge? Śaṅkara's response to this problem is to say that the means of knowledge do not conflict with each other, because a means of knowledge: "makes known something that is not within the scope of another means of knowledge."[52] If the *śruti* makes a statement that fire is cold and non-luminous, then it has to be assumed that the Vedic text means something else, because as Śaṅkara says, in a statement that is frequently quoted: "even a hundred Vedic texts cannot be a means of valid knowledge when they say that fire is cold and non-luminous!"[53] *Śruti* cannot override a matter that is proved by perception. If, however, the *śruti* makes a statement about metaphysical matters, which is its proper domain, and that statement is not metaphorical and is made with full purport, and that statement is found to be in conflict with perception, then the *śruti* overrides perception. To put the matter with greater precision: the knowledge revealed by the *śruti* does not actually negate perceptual *knowledge*, it does not negate something that is proved by perception, but it negates erroneous notions that are *assumed* to be true on the basis of perceptual data.[54] For example, the feeling that "I am unhappy" is perceptual and may well be assumed to be valid knowledge about myself, but according to the *śruti* the Self is Brahman which is free from all limitation and sorrow. In such a case, the *śruti* negates the erroneous self-knowledge even though it is based upon perception.[55] The *śruti* teaching of non-duality does not deny that there is a *perception* of duality, but it removes the erroneous idea, deriving from that perception, that duality is real. It is analogous to our perception of a blue sky. The conclusion that the sky is blue is based upon perception, but we know it is not really blue even though we continue to see it as blue. So too duality is perceived, but it is not a valid perceptual knowledge, and so the *śruti* sublates the notion of the reality of the perception but not the perception itself. Likewise, if an inference contradicts what the *śruti* explicitly says about metaphysical matters which are its own legitimate domain, then such an inference must be considered fallacious.[56]

The second issue concerns the ontological status of the Veda itself. In the *Brahmasūtrabhāṣya* an objection is raised along the following lines: if we accept that oneness is true then duality has to be false, but we see that the Upaniṣads themselves presuppose differences, such as the difference between the teacher and the pupil, and such distinctions would have to be untrue. But how can we accept that oneness is true when the Vedānta texts which are supposed to reveal it are based upon untrue dualities?[57] Śaṅkara replies that all our empirical transactions are valid until we know the truth, just as our dream is valid until we wake.[58] What Śaṅkara says here is that the *śruti* assumes real differences, like that of pupil and teacher, in order to enlighten the pupil, but after the pupil knows the truth the latter too sees that differences are unreal. For how else can the *śruti* teach except by assuming the standpoint of the one to be taught? Furthermore, the fact that the scripture relies upon unreal differences does not make the resultant knowledge untrue, as a true knowledge can result from an unreal cause. Śaṅkara illustrates this when he says that the person who awakens from a dream realises that the dream was unreal but he does not dismiss his knowledge of the dream as unreal.[59] Though the dream was false, the knowledge of the dream is true since it is not negated. Similarly, the Upaniṣad texts, though ultimately unreal along with the rest of the world, are able to generate true knowledge.

To conclude this section, I would like to refer to a discussion among Western scholars as to whether it would be more correct to see Śaṅkara as a theologian rather than as a philosopher. Richard De Smet has argued that while a number of notable modern Indian scholars have preferred to see Śaṅkara as a philosopher than as a theologian, his method is more correctly viewed as that of a theologian of the *śruti*. This view has gradually gained currency among Western scholars. Provisionally assuming the validity of this dichotomy, I feel that if we wish to call Śaṅkara a "philosopher" we could find justification for doing so provided that we define the meaning of "philosophy" in sufficiently broad terms, such as the search for First Principles and the investigation of reality so as to offer a coherent and meaningful picture of the world as a whole. Śaṅkara's teachings unambiguously present us with such a "world-view" where we can find interwoven ontology, epistemology and ethics. But if we define philosophy as a purely rational inquiry that proceeds by way of argument and is founded upon the supposition that human reason can of itself discover the underlying order (logos) of things, then clearly Śaṅkara is not a philosopher in this sense. The method of philosophy as practised by its Greek founders, Socrates, Plato and Aristotle, as an investigation into the order of things by means of rational discussion and argument, has defined the nature of philosophy in the West, and Śaṅkara does not fit into that mould.

If Śaṅkara is not a philosopher according to this narrower definition, can we say that Śaṅkara is a theologian? Theology is the rational discourse about God, and from the Christian centuries onwards this discourse has proceeded from a ground in revelation. About the nature of theology, Richard De Smet writes:

> ...the principle from which the validity of the theological conclusion derives is not the evidence of human reason, but the authority of an infallible testimony about the existence and the proper nature of the Absolute.[60]

And about the theological enterprise he writes:

> The purpose of this science of faith is (1) to ascertain the revealed testimony and the information it conveys, (2) to develop all the implications of such data, by means of demonstrations based upon authority and reasoning, and (3) to defend its conclusions against all opponents.[61]

According to this explanation we would have to agree that it would be more appropriate to see Śaṅkara as a theologian rather than as a philosopher in the narrower sense described above. It is most important to recognise the centrality of the *śruti* to Śaṅkara's thought, as well as to the Advaita tradition as a whole, and to view Śaṅkara as a "purely rational" philosopher would be to misunderstand the role of the *śruti* in his thought. Apart from the work of De Smet, the relation between Śaṅkara's thought and the *śruti* has also been clearly presented by Wilhelm Halbfass and by Anantanand Rambachan.[62]

It is most certainly correct to situate Śaṅkara within the theological realm of the Text, and Francis Clooney has expressed this point nicely:

> Today, if we may presume a more balanced and favourable attitude toward theology, we can understand more properly and fruitfully the relationship between the theological and philosophical domains of knowing. If we take seriously the temporal relationships among these ways of knowing, one may move from one to the other in either direction. One may first engage deeply in sacred texts, and later construct arguments and inquire into the foundations of knowledge that support what one reads; or, one may begin with the articulation of a rational discourse, and at a later point submit it to the demands of sacred texts, perhaps to ground it religiously, perhaps simply to illustrate and explain it. Advaita represents the former of these approaches, while modern readers have intended to interpret it according to the latter.[63]

While it is entirely appropriate and necessary to bring to light the centrality of the *śruti* for a correct understanding of Śaṅkara, Clooney's work highlights a danger inherent in this "either-or" discussion of Śaṅkara as either a philosopher or as a theologian, a discussion which presupposes the historical separation of these disciplines in the West. A separation of this kind has by and large not occurred in India where, for Vedānta, theology and philosophy, and the various branches of the latter, remain mixed together like the ingredients that blend to make a cake. Philosophy, theology, and their separation, are all part of the history of Western thought, and while highlighting the "theological" dimension to Śaṅkara serves as a salutary corrective to the mistake of seeing him as a "purely rational" philosopher, we should also note that the label of Advaita as "theology" has itself to be treated with some caution.

There are two areas, in method and in the final purpose, where those who would see Vedānta as "theology" can be found to err. Clooney regularly refers to the Advaitin as the "reader" of the text, but this brings Advaita too close to the approach of the Western theologian. This is evident from many of Clooney's statements, as for instance: "The permanent textuality of the Text ensures the possibility that one can learn Advaita from the outside in, by reading."[64] One can appreciate what Clooney is saying in so far as his study is focused on Śaṅkara's commentary on the *Brahmasūtra*, with its use of principles of interpretation borrowed from the Mīmāṁsā; but Clooney's approach to Advaita ("Since reading is the practice that both Advaita and Christian theologians have usually undertaken, ..." p.9) is somewhat misleading. Engaging with the Text by reading is an approach that is seen only in institutions of learning in India where Advaita is presented as an objective course of study leading to some traditional qualification, such as that held by a Vedic scholar, or else to a modern university degree, but it is not the way that a committed spiritual seeker, a *mumukṣu*, a *jijñāsu*, is advised to proceed, at least initially. Śaṅkara regularly employs the compounds: *śāstrācāryopadeśa* ("instruction by way of the scriptures and the teacher") and *vedāntācāryopadeśa* ("instruction by way of the Upaniṣads and the teacher"). These are not stray expressions, such ideas can be found throughout his works.[65] The regular compounding of the word "scripture" along with "teacher" *(ācārya)* should make it clear that Advaita is not just a matter of a serious, solitary, engagement with the Text. At some point it is a matter of the committed seeker seriously engaging the Text under the guidance of a competent teacher (a guru). Advaita's self-understanding, as a living, oral tradition, with a methodical transmission *(saṁpradāya)* of spiritual wisdom through the medium of a lineage of teachers *(paraṁparā)*, should not be lost sight of, and we should bear in mind the words of Śaṅkara on the subject in his commentary on the *Muṇḍaka* Upaniṣad: "even someone who knows the scriptures should not seek the knowledge of Brahman independently [without a guru]" *(śāstrajño 'pi svātantryeṇa brahmajñānānveṣaṇaṁ na kuryāt)*.[66] So in Advaita the method is not *just* to engage the Text through reading, but the method is to listen to the text from the mouth of the guru, to hear it orally transmitted and explained; and to present it as primarily an exercise of study, of "reading", is to deprive it of the methodology that it articulates for itself.

Secondly, while there are a number of traditions in Indian thought that may well be considered primarily theological, such as Viśiṣṭādvaita, which shares with normative Christianity the view that liberation is to be found in the next world, in Vaikuṇṭha (or in "Heaven" in the case of Christianity), Advaita considers liberation in this life to be the true aim of the spiritual seeker. This gives Advaita a rather different character from Western theology. In Advaita, the inquiry into the scriptures under the instruction of a guru is undertaken with the ultimate purpose of living-liberation *(jivanmukti)*. Although the *Brahmasūtra* is largely a meta-work discussing and harmonising the *śruti* texts, even it is engaged by the Advaitin with the purpose of resolving doubts in order to assist the rise of knowledge. And in Advaita knowledge ultimately means the immediate understanding of one's real nature as Brahman, as gained in this life itself. Thus the purpose for which Christian theologians and Advaitins approach their respective texts is different, and indeed, it would be hard to find a parallel among the former to the way in which we frequently find Śaṅkara versifying upon his own experience in his *Upadeśasāhasrī:*

> I am other than name, form and action. My nature is ever free! I am the Self, the supreme [i.e. unconditioned] Brahman. I am pure Awareness, always non-dual! (11.7)

Such is the soteriological outcome, the finding of one's real identity with the Absolute in this life, which is the reason Advaitins engage with the Text under the instruction of a competent guru. It is not the same in traditions where the concepts of *mokṣa* and *jīvanmukti* are absent, or at least are not a part of orthodox assent, as they are in Advaita. Since there are these differences in the method and in the goal, we should be wary of the potential misunderstanding that may occur if, while trying to understand one tradition, we inadvertently situate it too close to the orbit of another.

(3) Brahman as Īśvara and as the World

That there is an absolute reality is revealed by the *śruti*. This revelation serves to give the human mind a particular orientation which it otherwise may lack, and according to Śaṅkara, certainly would lack. In this section we shall attempt to determine Śaṅkara's understanding of the nature of Īśvara, the Lord, or "God", and the relation of the Lord to the absolute Brahman, by following Śaṅkara's statements taken largely from his commentary on the *Brahmasūtra*. Śaṅkara has not left us with a systematic discussion on the nature of Īśvara; this is certainly unfortunate considering the numerous discussions in his works on other topics, some of which, such as his lengthy altercations with the Mīmāṁsakas, are of little relevance today. So here we shall try to rethink the thoughts of Śaṅkara, as we find them in the *Brahmasūtrabhāṣya*, and arrive at an understanding that will, hopefully, be an accurate presentation of his views.

It is doubtful whether the existence of God can be proved by pure reason. There are well-known arguments for the existence of God: in India these were most notably developed by the Naiyāyikas, and such arguments met with strong counter-arguments, such as those of the Buddhists against the Naiyāyikas.[67] Among the various arguments for the existence of God, the argument from design (or "to design") might, at the outset, be deemed the most plausible: from the observation that the various phenomena in the world seem to exhibit order - the growth of trees and plants, the regular movement of the tides, the rotation of the earth and heavenly bodies etc. - and appear to exhibit signs of having an intelligent arrangement, we can infer the existence of an intelligent Being who has created a cosmos. However, even if we could infer the existence of God on the basis of the observation of an intelligently ordered world, we would not be able to know more than that a God exists. Śaṅkara does not even agree that we can infer the existence of God without the revelation of the *śruti.* He argues that inference cannot prove the possibility that there exists one God, as conceivably there could be more than one God, each carrying out some allotted task in the creation of the world, in much the same way as a variety of skilled people are seen to be required for the construction of a house.

Śaṅkara's view, as we have seen, is that metaphysical issues are the proper domain of the Vedic revelation alone and it is the latter that reveals the existence of a single, ultimate principle. Śaṅkara says that even though the *śruti* may be seen to be at variance over some of the details of creation, such as the mention of five elements in one Upaniṣad and three in another Upaniṣad, that is really of no consequence because it is not the purpose of the *śruti* to teach about creation. He says that knowing the details of creation does not serve any human goal (such as *dharma, artha, kāma* or *mokṣa).*[68] But it is important to note, he says, that the Upaniṣads unanimously teach about a single creator.[69] Thus according to Śaṅkara the consistent revelation of the Upaniṣads is that there is a single ultimate principle from whom this universe originated.

Though the valid testimony for the existence of God is solely from the *śruti,* Śaṅkara sees the statement in the *Bṛhadāraṇyaka:* "Under the mighty rule of this Immutable, O Gārgī, the sun and moon are held in their positions" (BU 3.8.9) as speaking about God in what amounts to a verification of the "argument from design". Śaṅkara says:

> ...Therefore [on the basis of the above *śruti* text] the existence of this Immutable is proved. For it is an invariable sign that heaven and earth remain in a fixed order and this is not tenable without a conscious Ruler who is free from the cycle of birth and death.[70]

But here, Saṅkara is not inferring the existence of God through the "argument from design", he is just saying that this is a valid argument since the *śruti,* in speaking about God, reveals it to be valid, but that does not mean that one could use it to infer the existence of God independently of the *śruti.*

In *Bṛhadāraṇyaka* Upaniṣad 1.4.7, there is a passage about the origination of the world: "This [universe] was then unmanifested. It manifested only as name-and-form." Could it be understood from this passage that the universe of name-and-form manifested spontaneously of its own accord? Arguing against this view, Śaṅkara says: "on the strength [of the context] it is implied that [the manifestation] depended upon the controller, the agent and the operation of the means."[71] In his comments upon this passage in *Brahmasūtra* 1.4.15, he argues that:

> From the way this world is manifest as name-and-form at the present time, [it is evident that] it manifests as having a controller. We should understand that the situation was the same at the beginning of the emanation of the world, for it is not tenable to conjecture something contrary to what is observed.[72]

He goes on to argue that the passive verb "it manifested" *(vyākriyata)* implies a manifesting agent, just as an expression like "the village is reached" implies a traveller.[73] Thus in the view of Śaṅkara, all the Upaniṣads reveal the existence of a single God as the creator of the world.

According to Advaita, God is not only the maker of the world, its intelligent cause, or "efficient cause" *(nimittakāraṇa),* but God is also its "material cause" *(upādānakāraṇa),* i.e., God is also the very constitutive "stuff" of the universe. In the Judeo-Christian and Islamic traditions God is the efficient cause of the world, but not its material cause. It is this latter aspect which is particularly important to understand, for it renders the Upaniṣadic perspective of the nature of God highly distinct from other major traditions, and this presents a considerable conceptual difficulty for those who partake, either explicitly or implicitly, in the Semitic understanding of God. The "Western" concepts of God tend to emphasise the transcendence of God; God is "out there", somewhere beyond the cosmos. This idea of God, as a personal Being who is located somewhere outside the cosmos, who is apart from this world, constitutes a subtle but powerful stumbling block to comprehending the Upaniṣadic-Advaitic understanding of God. This is true not only for those brought up in

Western traditions but also for Hindus who belong to those *bhakti* traditions that see God as located at some place, eg. in *Vaikuṇṭha*, and teach that *prakṛti* is the material cause of the world.

Before examining Śaṅkara's statements about God as the material cause, we will first look at the more familiar aspect of God as the intelligent, or efficient cause. We are able to know that God is the efficient cause on the basis of such *śruti* texts as: "He willed, 'I will be many, I will be born'." (TU 2.6.1), "It deliberated, 'I shall become many, I shall be born'." (CU 6.2.3). Śaṅkara says that free agentship is indicated by the statement "He willed", and since the passages previous to these indicate that nothing else then existed, and as there is no mention of any other first cause, the only legitimate conclusion is that Brahman must be the efficient cause of the world.[74] But if Brahman is the efficient cause of the world, some difficulties involved in the very idea of God as the first cause have to be addressed.

The first question is: why would God ever wish to create a world? Is there some purpose behind creation? If the creation has a purpose, God must have some need to fulfil, for rational actions take place only when we wish to accomplish something, not otherwise. But if God acts to fulfil some inner need, then the self-sufficiency on the part of the Lord would be called into question. However if the Lord acts irrationally, i.e., if the Lord acts without any purpose to the action, then the Lord could be compared to a insane person who acts solely out of a deranged state of mind without having regard to the consequences of the action. So why, then, does God create the world?

Such is the objection that Śaṅkara understands to be raised in *Brahmasūtra* 2.1.32. The following *sūtra* presents the reply to this objection and here the author of the *sūtras* uses the word "play/sport" *(līlā)*. Śaṅkara's reply is thus contextualised by the word *līlā* in the *sūtra*. Śaṅkara affirms that the Lord creates as in a *līlā* and he uses the word in its two principal meanings, in the sense of "sport" as well as in the sense of the "facility" with which an act is accomplished. He says just as a king or his minister, who has all that he requires, might yet engage in some sportive *(līlā)* activity, such as playing a game, without having something to accomplish by it, so does the Lord act solely from his own nature without having anything to accomplish. And though the creation of this universe may appear to us to be a mighty task, the Lord creates it with ease *(līlā)*, since he has unlimited powers. Śaṅkara rejects the suggestion that the Lord did not create, because there are texts to the contrary, or that the Lord's creation was an act of derangement, since the texts affirm the Lord's omniscience.

We can see that the *sūtra* uses the word *"līlā"* to avoid the specific objection that the act of creation implies some inner need on the part of the Creator. The solution proposed by the *sūtra* seems to render the creation rather pointless, but that was the price the author of the *sūtras* was willing to pay to avoid the difficulty concerning an implied imperfection on the part of the creator. Such is the dilemma in understanding God's creation of the world! Śaṅkara, however, does not seriously engage with the question, he is content to justify the view of the *sūtrakāra*. But he does make a final point: he says that we should not forget that the *śruti* texts dealing with creation are not at the level of the highest truth *(paramārtha)*, they are in the realm of conventional reality *(vyavahāra)*, and their real purpose lies elsewhere.[75] We shall return to this important point later.

The objection in the following *sūtra* is even more serious. If God is the cause of the world, then God is open to the charges of acting with partiality and with cruelty. The Lord has created a vastly unequal world: some beings, such as gods, experience sublime pleasures, while at the other end of the spectrum animals experience much suffering, and humans beings experience both, but with less intensity. Furthermore, the cruelty of inflicting suffering on creatures, and then finally destroying them, would prove abhorrent even to wicked people. Śaṅkara's response to these objections is again conditioned by the *sūtra* on which he is commenting. He says these faults are not applicable to God; they would apply if God created with complete independence, but that is not the case, for the Lord creates taking into account the merit and demerit accruing from the past lives of the souls. The Lord gives to each soul the result of their past deeds (karma) and thus there is neither partiality nor cruelty on the part of the Lord. But, it is further objected, all of these deeds only occur after creation has begun, before creation there was no karma to form the basis of differentiation of the souls into the bodies of gods and animals etc. So initially all beings must have been created equal.

Śaṅkara's response to this whole issue is to affirm that the cycle of worldly existence *(saṁsāra)* is beginningless *(anādi)*, and he gives the analogy of the beginningless causal relation that exists in the series of the seed and sprout. We have seen that such an argument puts Śaṅkara at odds with Gauḍapāda who, in 4. 20 of his *Kārikā,* argued that the illustration of the seed and the sprout cannot be used to illustrate a beginningless series, since we must first prove that the relation between seed and sprout is beginningless. However Śaṅkara is here faithfully following the argument of the *sūtrakāra,* who says: "...no, because *[saṁsāra]* is beginningless *(...na, anāditvāt)* (2.1.35). But at two other places in his *Brahmasūtrabhāṣya* Śaṅkara contradicts this very argument of beginninglessness. The most notable occurrence is at 2.2.37 where, arguing against the notion that the Lord is only the efficient cause of the world and not its material cause, Śaṅkara attacks some of the very arguments that he had supported in 2.1.34-36. He says that if one proposes that the Lord creates the world taking into account the karma of the souls (so as to avoid the defect that the Lord's creation, which is full of inequality, leads one to infer that the Lord is motivated by partiality), then Śaṅkara argues that in that case there would be a relationship of mutual dependence between the Lord and karma. And if one should seek to escape from this defect of mutual dependence by taking refuge in the beginninglessness of this relationship, then Śaṅkara will not allow it, for he says that beginningless does not solve the problem, it just extends the problem indefinitely.[76]

In such arguments as the above Śaṅkara attacks the idea that the Lord is solely the efficient cause of the world; yet in spite of such difficulties, he is nonetheless committed to accepting that the Lord is the efficient cause since, as we have seen, the Upaniṣads reveal this, as when it is said that before creation Being alone existed, without a second, and then: "that Being deliberated: 'I shall become many, I shall be born'." (CU 6.2.3). Such statements as these clearly tell that the Lord is both the efficient cause (as is seen by the word "deliberated") and the material cause of the world (as seen by the statement "I shall become many"). In reply to the objection that a deliberation before creation is seen on the part of efficient causes only, like potters etc. ("I shall make a pot"), but it is not seen that a material cause has any such deliberation, Śaṅkara replies that this is not a matter for inference based upon what we observe in the world, it is a matter for the *śruti* alone, and the *śruti* reveals that the Lord who deliberated is the material cause as well.[77] Śaṅkara also says that

Upaniṣad statements such as: "Through which [instruction], what is unknown becomes known" (CU 6.1.3) can only be logically possible if God is the material cause, because if God is only the efficient cause then God must always be other than the world, with the consequence that the Upaniṣadic proposition "by the knowledge of the One thing, everything becomes known" could never be fulfilled.[78] Thus God is at once the efficient as well as the material cause, and it is the latter aspect in particular that becomes a key to understanding the true nature of things according to Śaṅkara, as we shall try to show.

Śaṅkara's commentary on *sūtras* 2.1.14, 22 and 27 are especially helpful for grasping his understanding about the nature of reality. In *sūtra* 2.1.13 he raises an objection that if Brahman is the material cause, it would mean that Brahman has become everything, so Brahman must be both the subject and the object, but if that is the case the usual distinction between subject and object would break down. What would become of our normal, empirical understanding, of the division of subject and object? So the teaching that Brahman is the material cause is untenable as it contradicts experience. Śaṅkara replies that the fact that Brahman is the material cause does not upset our ordinary empirical understanding of the relationships of things in the world. He says that just as the modifications of the ocean, the waves, ripples, foam and so forth, are not different from the ocean which is nothing but water, but still there are the distinctions: "this is a wave, this is foam" etc., and though we make these distinctions we do not think that the wave etc. is something other than water, so too, there is no mixing up of our normal experience of subject and object even though everything is not other than Brahman.[79]

Śaṅkara commences 2.1.14 with the remark that the previous objection was answered by adopting the perspective of conventional life *(vyavahāra)*, but the differences that pertain to conventional life are not true from the level of ultimate reality *(paramārtha)*. Here Śaṅkara makes the important distinction between "levels" of reality, or rather "levels" in our understanding of reality, and he makes reference to this distinction some fourteen times in his discussion of this particular *sūtra*.[80] We have seen that Gauḍapāda too has spoken from two levels of truth (i.e. reality), for when he refers to the "ultimate truth" *(paramārtha)* in kārikā 2.32 he necessarily implies a level of conventional truth as well. It is through resorting to this distinction between "levels" of reality, an empirical reality and an ultimate reality, that Śaṅkara is able to harmonise different types of statements in the *śruti;* and it is through this distinction that he is also able to accept the experience of duality in empirical life and yet deny the reality of such experience from a higher understanding, and thereby show that from the ultimate *(paramārtha)* perspective there is Advaita, non-duality.

This is what he says at the beginning of 2.1.14:

> The refutation contained in the preceding *sūtra* was set forth by accepting the empirical division of the experiencer and the objects of experience. However this division does not exist from the standpoint of the highest truth, because these two, the effect and its [material] cause, are understood to be non-different. The effect is the manifold world consisting of space etc. and the supreme Brahman is the [material] cause. What we understand is that, in reality, the effect is "non-different", i.e., it does not exist separately from that [Brahman the material] cause.[81]

Śaṅkara justifies this reasoning by appealing to the reasoning supplied by the *śruti* itself. The *śruti* referred to is the famous *"vācārambhaṇa"* *śruti* (CU 6.1.4) which says: "By [knowing] a single lump of clay, everything that is made of clay would become known. A modification begins with speech, it is a [mere] name. The clay alone is true [i.e. real]." Explaining this *śruti*, Śaṅkara says that when the clay is known as clay, all that is made of clay, plates, dishes and so forth, would become known, since they all equally consist of clay. He cites the *śruti* just referred to and explains that a modification is begun just through speech which says "it is", and he goes on to say: "whereas there is no modification whatsoever existing as a real thing" *(na tu vastuvṛttena vikāro nāma kaścid asti).*[82]

The *"vācārambhaṇa" śruti* tells us that by knowing the material cause we know all of its modifications in so far as they are ultimately nothing but the material cause. It further states that the material cause is real and the modifications are ontologically unreal, their reality commences with language. While there is a transactional entity called a clay pot that fulfils practical functions like holding water etc., in reality there is no such entity as "pot" because the noun "pot" does not refer to a substance, it just refers to the clay which is the actual substance. Thus, according to this *śruti* text and Śaṅkara's explanation of it, our world is replete with nouns that lack ontologically real objects, because when our perspective shifts to the material cause we find that entities do not exist independently of the material cause itself. When the particular configuration of the material cause is predicated by "it is", a transubstantiation, as it were, occurs in the mind and the configuration acquires an inherent existence of its own: "pot is", "table is", "door is" etc. The idea that the modification of the material cause is a "thing" in its own right is erroneous, for the modification has no existence of it own since what truly exists is only the material cause in a particular configuration. This Upaniṣadic perspective, that the material cause alone is real and its effects are "unreal" - their independent substantiality is a mental construction based upon language - is very different from the Western tradition which seems to remain indelibly under the influence of Aristotle who, justifying a commonsense view of the world, made a distinction between Matter and Form and considered that both together constitute substance.

The teaching that Brahman is the material cause and that the world is its actual transformation *(pariṇāma)* leads on to the teaching that there is only an apparent transformation *(vivarta)*, once it is clearly understood that the effect of the material cause is not an entity in its own right. The material cause has not really become anything, since nothing "other" exists than the material cause itself. The teaching of real transformation is based on the idea that one thing changes into something else, but when it is discovered that there is no other thing except the material cause, what is it that the material cause has changed into? Thus, as has been pointed out by Dharmendra Nath Shastri, the *pariṇāmavāda* leads inexorably into the *vivartavāda*.[83] However we should note that a type of *vivarta* is already present in the Upaniṣads themselves, as is evident in *Chāndogya* Upaniṣad 6.1.4ff.

Although there is no transformation of the material cause into anything other than itself, there is nonetheless some change on the part of the material cause. Though the clay does not really change into a pot, since from the perspective of the clay there is no thing (which we call as "pot") that it changes into, the clay does undergo an alteration of its shape. It does not remain absolutely changeless, or immutable *(kūṭastha)*. So too Brahman, as the material cause of the world, has not changed *into* another thing, the world, since what we call as "world" is not an ontological entity in its own right; it is not something other than the material cause, Brahman itself. But if Brahman is the material cause, then, as in the case of the clay, some sort of alteration of Brahman must nevertheless occur. And if Brahman undergoes any sort of alteration a number of difficulties arise.

Such difficulties are as follows. If Brahman has parts it is conceivable that one part could transform while another part remains unchanged. But if Brahman has parts, Brahman would be a composite entity, and would thereby be subject to disintegration. Moreover we know that Brahman is without parts from the *śruti* texts that negate all attributes, such as: "Partless, actionless, peaceful, faultless, without taint" (ŚvU 6.19). Therefore Brahman must be without parts. But there is a difficulty here also, for if Brahman is without parts Brahman must undergo transformation in its entirety, and that goes against the *śruti* which repeatedly says that Brahman is without change. Furthermore, if Brahman transforms in its entirety into the world it would amount to saying that Brahman as such would cease to exist, for there would be no Brahman apart from the world, and the *śruti* teachings that Brahman is to be known would prove meaningless, because the world can be known without any effort on one's part, merely by looking. Thus the teaching that Brahman is the material cause that transforms is fraught with difficulty.[84]

Śaṅkara responds to such objections firstly by saying that there are *śruti* texts that deny that Brahman has parts and also deny that Brahman undergoes transformation:

> We understand Brahman to be absolutely changeless *(kūṭastha)* from the Upaniṣad texts that deny all modifications, such as: "That great birthless Self is undecaying, undying, immortal, fearless, Brahman" (BU 4.4.25), "This Self is to be described as 'not this, not this' " (BU 3.9.26), "Neither gross, nor minute" (BU 3.8.8). One and the same Brahman cannot be conceived as both having the attribute of transforming and being free from

> transformation. If you say that it could be like [the one body] can be motionless and also have motion, we say that is not so because there is the specification that Brahman is "absolutely changeless". The absolutely changeless Brahman cannot possibly be the locus of diverse attributes like motionlessness and motion.[85]

In this important passage Śaṅkara categorically states that Brahman undergoes absolutely no alteration. On the one hand Brahman is accepted as the material cause of the world, yet on the other hand Brahman is said to remain somehow absolutely unchanged. How are we to understand this?

In the following discussion Śaṅkara directly responds to the objection about partlessness and transformation raised above and he argues in two ways: firstly from *śruti,* then after raising a counterargument he puts forward his solution to the problem as he has gleaned it from his hermeneutics of the *śruti.* We learn from the *śruti,* he says, both that the world originates from Brahman and that Brahman continues to exist separate from its effects. What Śaṅkara says here is that although the world does not exist separately from Brahman, Brahman does exist separate from the world. *Śruti* texts such as: "one foot of him are all things, his three feet are immortal in heaven" (CU 3.12.6) clearly indicate, Śaṅkara says, that Brahman transcends the world. Since Brahman does exist apart from the world, the *śruti* texts teaching that Brahman is to be known thereby remain meaningful. Śaṅkara says we can legitimately conclude on the basis of the *śruti* that: "Brahman is unaltered" *(avikṛtaṁ brahma).*[86] This is an important statement for it means, according to Śaṅkara, that Brahman is the unchanged material cause. But, again, how are we to understand this?

Śaṅkara says:

> Brahman is *"śabdamūla",* i.e., the Upaniṣads are the means of knowledge about Brahman. The testimony of the senses etc. are not the means of knowledge about Brahman. Brahman has to be accepted just as it is presented in the Upaniṣads. And the Upaniṣads teach both these facts about

> Brahman: that it does not transform in its entirety and that it is partless.[87]

An objection is raised:

> Even the sacred texts cannot make known something contradictory, namely that the partless Brahman transforms, yet not entirely. If Brahman is without parts then either it would not transform at all or it would transform in its entirety. But if it transforms in some aspect and remains unchanged in some other aspect then it would follow from the supposition of these different aspects that Brahman has parts.[88]

Śaṅkara replies to this in an important passage where although he does not use the technical expression that the world is an "apparent transformation", a *vivarta,* of the unchanged Brahman, he does imply such a teaching:

> No, because we maintain that this difference of aspects [i.e. one aspect undergoes transformation while another remains unchanged] is constructed by Ignorance *(avidyā).* A thing does not come to possess parts just because of a difference of aspects that is constructed by *avidyā.* ...Brahman becomes the locus of all conventional [or empirical] reality, comprised of such things as transformation etc., due to this difference in aspect characterised by name-and-form, which is constructed by *avidyā,* which remains manifest or unmanifest and which cannot be categorically stated as either real [i.e. identical to Brahman] or otherwise [i.e. different from Brahman]. In the aspect pertaining to absolute reality, Brahman is beyond all conventional dealings and remains untransformed.[89]

There are a number of points raised in this and similar passages, such as his use of the word "Ignorance" *(avidyā)* and the expression "name-and-form" *(nāmarūpa),* which require analysis and clarification. We shall take up these issues in the following chapter, but here our main concern is to understand the "big picture", to follow Śaṅkara in his own understanding of Brahman, and particularly with regard to his understanding of Brahman as Īśvara.

What is clear from the discussion so far is that Śaṅkara is juggling a number of metaphysical issues and he is trying somehow to uphold them all. As he sees it, the *śruti* reveals that Brahman is the efficient cause of the world, thus Brahman is the Lord, or according to our usual understanding, God, the creator of everything. The *śruti* further reveals that Brahman, the Lord, is not just the efficient cause of the world but is its material cause as well. For Śaṅkara this is a fact, for the *śruti* consistently reveals such is the case. But the *śruti* also reveals that Brahman, while being the material cause, yet remains absolutely changeless, and therefore Brahman can undergo no transformation at all. The way that Śaṅkara can resolve the contradiction that Brahman becomes the world and yet somehow undergoes no change in the process is to interpret the *śruti* as speaking from two levels, from the perspective of absolute reality *(paramārtha)*, as well as from the perspective of empirical reality *(vyavahāra)*. We have seen that Gauḍapāda too taught from the perspective of two levels of reality.

Empirical reality *(vyavahāra)* is not something fictitious, it refers to the empirical world of objective reality, and according to this understanding the world arises from the Lord who is its material cause. God is therefore not just a hypothesis. The Lord exists, for we see that the world exists, and the *śruti* reveals that God is its cause. But there is still something more. Śaṅkara says that when we investigate the world we find that it consists of things which the Upaniṣads call "name-and-form" *(nāmarūpa)*, i.e., material forms which are called by certain names, and these are reducible to further "names-and-forms", and so on, until we find that the world, as a world, is not a substantial reality at all, even though it appears to be so. It is at this point, when the world has been reduced to its constituents of "name-and-form", when the concrete materiality of the world has been revealed as *mithyā*, that we pass from the *vyavahāra* to the "level" of the *paramārtha*, the ultimate reality. The metaphor of "level" is appropriate enough, for we know from the example of the laws of Newtonian and Quantum Physics that matter can be expected to simultaneously follow two different sets of "laws", according to whether it is viewed as a physical object or whether it is analysed from the perspective of its atomic and sub-atomic structure. At the level of *vyavahāra*, Brahman is the Lord who is the efficient and the material cause of the world. But from the absolute level the world is found to be an unreal appearance *(mithyā)*, and simultaneous with this understanding the Lordship *(īśvaratva)* of Brahman is also found to be an appearance, as is the individuality *(jīvatva)* of the Self. Appearances are always of something, and what appears as the world is Brahman itself, the One Being - an undivided pure Awareness - that is the reality of all that appears. It would be a mistake to say that the Lord (Īśvara) is reduced to mere fiction, because the Lord as the Creator cannot be denied just as the empirically existing world cannot be denied. And yet, ultimately, the Lord turns out to be none other than the attributeless Brahman, when the attributes of Brahman, through which Brahman is the Creator, are seen as *mithyā* along with the *mithyā* creation.

It would be futile to try to reconcile the two levels of *vyavahāra* and *paramārtha*, for they cannot be logically reconciled, though they may be grasped in an intuitive understanding. But Śaṅkara would say that this is the only way to do justice to the different statements about Brahman in the Upaniṣads without reducing any of them to metaphor, which is what Rāmānuja does in his interpretation of Brahman as the material cause. Śaṅkara's understanding of Īśvara is more fluid than what we find in later Advaita, where Īśvara is somewhat unceremoniously reduced to a formulaic proposition such as we can see, for example, in the following verse of Vidyāraṇya who expresses the point with a rather poetic flourish:

> Both jīva and Īśvara are the calves of the wish-fulfilling cow, the Kāmadhenu called *māyā*. Drink this duality as much as you like, but the truth is only non-duality.[90]

It is easy to see how Vaiṣṇava *bhaktas* would have reacted against such a clear-cut demarcation between the Absolute and Īśvara and the relegation of the latter to the realm of *māyā*. And yet despite the criticism that could be levelled at Vidyāraṇya, and also much of later Advaita, for the prominence given to the role of *māyā* which tends toward its virtual hypostatisation, Vidyāraṇya nonetheless must be fundamentally right, because if the *jīva* and Īśvara are considered to be real in an ultimate sense then an unbridgeable duality must exist between them, non-duality could never be possible, and the numerous statements in the Upaniṣads revealing their ultimate identity, such as "you are That *(tat tvam asi)*, would have no place. Such sentences as *"tat tvam asi"* would have to be interpreted metaphorically or construed to mean "you are His" *(tasya tvam asi)*. Śaṅkara would, I suspect, not disagree with Vidyāraṇya's statement, but neither does he put the matter so categorically. In his statements in the *Brahmasūtrabhāṣya*, his emphasis is more on saying that Īśvara, minus the Īśvara-ness *(īśvaratva)* brought about by phenomenal factors, is Brahman, rather than specifically saying that Īśvara is a creation of *māyā*. Let us see some of Śaṅkara's important statements on this subject of Īśvara in the *Brahmasūtrabhāṣya*.

Śaṅkara first raises the following objection:

> Since oneness is the sole concern of those who teach that the absolutely changeless Brahman is the Self, it follows that there is neither a Ruler nor those who are ruled, and so the assertion made earlier that Īśvara is the cause of the world stands contradicted.[91]

Śaṅkara gives a fairly lengthy reply that succeeds in clearly presenting his overall understanding of this matter, though he does so in a style in which the ideas are particularly compressed. He says:

> No, because omniscience depends upon the manifestation of the seed, i.e., name-and-form, whose nature is *avidyā*. ...Name-and-form is constructed by *avidyā*, it can neither be categorically stated as real [i.e. as identical to Brahman] or otherwise [i.e. as different from Brahman], it is the seed of the entire expanse of phenomenal existence, it constitutes the very self, as it were, of the omniscient Lord and is referred to in both the *śruti* and the *smṛti* as the *māyāśakti* and the *prakṛti* of the omniscient Lord. The omniscient Lord is other than the name-and-form, as we know from the *śruti*.... Thus Īśvara conforms to the limiting adjuncts of name-and-form made by *avidyā*, like space conforms to the

> adjuncts of a pot, a jar etc. And Īśvara, in the sphere of empirical life *(vyavahāra),* rules over the selves conditioned by the intellects [i.e. the *vijñānamayakośa],* who are called individual souls *(jīvas)* and who, though really one with his own Self, are like the space delimited by pots in that they conform to the body-sense-mind complex which is a product of name-and-form which is itself presented by *avidyā.* Thus the Lord's being the Lord *(īśvarasya īśvaratva),* his omniscience and his omnipotence, depend upon the limitation brought about by limiting adjuncts that are of the nature of *avidyā.* From the perspective of ultimate reality *(paramārthataḥ),* when, through knowledge, the Self is divested of all limiting adjuncts, the expressions pertaining to empirical life such as Ruler, ruled, omniscient etc. are not logically possible. Accordingly, it is said: "Where one sees nothing else, hears nothing else, knows nothing else, that is the Infinite" (CU7.24.1); "But when, to this knower of Brahman, everything has become the Self, then what would he see, and through what?" (BU 4.5.15) etc. Thus all Upaniṣads speak of the cessation of all empirical life *(vyavahāra)* in the state of ultimate reality *(paramārtha).*[92] ...However, in the sphere of empirical life, the empirical dealings from Īśvara onwards have been told in the *śruti:* "This One [i.e. the great, birthless Self: *mahān aja ātmā]* is the Lord of all, this One is the Ruler of beings, the protector of beings, the bank that serves as the boundary to keep these worlds apart" (BU 4.4.22).

On the basis of the *śruti* the existence of Īśvara has to be accepted, for the world exists, and Īśvara is revealed as its efficient cause and as its material cause. Therefore we should note that in the Upaniṣads the word Brahman does not always refer to the attributeless *(nirviśeṣa/nirguṇa)* Brahman as pure Being-Awareness, but it refers to Īśvara when the context has to do with the origination of the world. Like the Upaniṣads themselves, Śaṅkara often does not make the distinction particularly evident, and in the *Brahmasūtrabhāṣya* he frequently uses the terms Brahman, Paramātman, Parameśvara and Īśvara interchangeably. We will have occasion to refer again to this point in the following chapter. For Śaṅkara, the Lordship of the Lord is ultimately unreal *(mithyā)* as it partakes of the phenomenal realm, and that entire realm is negated by the statements "not this, not this" *(neti neti);* but the Being of the Lord is not unreal, because the Being of the Lord is nothing but the Being of Brahman, the Pure Awareness, Reality itself. Śaṅkara says as much in the following passage:

> When non-difference is awakened by the statements of non-difference such as: "you are That", then the condition of the individual soul as subject to *saṁsāra* vanishes, as does the condition of Brahman as the Creator: because the entire empirical world of duality, which is manifested by false knowledge, is sublated by right knowledge.[93]

The point to note about this passage is that Śaṅkara just says: "the condition of Brahman as the Creator vanishes" *(apagataṁ bhavati tadā...brahmaṇaś ca sraṣṭṛtvam)* and this indicates the fluidity of his understanding of Īśvara and the unconditioned Brahman, for it is the One Being, with or without the attributes of creatorship.[94] Later Advaitins, following in the footsteps of Śaṅkara, and further refining his thought, have tended to make clear-cut those distinctions that Śaṅkara left a little vague, perhaps deliberately so, keeping in view what can be seen in the Upaniṣads themselves. And in their attempt to define precisely the ontological status of Īśvara, the later Advaitins drew a rather heavy line, as it were, and placed the attributeless Brahman on one side of it and Īśvara on the other side along with *māyā.* I suspect that Śaṅkara would have avoided such a rigid categorisation, for although he certainly does make a distinction between Īśvara and the acosmic *(niṣprapañca)* Brahman, his line is a fine one: there is a sole Being that exists, and from the level of *vyavahāra* that Being *is* Īśvara, whereas from the acosmic, *paramārtha* perspective, it always remains the attributeless *(nirviśeṣa)* Brahman.

It is, however, this latter perspective alone that Śaṅkara considers to be the final purport of the *śruti.* The knowledge of how the world arose from Brahman, and even the knowledge that Brahman-Īśvara is its material cause, are only stepping stones for what the *śruti* intends to convey. The *śruti* fulfils itself in teaching that the individual soul is essentially none other than the changeless Brahman, beyond all *saṁsāra*, for it is only here that the self-transcendence that is the fruit of liberation can be found. He says:

> The scripture, as for instance the passage that begins: "this Self is described as 'not this, not this' " (BU 4.2.4) [and concludes by saying]: "O Janaka, you have reached That which is free from fear" (BU 4.2.4), shows that the fruit only accrues from the direct knowledge that the absolutely changeless Brahman is the Self. About this matter, this is the conclusion: in a context dealing with Brahman, when it is established that the result accrues only from the direct knowledge of Brahman as free from all attributes, then whatever in that context is not mentioned as the result, such as Brahman undergoing transformation into the form of the world, would find applicability only as a means to the direct knowledge of Brahman. That is in accord with the Mīmāṁsā principle: "whatever does not have a result of its own, but is mentioned in close proximity to something having a result, forms a part of the latter."[95]

And again he makes the same point:

> The *śruti* texts that speak of transformation of Brahman do not aim at teaching transformation, because we do not see a result from understanding that. Rather, the *śruti* speaking of the transformation of Brahman aims to teach that Brahman, free from all phenomenal life *(vyavahāra)*, is the true Self, for we see that there is a result in understanding that. As when the *śruti* begins: "this Self is described as 'not this, not this' " (BU 4.2.4) and [concluding] says: "O Janaka, you have reached That which is free from fear" (BU 4.2.4).[96]

In the following chapter we shall take up some of the important terms that have been referred to here, as well as some other matters central to Śaṅkara's teachings, and we shall examine these in the light of notable contributions by scholars to the study of Śaṅkara's thought.

---

1 J. Bader, *Conquest of the Four Quarters: Traditional Accounts of the Life of Śaṅkara.* Unpublished Ph.D Thesis. The Australian National University, 1991, p. 51. Bader says that all the eight "biographies" that he studied refer to the meeting of Śaṅkara and Govindapāda. There are no extant works of Govindapāda.

2 Bader., ibid., p.56. Cf. *Srīmat-Śaṅkaradigvijaya.* Sri Rangam: Vani Vilas, 1972, ch.5, v.105, p.60. Swami Tapasyananda (tr.), *Sankara-Dig-Vijaya: The Traditional Account of the Life of Sri Sankaracharya by Madhava-Vidyaranya.* Madras: Sri Ramakrishna Math, 1978, p.50.

3 In BSBh 1.4.14, p. 320, line 7f., (tr.) p.273, he cites GK 3.15. In BSBh 2.1.9, p.365, line 2f., (tr.) 318f., he cites GK 1.16. In 2.1.9, p.365, line 1, just before he cites GK 1.16, he refers to the word *māyāmātram* in GK 1.17 when he says: *māyāmātraṁ hy etat paramātmano' vasthātrayātmanā-avabhāsanaṁ rajjvā iva sarpādibhāvena-iti.* It is also possible, though not conclusive, that he salutes Gauḍapāda in US 18. 2.

4 The literature on the date of Ādi Śaṅkara is very extensive and it is not my intention to attempt a contribution to this question. H. Nakamura has discussed the date of Śaṅkara at length in his work, *A History of Early Vedānta Philosophy.* Delhi: Motilal Banarsidass, 1983, p.48-88. He places Śaṅkara at approximately 700-750 CE. Karl Potter, relying in part on the dating of Maṇḍanamiśra by Allen Thrasher, places Śaṅkara in the late seventh and early eighth centuries, i.e., about a century earlier than the frequently cited dates of 788-820. Karl. H. Potter, *Encyclopedia of Indian Philosophies (vol. 111): Advaita Vedānta up to Śaṃkara and His Pupils.* Delhi: Motilal Banarsidass, 1981, p.116. G.C. Pande places him between 650 and 700 CE., cf. his

work, *Life and Thought of Śaṅkarācārya.* Delhi: Motilal Banarsidass, 1994, p.52.

5 Eg. BSBh 1.1.5, p.107, line 8f, (tr.) p.51. 2.1.22 p.394, line 17, (tr.) p.349.

6 GK 3.3-9.

7 Eg. BSBh 2.1.9, p.365, line 1, (tr.) p.318. *māyāmātraṁ hy etat paramātmano' vasthātrayātmanā-avabhāsanaṁ rajjvā iva sarpādibhāvena-iti.* He then quotes GK 1.16. Cf. note 3 above. The rope-snake analogy in mentioned in GK 2.17-18.

8 BSBh 2.1.9, p.364, line 16, *evam avasthātrayasākṣī-eko-avyabhicārī, avasthātrayeṇa vyabhicāriṇā na saṁspṛśyate.*

9 Ibid, p.365, line 1, *māyāmātraṁ hy etat paramātmano' vasthātrayātmanā-avabhāsanaṁ rajjvā iva sarpādibhāvena-iti.*

10 US 16. 18. One may note that in this verse, Śaṅkara's expression: "their seed called deep sleep" *(tayor bījaṁ suṣuptākhyam)* resembles the expression *bījanidrā* in GK 1.13. With regard to the *Upadeśasāhasrī,* I am following the edition of Swami Jagadananda, *Upadeśasāhasrī: A Thousand Teachings of Śrī Śaṅkarācārya in two parts, prose and poetry,* Madras: Sri Ramakrishna Math, seventh ed., 1984. This edition is useful, in spite of occasional misprints, because it is easily available and inexpensive and it contains the text in Devanāgarī as well as an English translation. Professor S. Mayeda has brought out a largely excellent English translation, *A Thousand Teachings: the Upadeśasāhasrī of Śaṅkara,* Tokyo, University of Tokyo Press, 1979. The English translation of the Eighteenth chapter by A. J. Alston is also helpful, *"That Thou Art", Chapter XVIII of The Thousand Teachings of Śrī Śaṃkara,* London, Shanti Sadan, third edition 1982. A.J. Alston has recently published a complete

English translation of the *Upadeśasāhasrī*, which is available through the Shanti Sadan.

11 Eg. see US (prose) 2.86-89; (verse) 10. 4; 17. 18, 66. BUBh 2.1.18, p.729 line 15ff., (tr) p. 197; 4.3.19, p.888 line 16ff., (tr) p.456.

12 Cf. GK 3. 19, 21. Śaṅkara shares the same premise eg., US 16. 38 *(avasthāntaravattve hi nāśo'sya syān na saṁśayaḥ).* Also cf. BUBh 1.4.10, p.669 line 8f, (tr.) p. 101; 1.4.15, p.685 line 9, (tr.) p.127; 2.1.15., p.723 line 21f., (tr.) p.188; 2.4.12, p.766 line 14, (tr.) p.256; 3.4.2, p.808 line 24f, (tr.) p.328; 3.9.28, p.850 line 13f., (tr.) p.396; 4.3.20, p.890 line 27, (tr.) p.459; 4.4.6, p.917ff. line 27ff, (tr.) p.501. TUBh 2.1.1, p.283 line 8f., (tr.) p.291.

13 Cf. the discussion of this verse in chapter one, section 2: The *Vaitathyaprakaraṇa.*

14 US 18.94.

15 For example see US 9. 5; 13.5; 18.164, 167. Also BUBh 3.5.1, p.811 line 6ff. Mādhavānanda, p.333, translates: "...the reality of Brahman, though remaining as it is, naturally untouched by anything....". Also BUBh 3.5.1, p. 811 line 20f. Mādhavānanda, p.333, translates: "As the sky, fancied by the ignorant as being concave and blue, is really without these qualities, being naturally untouched by them, similarly Brahman, although fancied as being subject to hunger, thirst, etc., by the ignorant, ...really transcends these qualities, being naturally untouched by them...". Also BUBh 3.5.1, p.812 line 6f. Mādhavānanda, p.334, translates: "But that which is described as the witness of vision and so forth, ...is ever untouched by such relative attributes as hunger and thirst, as the sky is untouched by impurities like the clouds etc." For other instances where the nature of the Self is referred to as naturally "untouched" by

phenomena cf. BSBh 2.1.9, p.364f., line 16f., (tr) p.318: "So too, the witness of the three states, single and invariable, is not touched by the three variable states." Also CUBh 8.12.1, p.595 line 17f. (the text should read *nivartitāvivekaḥ*), (tr) p. 647; 8.14.1, p.604 line 4, (tr) p.668.

16 US 18. 133.

17 BGBh 18. v.66, p.294, line 23f., *adṛṣṭadarśanārthaviṣayatvāt pramāṇasya*, "For the scope of a means of knowledge is that it shows something which is not (already) seen."

18 BUBh 3.3.1, p.799, line 3f., (tr) p.312.

19 BUBh 1.1 (introduction), p.607f., line 11f., (tr) p.1. Also, BUBh 1.3.1, p.626, line 15f., (tr) p.32. BSBh 2.1.1, p.348f., line 9f., (tr) 302; 2.1.27, p.400, line 13f., (tr) p.355; 2.3.1, p.499, line 5, (tr) p.445. BGBh. 18.v.66, p.294, line 22f., (tr) p.757. AUBh (introduction) p.325, line 21f., (tr) p.9.

20 Ganganatha Jha (tr.), *Slokavartika*. Delhi: Sri Satguru Publications, 1983, p.31, v.68; also p.553. Ganganatha Jha, *Pūrva-Mīmāṁsā in its Sources*. Varanasi: The Banaras Hindu University, 1964, p.111, 123f., 135. BSBh 1.3.29, p.260, line 6, (tr) p.216.

21 BUBh 2.4.10, p.763, line 12f., (tr) p.251f. Also, BSBh 2.1.1, p.351, line 3, (tr) p.304.

22 BSBh 2.1.11, p.369, line 6 *(vedasya tu nityatve)*, (tr) p.323. BSBh 2.1.1, p.348f., line 9f., (tr) p.302.

23 BSBh 1.1.10, p.115, line 11, (tr) p.61.

24 BSBh 1.3.29, p.260, line 10f., (tr) p.217; 1.3.30, p.265, line 6f., (tr) p.221.

25 Jha, *Pūrva-Mīmāṁsā in its Sources*, op.cit., p.159f.

26 A.B. Gajendragadkar and R.D. Karmarkar (ed. and tr.), *The Arthasaṁgraha of Laugākṣi Bhāskara*. Delhi: Motilal Banarsidass, 1984, p.3.

27 BUBh 3.5.1, p.814, line 1f., (tr) p.336, "the ultimate aim of the Upaniṣads is to teach Self-knowledge".

28 BUBh 1.4.7, p.654, line 24, (tr) p.77, and p.658, line 23, (tr) p.84. BSBh 1.1.1, p.41, line 1f., (tr) p.11.

29 BSBh 1.1.7, p.111, line 1f, (tr) p.55.

30 BUBh 1.1, p.607, line 5f., (tr) p.1. Here, Śaṅkara explains that the verbal root *sad*, accompanied by the prefixes *upa* and *ni*, has the sense of completely destroying *saṁsāra*. Also, 2.1.20, p.733, line 10, (tr) p.202. Here, Śaṅkara mentions that according to the etymological meaning, the Upaniṣad "takes one to the Self", *Upa=samīpaṁ nigamayati*. See also, KaUBh (introduction) p.57, line 7f., (tr) p.93. Here, Śaṅkara gives an elaborate explanation with both the above meanings.

31 KaUBh (introduction) p.58, line 5f., (tr) p.94. BUBh 1.1, p.607, line 8f., (tr) p.1.

32 BSBh 2.3.40, p.548, line 14f. (tr) p.500: *vidhiśāstraṁ tāvad yathāprāptaṁ kartṛtvam upādāya kartavyaviśeṣam upadiśati, na kartṛtvam ātmanaḥ pratipādayati.* Even when a person comes to know the truth, the Vedic injunctions dealing with rituals do not become invalid, what happens is that the knowledge of non-duality removes the idea of difference upon which the whole edifice of ritualistic activity depends and so the knower of Brahman considers that the injunctions are no longer relevant or applicable. Cf. BUBh 4.5.15, p.947, line 6f., (tr) p.549.

33 BUBh 1.1, p.608, line 22f., (tr) p.3.

34 BSBh 1.3.25, p.246, line 4f., (tr) p. 204.

35 BSBh 2.1.11, p.368, line 7, (tr) p.322.

36 BSBh 2.1.3, p.354, line 10, (tr) p.307. Also BSBh 1.1.4, p.61, line 10f., (tr) p.21, and p.63f., line 4f., (tr) p.22; 2.1.14, p.379, line 6f., (tr) p.331. BUBh 3.9.26, p.845, line 16f., (tr) p.389. US 17. v.8.

37 BSBh 2.1.6, p.360, line 6f., (tr) p.313f. Also, BSBh 1.1.2, p.53f., line 4f., (tr) p.17. BSBh 1.1.4, p.63f., line 4f., (tr) p.22. BSBh 2.1.27, p.400, line 7, *śabdamūlaṁ ca brahma,* i.e., *śabdapramāṇakaṁ, na-indriyādipramāṇakam,* (tr) p.355.

38 BSBh 1.1.4, p.87, line 1f., (tr) p.36f.

39 Mādhavānanda tr. BUBh 2.1.20, p. 744, line 5f. and line 22f. (tr) p.218, 219. Also, 2.5.15 (tr) p.273, 274. 4.4.6, p.922, line 20 (tr) p.508: "..[this way] is ancient, being revealed by the eternal Śrutis, not modern like the misleading paths emanating from the intellect of the logicians."

40 BSBh 2.1.11, p.366f., line 13f., (tr) p.321.

41 Ibid p.369, line 4f., (tr) p.322f.

42 Wilhelm Halbfass, *Tradition and Reflection: Explorations in Indian Thought.* Albany: State University of New York Press, 1991, p.154.

43 BSBh 2.1.6, p.360f., line 13f., (tr) p.314.

44 Ibid., p.361, line 2f., (tr) p.314.

45 BUBh 1.4.10, p.669f., line 25f. (tr) p.102. So too BUBh 4.3.34, p.904, line 6f., (tr) p.480: "By implication *(arthāt* =by *arthāpatti)* the nature of ignorance too has been ascertained as the superimposition of attributes other than the true ones, and as not being a natural attribute of the self."

46 BUBh 2.4.1., p.758, line 1f., (tr) p.243.

47 BSBh 2.3.6, p.503, line 14f., (tr) p.450.

48 Ibid., p.506, line 10f., (tr) p.453.

49 BSBh 2.3.17, p.528, line 6f., (tr) p.475.

50 W. Halbfass, *Tradition and Reflection,* op.cit., p.180. Also, note the accurate discussion of the role of the *śruti* in Śaṅkara's teaching in K.S. Murty, *Revelation and Reason in Advaita Vedānta.* New York: Columbia University Press, 1959 [reprintedby Motilal Banarsidass].

51 Ibid., p.157.

52 BUBh 2.1.20, p.737, line 25f., (tr) p.209. Also, BGBh 18. 66, p.294, line 22f., (tr) p.757.

53 BGBh 18. 66, p.294, line 25f., (tr) p758. Also, BUBh 3.3.1, p.802, line 23f., (tr) 318.

54 BUBh 3.3.1, p.802, line 24f., (tr) p.318.

55 US 18. vv.6, 7, 217, 226, 227.

56 BSBh 2.3.7, p.511, line 2, (tr) p.457.

57 BSBh 2.1.14, p.376f., line 8f., (tr) p.329.

58 BSBh 2.1.14, p.376f., line 8f., (tr) p.329. Also, BUBh 1.4.10, p.670, line 10f., (tr) p.103; 5.1.1, p.953, line 10f., (tr) p.560f. BGBh 13. 2, p.192, line 22, (tr) p.504.

59 BSBh 2.1.14, p.378, line 3, (tr) p.330f.

60 R.V. De Smet, *The Theological Method of Śaṃkara.* Rome: Pontifical Gregorian University. Unpublished Dissertation, 1953, p.26.

61 Ibid., p.26.

62 The work of Halbfass has been referred to above. Anantanand Rambachan, *Accomplishing the Accomplished: The Vedas as a Source of Valid Knowledge in Śaṅkara.* Hawaii: University of Hawaii Press: Monographs of the Society for Asian and Comparative Philosophy, no. 10, 1991.

63 Francis X. Clooney, *Theology after Vedānta.* Delhi: Sri Satguru Publications [reprint], 1993, p.28.

64 Ibid., p.75.

65 The compound *śāstrācāryopadeśa* occurs seven times in his commentary on the *Bhagavadgītā* alone, along with variations such as *vedāntācāryopadeśa* . BG 2. 21, p.20, line 12; 2. 63, p.36, line 12; 8. 8, p.128, line 15; 13. 30, p.215, line 23; 13. 34, p.217, line 19; 18. 16, p.263, line 19; 18. 17, p.264, line 4; 18. 50, p.281, line 7; 18. 55, p.284, line 9. (Francis X. D'SA (ed.), *Word-Index to Śaṅkara's Gītābhāṣya.* Pune: Institute for the Study of Religion, 1985). Also cf. BUBh, 2.1.20, p.744, line 23; 2.4.2, p.767, line 5; 2.5.15, p.776, line 12. ChUBh, 6.15.2, p.537, line 12; 8.1.6, p.571, line 2. KaUBh 1.5.12, p.96, line 1. MUBh 2.2.7, p.162, line 22. US, 17.51-52 and prose portion ch. 1 and 2.

66 MUBh 1.2.12, p.153, line 5.

67 Cf. John Vattanky, *Gaṅgeśa's Philosophy of God.* Madras: The Adyar Library and Research Centre, 1984.

68 BSBh 1.4.14, p.320, line 2, *na hy ayaṁ sṛṣṭyādiprapañcaḥ pratipipādayiṣitaḥ. na hi tatpratibaddhaḥ kaścit puruṣārtho dṛṣyate śrūyate vā.* (tr) p.273. Toṭaka says the same idea in his *Śrutisārasamuddharaṇam,* cf. Michael Comans, *Extracting the Essence of the Śruti,* op.cit, v.44, p.33.

69 BSBh 1.4.14, p.318, line 10f., *satyapi prativedāntaṁ sṛjyamāneṣv ākāśādiṣu kramādidvārake vigāne, na sraṣṭari kiṅcid vigānam asti.* (tr) p.271. Further, p.320, line 4f., (tr) p.273. Though Śaṅkara will reconcile the variations in the account of creation in commenting on BS 2.3.1ff., he seems quite prepared here to accept that there are variations in the creation accounts of the *śruti,* and he thinks these variations are inconsequential because the *śruti* does not have its purport in teaching the details of creation.

70 BUBh 3.8.9, p.829, line 5f., (tr) p.362. The existence of Īśvara can also be inferred with reference to the superintendence of the distribution of *karma,* i.e., that the agent must experience the fruit of his or her past deeds. With reference to Īśvara and the distribution of the *karmaphala,* cf. BUBh 3.8.9, p. 829f., line 16f., (tr) p.363.

71 BUBh 1.4.7, p.655, line 10, (tr) p.78.

72 BSBh 1.4.15, p.322, line 1f., (tr) p.275.

73 Ibid.

74 BSBh 1.4. 23, p.340, line 5f., (tr) p.293. Also cf. 1.4.24.

75 BSBh 2.1.33, p.406, line 8f., (tr) p.361.

76 BSBh 2.2.37, p.489f., line 4f., (tr) 434. He also criticises the defence of beginninglessness in 2.2.30, p.477, line 9, (tr) p.424. Arguing against the Vijñānavāda, he says that the opponent cannot suppose a beginningless series of mental impressions *(vāsanā)* in order to obviate the need of accepting the existence of an external world that causes the impressions in the first place: "even if the mental impressions form a beginningless series, that would just lead to a baseless infinite regress on the analogy of the blind leading the blind."

77 BSBh 1.4.27, p.342, line 8f., *na hy ayam anumānagamyo'rthaḥ. śabdagamyatvāt tu-asyārthasya yathāśabdam iha bhavitavyam. śabdaś ca-īkṣitur īśvarasya prakṛtitvaṁ pratipādayati ityavocāma.* (tr) p.296.

78 BSBh 1.4.23, p.339, line 2f., (tr) p.292.

79 BSBh 2.1.13, p.272, line 3f. (in line 6 read *...anyatvaṁ bhavati* instead of the misprint *ananyatvaṁ bhavati),* (tr) p. 325.

80 BSBh 2.1.14, p.372, line 13, p.373, line 1, p.375, line 9, p.376, line 1, p.377, line 3, p.382, lines 10, 11 and 14 (twice), p.383, line 3 (twice), 4, 7 (twice).

81 BSBh 2.1.14, p.372f., line 13f. The above translation relied on that of Thibaut in part, (tr) p.326.

82 BSBh 2.1.14 p. 373, line 8, (tr) p.327.

83 D.N. Shastri, *The Philosophy of Nyāya-Vaiśeṣika and its Conflict with The Buddhist Dignāga School.* Varanasi: Bharatiya Vidya Prakashan, 1976, cf. pp.74, 79, 244. "One cannot, however, fail to note the contradiction involved in the theory that

the *dharmin* and the *dharmas* are two *different* things (aspects) and yet they are *identical.* Therein lies the weakness of the Sāṁkhya position. It was pointed out that the Sāṁkhya theory of *pariṇāma-vāda* (causation through change) glides inevitably into the Vedānta theory of *vivarta-vāda* (unreal causation)..." p.79.

84 BSBh 2.1.26.

85 BSBh 2.1.14, p.380, line 7f., (tr) p.332f.

86 BSBh 2.1.27, p. 400, line 6, (tr) p. 354f.

87 Ibid. p.400, line 7, (tr) p.355.

88 Ibid. p.400f., line 14f., (tr) p.355.

89 Ibid., p.401, line 5f., (tr) p.356.

90 *Pañcadaśī.* 6. 236.

91 BSBh 2.1.14, p.381, line 9f., (tr) p.333.

92 Ibid., p.381f, line 10f., (tr) p.333f. Thibaut's translation of this last sentence (p.382, line 14) is unacceptably free. He translates: "In this manner the Vedānta texts declare that for him who has reached the state of truth and reality the whole apparent world does not exist" (p.329f.) The sentence just reads: *evaṁ paramārthāvasthāyāṁ sarvavyavahārābhāvaṁ vadanti vedāntāḥ sarve.* Thibaut is potentially misleading in saying that: "the whole apparent world does not exist" which implies that there is nothing. Whereas for the Advaitin there is no world *qua* world, but there is the one Being, Brahman, appearing as a world.

93 BSBh 2.1.22, p.395, line 1f., (tr) p.349.

94 K.S. Murty remarks: "Brahman and Īśvara (God) are not two distinct things, but the same thing conceived from two different standpoints. Brahman is therefore referred to in many places as Parameśvara, i.e. the supreme Lord." K.S. Murty, *Revelation and Reason in Advaita Vedānta,* op.cit., p.4.

95 BSBh 2.1.14, p.381, line 3f., (tr) p.332f. Cf. *Śabarabhāṣya* on *Jaimini-Sūtra* 4.4.19. Also cf. BUBh 4.4.25, p.938f., line 26f., (tr) p.534, regarding Śaṅkara's statement on the ultimate purport of the *śruti.*

96 BSBh 2.1.27, p.401, line 10f. (tr) p.356.

CHAPTER FIVE

Remarks on: Īśvara, Jīva, Upādhi, Nāmarūpa and Avidyā

(1) Īśvara

Colonel G.A. Jacob is well-known for his immense and valuable labour in the field of Indian thought. This can be seen from his book: *A Handful of Popular Maxims current in Sanskrit Literature*, and it is especially evident with regard to Vedānta in his *Concordance to the Principal Upaniṣads*, as well as in his fine editions of old Vedānta texts.[1] Writing in 1893, in the Preface to his first edition of the *Vedāntasāra*, Jacob refers to Śaṅkara's use of the terms *para* and *apara* Brahman in the *Brahmasūtrabhāṣya*. Jacob says that writers of the Advaita school use the terms *para, mukhya* and *nirguṇa* to designate the pure unassociated Brahman, and *apara, amukhya,* and *saguṇa* to distinguish: "that portion of Brahma[n] which, through association with *avidyā*, is looked upon as God. The latter is also called *paramātman* and *parameśvara*."[2] Jacob argues that Śaṅkara draws a distinction between *para* and *apara* Brahman, but then proceeds to ignore the distinction, with the result that: "according to Śaṅkara's own showing, the terms *paraṁ* Brahman, *aparaṁ* Brahman, *para īśvara* and *īśvara* are all exactly synonymous."[3] He goes on to speculate as to the reason for this terminological confusion:

> To me, therefore, it seems impossible to come to any other conclusion than that the *viśiṣṭādvaitavādins* or some similar school, were in possession of the field in Śaṅkara's time, and that his own mind was so saturated with their doctrines as to be unable to shake them off even when propounding an antagonistic system.[4]

Leaving aside the vexed question as to the doctrinal orientation of the *Brahmasūtras* themselves, as well as the point concerning the commentaries on that text prior to Śaṅkara, Jacob's remarks embody a particular understanding that may be called into question. Even if it is the case, as Jacob says, that writers in the tradition of Advaita use the terms *para* Brahman and *nirguṇa* Brahman to indicate the Absolute Brahman and terms like *apara* Brahman and *saguṇa* Brahman to refer to Īśvara, the personal Lord, is that necessarily true for Śaṅkara? Or could Jacob be reading Śaṅkara in the light of the later Vedānta with which he became familiar? When Śaṅkara distinguishes between *para* Brahman and *apara*, or *saguṇa* Brahman, does he mean by the latter two terms Īśvara, as Jacob believes, or could he mean something else by the terms *apara* and *saguṇa* Brahman?

George Thibaut, in the Introduction to his largely excellent translation of the *Vedānta-Sūtras with the commentary of Śaṅkarācārya,* similarly equates *apara* and *saguṇa* Brahman with Īśvara, the personal God.[5] He then finds fault with Śaṅkara's overt distinction of a higher and lower Brahman.[6] But perhaps his own understanding is somewhat inaccurate, for in his laudable attempt to find conceptual clarity he may have categorised Īśvara too neatly, as merely *apara,* or *saguṇa* Brahman. The first question before us, then, is to try to determine whether such terms as "lower Brahman" *(apara* Brahman) and "Brahman with qualities" *(saguṇa* Brahman) do in fact directly correspond to Īśvara, the cosmic Lord.

The first occasion that Śaṅkara makes reference to two "forms", or "types", of Brahman is in his commentary on *Brahmasūtra* 1.1.11. Here he raises an objection that since the *Brahmasūtras* have now shown that an omniscient, omnipotent Īśvara is the cause of the origination, continuation and dissolution of the world, there is no necessity of the subsequent *sūtras.*[7] He replies by saying:

> Brahman is understood as having two forms: as qualified by limiting adjuncts, where difference is due to the modifications of name-and-form, and as the opposite of that, as free from all limiting adjuncts.[8]

Śaṅkara goes on to say that only when one is in the sphere of Ignorance *(avidyā)* does Brahman come within the sphere of all relations such as those involving someone who conceptually meditates *(upāsaka)* on Brahman which becomes the object *(upāsya)* of such a meditation. He concludes the passage by saying:

> Even though Brahman is just one, it is taught in the Upaniṣads with reference to having a connection with limiting adjuncts or as free from such a connection, depending on whether it is to be either conceptually meditated upon or to be known.[9]

Later passages help clarify what he means by the "lower" Brahman. In 1.2.2, he says:

> The Upaniṣad statements: "without vital breath, without mind, pure" (MU 2.1.2] refer to the pure [unconditioned] Brahman. Whereas this text: "consisting of mind, having the vital breath as its body" (CU 3.14.2) refers to the *saguṇa* Brahman.[10]

When Śaṅkara discusses the passage in the *Chāndogya* Upaniṣad where the phrase "consisting of mind, having the vital breath as its body" occurs, it is clear that he understands the entire passage to refer to Īśvara who, in turn, is described for the purpose of conceptual meditation *(upāsana)* as "consisting of mind, having the vital breath as its body" etc. According to Jacob, Thibaut, and indeed many others, Īśvara and the *saguṇa* Brahman are fully synonymous concepts, but I suggest that this is not entirely correct. While Īśvara can come under the general category of *saguṇa* Brahman, what Śaṅkara often has in mind by the terms *apara* Brahman and *saguṇa* Brahman is Īśvara Itself, but with the further predication of specific qualities (eg. "consisting of mind, having the vital breath as its body" etc.) that are to be superimposed for the purpose of meditation or worship. Therefore, while Īśvara is the *saguṇa* Brahman, the latter is not merely synonymous with Īśvara. Rather, what Śaṅkara generally means by *saguṇa* Brahman is Īśvara as further characterised by a series of conceptual qualities for the purpose of meditation or worship.

While the *nirguṇa* Brahman is the ultimate reality, when we are discussing any matter that pertains to the existence of the world, i.e., its origination, its arrangement etc., we are immediately dealing in the sphere of *vyavahāra,* and when we are in its domain we are always in the realm of Īśvara. All the statements about *saguṇa* Brahman occur in the course of discussions that presuppose the existence of the world, and therefore these statements are further predications about Īśvara, not upon *nirguṇa* Brahman per se. In *sūtra* 4.3.7 Śaṅkara treats the three terms *kārya* Brahman ("conditioned Brahman"), *saguṇa* Brahma and *apara* Brahman as synonyms, and he goes on to say that it is possible for souls to reach the conditioned Brahman, "because it has a location *(pradeśavattvāt)*."[11] Since at other places Śaṅkara denies that Īśvara has a form,[12] Īśvara cannot be referred to here by these terms. Rather, it is Hiraṇyagarbha, or Brahmā, the "first born" of the creation, who presides over the world to which souls journey on the path of gradual liberation *(kramamukti),* who is referred to as *saguṇa* Brahman in this passage. Therefore, *saguṇa* Brahman and Īśvara are not exactly synonymous terms: *saguṇa* Brahman is quite often a further specification about Īśvara for the purpose of conceptual meditation, and when that is so, the word refers, not to Īśvara pre se, but to Hiraṇyagarbha.

But if Īśvara is not merely equivalent to the term *saguṇa* Brahman then how does Īśvara fit into Śaṅkara's scheme of things, because Śaṅkara states that Brahman has only two aspects. Towards the end of the *Brahmasūtrabhāṣya,* he again makes this point:

> (query) Are there two "forms" of Brahman, a higher *(para)* and a lower *(apara)?* (reply) Yes indeed!..(query) What, again, is meant by the higher Brahman and the lower Brahman? (reply) Where Brahman is taught by words such as "not gross" and so forth, by way of the negation of distinctions consisting of name-and-form etc. created by *avidyā,* it is the *para* Brahman that is spoken of. And when that same *[para* Brahman] is taught for the purpose of conceptual meditation as qualified by some attribute belonging to name-and-form, by words such as: "consisting of mind, having the vital breath as its body, having an effulgent form" (CU 3.14.2), it is the *apara* Brahman.[13]

Here, he says that the same *nirguṇa* Brahman is the *saguṇa* Brahman when conceived as having various attributes. But when we see his comments on the *Chāndogya* Upaniṣad from which the quotation "consisting of mind" etc. is taken, it is clear that Śaṅkara considers the passage to be referring not to *nirguṇa* Brahman, but to Īśvara, and it is Īśvara who is described in this manner for the purpose of meditation or worship. So our conclusion is that, in spite of Śaṅkara's flexibility in employing terms, Īśvara should not be treated as merely the equivalent of *saguṇa* Brahman.

Rudolf Otto, in his book *Mysticism East and West*, has, I feel, made a worthwhile contribution to our understanding of Śaṅkara's conception of Īśvara, in so far as he has called attention to the theistic dimension that is prominent in a good deal of Śaṅkara's work, but which has not been sufficiently noticed, or has been misunderstood.[14] Otto does not wish to deny the ultimacy of the suprapersonal *nirguṇa* Brahman in Śaṅkara's thought, but Otto believes that: "The impersonal Brahman rests here [in the Advaita school of Śaṅkara]...on a theistic basis" and he argues that Śaṅkara, time and again, speaks in terms that can only be applicable to a personal Lord. According to Otto, Śaṅkara's teaching is grounded in a theism which it ultimately transcends in the higher knowledge of the *nirguṇa* Brahman. While there are differences between Śaṅkara's theism and the theism of the Semitic religions, Otto's work correctly understands Īśvara as having a more central position in Śaṅkara's thought than is often supposed to be the case.

There are numerous instances in the *Brahmasūtrabhāṣya* where Śaṅkara uses the two words, Īśvara (Lord) and Parameśvara (supreme Lord), in a synonymous fashion to refer to what can only mean a personal Lord. For example, he says: "the supreme Lord too, when he chooses, can assume a form made of *māyā*, for the benefit of the seekers."[15] We see statements referring to the "favour of the supreme Lord" *(parameśvarānugraha)*[16]; and we meet with numerous statements about the supreme Lord as the creator of the world *(parameśvaraśca sarvajagataḥ kartā sarvavedānteṣu-avadhāritaḥ)*[17]; we also hear that the liberating knowledge is from the grace of the Lord[18]; that the Lord is eternally without Ignorance[19]; that the Lord has entrusted certain duties to some special souls[20]; and that the Lord exists from all eternity *(nityasiddha Īśvara)*.[21] Although there are a couple of instances at the end of the

Brahmasūtra where it is not entirely clear whether Śaṅkara is referring by the word Īśvara to the supreme Lord, or to Hiraṇyagarbha (Brahmā), at other times when Śaṅkara uses the terms Īśvara and Parameśvara his use of those terms is consistent with the description of a single supreme Being, a personal God, who, as we have seen, is both the efficient and the material cause of the world.[22]

While there are thus many occasions when the terms Īśvara and Parameśvara can only refer to a personal supreme Lord, there are also numerous instances where Śaṅkara uses the words Īśvara and Parameśvara as synonyms for the supreme Self *(paramātman)* or the supreme, i.e., the unconditioned, Brahman *(paraṁ Brahman).* Such flexibility of language can also be seen in the *Bhagavadgītā,* where the words Parameśvara, Īśvara and Paramātman are seen to be directly equated: "He who sees the supreme Lord *(parameśvara)* residing equally in all beings..." (13.27), "seeing equally the Lord *(īśvara)* that is present equally everywhere..." (13.28), "the supreme Self *(paramātman)* is changeless, on account of being beginningless and free from attributes..." (13. 31, also 13.22). Śaṅkara too often uses Parameśvara and Paramātman synonymously. For example, in his commentary on *sūtras* 1.2.24 and 1.2.28 Śaṅkara uses the words Parameśvara and Paramātman interchangeably.[23] Similarly at other places, such as 1.3.7, he treats Īśvara and Paramātman interchangeably.[24] In 1.3.10 Śaṅkara introduces a topic with the question whether the word *"akṣara"* ("immutable"), as occurring in *Bṛhadāraṇyaka* Upaniṣad 3.8.8, refers to the syllable OM or to the supreme Lord *(parameśvara).* He states the final position saying: "the supreme Self is what is meant by the word *akṣara"* and he later sums up saying that the *akṣara* is none other than the "supreme Brahman itself" *(akṣaraṁ param eva brahma).* Again, in 1.3.11, in continuation of the topic, he refers to Parameśvara and then finally, in 1.3.12, to *paraṁ* Brahman. So we can see that Śaṅkara employs all these words: Parameśvara, *para* Ātman and *paraṁ* Brahman, when discussing the single word *akṣara.* And this is not the only occasion in the *Brahmasūtrabhāṣya* when he uses these terms synonymously, on other occasions too he uses the words Īśvara, Parameśvara, Ātman and Brahman interchangeably.[25]

This seemingly indiscriminate use of specialised terms prompted Paul Hacker, one of the most careful students of Śaṅkara's language in the *Brahmasūtrabhāṣya,* to express the opinion that: "...we must consider an aversion for definitions and a cavalier attitude toward conceptual systematization as a general distinguishing feature of the thought of Ś[aṅkara]."[26] Through his careful study Hacker has drawn attention to this problem of usage in regard to the above terms and he has also noted its solution, at least as far as Advaitins are concerned, though he has perhaps not given it due significance. The point I am referring to is the distinction in Advaita between conventional reality *(vyavahāra)* and ultimate reality *(paramārtha)*. Hacker makes the comment: "...in keeping with the basic illusionistic dogma of his system, Īśvara and *paraṃ* Brahma or Paramātman, which he [Śaṅkara] intuitively (and possibly under the influence of non-illusionistic predecessors) was inclined not to distinguish, can occasionally be kept apart."[27] Here Hacker is saying that Śaṅkara, in keeping with his "illusionistic" doctrine, does occasionally make a distinction between *paraṁ* Brahman and Īśvara.

Hacker shows that when Śaṅkara does distinguish between *paraṁ* Brahman and Īśvara, he does so in the context of the "levels" of reality, *vyavahāra* and *paramārtha*. Hacker says:

> Even in the theory of creation the concepts Īśvara and *(paraṃ)* Brahma or Paramātman are largely interchangeable, through not everywhere. One can say that this interchangeability extends throughout the whole theory of creation, with the single exception of the statement that the *īśvaratva* of Īśvara is illusory. To say that the *brahmatva* of Brahman is ultimately unreal is of course impermissible. ...Only where the "division into ruler and ruled" *(īśitṛ-īśitavya-vibhāga)* is assigned to the *vyāvahāriky avasthā*, or where the *īśvaratva* of Īśvara is called illusory (II, 1, 14), is it said that this division does not really pertain to Brahman or Ātman, or does so only from the empirical standpoint. Only in such places are Īśvara and Brahman or Paramātman presented as two distinct things.[28]

We have also shown, toward the end of the previous chapter, that whenever Śaṅkara makes the distinction between Īśvara and the absolute Brahman, he keeps in view the sphere of empirical reality and of ultimate reality:

> Thus the Lord's being a Lord *(īśvarasya īśvaratva)*, his omniscience and his omnipotence, depend upon the limitation brought about by limiting adjuncts that are of the nature of *avidyā*. From the perspective of ultimate reality *(paramārthataḥ)*, when, through knowledge, the Self is divested of all limiting adjuncts, the expressions pertaining to empirical life such as Ruler, ruled, omniscient etc., are not logically possible. Accordingly it is said: "Where one sees nothing else, hears nothing else, knows nothing else, that is the Infinite" (CU 7.24.1); "But when, to this knower of Brahman, everything has become the Self, then what would he see, and through what?" (BU 4.5.15) etc. Thus all Upaniṣads speak of the cessation of all empirical life *(vyavahāra)* in the state of ultimate reality *(paramārtha)*. ...However, in the sphere of empirical life, the empirical dealings from *Īśvara* onwards have been told in the *śruti:* "This One [i.e. the great, birthless Self: *mahān aja ātmā]* is the Lord of all, this One is the Ruler of beings, the protector of beings, the bank that serves as the boundary to keep these worlds apart" (BU 4.4.22).[29]
>
> When non-difference is awakened by the statements of non-difference such as: "you are That", then the condition of the individual soul as subject to *saṁsāra* vanishes, as does the condition of Brahman as the creator *(brahmaṇaśca sraṣṭṛtvam):* because the entire empirical world of duality, which is manifested by false knowledge, is sublated by right knowledge.[30]

So we can see that Śaṅkara makes a distinction between Īśvara and the absolute Brahman in the context of the important distinction between empirical and absolute reality.[31] Such a view accords with his hermeneutics of the *śruti*, for his understanding is that the "negative", or *nirguṇa* texts, convey the ultimate message of the *śruti*, and he sees discussions concerning creation as preparatory for the knowledge of oneness. To illustrate these two points, we shall cite from Śaṅkara's commentary on *Brahmasūtra* 4.3.14, where he says:

> (objection) From the *śruti* texts that speak of Brahman as the cause of the origination, continuance and dissolution of the world, we can see that Brahman has manifold powers. (reply) No, because the Upaniṣad statements that deny distinctions can convey no other meaning. (objection) The texts dealing with origination etc. likewise convey no other meaning. (reply) No, because they are meant to teach oneness. For when the scripture teaches, through the illustrations of clay and so forth, that the Being, i.e., Brahman, is the one reality and that modifications are unreal, it cannot have the aim of teaching about origination. (objection) Why are the *śruti* texts that deal with origination etc. auxiliary to the texts that deny distinction, and not the reverse? (reply) That is because the texts denying distinctions have a meaning that leaves nothing wanting. For when the oneness, the eternity, the purity etc. of the Self has been understood, no further expectation arises, because it is logically possible for there to be the conviction that the final purpose has been attained. ...But it cannot be said that the texts about creation have the capacity to teach a meaning that leaves nothing more to be desired. It is evident that they have another meaning. ...for these texts dealing with origination etc. aim at conveying the understanding of the oneness of the Self.[32]

From the absolute perspective, Śaṅkara does distinguish between Īśvara and the absolute Brahman, the sole Being that is pure Awareness. If he did not make such a distinction then his teaching would be a kind of monistic theism, but it would not be non-dualism *(advaita)*. At the level of *vyavahāra,* when the discussion has to do with the cosmos, the teaching of the Upaniṣads is that the Lord existed before the creation of the universe and the Lord has become the universe and everything in it ("I shall become many, I shall be born".). Śaṅkara accepts this, but he also accepts that there are *śruti* statements that deny all distinctions *("neti neti", "asthūla"* etc.), and unlike Rāmānuja, who gives a restricted meaning to the statements of negation as denying only evil qualities *(heyaguṇa)* that are opposed to the purity of the Lord's nature, Śaṅkara says that the statements of negation have unrestricted force and deny all distinctions whatsoever. And so Śaṅkara ultimately arrives at non-dualism, through the negation of all "name-and-form", with the result that the irreducible essential nature of the Lord, pure Awareness, is found to exist absolutely.

When Śaṅkara distinguishes between Īśvara and the absolute Brahman, Īśvara would have to be considered as *saguṇa* Brahman. However in the contexts where Śaṅkara uses the terms Brahman, Paramātman, Parameśvara and Īśvara interchangeably, *saguṇa* Brahman would then be generally Hiraṇyagarbha-Brahmā rather than Īśvara per se. Different hypotheses can plausibly be put forward, historical as well as psychological, as to why Śaṅkara often uses these four terms interchangeably in his *Brahmasūtrabhāṣya.* I suggest a philosophical reason: he often does not make the distinction explicit, in the same way as the Upaniṣads often do not do so, because for him *paraṁ* Brahman and Īśvara are not two distinct things, they are in fact one and the same Being. At the level of *vyavahāra,* i.e., in the context of the world, reason seeks to know about the efficient and material causes of the world, and the Upaniṣads reveal the existence of a supreme Being who is both the efficient and the material cause. But in the highest knowledge, when all name-and-form is found to be merely apparent ("But when, to this knower of Brahman, everything has become the Self, then what would he see, and through what?" (BU 4.5.15) Etc.), it is not that Īśvara is then found to be a fiction, but it is rather that the Īśvaratva of Brahman (or the *sraṣṭṛtva* of Brahman) "vanishes" *(apagata,* literally "goes away") in so far as the attributes of Creatorship etc. cannot be located in the undifferentiated Being that is pure Awareness. When everything has the single "eye of Awareness" *(prajñānetra,* AU 3.1.3), a division of "ruler and ruled" *(īśitṛ-īśitavya-vibhāga)* etc. can no longer be found.

Śaṅkara's interchangeable usage of the four terms can no doubt be confusing. But his perspective is more fluid, and can perhaps better accommodate the aspirations of religiosity, than the more rigid definitions of some of his successors. We may, perhaps, put it this way: we can either say there is one Being, the unconditioned Brahman *(paraṁ brahman),* which appears as Parameśvara, the supreme Lord (i.e. Īśvara), or, we could also express this more theistically and say that there is one

Being, Parameśvara, who has become everything, and whose essential nature is *paraṁ* Brahman, the unconditioned pure Awareness. Sometimes Śaṅkara seems to express this latter understanding:

> The supreme Lord *(parameśvara)* is just one, absolutely unchanging, whose very nature is Consciousness, who, by *avidyā*, is thought to be manifold, like a magician through *māyā*. There is no other principle of Consciousness.[33]

Thus we could speak of *paraṁ* Brahman as having a lower aspect, i.e., Īśvara, or, we could speak of Īśvara as having a higher aspect, and since Īśvara has two aspects, the *īśvaratva* and the *paraṁ* Brahman, Śaṅkara can, and probably does, use the word "Īśvara" to refer to either aspect. This is perhaps a reason for some of the confusion surrounding his usage of the terms Īśvara and Parameśvara in the sense of *paraṁ* Brahman. Sometimes he refers to this higher aspect of Īśvara, equivalent to the *paraṁ* Brahman, as the "nature belonging to the supreme Lord" *(pārameśvararūpa):* "When the nature belonging to the supreme Lord, as free from all distinctions, is being taught, then the scripture says: 'without sound, without touch, without form, changeless' (KaU 1.3.15)."[34] Thus Śaṅkara's understanding of Īśvara can accommodate a number of perspectives. Since Īśvara is the cause of the world, Śaṅkara is able to speak of Īśvara in theistic terms; since Īśvara is the material cause of the world he can say, in a monistic fashion, that Īśvara alone exists. And at the level of ultimate truth, when, through the understanding of the *mithyātva* of all limiting adjuncts *(upādhi)* of name-and-form, everything is seen to be not an other to pure Awareness, the distinctions of jīva and Īśvara no longer apply, and it is the *paraṁ* Brahman, the very essential nature of the Lord Itself, that is the final reality.

By way of concluding this section I would like to discuss a modern interpretation of Śaṅkara's teaching concerning the nature of Brahman, an interpretation put forward by some Christian scholars, notably by the Jesuit, Richard De Smet. Dr De Smet maintains that the description of the *para* Brahman as "impersonal" became common from the nineteenth century and it is the legacy of a philosophical reduction of the concept of "person", initiated by F.H. Jacobi, so as to apply only to human individuals.[35] De Smet calls into question the correctness of applying the term "impersonal" to the *para* Brahman, for in his view the *para* Brahman of Advaita is actually equivalent to the *deus simplex* of Christian scholastic thought.[36] Thus De Smet says, ..."the personal God of Christianity is really the Absolute", by which he means that the personal God of Christianity is equivalent to what Śaṅkara means by *para* Brahman.[37] The issue before us is to determine whether the interpretation of Śaṅkara that De Smet presents, in order to demonstrate the equivalence of the *para* Brahman and the *deus simplex* of Christian theology, is valid. Further to this, I will offer some remarks regarding the term "personal" in relation to the *para* Brahman.

From what I have said earlier in this section, as well as in the previous chapter, it should be clear that I think the distinction between Brahman as Īśvara, the personal Lord, and Brahman as the unconditioned Absolute is more fluid in Śaṅkara's understanding than in that of some of his successors. Perhaps comparisons between Śaṅkara and the great theologian-philosophers, such as Thomas Aquinas (and more especially Meister Eckhart), may prove rewarding. Although I do not know a great deal about the thought of Thomas Aquinas, I doubt whether the *para* Brahman of Śaṅkara and the God of St Thomas Aquinas can be equated as readily as Father De Smet would have us believe, and further, I consider that De Smet has been able to draw some close comparisons between the two by interpreting Śaṅkara, on at least one important issue, in a way that erroneously brings him into closer conformity with a Western theological perspective.

In the thought of Thomas Aquinas the "pure perfections", such as the virtues of wisdom and goodness, can be predicated of God only analogically. Though these perfections do really exist in God, the human mind can know them only in an imperfect manner, by way of analogy derived from the imperfect presence of such virtues in ourselves who have a real relation of ontological dependence upon God as our efficient cause and the source of whatever virtues we possess. It is evident that if there is to be an analogical predication of qualities to God, on the basis of those found to exist in the human person, it would be difficult to avoid some anthropomorphism in our understanding of the nature of God. According to F.C. Copleston:

> In Aquinas' account of our natural knowledge of the divine nature there is, then, a certain agnosticism. When we say that God is wise we affirm of God a positive attribute; but we are not able to give any adequate description of what is objectively signified by the term when it is predicated of God.[38]

And further:

> As Aquinas says clearly, a certain measure of 'agnosticism' is inevitable. It could be avoided only by relapsing into anthropomorphism...[39]

What is meant here by the term "agnosticism" is that our knowledge of God is necessarily imperfect and inadequate.[40] Judging from Father Copleston's explanation of Thomas Aquinas, there is perhaps some similarity between the simple divine essence in the thought of St Thomas and the *nirguṇa* Brahman of Śaṅkara. But there is, nonetheless, an important difference, in so far as the absolute Being for the Christian theologian is a Being that acts, whereas for Śaṅkara, simple Being precludes the idea of action.[41] This difference is evident from the fact that in Christianity God acts to really create the world, out of sheer nothing, such that the multiplicity of created things are entirely dependent ontologically upon the will of God for their continuing in existence. And, taking over the conception of God from the Old Testament, the God of Christianity is actively involved in the historical process of the world itself.

Of course it is only in relation to the fact of the existence of the world that any discussion arises, in natural theology, of the existence of God as its creator. The arguments for the existence of God, such as those of Thomas Aquinas, proceed on the basis of divine causality from the observation of the existence of finite things. Śaṅkara would have no theoretical difficulty in accepting the validity of such arguments (though he thought that the existence of God cannot be proved independently of revelation). However Śaṅkara makes it clear that from the standpoint of the highest truth, or ultimate reality *(paramārthataḥ):* "...all Upaniṣads speak of the cessation of all empirical life in the state of ultimate reality *(evaṁ paramārthāvasthāyāṁ sarvavyavahārābhāvaṁ vadanti vedāntāḥ sarve)*".[42] Such a statement should not be overlooked, as it tends to be, by those who would see an equivalence between the *para* Brahman of Śaṅkara and the nature of God according to Thomas Aquinas. Therefore the *para* Brahman of Śaṅkara is ultimately acosmic, in the sense that while Brahman is the material cause of the world, the so called real things that comprise the world are found to be, in fact, not truly existing in the way they present to commonsense. They are only apparently existing, they are ontologically *mithyā*, because the product of a material cause has no existence of its own, its existence is just the existence of the material cause itself. And when there is the ascertainment that the entire world is *mithyā*, since it does not exist as an entity in its own right separate from Brahman the material cause, there is then the discovery that Brahman has not actually *become* the world: because the word "world" does not correspond to a "thing", a reality that could stand as the object of the process of becoming (and the idea of the world as a separate "thing" is implied in any doctrine of a real creation, either where God transforms into the world or creates the world *ex nihilo)*. And thus Brahman, as the intelligent and material cause of a *mithyā* effect, moves beyond our notion of a real relation between cause and effect. And since the Upaniṣads specify that Brahman is unchanging spirit, the insight reached by Advaita is that Brahman does not change into the world but only *appears as* the world. I have tried to show the steps to this conclusion in the previous chapter (though it should be noted that, for truly understanding Advaita, these steps are not just to be understood as propositional knowledge, but they have to become "existentially" meaningful, especially the understanding of Brahman as the material cause).

Thus there is a major difference between the Advaita of Śaṅkara, stemming from the Upaniṣads, and the theology of Thomas Aquinas, erected largely upon the thought of Aristotle, and that difference concerns the reality of the "effect". When Richard De Smet finds a close parallel between Śaṅkara and Aquinas, this is done by glossing over the ontological *mithyātva* of the effect in the thought of Śaṅkara. For example, De Smet writes of a *tādātmya* relation between the material cause and its effect as a relation of: "constant ontological dependence" between the effect and the cause.[43] But while this may seem to be a correct presentation of Śaṅkara, it is not really so, because it grants more reality to the effect than Śaṅkara is prepared to allow. For Śaṅkara, the effect is not a thing in itself, it has no being of its own: its being is the being of the material cause. This important perspective can be traced to the famous *"vācārambhaṇa"* passages of the *Chāndogya* Upaniṣad (6.1.4 f., also 6.4.1 f.), where effects are shown to be "name-and-form", i.e., to be constructed as ontological realities by language, whereas they actually have no independent being of their own apart from their material cause. Such a perspective, that an effect is not a thing in its own right, that it is not really a substance, for it is ontologically reducible to its material cause, is a very different perspective from the Western tradition which has remained long under the influence of Aristotle's defence of commonsense realism which looks to the reality of form. Aristotle taught that while substance is the combination of matter and form, it is actually the form that imparts substantiality to matter, since he considered that a substance should be something individual and definable. A substance is when matter receives the impression of a particular form. A clay-pot is a substance, for the pot is an individual definable "thing". For Śaṅkara, however, closely following the metaphysical perspective of the Upaniṣad just mentioned (where no such distinction is made between essence and existence, between "what" a thing is and that "by which" it is), the pot is not a substance, because it has no existence of its own, its existence depends entirely upon the existence of the material cause. Strictly speaking, a pot is not a "thing", it is not really a noun, it is an adjective to clay.

Thomas Aquinas, along with the Western tradition in general, has inherited from Aristotle the tendency to hypostatise form. This can be seen in Aquinas' conformity to commonsense and to ordinary linguistic usage by making a metaphysical distinction between essence (substance) and its existence. But Śaṅkara would consider all this to be so much sophisticated manoeuvring in the defence of commonsense realism, somewhat akin to the attempt by the Nyāya-Vaiśeṣika to defend realism utilising the concepts of *asatkāryavāda* and *samavāya*.[44] What we ordinarily conceive as a substance does have a practical reality *(vyavahāra)*, but when considered from the perspective of its material cause it is found to have no being of its own, and that means it is not a "thing" in its own right. Consequently, De Smet is not correct in speaking of the: "relation of the effects to their divine Cause",[45] because there can only be relations between things, but since the effect is not really a "thing" it cannot enter into a relation with its material cause. It is not that, as he says: "the relation is not real in both terms", because according to Śaṅkara there is no possibility of a relation at all. There can be no *tadātmya* "relation" between the clay-pot and the clay, because the pot is not a "thing", which it must be if it is to enter into relation with the clay. Similarly, there can be no "relation" between the *mithyā* world and the *para* Brahman, because they are not two things.

Can the *para* Brahman be called "impersonal"? The word "impersonal" depends, of course, on the definition of what it means to be a person. The definition of person would most likely contain reference to the ability to think rationally and to the capacity for self-reflection.[46] Together with thinking and self-consciousness, the conception of a person is also likely to include the capacity to enter into relationship, and so relationality, along with rationality and reflexivity, would be applicable to the concept of person. If this is so, then we may say that Īśvara can be considered a personal deity (though Śaṅkara's presentation of Īśvara is not very determinate), for Īśvara is related to the world as its intelligent and material cause, and Īśvara even chooses to incarnate. Thus the concept of Īśvara becomes increasingly definite as we pass from the abstraction of metaphysics to the dimension of popular religious life. *Para* Brahman, on the other hand, does not seem to fit the definition of "person" and so might be considered as "impersonal". But "personal" and "impersonal" are Western ascriptions that do not form a part of Vedānta's own discourse, and I would prefer to say that instead of calling *para* Brahman "impersonal", with the negativity that such a term may convey, *para* Brahman is suprapersonal in so far as it does not fit our category of "person". But even if we say that *para* Brahman is "impersonal" it does not mean that the *para* Brahman is some sort of inert foundation upon which the world is fabricated, like a house is erected on a concrete slab. For Īśvara and the *para* Brahman are not separate entities, it is just that the attributes of "overlordship" *(īśvaratva)*, that are relational to the world, "dissolve" - from the *paramārtha* perspective, when the real world together with its real causal relations are seen as ontologically *mithyā* - into the *para* Brahman that is pure Awareness (or pure Spirit), to which the attributes of personality, even those of an ultimate *īśvaratva*, cannot finally be predicated. As we said before, from the *paramārtha* perspective, the attributes of Creatorship etc. cannot be located in the undifferentiated Being that is pure Awareness.

(2) Jīva

I do not intend to discuss in elaborate detail the nature of the individual soul *(jīva).* I will just present the main ideas and proceed to highlight a couple of points. The individual self, or "soul", has no inherent being of its own as an individual. Yet it does have inherent being, for its essential nature is none other than the being of Brahman. Brahman itself, conditioned by limiting adjuncts *(upādhi),* is called as an individual soul *(jīva).* Śaṅkara says in this regard:

> The meaning that all exponents of Vedānta have to accept is this: the difference between the individual self *(vijñānātmā)* and the unconditioned Self *(paramātmā)* is not absolutely real, it is brought about by limiting adjuncts such as the physical body etc., which are composed of name-and-form and which are presented by Ignorance *(avidyā).*[47]

Individuality is contingent upon the limiting adjuncts *(upādhi)* of the body-mind and it is therefore unreal. But the fundamental being of the individual self is not unreal, because that is none other than the Being of Brahman.

The limiting adjuncts are physical *(sthūla)* as well as subtle *(sūkṣma).* The former is the physical body *(sthūlaśarīra),* it is a product of the five material elements (space, air, fire, water and earth), and it undergoes the sixfold modifications ending with death (the body is born, exists, grows, alters, declines and dies). There is also a subtle adjunct called the subtle body *(sūkṣmaśarīra).* It too is a material entity, for it is also composed of the five elements, though in their subtle form.[48] The subtle body does not perish at the time of the death of the physical body, but it passes on to a new physical body.[49] The subtle body has seventeen constituents.[50] These are subtle by definition and they are not to be confused with their locations in the physical body. The seventeen constituents are generally said to be as follows: the five organs of perception (the sense of hearing, touch, sight, taste and smell), the five organs of action (speech, hands, feet, evacuation and generation), the mind, the intellect, and the life-force *(prāṇa)* which is divided fivefold on account of its five different functions (expiration also specifically called *prāṇa,* inspiration and excretion called *apāna,* exertion called *vyāna,* expulsion called *udāna,* and digestion called *samāna).*[51] The subtle body is the primary limiting adjunct of the soul, and among the various components of the subtle body it is the mind and the intellect that together are the principal factor contributing to the individuality of the soul.

The distinction between mind *(manas)* and intellect *(buddhi)* is due only to the difference in function of a single inner-instrument *(antaḥkaraṇa).* Śaṅkara says that this inner-instrument is referred to by various names, as *manas, buddhi, vijñāna* (i.e. *ahaṅkāra)* and *citta,* according to whether one or another of its various functions are highlighted.[52] Thus when discursive or speculative thought is referred to, or when indecisive thought is predominant, then the inner-instrument can be called *manas,* or mind, i.e., the faculty of thought. When ascertainment or knowledge is dominant then it can be called *buddhi,* or intellect, i.e., the faculty of knowledge. When the aspect of egoism is emphasised it is referred to as *ahaṁkāra,* or "I". And when feeling (and memory) are referred to it can be called *citta.* The inner-instrument (which we will call by the general term "mind") is the most important adjunct *(upādhi)* of the Self, because it is the only place where Self-knowledge can occur.[53] It is also the place where the primary mistake is made about the true nature of the Self, in that the pure Awareness-Self is first identified with the operations of the mind itself.

The aspect I particularly wish to highlight in this section is the crucial distinction that Advaita makes between cognitive activity and the real Self, Awareness as such. Śaṅkara, in his commentary on the *Bṛhadāraṇyaka* Upaniṣad, gives this definition of Self:

> The word "Self" *(ātman)* means the Light which is different from the body, the sense organs and the combination of their parts; it illumines the body and the organs like an

> external light such as the sun etc., and is itself not illumined by anything else.[54]

In his *Upadeśasāhasrī*, Śaṅkara tells us on more than one occasion that the Self is of the nature of pure Awareness and is distinct from cognition. For example:

> The modification of the mind, which is produced by the operation of the eye and which takes on the form of the object, is indeed always seen by the eternal Seeing of the Self.[55]

Śaṅkara refers to this point in the *Bṛhadāraṇyakabhāṣya* while commenting upon the cryptic statement by Yājñavalkya, "you cannot see the Seer of seeing" (BU 3.4.2). Śaṅkara says:

> The Self is the Seer of seeing. Seeing is of two types: ordinary and the truly real. The ordinary seeing is a modification of the internal-organ [i.e. mind] as connected with the eye. It is an act, so it arises and perishes. Whereas the Seeing that belongs to the Self is like the heat and the light etc. of fire [i.e. it is the very nature of the Self]. As it is the very nature of the Seer, it does not arise and does not perish. It seems to be connected with the [ordinary] seeing that is a [mental] activity and functions as a limiting adjunct, and in this way it comes to be referred to as the "Seer". And on the basis of the difference [between the real Seeing and the ordinary seeing] there is the designation "Seer" [which refers to the real Seeing] and "seeing" [which refers to the ordinary seeing].[56]

In the *Aitareyabhāṣya*, Śaṅkara succinctly states this important teaching:

> This is the correct understanding. The eternal Seeing belonging to the Self apprehends the "external",

> impermanent, seeing. But because the "external" seeing has the impermanent properties of arising and ceasing etc., the Seeing that is the Self, which apprehends that ["external" impermanent seeing], seems to be like that [impermanent seeing], and that is the reason people are confused [and regard the real Seeing] as impermanent etc. The case is analogous to the way one's vision seems to revolve when its object is something such as a whirling firebrand.[57]

Śaṅkara considers that the words seer, hearer, thinker etc. do not refer to the true Self as understood in Advaita. They literally refer to the "person" who has the natural identification with the faculties of sight, sound, thought and so forth. The Self can, however, be directly indicated by these words, if the hearer is ready to negate the literal sense of the words and grasp their implied meaning as the unobjectifiable "subject", the pure Awareness itself. We shall discuss this important topic of indication *(lakṣaṇā)* in the following chapter, but it is worthwhile noting here that the method of indication is in accord with Yājñavalkya's teaching in the *Bṛhadāraṇyaka* Upaniṣad, for Yājñavalkya uses this technique of language to directly indicate the Self as the non-objectifiable, invariable, Awareness:

> This Immutable, O Gārgī, is the unseen Seer, the unheard Hearer, the unthought Thinker, the unknown Knower. There is no other seer than This, there is no other hearer than This, there is no other thinker than This, there is no other knower than This.[58]

Śaṅkara comments elsewhere in the *Bṛhadāraṇyaka:*

> This supreme [i.e. unconditioned] Self, the witness of the cognitions of all beings, has been described as "not this", "not this" etc. Apart from whom there is no other seer, hearer, thinker and knower. It is undifferentiated, present in all beings, and is by nature always pure, awake and free *(nityaśuddhabuddhamuktasvabhāva)*.[59]

It is this dimension of pure Awareness - which is Being itself - that constitutes the essential core of the person. Paul Hacker has expressed the Advaita understanding with lucidity and his words deserve to be quoted at length:

> The Vedāntic concept of the person thus draws a sharp line within the inner realm of what we may call the "soul". Even the 'I' and the "subject" are affected by it. Tentatively and, after the process of reduction has been completed, finally as well, these words also describe the core of the person. For, in the opinion of the Advaita Vedānta, the meaning of these terms includes, in addition to nonauthentic ingredients, also the authentic person; after reducing it to the personal core, the words remain applicable. The 'I' is a mixture of what is mental and nonauthentic, and the authentic core of the self, of the objective and the subjective. Advaita Vedānta goes a part of the way with its sister school, the (Pūrva) Mīmāṃsā, which defines the soul or the self as that which is meant by the word 'I'. But finally it moves away from the Mīmāṃsā and discards what is mental in the 'I'. It is only after this reduction that it can again use the word 'I' with reference to the self. In the realization of the Upaniṣadic sentence "I am Brahman", the identification with Brahman, whose being is true, *removes* the "I-ness" of the 'I'. Only by the amalgamation of the self and the psyche or mind is it possible for the 'I' which misapprehends itself, to act and suffer. Thus, the concept of the subject, too, is applicable to the self only after the reduction of the contents. This reduction must remove that which is functional and incidental in the subject from the content of the term; what remains is pure nonobjectifiable consciousness.[60]

There are two points here to be noted. The first is that the terms 'I' and 'subject' "remain applicable" even after discarding the objective and thereby nonauthentic aspects of the person. Thus the essential core of the person remains as 'I' in the most fundamental sense. The pure

Awareness, which the Advaitin calls the Self, is, then, identical to the core sense of Self-hood and it is not meant to be considered as a mere abstraction.

This leads to the second point. This pure Awareness, which constitutes the core of the person, also provides the sense of fundamental identity to the person. Hacker does not explicitly mention this in the passage cited above, though he refers to this issue elsewhere and in concluding his discussion he says:

> The self pervades not only the psyche but all the constituents of a human being. It thus binds these constituents together into a whole. It is the principle of existential unity in a human being.[61]

For Advaita, it is pure Awareness - identical with Being itself - which is the core, or Self, of all that exists, and in the case of the human person it is this Awareness-Being that lies at the centre of the feeling of the existential self-identity of a person. To turn for a moment to a comparison with Western philosophy, it is well known that Rene Descartes discovered the indubitable certainty of his existence in the fact that he is: "a thing which thinks".[62] But in so equating his existence with the activity of thinking, the consequence would be that if Descartes is not thinking then he cannot prove that he exists. Although what Descartes says may be logically true, it is not existentially true, for in reflecting upon oneself following a period of absent-mindedness, when we are not aware of our concrete existence, we do not feel that we did not exist during that time. David Hume considered the "self" to be a bundle of perceptions among which no substantial entity could be found that we might call a self. He accounted for the sense of personal identity on the basis of memory, which provides a resemblance among cognitions so that the imagination can then synthesise a personal identity. And because of memory we can have a cause-effect relation between cognitions, which can be extended beyond even what we can remember, so that there appears to be a personal identity even about matters of which the memory has been lost.[63] However, Hume's explanation failed to satisfy Hume himself, for in his Appendix to *A Treatise of Human Nature* he confessed his inability to account for the principle of connection that binds together all the particular perceptions and gives them a unity. He put it down to feeling, we only *feel* a connection among what are actually discrete thoughts.[64] But Śaṅkara, while perhaps granting that memory does provide a functional demonstration of personal continuity, would maintain that the existential sense of personal identity is grounded in the feeling of Being that lies at the core of the person, and he would further maintain that this Awareness-Being "core" is self-luminous and is presupposed in any proof. Thus the Advaitin would say that it is the feeling of Being [i.e. Brahman] that provides the true sense of existential identity. Hacker has brought our attention to this notable point about the spiritual self providing the existential unity of the person; and he refers as well to the important matter of the self-luminosity of the Self, which we will have occasion to discuss in the following chapter.

(3) Upādhi

The word *upādhi* is the most important technical expression in Advaita and as such it deserves to be mentioned, even if only briefly. An *upādhi* refers to a thing that apparently conditions something else by transferring its properties to that other thing on account of the proximity between them.[65] The standard illustration is that of a red flower which transfers its property of redness to a clear crystal due to their proximity. In this instance the red flower is the *upādhi* of the crystal. Śaṅkara uses the word *upādhi* in this same sense, i.e., as an adjunct, or limiting condition, which brings about a seeming limitation to something else. Another common illustration, which Gauḍapāda has used, is how the form of a pot causes an apparent limitation with regard to space.[66] Even though space is undivided, we nonetheless think of a circumscribed "pot-space" when we think of it with reference to the limiting adjunct of the pot. In his commentary upon the *Bṛhadāraṇyaka* Upaniṣad 3.8.12, Śaṅkara raises the important question as to what is the difference between Brahman, God *(Īśvara)*, and the individual self *(jīva)* and he answers the question by saying that these distinctions are made only on the basis of limiting adjuncts. He says:

> What then is the difference among them? We say that it is brought about by limiting adjuncts. Intrinsically there is no difference or identity among them, because they are in essence undifferentiated, divisionless Consciousness, analogous to a lump of salt. For there is the *śruti:* "without before or after, without interior or exterior. This Self... is Brahman" (BU 2.5.19). And in the *Atharvaṇa* we hear: "coextensive with all that is external and internal, unborn" (MU 2.1.2). Therefore, the Self that is free from all adjuncts is referred to - for the reasons that it cannot be directly designated, that it is without qualifying attributes and on account of its oneness - as: "not this, not this".
> The Self, having the limiting adjuncts of the body and sense organs which are qualified by ignorance, desire and action, is called the transmigrating individual self *(jīva)*. The Self, having as its limiting adjunct the power of eternal and unsurpassed knowledge, is called the Internal Ruler *(antaryāmī)* and Īśvara.
> That very Self, free from limiting adjuncts, absolute and pure, is called from its own standpoint the Immutable and the supreme [i.e. unconditioned] *(para)*. As qualified by various limiting adjuncts of the body and organs, whether of Hiraṇyagarbha, the manifest *(virāṭ)*,[67] the [presiding] deities, the species, the individual, human beings, animals and spirits etc., the Self acquires those names and has those forms.[68]

Śaṅkara considers that all the Upaniṣad texts which seem to speak of difference can be harmonised with the texts that speak of non-duality when they are looked at in this way: difference is not intrinsic to Brahman, but it is brought about in appearance by the presence of various limiting adjuncts that are the modifications of name-and-form *(nāmarūpa)*.[69]

(4) Nāmarūpa

We have seen that Īśvara is both the efficient as well as the material cause of the world, since the Upaniṣads speak of no other efficient cause, nor do they speak of an independently existing material, such as the *Prakṛti* (or *Pradhāna)* that the followers of Sāṅkhya infer to be an independently existing material cause. When Śaṅkara speaks of the material that constitutes the world, he often calls it *"nāmarūpa"*, "name-and form". The term *"nāmarūpa"* occurs in a number of Upaniṣads, most notably in *Bṛhadāraṇyaka* 1.4.7 and *Chāndogya* 6.3.2 and 8.14.1.[70] What is *nāmarūpa?* Śaṅkara understands the term to mean the primary stuff out of which the world is made. The world in toto is the evolution, or manifestation, of this primary material called name-and-form. The five elements are name-and form, and so too their products, the physical body as well as the subtle body, are "name-and-form".[71]

The expression "name-and-form" *(nāmarūpa)* is explained in the *Bṛhadāraṇyaka* 1.4.7 as a description of the manifest world of "named things":

> It [the world] manifested only as name-and-form: "this thing [i.e. X] has this form and it has such and such a name." To this day it [the world] is manifest only as name-and-form: "this thing has this form and it has such and such a name."

Here, name-and-form is a description of the world as it now stands revealed, for the manifest world contains innumerable forms to which various names are ascribed: such and such a form has such and such a name. Name-and-form is not used in this passage as a nomenclature for fundamental matter itself, whereas for Śaṅkara the expression name-and-form becomes a convenient label to refer to the constituent material of the universe. For Śaṅkara, the differentiated universe, beginning with the five material elements and continuing through all their various combinations, can be referred to as "name-and-form".

However by the term "name-and-form" Śaṅkara does not just mean the material of the visible, or manifest universe, but he also means the material that existed in a subtle and unmanifest condition, even before the universe was manifested. We can see the origin of this conception in

Bṛhadāraṇyaka 1.4.7, which commences with this statement: "That *(tat)* this *(idam)* [universe] was then unmanifested. It manifested only as name-and-form *(tat-ha-idaṁ tarhi-avyākṛtam āsīt, tad nāmarūpābhyām eva vyākriyata).*" Commenting upon this passage, Śaṅkara says the Upaniṣad wants to show that just as we can infer the existence of a tree in a seed form through the observation of its various effects, such as a sprout etc., so too, we should know that this manifest universe existed in an unmanifested "seed-state" *(bījāvasthā)* prior to its manifestation.[72] He says that the word "that" *(tat)* in the passage refers to the universe as it existed in its "seed-state", prior to its origination, while the word "this" *(idam)* refers the perceptible universe with its now differentiated names-and-forms. The grammatical co-ordination of the two words "that" and "this" which refer to the universe in its past and present states respectively, shows the identity of the universe in its causal and its effect states. Śaṅkara here accepts the position known as *satkāryavāda,* the doctrine that the effect pre-exists potentially in its material cause.[73] Śaṅkara is saying that the doctrine of *satkāryavāda* holds good when we are talking about relations between "matter" itself, for we can observe that gross matter emerges from more subtle, embryonic states of matter. But Śaṅkara does not accept that a relation of *satkāryavāda* actually exists between Brahman and the subtle matter, because Brahman is relationless *(asaṅga)* from its own standpoint.

As we have just seen, name-and-form is a term that refers to the constituent material of the universe; and that material can exist both in a manifest and in an unmanifest condition. Since it is the same material, in either a manifest or an unmanifest state, Śaṅkara sometimes uses the word *nāmarūpa* to refer just to the unmanifest condition of the primary stuff of the world, as when he calls name-and-form the "seed of the world" *(nāmarūpayor jagadbījabhūtayoḥ).*[74] On other occasions, he refers to this unmanifest condition by more specific terms. On the basis of the above Upaniṣad passage ("That... [universe] was then unmanifested" *(tat...tarhi-avyākṛtam āsīt)*), where we see the use of the word "unmanifested" *(avyākṛtam),* Śaṅkara often refers to the primary material, in its subtle, unmanifest condition, by the word *avyākṛta* ("unmanifested" or "unevolved"). Sometimes he refers to it by the word *avyakta* ("unmanifested"). And sometimes, but only in certain contexts, by the word *akṣara* ("imperishable"). Śaṅkara also refers to this condition of the unmanifested primary material, i.e., the *avyākṛta*, *avyakta*, or (sometimes) *akṣara*, as "the potentiality belonging to name-and form" *(nāmarūpabījaśakti)*.[75] Here, the expression *bījaśakti* seems to be a *karmadhārya* compound, since he uses this expression by itself on a number of other occasions,[76] and it would mean a "seed-potency" *(bījarūpā śaktiḥ)*. The idea seems to be that what is meant by the words *avyākṛta* etc. is the potentiality inherent in the unmanifest name-and-form. And this "potentiality" is called by the word *śakti* ("power") because it is: "the combination of all powers of causes and effects"[77] and it is also called *bīja* ("seed") as it is: "the seed for all bodies and organs".[78] This unmanifest name-and-form *(avyākṛtanāmarūpa)*, which is the potential condition for the manifest name-and-form, constitutes the subtle limiting adjunct *(upādhi)* of the Lord, and when the Lord creates the world, it is by way of the manifestation of this subtle *upādhi* called unmanifest name-and-form.[79]

We shall discuss further this concept of the "potentiality" *(bījaśakti)* of the unmanifest name-and-form in the next section. At present we shall confine ourselves to the question of the ontological status of this constitutive material that Śaṅkara calls name-and-form. There are a number of occasions in the *Brahmasūtrabhāṣya*, as well as elsewhere, when Śaṅkara qualifies the expression *nāmarūpa* by a particular phrase, *tattvānyatvābhyām anirvacanīya*, which means: "indeterminable, or inexpressible *(anirvacanīya)*, as *tattva* or as something else *(anya)*." Paul Hacker has drawn attention to this significant, but enigmatic phrase, and has asked the pertinent question: "what does the word *tattva* in the compound mean?"[80] The meaning of the whole expression hangs upon the meaning of the word *tattva*. Hacker lists four occasions in the *Brahmasūtrabhāṣya* where *nāmarūpa*, or *avyakta*, is described as not determinable as either "*tattva*" or as something else. He proposes two possibilities regarding the meaning of the word *tattva*. Firstly, he says it could be the abstract form of a demonstrative pronoun *(tat)* which must then refer to some previously or subsequently mentioned noun. The expression would mean that *nāmarūpa* is indefinable as either "being of the nature of 'that' *(tattva*= Brahman, or Īśvara, or Parameśvara, depending on which of these words occur in one of the passages), or as being something other than that". Thus the meaning would be that *nāmarūpa* cannot be categorically determined as either identical to Brahman or as something other than Brahman.

Hacker rejects this possibility, because in one of the four instances (1.4.3) the noun Parameśvara is not in sufficient contiguity with *tattvānyatva* to justify the pronominal use of the word *tattva.* He says that the issue is decided in the passage (2.1.14) where the next sentence to the one under discussion states: "...Īśvara is other than name-and-form." Hacker says: "this emphasis on difference would be unintelligible if, by means of the *tattvānyatvābhyām* occurring just one line before, it were meant that name and form are neither different nor identical with Īśvara."[81] The second possibility is that the word *tattva* means "essence", i.e., "reality", and does not refer to a preceding or following noun. Hacker accepts this explanation and he believes that the whole expression means that *nāmarūpa* cannot be determined as real ("that") or as something else, because the *nāmarūpa* does not exist in a stable state of being. Hacker says: "one can never say, 'It is that' or 'It is something else', for just as it wanted to unfold itself in the primal state, so now it always wants to transform itself and is never anything constant."[82]

I do not believe that Hacker has accurately explained the meaning of *tattvānyatvābhyām anirvacanīya,* and his own explanation, according to the grammar of the texts, is somewhat forced.[83] Accepting his argument that *tattva* is not an abstract pronominal form, the expression *tattvānyatvābhyām anirvacanīya* would then mean: "not determinable as a reality or as something else". But the expression would be better understood in an ontological sense, as referring to the ontological status of *nāmarūpa,* rather than as a cosmological statement about the unstable nature of the primary material that is always ready to transform itself.

There is another instance of this expression that deserves consideration. It occurs in Śaṅkara's commentary upon the *Bṛhadāraṇyaka* Upaniṣad. The passage reads:

> It is *nāmarūpa* that constitutes the limiting adjunct of the Supreme Self, and in becoming manifest, *nāmarūpa* cannot be categorically stated as either a real thing *(tattva),* or as something else, analogous to [the relation between] foam and water.[84]

The illustration of the foam and water occurs a number of times in Śaṅkara's works[85] and his use of this illustration may help us clarify the meaning of the expression *tattvānyatvābhyām anirvacanīya.* While commenting upon an earlier passage in the *Bṛhadāraṇyaka* Upaniṣad, Śaṅkara said:

> The unmanifest *nāmarūpa* which is identified with that [supreme Self], becomes manifest, like dirty foam from clear water. The [supreme Self] is distinct from *nāmarūpa.*[86]

A passage from the *Upadeśasāhasrī* provides the clearest account of his use of this illustration:

> The unmanifest name-and-form, in the course of becoming manifested from the Ātman, became the name and the form "space".[87] That element known as space arose in this way from the Supreme Self, like dirty foam from clear water. The foam is not water, nor is it something entirely different from water, for it is not seen apart from water. The water, however, is clear and is other than the foam which is a form of dirt. Similarly, the Supreme Self is other than the name-and-form which corresponds to the foam; the Supreme Self is pure, clear and different from that name-and-form. The name-and-form was unmanifested and in the course of becoming manifest it became the name and the form "space", corresponding to the foam.[88]

We see here that the first element of manifest *nāmarūpa*, the element space, arose "from the supreme Self, like dirty foam from clear water." The foam, "is not water, nor is it something entirely different from water, for it is not seen apart from water." On the basis of this analogy, we can see that the *nāmarūpa* (to which the foam refers in the illustration) must be ontologically indeterminable: it is not identical to Brahman, just as the foam is not identical to water; nor is it entirely different from Brahman, as it does not have an independent existence. Thus *nāmarūpa* cannot be determined as identical to the only ontological reality, Brahman, nor can it be determined as something other than Brahman. So even though the word *tattva* is not a pronominal form, and therefore has no grammatical relation to Brahman in the various contexts where the expression *tattvānyatvābhyām anirvacanīya* occurs, when the expression says that *nāmarūpa* is indeterminable as a reality *(tattva)* it must mean that *nāmarūpa* is not determinable as identical to Brahman, since Brahman is the only reality. The Supreme Self, however, is explicitly said in the above passage to be: "other than the name-and-form". Thus while *nāmarūpa* [A] is indeterminable as identical or different from Brahman [B], the latter is independent of, or "untouched" by, the former. This is exactly the meaning of this passage in the *Brahmasūtrabhāṣya* 2.1.14:

> Name-and-form is constructed by *avidyā*, it can neither be categorically stated as real or otherwise; it is the seed of the entire expanse of phenomenal existence; it constitutes the very self, as it were, of the omniscient Lord and it is referred to in both the *śruti* and the *smṛti* as the *māyāśakti* and the *prakṛti* of the omniscient Lord. The omniscient Lord is other than the name-and-form, as we know from the *śruti*... .[89]

Hacker's objection referred to above ["this emphasis on difference would be unintelligible if, by means of the *tattvānyatvābhyām* occurring just one line before, it were meant that name and form are neither different nor identical with Īśvara."[90]] misses the point of Advaita, which is that while *nāmarūpa* is not determinable as real or as something else, i.e., as identical to Brahman or as different from Brahman, the latter is different from the former [A is non-separate from B, though B is independent of A]. This is entirely consistent with Śaṅkara's statements in both his *Bṛhadāraṇyaka* commentary and the *Upadeśasāhasrī*, cited above. So although Hacker is most probably right that the word *tattva* is not a pronoun referring to Brahman, and that it literally means "thatness", i.e., "essence", or "reality", the term nonetheless ultimately refers to Brahman because Brahman is the final measure of reality. This interpretation harmonises with a kārikā of Gauḍapāda cited earlier:

> This plurality does not exist as identical to the Self nor even does it somehow exist of its own accord. Those who know reality, know that nothing exists different [from the Self] or as identical [to the Self].[91] [2.34]

The expression *tattvānyatvābhyām anirvacanīya* is not a cosmological expression, but it is a statement about the ontological reality of the material of which the world consists.[92]

In a passage in his commentary upon the *Bṛhadāraṇyaka* Upaniṣad 3.5.1, Śaṅkara says that ultimately *nāmarūpa* has no independent existence apart from Brahman and therefore it does not constitute a second thing to Brahman. This passage is significant, because it indicates what he means by non-duality: that while *nāmārūpa* is non-separate from Brahman, Brahman is independent of *nāmārūpa* .

> [Objection] If you admit the existence of the limiting adjunct of name-and-form, the *śrutis* such as "one only, without a second" (CU 6.2.1) and "there is no diversity whatsoever here" (BU 4.4.19) will be contradicted.
> [Reply] No. This has been refuted through the illustration of the water and foam and illustrations like clay [and the pot] etc. But when, from the perspective of the highest truth *(paramārtha),* those who follow the *śruti* seek to ascertain whether name-and-form is different from the Supreme Self, the fact is that it is not a different thing, just as the modifications of clay [are not different entities from clay]. It is just like the foam of water and the modifications such as pots etc. The *śrutis,* "one only, without a second", "there is no diversity whatsoever here" etc. are understood as having regard to that highest truth. But when, on account of natural ignorance, Brahman - though remaining in its own condition like the rope, the mother-of-pearl and the sky, and inherently untouched by anything - is not ascertained, through discrimination, from the limiting adjuncts of the body and the sense organs which are the effects of name-and-form, there results the

> natural outlook that one is identical to the limiting adjunct of name-and-form. Then there is all this phenomenal life consisting of the existence of different entities.[93]

The name-and-form is ontologically *mithyā (tattvānyatvābhyām anirvacanīya),* and therefore there is the possibility of Advaita, because name-and-form does not constitute a second reality to Brahman.

(5) Avidyā

In this section we will discuss the concept of *avidyā,* and its relation to *nāmarūpa,* in the light of the important article by Paul Hacker, *"Distinctive features of the Doctrine and Terminology of Śaṅkara:* Avidyā, Nāmarūpa, Māyā, Īśvara".[94] We will then refer to a contemporary debate in Advaita circles about the nature of *avidyā,* as can be found in the writings of Śrī Saccidānandendra Sarasvatī.

In the introductory portion to his *Brahmasūtrabhāṣya,* Śaṅkara defines *avidyā* as synonymous with superimposition *(adhyāsa):* "The wise consider this superimposition...to be *'avidyā'.*" Hacker sees this statement, occurring right at the beginning of the commentary, as providing a clear understanding of what Śaṅkara means by *avidyā,* namely that it means the same as *adhyāsa.* Hacker goes on to say that when Śaṅkara uses the term *mithyājñāna* ("false cognition") he uses it in the same sense as *avidyā.* He says that this distinguishes Śaṅkara from later Advaitins for whom *avidyā* is the cause of *mithyājñāna.* Hacker goes on to explain:

> For Ś.'s successors and even several of his contemporaries and precursors, *avidyā* is something quite unique: [it is] the material cause of all errors and the entire manifold world... . Ś., on the other hand, considers *avidyā* to fall under another, more general concept: *avidyā* is a *kleśa.* It is the first, most important, and most dangerous member in a chain of other *kleśas* which are caused by it. This point of view is very close to that of the Yoga system [cf. *Yogasūtra* 2.3].[95]

> *Avidyā* is for Ś., in contrast to other Advaitins, more an affliction of the psyche *(kleśa)* than a cosmic power *(śakti)*.[96]

What Hacker says is plausible, as can be seen from a number of Śaṅkara's statements, for example: "*avidyā* is the idea of Self in regard to the body etc. which are not the Self."[97] But this explanation of *avidyā*, as meaning just *adhyāsa*, encounters a difficulty when we find that the world is spoken of as "caused" *(kṛta)*, "presented" *(pratyupasthāpita)* or even "superimposed" *(adhyasta)* by *avidyā*.[98] And the latter instance, in particular, seems to indicate that *avidyā* and *adhyāsa* cannot always be treated as synonyms, for it is hardly intelligible to say that something is "superimposed by superimposition". In spite of providing such examples, Hacker can still affirm that: "in his [Śaṅkara's] case *avidyā* is never designated as the material cause of the physical world."[99]

Hacker, however, restricts the scope of his original assertion, because later in his article he acknowledges that there are occasions when the terms *nāmarūpa* and *avidyā* are expressly related. He cites a number of passages, but perhaps the most important are from the *Brahmasūtrabhāṣya* 1.4.2-3, and 1.4.9. Hacker translates these passages:

> [The Upaniṣad passage BU 1.4.7] shows that 'this', i.e., the world, which is fragmented in manifest names and forms, can, in its original state, when it exists in a state of seed potency in which name and form are not yet unfolded, be designated by the word 'the unmanifest'. ...But we recognize that this original state of the world is dependent on the highest Lord and does not exist independently. And it is necessary to assume that there is such an [original state], for it serves a purpose. For without it a creative activity on the part of the highest Lord would not be possible, since He cannot act if He is without potency. Moreover, those who are liberated are not born again. Why? Because [for them] that seed potency is burned up by knowledge. For the seed potency is essentially ignorance, which can be referred to by the word 'the unmanifest'; which has the highest Lord as its substratum; and which is the great sleep

> consisting of *māyā* in which the souls lie, not yet awakened to their true nature, wandering in *saṃsāra*. The same 'unmanifest' is sometimes designated by the word 'ether' ...[citation of BU 3.8.11)....Sometimes it is expressed by the expression 'the imperishable' ...[MU2.1.2]....Sometimes it is called *māyā*... [ŚvU 4.10]....[100]
>
> Precisely this divine power of creation, in which name and form are un-unfolded, is intended as the original state of name and form in this Vedic verse (ŚvU 4.5).[101]

Hacker recognises that in the context of the above passages Śaṅkara speaks of a *śakti* as something "material". Hacker says: "But this power is not just a capacity. It is also a substance out of which God forms the world: the *śakti* of Īśvara is a *bīja-śakti*."[102]

Hacker's line of thought may be summarised as follows. For Śaṅkara the "unmanifest name-and-form" *(avyākṛta [nāmarūpa]* or *avyakta [nāmarūpa])* is a type of subtle primary material that exists as a "seed potency" *(bījaśakti)*. This *avyākṛtanāmarūpa* is closely related to *avidyā*, but it is not quite identified with *avidyā*, for Śaṅkara frequently constructs compounds where it is said that *nāmarūpa* is "made" *(kṛta)*, "brought forth" *(pratyupasthāpita)*, or "superimposed" *(kalpita, adhyasta* etc.) by *avidyā*.[103] In these senses the meaning of *avidyā* still remains vague. Occasionally the *avyākṛtanāmarūpa* is said to be of "the nature of *avidyā*" *(avidyāmaka)*. So though *avyākṛtanāmarūpa* and *avidyā* may not be identical concepts, they are closely related, and at times they are even equated. Hacker says, and I believe his view to be accurate, that what later Advaitins have done is to discard the concept of the unmanifest *nāmarūpa* and attribute its capacities directly to *avidyā*. Thus *avidyā* is said to be the material cause *(upādāna)* and indeterminable *(anirvācya)*, terms which in Śaṅkara's works apply only to the *avyākṛtanāmarūpa*.[104]

According to Hacker, *avidyā* is used in two senses, both as the equivalent of *adhyāsa* and as identified with the *avyākṛtanāmarūpa*, the material cause of the world. He says that when the word *avidyā* is used by itself it means the same as *adhyāsa*. But on some occasions *avidyā* (also *māyā)* and *avyākṛtanāmarūpa* mean one and the same thing, but that is only when they are specifically identified, and "only when they are explicitly referred to as the prime matter of the universe."[105] We can see that although at the beginning of his article Hacker says categorically that: "for Ś. *avidyā* is the same as *mithyājñāna*" (i.e. *adhyāsa*), he modifies this view later in the article and rightly acknowledges that there are occasions when Śaṅkara equates the terms *avidyā* and *māyā* with *avyākṛtanāmarūpa*, regarding the latter as a power, or *śakti*.

There is no such latitude shown in the writings of Śrī Swami Saccidānandendra Sarasvatī, who stoutly maintains that according to Śaṅkara *avidyā* means only *adhyāsa* and that Śaṅkara does not entertain any notion of *avidyā* as a power, or *śakti*. He further argues that from Padmapāda onwards the entire Advaita tradition deviates from the teachings of Śaṅkara and that Sureśvara alone is faithful to the original teaching. The controversial writings of Saccidānandendra, in fluent Sanskrit as well as in English, have become influential in some Vedānta circles in India, especially around Mysore and Bangalore, and also in Delhi. If fact, if there has been a debate internal to the Śāṅkara tradition of Advaita over the last fifty years, it is the dispute between the protagonists of the views of Saccidānandendra and those who would defend the standard position. Given the significance of this issue for Advaita I intend to discuss it at some length, though it could well be treated to a monograph in its own right.[106]

In order to understand the thought of Saccidānandendra in its proper context we should first review the major work of his "guru", K.A. Krishnaswamy Iyer.[107] Saccidānandendra (formerly Y. Subba Rao) came under the influence of K.A. Krishnaswamy Iyer when, as a student at Central College, Bangalore, he received boarding and lodging at the house of Krishnaswamy Iyer who was then a teacher at that College. Later, when Subbha Rao was himself a school headmaster in Bangalore, it is said that he: "once again came under the benign patronage and guidance of K.A. Krishnaswamy Iyer."[108] A brief biographical account of Saccidānandendra records their relationship:

> Under the paternal care and guidance of Kṛishṇaswāmy Iyer he was able to realize as to how much injustice had been done to genuine, traditional Vedānta, in general, and to Śaṅkara, in particular. With a view to getting rid of all

> doubts and anomalies both Kṛishṇaswāmy Iyer and Subbharāya met Hānagal Virūpākṣa Shāstri and raised the issue. They were shocked out of their wits, so to speak, when Shāstriji, in reply to a pertinent query, answered that - "For Prārabdha Karma to remain, a remnant part of Avidyā alone is the cause; in other words, in Jñānis too there remains a little bit of ignorance."
>
> On their own, both the mentor Iyer and the pupil Subbharāya considered seriously the paradoxical question - "...how at all could such a spurious admixture of fallacious, highly imaginative Avidyā doctrines get into the mainstream and where from?" Lo and behold! They could pin-point and point out that the distorted interpretations of the original Bhāshya sentences by the Vyākhyānakāras [sub-commentators] were in themselves the real culprit and had played the role of the 'villain of the piece', so to speak, in this whole bizarre drama.[109]

When we look at the major work of K.A. Krishnaswamy Iyer, *Vedanta or The Science of Reality,* first published in 1930, and subsequently republished by the Adhyatma Prakasha Karyalaya founded by Swami Saccidānandendra, we can see that it contains most of the ideas that were so trenchantly argued by Saccidānandendra himself. That the author of *Vedanta or The Science of Reality* was a keen student of Western philosophy and literature is obvious, for six chapters of his book are given over to an examination of Western philosophy. Kant is discussed sympathetically, and so too is Hegel. However the purpose of these chapters is not to elucidate Western philosophy to an Indian audience, but to show the limitations of Western thought when compared to the perfect science of Vedānta, as understood by the author. It is evident that the whole work is written against a background of Western thought. For instance, expressions reminiscent of the thought of Hegel can occasionally be seen, as when Krishnaswamy Iyer says: "The world is perfecting itself, and history is on the march of the cosmic spirit towards its self-realization."[110] And just as Hegel wrote of a transcendence of opposites, of subject and object, into a higher "self-consciousness", Krishnaswamy Iyer too speaks of the transcendence of subject and object in the state of deep sleep, which is nothing but pure Consciousness itself.[111] In fact we may hypothesise at the outset that Krishnaswamy Iyer put forward a teaching of Vedānta that received its fundamental impetus - in terms of its central aim, which was to demonstrate Vedānta rationally, on the basis of an analysis of common, empirical experience - from some of the then current ideas of the West; and the works of Śrī Saccidānandendra Sarasvatī are but a refinement of that initial "Western inspired" teaching, and are an attempt to integrate it into the arena of traditional Vedānta by arguing for its validity as the correct interpretation of Śaṅkara.

Krishnaswamy Iyer argues that Vedānta is a science of reality. The word "science" indicates that Vedānta proceeds by way of an empirical method, that its conclusions are testable and result from a rational investigation of common experience, rather than from some kind of private, mystical "experience". As the author writes in his Introduction: "For it [Vedānta] is a science, and like the truths of mathematics or physics, its declarations are verifiable by immediate reference to the facts of life."[112] The empirical method that he puts forward is the analysis of three conditions with which everyone is familiar: waking, dream and deep sleep. This method is ultimately based upon the Upaniṣads, particularly the *Māṇḍūkya* Upaniṣad. But having received the initial insight from the Upaniṣads, Krishnaswamy Iyer does not dwell on the Upaniṣads at any length, for he principally wants to demonstrate the essential rationality and universal applicability of the Vedāntic understanding, and so he keeps his sources in the background. In the following words he presents a summation of his teaching:

> Life manifests itself in three typical states. Of these, waking and dream cannot be identified, each [exists] by itself; and sleep is considered as such because the waking intellect finds it a pure negation of all that is familiar to it as life. But sleep by itself is Pure Consciousness, that is, consciousness free from the subject-object form, and that is the essence of the human spirit. It is *not* unconsciousness, which we can never conceive. The three states do not succeed each other, but are absolutely independent, and our memory of sleep and dream is not memory in the common

> conception of the term. Time, space and causation characterise waking and dream, but their dominion is *within* each of the latter, not outside, so that the states have no connection of any sort with one another. I cognize the states, hence I am in each of them and yet I isolate myself from dream and waking when I, as now, contemplate them, and in sleep I am wholly identical with Pure Consciousness which is my essence, what I am truly. Pure Consciousness never changes, as it transcends time and causation, and hence essentially I am ever one with it.[113]

He says here that: (a) there are three distinct states of consciousness which everyone experiences: waking, dreaming and deep sleep. (b) Waking and dream are unconnected. It is not the case that dream is ontologically dependent on the waking state, rather they are entirely distinct states in terms of space and time, and there is a different ego subject in each state: the waking ego does not dream, nor does the dream ego awaken. (c) The subject-object relationship that exists between the ego and the world in these two states is entirely concomitant with the state itself. Thus each state is inclusive of its own world. Just as the dream ego and the dream world simultaneously arise and disappear, so does the waker and the waking world, and it is illegitimate to believe that the waking world continues to exist when one is dreaming. (d) Since the states of waking and dream are transient, the knowledge of them as a series is only due to the persistence of a principle distinct from them, i.e., the unchanging Witness Consciousness, or Pure Consciousness. (e) Strictly speaking, deep sleep is not a "state" at all, for in sleep there is Pure Consciousness and nothing else. (f) The fact that the state of deep sleep as pure Consciousness itself - free from all subject-object relations which are concomitant to the states of waking and dream - can be intuited from a rational reflection on everyday experience, means that no special spiritual experience is required above and beyond reflection upon one's ordinary experience. (g) Pure Consciousness, which we call as "deep sleep", while remaining intrinsically unchanged (for that too is our experience), somehow - inexplicably - splits itself into both subject and object in the waking and dream states.

We can see that Krishnaswamy Iyer has essentially based his philosophy upon the examination of the states of experience as revealed in the *Māṇḍūkya* Upaniṣad. But he has interpreted this Upaniṣad in a most radical manner, as teaching that the states of waking and dream are entirely discontinuous worlds.[114] Krishnaswamy Iyer says that it is illegitimate to reason beyond what is actually given in experience itself. It is natural, but erroneous, to believe that the waking world persists during dream or sleep, because to do so is to reason from the experience of the waking state. For in dream and sleep there is no knowledge whatsoever of the waking world, and it is only from the waking perspective that we call dream unreal and we call sleep as a state of unconsciousness. In fact, dream is equally as real or as unreal as the waking state itself, for dream has its own space and time that we call unreal only from the perspective of the waking state. So too sleep can be called an experience of unconsciousness only from the standpoint of the waking state, whereas in fact it is Pure Consciousness, free from subject and object. This intuition of Pure Consciousness, as the invariable Witness of the states of waking and dream, can be arrived at by anyone who is prepared to reflect on the three states of experience without giving an unwarranted bias to the waking state, which, he adds, is the major fault of Western philosophy.

There is no doubt that Krishnaswamy Iyer is teaching Advaita, but it is of a very radical type which does not seem to me to reflect the bulk of the teachings of the Upaniṣads, nor the teachings of Śaṅkara, nor even of Gauḍapāda. Krishnaswamy Iyer repeatedly appeals to one's intuition: this knowledge of Pure Consciousness is arrived at by intuition, through an unbiased reflection on our own experience. But while it is true that our conclusions about dream and sleep are only from the standpoint of the waking state, I feel that it is counter-intuitive to hold that the waking world does not exist during dream or deep sleep. Krishnaswamy Iyer recognises, of course, that we feel and act as though the waking world persisted while we were asleep, but he argues that this is a fallacious inference based upon the uncertain testimony of memory which is "unreliable as a means of ascertaining the absolute truth" (p.107). However, later, he himself relies on memory, in this case the memory of the absence of subject and object in sleep, to imply the presence of an unchanged Witness Consciousness (p.168). So while he disregards the testimony of memory in one sphere, he does utilise it when he wishes to prove something else.

Furthermore, it is hard to see how his teaching, which does not posit a common world persisting in dream or sleep, can avoid some sort of solipsism involving parallel worlds, where each *jīva* transacts in its own world that is individually manifested by God, and which is so similar to the worlds of the other *jīvas* that common interaction is possible. While the teaching of Krishnaswamy Iyer has a place for a conception of God - as the dynamic consciousness that manifests the worlds of waking and dream - since he does not believe that there is the objective manifestation of a world by God, he seems to have to logically accept a kind of solipsism, though he wishes to deny it at a practical level (p.253).

Further, if sleep is essentially nothing but pure Consciousness then there are really only two states of ordinary experience, waking and dream. What is called "sleep" from the waking standpoint is actually the "state" of pure Consciousness that underlies these two. Thus when he refers to the syllable OM (AUM) as presented in the *Māṇḍūkya*, he says that: "A stands for all waking experience, U for dream experience and M for deep sleep or Pure Consciousness".[115] But that is not correct, because the *Māṇḍūkya* speaks of three states of ordinary experience, as well as the "fourth state", the underlying Consciousness. The letter A represents the waker and the waking world, the letter U represents the dreamer and the dream world and the letter M represents sleep. The Upaniṣad then speaks of the "non-letter" *(amātra)* which is the underlying Self. Thus the *Māṇḍūkya* speaks of three ordinary states, waking, dream and sleep, plus the underlying "fourth" *(turīya)*. But Krishnaswamy Iyer can, and does. speak only of two ordinary states.

Finally, while he wishes to present the view that what we call deep sleep is nothing but pure Consciousness, he occasionally suggests that something is required to account for our experience of the personal continuities that reappear upon waking, as when he says: "In deep sleep personality cannot be predicated of reality but must be assumed to have remained in a germinal or latent condition".[116] What this "germinal condition" is, he does not say. Swami Saccidānandendra recognised that there were still some vestiges of the influence of the *Pañcadaśī* in the thought of Krishnaswamy Iyer, and he pointed this out in his own Introductory Remarks to the second edition.

For the most part, the fundamental ideas of Krishnaswamy Iyer are replicated in the work of his "pupil" Saccidānandendra Sarasvatī. This is especially so in the case of his earliest and most important polemical work, *Mūlāvidyānirāsa.*[117] Here, Saccidānandendra sets out to refute the belief that Gauḍapāda, Śaṅkara or Sureśvara taught the view current in later Advaita, that there exists a causal power called, among other names, Ignorance *(avidyā).* According to this view, *avidyā* is ontologically *mithyā,* i.e., it is categorically indeterminable as either absolutely real *(sat)* or as totally unreal *(asat);* but since it is not totally unreal, it must have some sort of positive existence *(bhāvarūpa).* This power called *avidyā* conceals the true nature of reality, and it brings about the projection of the world. Though it is removed by the knowledge of the Self as Brahman, its impressions still persist subsequent to the rise of such knowledge, for it is only in this way that the continued existence of the person who is liberated while living in the world *(jīvanmukta)* can be explained. Saccidānandendra argues that all such ideas are the inventions of later commentators beginning with Padmapāda, who said:

> Beginningless Ignorance *(avidyā)* is referred to in various ways in the *śruti,* the *smṛti, itihāsa* and the *purāṇas:* as "name-and-form" *(nāmarūpa),* the "unmanifested", or "unevolved" *(avyākṛta),* Ignorance *(avidyā), māyā,* "Nature" *(prakṛti),* "non-perception" *(agrahaṇa),* "the unmanifest" *(avyakta),* "darkness" *(tamas),* "the Cause" *(kāraṇa),* "Dissolution" *(laya),* "Power" *(śakti),* "the Great Sleep" *(mahāsupti),* "Sleep" *(nidrā),* "Imperishable" *(akṣara)* and as "Space" *(ākāśa).*[118]

According to Saccidānandendra, Gauḍapāda, Śaṅkara and Sureśvara taught no such doctrine of a positively existing causal *avidyā.* When Śaṅkara uses the term *avidyā* he just means superimposition *(adhyāsa),* for that is how he himself explained *avidyā* at the beginning of his *Brahmasūtrabhāṣya:* "Learned people consider that the superimposition, so defined, is "ignorance" *(avidyā).*"[119] Saccidānandendra says we need not try to trace the cause of superimposition, and indeed we cannot, since the idea of cause and effect depends upon superimposition, as does all our epistemological activity beginning with knowership itself. However, if one still seeks for the origin of superimposition, he says superimposition can be said to be "caused" by a sheer absence of knowledge *(jñānābhāva)* amounting to non-discrimination *(aviveka)*, which results in superimposition. Saccidānandendra says that in the work of Śaṅkara the nature of *avidyā* is:

> the mutual identification between the Self and the not-Self and the superimposition of their attributes. Various expressions signifying *avidyā* are found in the commentary, such as: "superimposition" *(adhyāsa, adhyāropa)*, "erroneous inversion" *(viparyaya)*, "error" *(viparyāsa)*, "wrong knowledge" *(mithyājñāna)*, "wrong cognition" *(mithyāpratyaya)*, "misapprehension" *(anyathāgrahaṇa)*, "darkness" *(tamas)*, "confusion" *(bhrānti)* and "delusion" *(moha)*.[120]

And he distinguishes the above terms from other terms used by Śaṅkara, all indicating the mere absence of discriminative knowledge *(jñānābhāva)*:

> This absence of discrimination is taught in the Commentary by a variety of synonyms all referring to a want of knowledge: "Ignorance", i.e., absence of knowledge *(ajñāna)*, "non-apprehension" *(agrahaṇa)*, "not knowing" *(anavabodha)*, "not understanding" *(anavagama)* and "not awakening" *(apratibodha)*. At some places [the absence of discrimination], in so far as it is the cause of the wrong knowledge *(mithyājñāna)* [i.e. superimposition], is also referred to as the "cause" *(kāraṇa)*, "seed" *(bīja)* and "sleep" *(nidrā, supti)*, and when that is so, wrong knowledge is then spoken of as the "effect" *(kārya)*, "result" *(phala)* or as "dream" *(svapna)*.[121]

Thus according to Saccidānandendra, *avidyā* means superimposition and it is only in later Vedānta, beginning with Padmapāda, that a causal power called *avidyā* is postulated as the cause of superimposition.

For Saccidānandendra, the assault on the concept of a causal power called *avidyā* is not just a theoretical exercise, it is important because of its soteriological consequences. In order to appreciate this, we need to focus upon some of the central ideas of Saccidānandendra's teaching. In his commentary upon the *Taittirīya* Upaniṣad, Śaṅkara provides the following definition of reality:

> Something is real when, once it is ascertained to be in a certain condition, that condition is not found to alter. Conversely, if a thing is ascertained to be in a certain condition but that condition alters, that thing is said to be unreal. Therefore that which undergoes change [or modification, *vikāra]* is unreal.[122]

Saccidānandendra cites this definition and applies it to the context of the three states of experience, waking, dreaming and deep sleep, and he says that if the causal power called *avidyā* is present in all these states of experience, as the tradition of Advaita accepts, then *avidyā* must be, by definition, real, and so it could not be removed.[123] Such a consequence would, of course, be unwelcome for Advaita. But since Saccidānandendra argues that a positively existing causal power is an erroneous concept fostered on the teachings of Gauḍapāda and Śaṅkara by later commentators, he is able to escape from this conclusion by denying the existence of such an *avidyā* altogether. And he is able to show that there is a situation within the experience of everyone where *avidyā* in the meaning of superimposition completely ceases, and that is the "state" of deep sleep. Although superimposition, starting with knowership and involving the experience of duality, is present in waking and in dream, it is entirely absent in deep sleep. Thus Saccidānandendra points to deep sleep as a "state" that is entirely free from duality and is, in fact, nothing but pure Consciousness itself.

Saccidānandendra says:

> The Veda....teaches that dreamless sleep is a state where the Self rests in its own nature, bereft of the suffering entailed by the superimposition of plurality.[124]

In the same way as Krishnaswamy Iyer, Saccidānandendra proceeds primarily by way of a reflection upon the three states of experience, as revealed in some Upaniṣads, principally the *Māṇḍūkya*, and he argues that while superimposition and duality are concomitant with the states of waking and dream, there is no duality in deep sleep, for deep sleep is not a state at all, it is nothing but pure Consciousness. Only from the perspective of waking can deep sleep be considered a "state", whereas it is actually the underlying reality, pure Consciousness itself, which somehow - inexplicably - appears to transform into the world of waking and into the world of dream.

A consequence of this understanding is that a reflection on the everyday experience of waking, dream and dreamless sleep, as guided by the Upaniṣad teaching, is sufficient for liberation, and Saccidānandendra is dismissive of *samādhi*- orientated practices involving control of the mind. This is because knowledge of reality does not require the generation of any special type of experience; what is necessary is the intuition of the invariable pure Witness-Consciousness that underlies the states of waking and dream and exists on its own in the "state" which, from the perspective of waking, we call as deep sleep.

In keeping with his strictly empirical and phenomenological method of analysis Saccidānandendra says that the states of waking and dream are ontologically equivalent: they are equally real or equally unreal and we have no logical grounds for maintaining that the waking state has a greater reality than dream, for it is our experience, he says, that both waking and dream arise and disappear, and when one is present the other is completely absent.

> The world that is perceived in any given state (waking or dream) of subject-object consciousness is peculiar to that state, and cannot be separated from it.[125]

> ...it is right to dismiss the worlds of waking and dream as mere false appearances. For they are only perceived in the states which condition them, and in dreamless sleep they disappear.[126]

> What we teach is that the universe that is seen in waking is related only to the waking state, and is not perceived or found in any other state.[127]

Like Krishnaswamy Iyer, Saccidānandendra argues that the states of waking and dream exist in their own space-time and we are not entitled, out of bias in favour of the reality of the waking state, to cling to the belief that the waking world continues during dream or sleep. When there is dream there is no waking world, just as in waking there is no dream world, and in deep sleep there is no experience of any world at all. He says that there is no common time frame between waking, dream and the "state" we call deep sleep. And when that is accepted, the consequence is that waking and dream cannot be causally related. He says:

> Perhaps you will say that it is possible to infer the existence of time interpenetrating and supporting the states of waking, dream and dreamless sleep, because they come and go. ... But this argument is not correct. For in dreamless sleep no one has experience of time. The claim that the three states (of waking, dream and dreamless sleep) come and go and belong to a single time series is in contradiction with experience, and should therefore be rejected as an error. ...And when that has been conceded, one cannot make out that they stand to one another in the relation of cause and effect.[128]
>
> ...it is a mistake to suppose that dreams consist of impressions (vāsanā) of waking experience.[129]
>
> So we should conclude with confidence that the world perceived in waking and the world perceived in dream are both equally illusory. For the appearance of both is of limited duration, and they cease to exist in dreamless sleep.[130]

To sum up the main teachings of Saccidānandendra: (1) on the basis of the definition of unreality as what is subject to change, waking and dream are found to be equally unreal. (2) The Witness Consciousness is real, as it persists in waking and dream - for change could not be known without an unchanging principle that is the witness of change - and it alone exists in the state called deep sleep. (3) There is no causal power called *avidyā* and therefore in deep sleep there is nothing but the Self, pure Consciousness, free from all duality. (4) Liberation consists in the intuition of the pure Self as the Witness, together with the sublation - by knowledge - of the superimposition of waking and dream. What is required for liberation is reflection on the states of experience, leading to the sublation of the false and the intuition of the Self as the invariable Witness Consciousness. Liberation is not the outcome of any extraordinary experience and so it does not demand control of the mind leading to states like *samādhi*.

We should note that the most important aspect of his teaching is that deep sleep is not a state, but is pure Consciousness itself, and pure Consciousness can be intuited through a rational reflection upon one's everyday experience of the three states. His lengthy disquisition against the concept of a causal power called *avidyā* is primarily intended to negate the presence of such a power in deep sleep, so that the latter can be shown to be nothing but pure Consciousness itself; and pure Consciousness and non-duality can thereby become available as facts to be intuited by anyone capable of right reflection.

The teaching of Krishnaswamy Iyer and Saccidānandendra Sarasvatī (for it is fundamentally the same teaching) presents Advaita in an essentially rational form, since it asks us just to reflect in an unbiased manner upon our own experience. Their presentation of Advaita, however, is not free from difficulties. In Advaita, there are two methods to reveal the unreality *(mithyātva)* of things. The first involves the idea of change and permanence; what deviates *(vyabhicāri)* and what persists *(avyabhicāri)*. Change involves coupling being and non-being, for something must first cease to exist in order for change to even occur, but how can something that no longer exists be considered real? The equation of change with unreality can be seen in Gauḍapāda: "What does not exist at the beginning and at the end, likewise [does not exist] even in the present."[131] Śaṅkara too defines unreal and real in terms of change and the absence of change, as we can see from the definition in his *Taittirīya* commentary, cited earlier. There is another important method of discerning what is *mithyā*. This can be seen in the teaching of the *Chāndogya* Upaniṣad (6.1.4; 6.4.1ff.) and it can also be found in the writings of Śaṅkara, as for example: "What we understand is that, in truth, the effect is 'non-different', i.e., it does not exist separately, from that [Brahman] the [material] cause."[132] This method consists in the determination that a thing is *mithyā* when its existence cannot be established independently from the existence of its material cause *(adhiṣṭhāna-ananyatva)*, as can be seen in the case of a clay-pot in relation to its material cause, clay. The clay-pot is *mithyā*, because it has no existence of its own, its existence is just the existence of the material cause.

Saccidānandendra understands *mithyā* according to the first method, but he does not appear to make use of this other important way of determining something to be *mithyā*. The consequence is that he considers it is the changeability of the states of waking and dream that determine their unreality *(mithyātva)*, and that pure Consciousness can be ascertained only through the negation *(bādhā)* of these two states. His approach places considerable emphasis on the continued negation, by knowledge, of the states of waking and dream. However, if he took the second approach to understanding *mithyā*, then his focus would be more on the appreciation of the presence of pure Consciousness even in the waking state itself, since the latter stands to the former like the pot stands to the clay.

Furthermore, in his attempt to avoid contaminating the state we call deep sleep with a causal power called *avidyā* he actually maintains that unreal things do not require any material cause in order to appear:

> But could we not say that we are forced to assume the presence of Ignorance in dreamless sleep on the ground that the perception of the waking world afterwards would otherwise be inexplicable? Examples such as that of the manifestation of illusory silver in mother-of-pearl, followed by its cancellation and abolition, are found to be inexplicable without appeal to positive Ignorance as the material cause of the false appearance. And in the same

> way, does not the perception of the waking world prove the presence of positive Ignorance in dreamless sleep as the material cause of the waking world? [reply] Not so! For an illusory object does not require a material cause. We cannot say that a thing belongs to a system of causes and effects and at the same time is false.[133]

His teaching is that the waking and dream worlds, as they are unreal *(mithyā),* require no material cause in order to appear. But this is an extraordinary assertion that has no foundation in the Upaniṣads which are unanimous in their view that Brahman is the material cause of the world. Nor can it find justification in the commentaries of Śaṅkara who repeatedly speaks of Brahman as the material cause of the world.

Saccidānandendra does not see a causal relationship between waking and dream, they are entirely independent states in their own space and time, and when dream exists the world of waking does not exist. It is hard to see how this teaching avoids solipsism, even though Krishnaswamy Iyer and Saccidānandendra believe that it does not entail this outcome. Their arguments, however, are unconvincing. For if we believe that the waking world vanishes when a person is in dream or sleep (and though we cannot prove that it does not vanish, we equally cannot prove that it does) then there can be no common world of experience, and it is hard to avoid the conclusion that the appearance of a waking world is unique to each individual in the waking state, just like the appearance of a dream world is unique to each dreamer. This is in keeping with the teaching of *dṛṣṭisṛṣti,* i.e., the creation of the world is concurrent with the perception of the world, rather than the commonsense view of *sṛṣṭidṛṣṭi,* that the world is created and therefore it is seen. The latter view is supported by the majority of the statements in the Upaniṣads and it is also the position of Śaṅkara. In his *Mūlāvidyānirāsa,* Saccidānandendra says nothing about the existence of a creator, Īśvara, and this omission is significant, for the existence of Īśvara is normally associated with the explanation of the existence of the physical world. His denial of an objectively existing world, and his silence about Īśvara, are both consistent with the ultimate subjectivism of his position.

While there may be statements in the Upaniṣads that could be interpreted to support Saccidānandendra's contention that deep sleep is equivalent to pure Consciousness, there are other statements in the Upaniṣads that clearly do not support that position. Let us take one notable instance. The *Māṇḍūkya* Upaniṣad refers to the "fourth" *(turīya)*, i.e., the pure Consciousness-Self that underlies the three states of waking, dream and deep sleep. By using the word "fourth" the Upaniṣad specifically says that the third state, deep sleep, is not to be equated with the highest reality, and from this one could go on to postulate the presence of *avidyā* in deep sleep. However, according to Saccidānandendra, there can be no "fourth state", because deep sleep is nothing but pure Consciousness itself. Saccidānandendra acknowledges the difficulty that the word *turīya* has for his teaching and in the course of defending his position he says:

> ...the Veda does not teach the existence of any 'fourth state'. The Māṇḍūkya Upanishad does not intend to convey the existence of another 'state' beyond dreamless sleep.[134]

> The Vedas do not speak of any 'pure state' beyond dreamless sleep. If the Vedic texts speak of 'dreamless sleep and "the Fourth"' one is forced (by the teaching of the Veda taken as a whole) to take the two terms as having equivalent value.[135]

Saccidānandendra is not on strong ground here, for it is hard to refute the evidence provided by the direct mention of the word "fourth" *(turīya)* in the *Māṇḍūkya* Upaniṣad, and the Upaniṣad also explicitly refers to sleep as only the "third quarter" *(tṛtīyaḥ pādaḥ)*.

It is my opinion that many post-Śaṅkara Advaitins have, possibly in response to probing questions from their opponents, tended to focus rather excessively on the problem of the nature of *avidyā*, or *māyā* (treating here the two terms as identical in meaning); and perhaps also coming under the ubiquitous influence of the Sāṅkhya concept of *prakṛti* they have tended to materialise *avidyā-māyā* and treat it as a virtual reality in its own right. Of course it is *avidyā-māyā* that is postulated as the necessary bridge at the inexplicable juncture between the realms of *vyavahāra* and *paramārtha*. But even while Advaitins freely admit that the juncture between the *vyavahāra* and the *paramārtha* is incomprehensible and hence inexplicable and to say that it is *avidyā* or *māyā* ultimately means just that - they have nonetheless reified *avidyā-māyā* to the extent that it has almost become an entity it its own right. This approach has resulted in the often clear subordination of the concept of Īśvara to that of *māyā*, whereas I believe it would be more beneficial, both religiously and philosophically, to frankly acknowledge the inexplicability of the relation between the *vyavahāra* and the *paramārtha* and to keep Brahman as the central concern throughout. And Brahman is always equivalent to Īśvara from the cosmic perspective of the existence etc. of the world *(vyavahārataḥ)*, which is a fact many Advaitins seem to overlook. It is only from the acosmic perspective of the highest truth *(paramārthataḥ)*, which necessarily entails the understanding of the *mithyātva* of the world, that the Īśvara-ness of Brahman is found to disappear, leaving Brahman ever untransformed.[136]

That being said, there is sufficient evidence in the writings of Śaṅkara for us to acknowledge that he accepts some sort of veiling and creative power which we may call *māyā* or *avidyā*. We see that Gauḍapāda says:

> This unborn [non-dual, *turīya-ātman]* becomes different just through *māyā*, not otherwise. For if it becomes different in reality, the immortal would become mortal. [3.19]

Gauḍapāda hints that *māyā* is some kind of "power" when he says: "The Self, the effulgent one, apparently creates itself through itself due to its own *māyā* [2.12]." In the commentaries of Śaṅkara there are more explicit affirmations that *māyā* and *avidyā* refer to the power, or potency *(śakti)*, inherent in unmanifest name-and-form. For instance, in *Muṇḍaka* Upaniṣad 2.1.2 the statement occurs: "the Puruṣa is....beyond the transcendent imperishable *(puruṣaḥ....akṣarāt parataḥ paraḥ)*." Śaṅkara comments here that the "imperishable" *(akṣara)* means the "unmanifested" *(avyākṛta)*, and he says that it is a "limiting adjunct *(upādhi)* which is the seed of name-and-form", and that it is the *upādhi* of the supreme Being *(puruṣa)* who is intrinsically without any *upādhi*.[137] In his commentary upon *Brahmasūtra* 1.2.22, he repeats this identification and further explains the *Muṇḍaka* passage:

> The imperishable means the unmanifested. It is in the form of the power *(śakti)* that is the seed of name-and-form. It contains the subtle elements, it has Īśvara as its basis, it constitutes His limiting adjunct, and while higher than its own modifications, it is unmodified.[138]

In *Kaṭha* Upaniṣad 1.3.11 there is the statement: "Puruṣa is higher than the unmanifested" *(avyaktāt puruṣaḥ paraḥ)*. Here, Śaṅkara says:

> The unmanifested *(avyakta)* is the seed *(bīja)* of the whole world, it is the essence of unmanifested [or unevolved] name-and-form,[139] it is in the form of a combination of all the powers of causes and effects, it can be referred to by such terms as "unmanifested" *(avyakta)*, "unmanifested" [or unevolved] *(avyākṛta)*, "space" *(akāśa)*[140] etc., it entirely depends upon the supreme Self, it is like the power of a banyan tree in a tiny banyan seed.[141]

Śaṅkara most clearly presents the view that the "unmanifested" is a kind of potentiality, or power *(śakti)*, when he says in his commentary upon *Brahmasūtra* 1.4.3:

> We accept that this prior condition of the world is dependent upon the highest Lord, not something that exists independently. And that [prior state] must necessarily be accepted, for it is important. Without it the highest Lord cannot be shown to be a creator, for activity is not possible if He is without the power. And the reason why the liberated souls have no further birth is that the seed-potency *(bījaśakti)* [of name-and-form] is scorched by knowledge. For that seed-potency is of the nature of ignorance *(avidyātmikā)*. It is referred to by the word "unmanifested" *(avyakta)*, it has the supreme Lord as its basis, it is full of wondrous magic, it is a great sleep in which the transmigrating souls are lying without awakening to their own true nature.[142] The *śruti* refers to the "unmanifested" at some place by the word "space" *(akāśa)* (BU 3.8.11), at

> some other place by the word "imperishable" (MU 2.1.2), and at another place it is indicated by the word *"māyā"* (Śv 4.10). *Māyā* is surely unmanifested, because it cannot be ascertained as either real or as unreal.[143]

Another significant reference occurs in his commentary upon *Brahmasūtra* 1.4.9, where the topic under discussion concerns the word "unborn" *(ajā)* occurring in *Śvetāśvatara* Upaniṣad 4.5. Śaṅkara says it is evident from a study of the context that the word *ajā* in the mantra refers to:

> the same divine power *(saiva daivī śaktiḥ)* [mentioned in other passages, ŚvU 1.1-3, 4.10.], which is of the nature of unmanifested name-and-form *(avyākṛtanāmarūpā)*, and which is the prior condition of [manifest] name-and-form *(nāmarūpayoḥ prāgavasthā)*.[144]

From such important passages as these, we can see that Śaṅkara accepts the empirical existence of some power, frequently called as *avyākṛta*, *avyakta*, or *māyā*, which is the seed-potency *(bījaśakti)* belonging to unmanifest name-and-form. Unmanifest name-and-form *(avyākṛtanāmarūpa)* is of the nature of *avidyā* because the delusion of its reality can be dispelled by knowledge, and so the word *avidyā* primarily signifies the mysteriously concealing, and ultimately unreal aspect, of the unmanifest name-and-form. It is possible that Śaṅkara uses the word *avidyā* in this sense - referring to both the deluding and unreal dimension of the unmanifest name-and-form - when he uses the word *avidyā* as the enigmatic first member in the compounds: "made by *avidyā*" *(avidyākṛta)*, "presented by *avidyā*" *(avidyāpratyupasthāpita)*, "fashioned by *avidyā*" *(avidyākalpita)* and "caused by *avidyā*" *(avidyānimitta)*, which are to be found throughout his commentary on the *Brahmasūtra*. While *avidyā* is at times specifically equated with superimposition, that need not invariably be the case, as when he makes such compounds as *avidyādhyāropita* "superimposed by *avidyā*", which would be unintelligible if *avidyā* also meant superimposition.[145] If *avidyā* refers to the delusive and unreal aspect of the unmanifest name-and-form then the latter can be seen as having two characteristics, a deluding and unreal aspect *(avidyā)*, as well as a creative aspect since it is the primary material of the world. It is then not difficult to see how later Advaita, by discarding the term "unmanifest *nāmarūpa*" and subsuming its function into the single term *avidyā*, could look upon *avidyā* as having the double aspect of concealing *(āvaraṇa)* and projecting *(vikṣepa)*. While post-Śaṅkara Advaita has developed and reified the concept of *avidyā*, we do not find the fundamental discontinuity between Śaṅkara and later Advaita as proposed by K.A. Krishnaswamy Iyer and Swami Saccidānandendra Sarasvatī.

1 G.A. Jacob, *A Handful of Popular Maxims current in Sanskrit Literature.* Delhi: Nirajana, 1983 [first published 1900-1904]. G.A. Jacob, *A Concordance to the Principal Upaniṣads and Bhagavadgīta.* Delhi: Motilal Banarsidass, 1971 [first published 1891. G.A. Jacob (ed), *The Naishkarmya-Siddhi of Sureśvarāchārya with the Chandrikā of Jnānottama.* Bombay: Government Central Book Depot (Bombay Sanskrit Series No.XXXVIII), 1906. G.A. Jacob (ed), *Vedāntasāra of Sadānanda with the Commentaries of Nṛsiṃhasarasvatī and Rāmatīrtha.* Varanasi: Krishnadas Academy, 1975 [first published 1893].

2 G.A. Jacob, *Vedāntasāra,* op.cit., p.vii.

3 Ibid., p.ix.

4 Ibid.

5 George Thibaut (trans.), *Vedānta Sūtras with the commentary of Śaṅkarācārya* (Two Parts). Delhi: Motilal Banarsidass, 1980 [first published 1904], Introduction pp.xxvii and xxx.

6 Ibid., p.cxiii, cxv ff., cxxiii ff.

7 BSBh 1.1.11, p.116, line 3f., (tr) p.61f.

8 Ibid p.116, line 7, (tr) p.62.

9 Ibid., p.118, line 1, (tr) p.64.

10 BSBh 1.2.2, p.164, line 6f., (tr) p.112.

11 BSBh 4.3.7, p.879f. line 10f., (tr) p.879. This is the opinion of the ācārya Bādari, which Śaṅkara accepts.

---

12 BSBh 2.2.40, p.492, line 9, (tr) p.438.

13 BSBh 4.3.14, p.889, line 6f., (tr) p.891f.

14 Rudolf Otto, *Mysticism East and West*. New York: Living Age Books, 1957. Cf. Ch. X, p.115f (# 9).

15 BSBh 1.1.20, p.133, line 6, (tr) p.80f.

16 BSBh 1.3.30, p.262, line 8, (tr) p.218.

17 BSBh 1.4.16, p.326, line 3, (tr) p.279. Also, for example the following: "In this cycle of creation the supreme Lord fashioned the world consisting of the sun and moon and so forth just as it was made in the previous cycle." (1.3.30, p.265, line 2, (tr) p.220f.). "We have shown that the Upaniṣads have their purport in teaching that the Lord is the cause." (2.1.1, p.348, line 7, (tr) p.302). "Texts such as: 'Under the mighty rule of this Immutable, Gārgī, ...' (BU 3.8.9) declare that the entire moving world is under the control of the Lord." (2.2.3, p.420, line 7f., (tr) p.373).

18 BSBh 2.3.41, p.552, line 11, (tr) p.504.

19 BSBh 3.2.9, p.637, line 5 (tr) p.605.

20 BSBh 3.3.32, p 733, line 9f., (tr) p.703.

21 BSBh 4.4.17, p.902, line 9, (tr) p.908; also 4.4.18.

22 Regarding the usage at the end of the BS, Paul Hacker mentions that in 4.4.17 *(īśvarasāyujyaṁ vrajanti)*: "...here, at least once, īśvara is a synonym of *saguṇa brahma.*" Cf. "Distinctive Features of the Doctrine and Terminology of Śaṅkara: Avidyā, Nāmarūpa, Māyā, Īśvara" in Wilhelm Halbfass (ed.), *Philology*

and Confrontation: Paul Hacker on Traditional and Modern Vedānta. Albany: State University of New York Press, 1995, p.93.

23 Gambhirānanda sometimes mixes the two words up, translating the word Paramātman as "God" in 1.2.24, p.147; and Parameśvara as "supreme Self" in 1.2.28, p.154 and 1.2.32, p.158.

24 BSBh 1.3.7, p.210, line 8: *īśvarakṣetrajñau-ucyete*, line 11: *paramātmā*.

25 In 2.1.33, Śaṅkara uses the words Īśvara and Parameśvara as synonyms, p.406, line 2 *(īśvara)*, line 5 *(parameśvara)*. In 1.4.23, p.339, line 3, he says that Brahman is the material and the efficient cause; on p.340, line 7 he again speaks of Brahman, but on line 10 he says Ātman is the efficient and material cause. In sūtra 2.2.37, p.488, line 2, he refers back to 1.4.23 and says that it was established there that Īśvara is the material and efficient cause.

26 Paul Hacker, "Distinctive Features of the Doctrine and Terminology of Śaṅkara: Avidyā, Nāmarūpa, Māyā, Īśvara" in Wilhelm Halbfass (ed.). *Philology and Confrontation: Paul Hacker on Traditional and Modern Vedānta*, op.cit., p.95.

27 Ibid., p.95.

28 Ibid., p.91.

29 BSBh 2.1.14, p.382f, line 10f., (tr) p.334f. Also, for another comment on the *vyāvahārika* aspect of Īśvaratva, cf. 3.2.38, p.665, line 2, (tr) p.640.

30 BSBh 2.1.22, p.395, line 1f., (tr) p.349.

31 I agree with Jacqueline Hirst that we cannot find a neat distinction between the *paraṁ* Brahman and Īśvara in Śaṅkara's thought, as we can see in later Advaita. However, I do think that Śaṅkara makes it clear that there is a final distinction, and that it is to be found at the *pāramārthika* perspective. Cf. Jacqueline Hirst, "The Place of *Bhakti* in Śaṅkara's Vedānta", in Karel Werner (ed.), *Love Divine: Studies in* Bhakti *and Devotional Mysticism.* Durham Indological Series No. 3. Surrey: Curzon Press, 1993.

32 BSBh 4.3.14, p.884f., line 5f., (tr) p.885f.

33 BSBh 1.3.19, p.238, line 2f., (tr) p.195.

34 BSBh 1.1.20, p.133, line 8f., (tr) p.81. Here he says: *nirastasarvaviśeṣaṁ pārameśvaraṁ rūpam.* In 1.2.4, p.145, line 13, (tr) p.92f., he says: *nirastasarvaviśeṣasambandhaṁ paraṁ brahma....* So it is evident that the *pārameśvaraṁ rūpam* is the same as *paraṁ* Brahman. Regarding the term *pārameśvaraṁ*, cf. also BSBh 1.3.19, p.237, line 15; 3.4.8, p.785f., line 18f.

35 See Bradley Malkovsky, "The Personhood of Śaṁkara's *Para Brahman*", *The Journal of Religion,* Volume 77, Number 4, October 1997, p.559f. Cf. R.V. De Smet, "Towards an Indian View of the Person" in Margaret Chatterjee (ed.), *Contemporary Indian Philosophy,* series 2. London: Allen and Unwin, 1974, p.53f.

36 Malkovsky, ibid., p.560. De Smet, ibid., p.54. Cf. also, the remarks by P. Fallon, in R. De Smet and J. Neuner (eds), *Religious Hinduism,* op.cit. p.112.

37 De Smet, ibid., p.54.

38 F.C. Copleston, *Aquinas.* Middlesex: Penguin Books, 1970, p.136. Also the discussion on Aquinas in his *A History of*

Philosophy, vol. 11, Medieval Philosophy: Augustine to Scotus. London: Burns Oates and Washbourne, 1950.

39 Ibid., p.138.

40 Ibid., p.139.

41 Cf. the significant comment by Paul Hacker: "Although Śaṅkara, just as Thomas Aquinas, taught the absolute *simplicitas* of the absolute, the Hindu was radically different from the Christian insofar as he was incapable of thinking of the absolute being as *actus.*" "Being and Spirit in Vedānta" in Wilhelm Halbfass (ed.), *Philology and Confrontation: Paul Hacker on Traditional and Modern Vedānta,* op.cit., p.194, also cf. p.205.

42 BSBh 2.1.14, p.382, line 14. For the full passage see chapter four, note 92.

43 R V. De Smet, "Śaṅkara and Aquinas on Creation", *Indian Philosophical Annual.* University of Madras, vol. 6, 1970, p.118.

44 See the critique of the Nyāya-Vaiśeṣika view of substance made by Toṭaka, the disciple of Śaṅkara, in Michael Comans, *Extracting the Essence of the Śruti: The Śrutisārasamuddharaṇa of Toṭakācārya.* Delhi: Motilal Banarsidass, 1996, vv.135-147, pp.89ff.

45 R V. De Smet, "Śaṅkara and Aquinas on Creation", op.cit., p.117.

46 Locke defined "person" as: "a thinking, intelligent being, that has reason and reflection, and can consider itself as itself, the same thinking thing, in different times and places; which it does only by that consciousness which is inseparable from thinking, and seems to me essential to it." Cf. the entry on "Persons" in Paul

Edwards (ed.), *The Encyclopedia of Philosophy:* New York: Macmillan, 1967.

47 BSBh 1.4.22, p.335, line 6f., (tr) p.289. Difference is entirely based upon *upādhi,* cf. also, 1.1.5, p.107, line 7f., (tr) p.51; 1.1.31, p.156, line 13f., (tr) p.105; 2.3.17, p.528, line 6f., (tr) p.475; 2.3.18, p.529, line 5, (tr) p.476; 2.3.30, p.539, line 16f., (tr) p.490; 2.3.49, p.560, line 12f., (tr) p.515; 3.2.9, p.637, line 11f., (tr) p.606. BUBh 2.1.20, p.745, line 2, (tr) p.220; 3.5.1, p.810, line 23f., (tr) p.332.

48 US (prose) 1.22. Also cf. CU 6.5.1-4, 6.6.1-5.

49 BSBh 4.2.10, p.862, line 14, (tr) p.858. BUBh 4.3.35, p.905, line 8f., (tr) p.482; 4.3.36, p.906, line 17f., (tr) p.483.

50 BUBh 3.7.2, p.821, line 9, (tr) 348; 4.3.20, p.889, line 13, (tr) p.457.

51 Concerning the function of the five *prāṇas,* cf. BSBh 2.4.12, p.580, line 15f. (tr) p.540. BUBh 1.5.3, p.699, line 5f., (tr) p.149.

52 BSBh 2.3.32, p.541, line 9f., (tr) p.493; 2.4.6, p.572, line 8f., (tr) p.529f. BUBh 1.5.3, p.698, line 16, *(manasaḥ =antaḥkaraṇasya),* (tr) p.148; 2.1.19, p.730, line 16, *(buddheḥ = antaḥkaraṇasya),* (tr) p.199.

53 KeUBh 2.4, p.27, line 6f., (tr) p.63. TUBh 2.1.1, p.286, line 4f., (tr) p.299. BGBh 2.21, p.20, line12, (tr) p.68.

54 BUBh 4.3.6, p.864, line 14f., (tr) p.421.

55 US (verse) 13. 6.

56 BUBh 3.4.2, p.807, line 18f., (tr) p.327; also cf., 1.4.10, p. 673, line 13f., (tr) p. 109.

57 AUBh 2.1, p.341, line 21f., (tr) p.52f.

58 BU 3.8.11; also cf., 3.4.2; 3.7.23; 4.4.18.

59 BUBh 4.4.12, p.925, line 3f., (tr) p.512.

60 "The Idea of the Person in the Thinking of Vedānta Philosphers" in Wilhelm Halbfass (ed.), *Philology and Confrontation*, op.cit., p.155f.

61 "Śaṅkara's Conception of Man" in Wilhelm Halbfass (ed.), *Philology and Confrontation*, ibid., p.184 (cf.pp.182-84, also 225).

62 Rene Descartes, *Discourse on Method and the Meditations*. Middlesex: Penguin Classics, 1986 (Second Meditation) p.105.

63 Antony Flew (ed), *David Hume on Human Nature And the Understanding*. London: Collier Macmillan, 1962, (cf. From *A Treatise of Human Nature)* p.266-267.

64 Ibid., p.284.

65 The etymology of the term is understood as: *upa=samīpavartini, ādadhāti=saṁkrāmayati svīyaṁ dharmam iti-upādhiḥ*. B. Jhalakikar (revised V.S. Abhyankar), *Nyāyakośa, Dictionary of Technical Terms of Indian Philosophy*, Poona: Bhandarkar Oriental Research Institute, 1978, p. 177.

66 Cf. chapter one, section (3) The *Advaitaprakaraṇa* of the *Gauḍapādakārikā*.

67 Reading *vyākṛta* instead of *avyākṛta*.

68 BUBh 3.8.12, p.832 line 13ff., (tr) p.367. Also cf. BUBh 4.3.18, p.887, line 21f., (tr) p.455; 5.1.1, p.951, line 1, (tr) p.557. BSBh 1.1.5, p.107, line 7ff., (tr) p.51; 2.3.17, p. 527, line 14f., (tr) p.474f.; 2.3.45, p.556, line 7, (tr) p.509; 2.4.20, p.590 line 1, (tr) p. 549. AUBh 3.1.3, p.349, line 10f., (tr) p.73. MUBh 2.1, p.154, line 8ff., (tr) p.114.

69 BUBh 1.4.6, p.653, line 7ff., (tr) p.74ff.; 3.8.12, p.832 line 24ff., (tr) p.368.

70 Also MU 3.2.8. PU 6.5.

71 BSBh 1.3.41, p.286f, line 7f., (tr) p.239, "Apart from Brahman, there can be no other thing than name-and-form, because the entire world of modifications is manifested 'just as name-and-form' (BU 1.4.7)." BUBh 2.2.1, p.745, line 8, *bhūtāni ca nāmarūpātmakāni*, (tr) p.221. 3.5.1, p.810., line 23 *nāmarūpavikārakāryakaraṇalakṣaṇasaṅghāta*, (tr) p.332. Also PUBh 6.5, p.139, line 18, (tr) p.503.

72 BUBh 1.4.7, p.654, line 22f., (tr) p.77. Also, BSBh 1.4.2, p.296, line 8f., (tr) p.248.

73 BUBh 1.4.7, p.655, line 7, (tr) p.78, "From this it is clear that a non-existent effect is not produced, nor an existent effect lost." Also, cf. BUBh 1.2.1, p.613, line 12f, (tr) p.12; 1.2.1, p.614ff, line 17f., (tr) p.14f.

74 CUBh 8.14.1, p.604, line 2, (tr) p. 668; and US (prose) 1.18.

75 BSBh 1.2.22, p.191, line 7, (tr) p.143; also cf. 1.4.2, p.296, line 9, (tr) 248.

76 BSBh 1.4.2, p.296, line 9, (tr) p.248; 1.4.3, p.297, line 6, (tr) p.249.

77 KaUBh 1.3.11, p.82, line 8, (tr) p.161.

78 MUBh 2.1.2, p.155, line 8 (reading: *sarvakāryakaraṇabījatvena*, some editions read: *sarvakāryakāraṇa...)*, (tr) p.117.

79 As an *upādhi* of the Lord, or supreme Self cf. BSBh 1.2.22, p.191, line 6, (tr) p.143. BUBh 2.4.10, p.763, line 15f., (tr) p.252. There is also a noteworthy passage in TUBh 2.6.1, p.298, line 23f., (tr) p.332, which says:
"[Becoming many] takes place through the manifestation of name-and-form which exists in the Self and is unmanifested. When the name-and-form which exists in the Self and is unmanifested, becomes manifest, it becomes manifest without abandoning the Self as its essential nature, i.e., it is manifest in all its various conditions remaining non-separate from Brahman in space and time. That manifesting of name-and-form is what is meant by Brahman becoming many. In no other way is it logical that the partless Brahman becomes many..."

80 "Distinctive Features of the Doctrine and Terminology of Śaṅkara: *Avidyā, Nāmarūpa, Māyā, Īśvara*" in Wilhelm Halbfass (ed.), *Philology and Confrontation*, op.cit., p.71.

81 Ibid., p.72.

82 Ibid, p.73.

83 To substantiate his own view, Hacker appears on this occasion to be somewhat cavalier in his explanations of the texts. Referring (ibid., p.73) to BSBh 1.4.3 p.298, line 1, *avyaktā hi sā māyā, tattvānyatvanirūpaṇasyāśakyatvāt,* he explains it as: "it is said clearly that *māyā* does not admit of a determination as *tat* or

anyat, because it exists as *avyakta*...", but the translation should be the other way around, as he translates on p.83: "*Māyā* is, namely, 'unmanifest' *{avyakta}*, since one can neither describe it by saying, 'It is this', nor by saying, 'It is something else'." More problematically, in referring to 2.1.27, p.401, line 7f., *avidyākalpitena ca nāmarūpalakṣaṇena rūpabhedena vyākṛtāvyākṛtātmakena tattvānyatvābhyām anirvacanīyena*..., he explains the passage his way (ibid., p.73): "'the diversity of forms *(rūpabheda)* which is name and form' is 'determinable neither as a that nor as something else', because it is (sometimes) 'unfolded' and (sometimes) 'not unfolded'...". This explanation takes *vyākṛtāvyākṛtātmakena* as having *vaiyadhikaraṇya* with *tattvānyatvābhyām anirvacanīyena* in that the latter is due to the former, whereas they clearly have *sāmānādhikaraṇya*, which is the way that both Gambhīrānanda, p.356 and Thibaut, p.352 have translated the passage.

84 BUBh 2.4.10, p.763, line 15ff., (tr) p. 252.

85 Some other instances of the illustration of the foam and water are BUBh 1.4.7, p.655, line 15ff, (tr) p.78; 3.5.1, p.811, line 2f, (tr) p.332. CUBh 8.14.1, p.604, line 1ff, (tr) p.668. AUBh 1.1.2, p.330f., line 24f., (tr) p.22f. US (prose portion) 1.19.

86 BUBh 1.4.7, p.655, line 15ff, (tr) p.78.

87 Cf. This passage is modeled upon TU 2.1.1.

88 US (prose portion) 1.19.

89 BSBh 2.1.14, p.382, line 2f., (tr) p.333f.

90 "Distinctive Features of the Doctrine and Terminology of Śaṅkara: *Avidyā, Nāmarūpa, Māyā, Īśvara*" in W Halbfass (ed.), *Philology and Confrontation*, op.cit., p.72.

91 Cf chapter one, (2) The *Vaitathyaprakaraṇa.*

92 S. Mayeda, *A Thousand Teachings,* op.cit., p. 59 n.17 and p. 230 n.41, follows the views of Paul Hacker. Hacker's view is also followed by Allen Thrasher who, in his study of the thought of the *Brahmasiddhi* of Maṇḍanamiśra, remarks that: "It is possible that Maṇḍana was influenced in his use of *anirvacanīya* by a misreading of the places where Śaṃkara uses the *tattvānyatvābhyām anirvacanīya* formula." Cf. Allen Wright Thrasher, *The Advaita Vedānta of Brahma-siddhi,* Delhi: Motilal Banarsidass, 1993, p.28. It hardly seems plausible to presume such a misreading on the part of a scholar like Maṇḍana.

93 BUBh 3.5.1, p.810f., line 27f., (tr) p.332f.

94 Wilhelm Halbfass (ed.), *Philology and Confrontation,* op.cit., p.57ff.

95 Ibid., p.59.

96 Ibid., p.60.

97 BSBh 1.3.2, p.207, line 11f., (tr) p.162.

98 Wilhelm Halbfass (ed.), *Philology and Confrontation,* op.cit., p.63.

99 Ibid., p.64.

100 Ibid., p.83. BSBh 1.4.2, p.296, line 8f, and 1.4.3, p.297, line 2f.

101 Ibid., p.83f. BSBh 1.4.9, p.308, line 3f.

102 Ibid., p.84.

103 Ibid., p.75.

104 Ibid., p.68, also p.76, where, referring to the view of other teachers of Śaṅkara's school, Hacker says: "...according to whose interpretation the prime matter of the cosmos falls together with the magical potency of illusion, *avidyā*, and with *māyā*, so that the term *nāmarūpa* becomes dispensable as a designation of the seed of the cosmos."

105 Ibid., p.85.

106 Martha Doherty has completed a doctoral dissertation at Harvard University on the topic of *Avidyā*, in which she discusses Swami Saccidānandendra's ideas in detail. I would like to acknowledge the assistance she has given by showing me two draft chapters of her thesis which discuss the work of Swami Saccidānandendra.

107 K.A. Krishnaswamy Iyer, *Vedanta or The Science of Reality.* Bangalore: Adhyatma Prakasha Karyalaya, 1991 [First Ed. 1930]. The Publisher's Note to the Third Edition says that: "...the eminent *Vedantin*, K.A. Krishnaswamy Iyer, was Swamiji's guide and *guru*. Not a day passed during the life time of the Swamiji without his remembering and paying tribute to the solid contribution made by K.A. Krishnaswamy Iyer to the world of *Advaitic* literature" (p.X11). Swami Saccidānandendra himself says, in his Introductory Remarks To The Second Edition (1965), that contact with Krishnaswamy Iyer has: "...helped me in no small measure to understand the rational caste of Upanishadic teaching" (p.XXX111).

108 D.B. Gangolli, *Sri Satchidanandendra Saraswati Swamiji.* Holenarsipur: Adhyatma Prakasha Karyalaya, 1997, p.16.

109 Ibid., p.16f.

110 K.A. Krishnaswamy Iyer, *Vedanta or The Science of Reality*, op.cit., p. 89.

111 Ibid., "The assertion of Hegel that Self-consciousness transcends the self and the not-self and denies both by its transparent oneness, is a happy hit of genius which in the condition of deep sleep is verified daily by every being." p. 56, also p.137.

112 Ibid., p.16.

113 Ibid., p.457f.

114 Such an interpretation could indeed be inferred from the passages of that Upaniṣad, though I do not believe that it ought be inferred, for this interpretation has nothing to do with the principal idea of the Upaniṣad which is, essentially, the indication *(lakṣaṇā)* of the true nature of the acosmic *(prapañcopaśama)* Self by means of *anvaya* (i.e. by showing the Self as the invariable substratum of the three states) and *vyatireka* (i.e. by showing the discontinuity of the states). I do not believe that we need to read into the text a kind of solipsism. For more details cf. chapter one.

115 K.A. Krishnaswamy Iyer. *Vedanta or The Science of Reality*, op.cit., p.204.

116 Ibid., p.199.

117 Satchidanandendra Sarasvati, *Mūlāvidyā Nirāsaḥ; athavā Śrī Śaṅkara Hṛdayam.* Holenarsipur: Adhyatma Prakasa Karyalaya, 1929. Translated by A.J. Alston under the title: *The Heart of Śaṃkara.* London: Shanti Sadan, 1993. All references to the *Mūlāvidyā Nirāsaḥ* are to the translation by A.J. Alston.

118 PP p.98f., (MRI) p.173f., (tr.) p.66f.

---

119 BSBh p.19, line 2, (tr) p.3.

120 Sacchidanandendra Sarasvati, *Vedānta-prakriyā-pratyabhijñā.* Holenarsipur: Adhyatma Prakasa Karyalaya, 1964, p.32f. Cf. A.J. Alston, *The Method of the Vedanta.* London and New York: Kegan Paul International, 1989, p.48.

121 Ibid. In his last book, *Misconceptions about Śaṅkara* (Holenarsipur: Adhyatma Prakasa Karyalaya, 1973) Saccidānandendra says, p. 11, that the word *māyā* is: "the name given to *Prakṛti* or name and form in seed form, which gives rise to all the different phenomena."

122 TUBh 2.1, p.283, line 8f., (tr) p.291.

123 [*Mūlāvidyā Nirāsaḥ* trans. as] *The Heart of Śaṃkara*, op.cit., para 27, p.27f. Saccidānandendra cites this definition by Śaṅkara in para 68, p.78.

124 Ibid., para 151, p.158.

125 Ibid, para 69, p.80.

126 Ibid, para 70, p.81.

127 Ibid., para 74 (1), p.83.

128 Ibid., para 60, p.66.

129 Ibid., para 60, p.67.

130 Ibid., para 95, p.106.

131 GK 2.6

132 BSBh 2.1.14, p.372f., line 13f. (tr) p.326.

133 *The Heart of Śaṃkara*, op.cit., para 40, p.40f.

134 Ibid., para 153, p.159.

135 Ibid., para 154, p.163.

136 BSBh 2.1.27, p.401, line 7f., (tr) p.356. *avidyākalpitena ca nāmarūpalakṣaṇena rūpabhedena vyākṛtāvyākṛtātmakena tattvānyatvābhyām anirvacanīyena brahma pariṇāmādisarvavyavahārāspadatvaṁ pratipadyate. pāramārthikena ca rūpeṇa sarvavyavahārātītam apariṇatam avatiṣṭhate. vācārambhaṇamātratvāc cāvidyākalpitasya nāmarūpabhedasya-iti na niravayavatvaṁ brahmaṇaḥ kupyati.*

137 MUBh p.155, line 7f, (tr) p. 116f. Also, p.154, line 17f, (tr) p.115.

138 BSBh 1.2.22, p.191, line 7f, (tr) p.143. I understand the term *śakti* to be in apposition with *bīja* and the expression "seed-potency" *(bījaśakti)* to refer to the unmanifested name-and-form, *avyākṛtanāmarūpa,* on the strength of Śaṅkara's commentary upon MU 2.1.2, where he says, *nāmarūpabījabhūtāt avyākṛtākhyāt,* p.154, line 17. The commentators Govindānanda and Ānandagiri, however, both understand *bīja* to refer to Īśvara, i.e., *nāmarūpayor bījam īśvaraḥ tasya śaktirūpam.* Paul Hacker has referred to this point, cf., "Distinctive Features of the Doctrine and Terminology of Śaṅkara: *Avidyā, Nāmarūpa, Māyā, Īśvara*" in W Halbfass (ed.), *Philology and Confrontation,* op.cit., p.98, n.28.

139 Following the reading *avyākṛtanāmarūpasatattvam.*

140 Cf. BUBh 4.1.2, p.852, line 22, (tr) p.401; 4.4.17, p.927, line 6, (tr) p.516.

141 KaUBh 1.3.11, p.82, line 7f., (tr) p.160f.

142 Cf. GK 1.16.

143 BSBh 1.4.3, p.297f., line 2f., (tr) p.249.

144 BSBh 1.4.9, p.308, line 3f., (tr) p. 261f.

145 BSBh 2.1.9, p.364, line 12f., (tr) p.318; 4.3.14, p.888, line 19, (tr) p.891.

CHAPTER SIX

The Means (sādhana), the End (sādhya) and their Relation

(1) The method in the Upaniṣads as interpreted by Śaṅkara

Śaṅkara sees the Upaniṣads as the source of spiritual understanding. It is in the Upaniṣads that we discover the nature of the reality underlying the phenomenal world, and the Upaniṣads also show ways by which that reality can be known. For Śaṅkara, and the Advaita tradition as a whole, the Upaniṣads are truly the means of knowledge *(pramāṇa)* in matters of the spirit.

The Upaniṣads tell that the reality about which they speak is not an object of the senses:

> That which one does not see with the eye (KeU 1.7)
>
> Nobody sees Him with the eye (Ka U 2.3.9)
>
> It is not comprehended through the eye (MU 3.1.8)

If the metaphysical reality, Brahman, is not an object of the senses, then the primary means of knowledge through which we know anything in the world, namely sense-perception, has no scope to reveal Brahman. And if that is so, one's own independent speculation would be ruled out, since inference depends upon the data supplied by the senses. The Upaniṣads teach this very conclusion, as we can see from the often quoted statement in the *Taittirīya* Upaniṣad:

> From which words turn back, not reaching, along with the mind (TU 2.4.1; 2.9.1)

But if the Upaniṣad says that words "turn back", does not the Upaniṣad negate itself as a means of knowledge? For the Upaniṣads are only in the form of words, and if Brahman cannot be revealed by words, then the Upaniṣads - which state that Brahman exists, but also state that there is no way of knowing Brahman, since it is neither a sense-object, nor an object of language, nor of thought - would show themselves to be impotent to reveal Brahman. The consequence is that the Upaniṣads would be meaningless.

There is a single way out of this difficulty, and it is that the Upaniṣads do reveal the nature of Brahman through language, but only though a particular type of language. Richard De Smet expresses the matter thus:

> Since all words belong to the realm of secular knowledge and designate primarily sense-objects only, it is clear that they can be employed by the *Śruti*, or by the guide in *Brahma-jijñāsa*, only in two ways: either in some secondary....meaning, or in their negative forms, for there is no other way of detaching them from their primary application which has no scope with respect to Brahman.[1]

Śaṅkara says that words can function in only four ways. Either a word refers to something which is a member of a generic class, a noun, such as the word "cow"; or it refers to a quality of a thing, such as white or black; or it refers to some action, such as cooking or reading; or to a relationship between things, such as: "He is rich", "He owns many cows".[2] Since Brahman is not a sense object, Brahman cannot be denoted by words which are normally employed, in any of these four ways, to refer to sense objects. So if the *śruti* is to reveal Brahman through language - and that is the only way that the *śruti*, which is in the form of words, could reveal Brahman - but language is structured in such a way that it can speak only of sense objects, then the *śruti* has to find another way to use language. It does just this, when it employs the language of negation and uses words in an implied meaning.

It is well known that the *śruti* uses the language of negation to refer to Brahman, as when it says:

> That which is invisible, ungraspable, without source, without features, without eyes or ears, hands or feet... (MU 1.1.6)

And of course there is the famous negation found in the *Bṛhadāraṇyaka* Upaniṣad:

> Now therefore the description [of Brahman]: "Not this, not this." Because there is no more appropriate description than this: "not this" *(iti na)* (BU 2.3.6).[3]

Śaṅkara writes that the negation "not this, not this" serves to remove differences brought about by limiting adjuncts. He says that words function with reference to some attribute or the other, and that is the case even in regard to the positive descriptions of Brahman given in the *śruti*, such as: "Brahman is Consciousness, Bliss" (BU 3.9.28), and "absolutely uniform Consciousness" *(vijñānaghana eva)* (BU 2.4.12). Even here, he says, words refer to Brahman:

> ...by way of name, form and action that are superimposed [on Brahman]. But when the true nature of Brahman is sought to be described, free from the distinctions of all limiting conditions, it cannot be described by any means. This is the only procedure, the description: "not this, not this", which is by way of negation of all existing descriptions.[4]

And again, in responding to a query that surely statements like: "Brahman is Consciousness, Bliss"; "absolutely uniform Consciousness"; "Brahman is Being, Awareness, Infinite" *(satyaṁ jñānam anantaṁ brahma)* (TU 2.1.1) do define Brahman as pure Awareness, he says:

> That is true, but even so, words like "Consciousness" etc. refer to Brahman just by way of the limiting adjuncts of the mind, body and the senses.[5]

The "negative method" in general, and these statements of Śaṅkara which belong to that method, pose some problems. Firstly, is the statement of negation, "not this, not this" *(neti neti)*, intended to be open-ended? The Upaniṣad teaching would be nihilistic if the negation process is without termination. Secondly, how can we know Brahman by negating what it is not? If the method the Upaniṣads employ to reveal Brahman is ultimately a negative one, if the Upaniṣads just tell us what Brahman is not, there can be no positive knowledge of that reality whose existence they proclaim, and once again the charge could be made that the Upaniṣads are meaningless.

The first objection is easily met. Śaṅkara emphatically asserts that negation would be fruitless unless something stands unnegated. Further, he contends that if nothing remains after the process of negation, then anything that is sought to be negated by that process could not be negated and would become, *de facto*, real:

> Something that is not real is negated on the basis of something real, as in the case of the snake etc. on the rope etc. That [denial of something unreal with reference to something real] is possible when some positively existing thing is left over. If everything is denied, what positively existing thing would remain? If nothing else remains, the thing that is sought to be denied could not be denied and it would thereby become real. Negation would become logically impossible.[6]

Śaṅkara considers that the negation taught by repetition in the statement "not this, not this" *(neti neti)* removes all superimpositions from Brahman which then stands unnegated in its own true nature. He makes this same point in a number of his works, as for instance in the *Brahmasūtrabhāṣya:*

> When there is the repetition ["not this, not this", what happens is that] from the denial of all objects in their totality, That which is not an object, the inner-Self, is Brahman; and the desire to know Brahman ceases. Hence the definitive conclusion is that [the statement "not this,

> not this"] negates the phenomenal world, which is superimposed in Brahman, and leaves Brahman remaining.[7]

To cite a couple of instances from the *Upadeśasāhasrī:*

> As [the Self] cannot be negated, it is left as the remainder [by the statement] "not this, not this". "I am not this, I am not this" - in such a way It becomes clearly known. [2.1][8]
>
> The sense of agency etc. has been superimposed upon the Self, the Pure Awareness, by the mind. "Not this, not this" negates all of it , along with the mind itself. [18. 25]

Śaṅkara says that once the removal of superimposition has taken place, the Ātman then stands self-revealed. That this is his view is evident from the juxtaposition of two verses in the *Upadeśasāhasrī,* where in the verse following the one just cited above we read:

> Perception, self-luminous, Seeing, innermost, always unchanging, immediately evident, within all, the Witness, the principle of Consciousness, constant, free from qualities and without a second. [18. 26]

It is clear that negation is meant to exclude all limiting conditions from the Self which then stands as it is: as pure Consciousness which is not an object of the senses, the mind or speech. This also begins to answer the second objection raised above, namely that no positive knowledge can be achieved through mere negation. What Śaṅkara is saying is that the absolute Self is never remote or indirect *(parokṣa),* for its nature is self-revealing Consciousness, and as such, it must always be immediately evident *(aparokṣa).* The negation *"neti neti"* removes, through discriminative insight, all the limiting conditions and their attributes from the Self, which then stands revealed as it truly is. But I believe that if this insight occurs, it is not simply the outcome of the negation process, rather it is because the true nature of the Self is indicated through the negation process itself. This requires further explanation, but to state my conclusion at the outset, I believe that the "way of negation" should not be understood as a separate method apart from the method of "indication" [or "implication"] called *lakṣaṇā*, where the Self is indicated through the secondary, or the implied meaning, of a word. Thus I believe there is a single method in the hermeneutics of liberation in the Advaita of Śaṅkara, and this method necessitates the use of *lakṣaṇā*. For example, firstly, the context is taught, i.e., Brahman, Ātman, the Lord, the nature of the *upādhis* etc. Then all the *upādhis* that pertain to the individual body-sense-mind complex, as well as the *upādhis* to do with the cosmic Lord, i.e., the "Creatorship" on the part of Brahman, are negated in the final denial characterised by the statement "not this, not this", so that the true nature of the Self, that is already contextually known, is simultaneously and directly indicated through the negation process as the pure Awareness "basis" that now exists undivided *(akhaṇḍa)* following the negation of all *upādhis*. Thus the language of negation and the language used in a secondary, or implied sense *(lakṣaṇā)*, are not two different ways of proceeding; they form a single method of revealing the Absolute. If this is so, which I will try to show, then the statements by Śaṅkara in his various commentaries can also be shown to be consistent in their method of revealing the Self as Brahman.

In speaking about the method of the *śruti*, Karl Potter expresses the view:

> Ultimately, however, scripture can provide no positive key to liberation, because the key lies in removing ignorance, a negative step; so the highest view of all is that of *apavāda*, that reality is "not this, not this" *(neti neti)*.[9]

It is true that for Śaṅkara the Upaniṣads culminate in the statement *"neti neti"* which negates all superimpositions in their entirety. But the negation itself functions in the context of *lakṣaṇā*, for our ignorance of something cannot be removed without pointing out the nature of the thing about which there is ignorance. It is not sufficient merely to say: "not a snake, not a snake!", the substratum of the error must also be positively pointed out ("this is not a snake, it is a rope!") in order to provide a knowledge that is truly liberating. I believe that negation *(apavāda)* is throughout coupled with the positive indication of reality through *lakṣaṇā*. While Professor Potter does makes reference to *lakṣaṇā*, he does not discuss the significance of this matter.[10]

Richard De Smet highlights the importance of the method of indication [implication] *(lakṣaṇā)* in Advaita. Whilst distinguishing both a negative and a positive method, the latter characterised by *lakṣaṇā*, he is of the opinion that the negative way is but an intermediary step to the positive method of indication, and though he does not say that there is but a single method, consisting of negation cum indication, he does come close to that view:

> The function of the context cannot be too much emphasised. The Vedāntic definitions of Brahman are usually prepared by a series of progressive *adhyāropas* [erroneous imputations] which pedagogically direct the mind to focus its attention on the highest reality; then, these approximations are contradicted and neutralised by the *"neti neti"* method, and, finally, the true definition is enunciated in terms denoting pure perfections, which through implication, are elevated to signify the absolute Brahman-Ātman.
>
> Thus the whole context directs the pupil to perform the act of implication.[11]

Anantanand Rambachan mentions three methods: (1) the method of superimposition *(adhyāropa)* and de-superimposition *(apavāda)*, (2) the method of negation *(neti neti)*, and (3) the method of implication *(lakṣaṇā)*. Among these, he sees the first two as being fulfilled by the latter and he says:

> One cannot overestimate the importance of *lakṣaṇā*... . It is integral to Śaṅkara's rationale for the *Vedas* as a *pramāṇa* of *brahman*. After his justification of the *Vedas* as a source of knowledge by showing the limitations of all other *pramāṇas* with regard to *brahman*, the problem of the

> latter's inexpressibility through words, which are unavoidably finite in their reference, still remains. In response to this dilemma, Śaṅkara proposes *lakṣaṇā* as the method of surmounting *brahman's* inexpressibility.[12]

Rather than three distinct methods, I see superimposition and its removal *(adhyāropa-apavāda)* and the way of negation *(neti neti)* as constituting a single technique that unites with indication: thus there is but one method, and it consists of negation cum indication. Both De Smet and Rambachan highlight the importance of *lakṣaṇā* in revealing the nature of the Infinite through words, given that words are acknowledged to be, as Rambachan says, "unavoidably finite in their reference." I believe these authors to be entirely correct in the importance they give to the use of the implied meaning of words. And I further agree with Rambachan that this is the only way to solve the problem of the unknowability of Brahman which would result if the words of the Upaniṣads only negate, but do not also reveal.

Both these authors have difficulty, however, in producing sufficient illustrations of Śaṅkara's use of *lakṣaṇā* to justify their assertion of its fundamental importance to his hermeneutical method. While they are able to give instances of his use of *lakṣaṇā*, they cannot adduce as many as one would expect if *lakṣaṇā* is so central to his thought. To supplement a lack of references by Śaṅkara they have to rely on explanations from later Advaita. As well as sharing their assertion of the importance of *lakṣaṇā*, I share something of their difficulty in demonstrating numerous instances of its use, though I can show some additional cases. But first, it may be worthwhile to explain briefly what exactly is meant by *lakṣāṇā*, following the classical Advaita account.

A word has a primary meaning *(vācyārtha/ mukhyārtha)* which is revealed through its express sense *(śakti)*. But a word, or a group of words, can also have a secondary, or implied meaning *(lakṣārtha)*, where the meaning is conveyed through indication *(lakṣaṇā)*, as for example: "the village is on the Ganges". Here, the primary meaning of the sentence is not intelligible according to our usual understanding of the site of a village, and so, in order to make sense of the meaning of the speaker's utterance, we have no alternative but to give up the literal meaning of the words and find a meaning that is implied through the literal meaning, namely that the village is situated, not at some distance from the Ganges, but right upon its bank.

Advaitins agree with the Mīmāṁsakas that it is not correct to resort to an implied meaning so long as the literal, or primary meaning, makes sense. It is only when an utterance is made with purport, i.e., it is not nonsensical, but the purport is unintelligible according to its direct or literal meaning, that we are entitled to seek a meaning that is implied through the words. Thus *lakṣaṇā* requires that the direct meaning is unintelligible in the context, and further, it requires that some relation exists between the primary meaning and the secondary, or implied meaning, so that we can move from the former directly to the latter. This movement of thought is performed by implicatory reasoning called "necessary presumption" *(arthāpatti)*, which requires the postulation of a fact to explain another known fact which would otherwise remain unintelligible. The standard example of *arthāpatti* is: "fat Devadatta does not eat during the day" *(pīno devadatto divā na bhuṅkte)* where, under normal circumstances, we can only make sense of this unintelligible fact by assuming that Devadatta must be eating during the night. When the express meaning of a statement contradicts reason, we can either abandon the statement as nonsensical, or look for an implied meaning. If that statement is made in all seriousness, with the intention to convey a particular piece of information, we are not entitled to just abandon it as nonsense, and we must therefore look for some implied meaning that alone, and immediately, will make sense of the otherwise unintelligible utterance.

Śaṅkara says all words are finite in their scope, for they function, as we saw, in one of four ways: they can refer to nouns, i.e., to things of a certain class *(jāti)*, such as "pot"; or they can refer to the properties of things, such as the adjective "white" in the phrase "white pot"; or to actions such as "he drops the white pot"; or to relationships as in "that white pot belonged to Devadatta". Since all words have only a finite meaning, no word can directly reveal the Infinite. Even words like "awareness" cannot directly express the reality of which the Upaniṣads speak, for the word "awareness" literally refers to conscious states of mind. No word in its literal, or express sense, is able to reveal Brahman; yet the Upaniṣads are only in the form of words. Thus we seem to be at an impasse. The only way the Upaniṣadic words can directly reveal

Brahman is to indicate Brahman through their secondary, or implied meaning *(lakṣaṇā)*. There is no other way that the words of the Upaniṣads can reveal the nature of Brahman. And they can do this if a relationship exists between the literal and the implied meanings, as we will explain further below.

Indication *(lakṣaṇā)*, as discussed in later Advaita writings, is said to be of three types:

(1) *Lakṣaṇā* where the primary meaning is completely given up *(jahallakṣaṇā)*. As in the statement: "the village is on the Ganges", where the direct meaning, "on the Ganges", is unintelligible as the location of a village. In order for this statement to make sense, the direct meaning of the words "on the Ganges" is completely abandoned, and it is substituted by an implied meaning that is connected to the direct meaning, and thus by implying "on the bank" the statement becomes intelligible.

(2) *Lakṣaṇā* where the primary meaning is not given up, but an additional meaning is implied *(ajahallakṣaṇā)*. For example in the statement: "protect the curd from the crows", the direct meaning of the word "crows" is not abandoned, but an implied meaning of: "and anything else", is added.

(3) *Lakṣaṇā* where a part of the direct meaning is given up and a part of it is retained *(jahadajahallakṣaṇā* or *bhāgatyāgalakṣaṇā)*. In the usual example, "this is that Devadatta", the word "that" refers to Devadatta as he was in the past, eg., a young student at Benares, and the word "this" refers to Devadatta as he is right now, an old man living in Delhi. The statement of identity is logically untenable, because the old man is not the same as the young man, so how can we say this person is identical to that person? The statement, when interpreted through implication, becomes intelligible to commonsense if we retain the substantial identity of the person and give up the two incompatible attributes associated with different places and times. Setting aside the opposing conditions, we recognise the essential identity: "this is that Devadatta!"

Of these three types of *lakṣaṇā*, Advaitins tend to use the third type in their hermeneutics of the Upaniṣads. In the introduction to his translation of Śaṅkara's *Upadeśasāhasrī* Sengaku Mayeda expresses the opinion that the use of *lakṣaṇā* was an innovation by Advaita teachers subsequent to Śaṅkara.[13] But that is not so. For although Śaṅkara does not discuss the significance of *lakṣaṇā*, and though he does not refer to *jahadajahallakṣaṇā* by name, he most certainly does use *lakṣaṇā* in his interpretation of Upaniṣad sentences. We can see this by referring to three important instances where he employs *lakṣaṇā* as the key to unlocking the meaning of the Upaniṣads.

The first occurs in his explanation of an important passage in the *Taittirīya* Upaniṣad which gives the essential definition of Brahman.[14] The passage is: "The knower of Brahman attains the supreme. Concerning that, there is this verse: 'Brahman is Being, Awareness, limitless'." (TU 2.1). Śaṅkara's commentary upon this portion of the *Taittirīya* is one of his great exegetical pieces of writing and it is worthwhile to see the way in which he interprets the sentence of definition: "Brahman is Being *(satya)*, Awareness *(jñāna)*, limitless *(ananta)*." In this sentence, the word "Brahman" is the only noun while the three words *"satya"*, *"jñāna"* and *"ananta"* are adjectives which are co-referential with the noun Brahman. Thus the sentence says that Brahman is *satyam*, Brahman is *jñānam* and Brahman is *anantam*.[15] Śaṅkara firstly defines the word *satya*. He says that "real" *(satya)* means freedom from change. He shares this definition in common with Gauḍapāda.[16] Śaṅkara says something can only be called *satya*, true or truly real, if it does not undergo any change:

> Something is real when, once it is ascertained to be in a certain condition, that condition is not found to alter. Conversely, if a thing is ascertained to be in a certain condition and that condition alters, that thing is said to be unreal. Therefore, that which undergoes change [or modification, *vikāra*] is unreal.[17]

So the word *satyam*, because of its apposition with the word "Brahman", distinguishes Brahman from all things that change.

The word *jñāna,* he says, means "knowledge" or "awareness", and this reveals that Brahman is not insentient. According to Śaṅkara, the word *jñāna* finally means, not the agent of knowing, i.e., an individual knowing personality or ego, but Awareness *per se.* How does he arrive at his conclusion? He says that the word *jñāna* is:

> a distinguishing characteristic of Brahman along with the words *satya* and *ananta.* The words *satya* and *ananta* cannot be logically applied if Brahman is an agent of knowing, because as the agent of knowing, Brahman would undergo change, and how then could it be real *(satya)* and limitless *(ananta)?* What is not separate from anything is "limitless" *(ananta).* If Brahman is the agent of knowing, it is separate from both the object of knowledge and the instrument of knowing, and hence it could not be limitless.[18]

We can see here that Śaṅkara interprets the word *jñāna* to mean pure (i.e. mere or simple) Awareness because it is used as a defining characteristic of Brahman along with the words *satya* and *ananta.* The word *satya* negates change and *ananta* negates limitation. Since the word *jñāna* is co-referential with the word *satya, jñāna* must also be *satya,* i.e., *jñāna* must be real, and real means changeless, and that would not be the case if *jñāna* referred to knowership. And since the word *jñāna* is also co-referential with the word *ananta, jñāna* too must be *ananta,* i.e., without boundary. The word "Brahman" has its own etymological meaning of "vast". The two words, *satya* and *jñāna,* reveal what Brahman ("the vast") actually is, while the word *ananta* functions by way of negating finitude from the other terms.[19] Thus Brahman is *satya* which is *ananta,* and *jñāna* which is *ananta.* Hence the definition of Brahman, which gives primary importance to the term *jñāna,* is: Brahman is Awareness, which is identical to Being itself, and which is without any boundary.[20]

The above definition of Brahman was reached by indication *(lakṣaṇā),* for Brahman is not the literal meaning of a word, even of the words *satya* and *jñāna.* Śaṅkara says the word *satya* literally refers to things that are real in our ordinary experience, pots and pans etc., and he says the word *jñāna* literally refers to the properties of the mind, i.e, to cognitive-states, which is what we would ordinarily understand by the word "awareness".[21] And so Brahman is not the literal denotation *(vācyārtha)* of either of these words. But he says that the nature of Brahman is indicated by the words *satya* and *jñāna*, even though it is not directly expressed by those words *(tallakṣyate na tu ucyate)*.[22] How is this indication possible? He says it is because:

> the words *satya* etc., on account of their occurring in mutual proximity to each other, mutually restrict and are restricted by one another, and in this way they distinguish Brahman from the literal meanings of the words *satya* etc. and they convey the definition of Brahman.[23]

Śaṅkara says the co-referentiality of the words serves to remove the limitations from the words. Each word retains its own root meaning, but now in an unlimited sense. The word *satya* retains its primary meaning of "being", but on account of its apposition with the word *ananta* it gives up its usual meaning, where it refers to some or other existing thing, so that it now means "limitless Being". Similarly, *jñāna* retains its primary meaning of "knowing", but due to its apposition with the word *ananta* it gives up its usual meaning of cognition and comes to mean "limitless Awareness".

Thus Brahman is indicated, but is not directly expressed *(tallakṣyate na tu ucyate)*, by the words *satyaṁ jñānam anantam*. The indication is that of the *jahadajahallakṣaṇā* (or *bhāgatyāgalakṣaṇā)* type, where part of the primary meaning is given up and part is retained. The direct meanings of the words *satya* and *jñāna*, "being" and "awareness", are retained; but the limited, conventional understanding of those two words, is abandoned on account of their mutual juxtaposition and their co-referentiality with the word *ananta*, so that what they come to indicate is: unqualified "Being", unqualified "Awareness". While Śaṅkara has not used the term *jahadajahallakṣaṇā*, a term that gained currency in later Advaita, he has nonetheless used indication, and the type of indication he employed is *jahadajahallakṣaṇā*. Those who would see the statement *satyaṁ jñānam anantaṁ brahma* as not revealing the nature of Brahman through *lakṣaṇā*, but as merely performing a negative function of denying the contraries of the terms, i.e., Brahman is not unreal, not insentient, and not finite, have not studied Śaṅkara's full commentary on this passage with sufficient care.[24]

Concerning the well known Upaniṣad statement referred to earlier: "From which [Brahman] words turn back, not reaching, along with the mind" (TU 2.4.1; 2.9.1), Śaṅkara says that *śruti* sentences such as these mean that the nature of Brahman cannot be directly expressed through language used in its literal sense.[25] But we should understand that this is not to say that Brahman cannot be directly indicated through words when they are used in an implied sense, as in the case of *satyaṁ jñānam anantaṁ brahma.*

We referred earlier to a quotation from Śaṅkara, where in response to the objection that Brahman can be literally defined by the words: "Brahman is Being, Awareness, Infinite" *(satyaṁ jñānam anantaṁ brahma)* (TU 2.1.1), for the reason that Awareness is properly the characteristic of Brahman and not of anything material, Śaṅkara replied: "That is true, but even so, words like "Consciousness" etc. refer to Brahman just by way of the limiting adjuncts of the mind, body and the senses."[26] We ought now to understand this statement in the light of his extensive treatment of the sentence *"satyaṁ jñānam anantaṁ brahma"* in the *Taittirīya* Upaniṣad, where he says that though these words *satya* and *jñāna* cannot define Brahman by their express sense, for they literally refer only to our common understanding of what is real, or to our ordinary understanding of what constitutes consciousness, they do define Brahman through indication, and that is possible because of the mutual juxtaposition of the three terms which serves to release both terms, *satya* and *jñāna*, from their finite meanings.

Another important occasion where Śaṅkara uses *lakṣaṇā* is in his explanation of the *mahāvākya, tat tvam asi* ("you are That"). Although Śaṅkara does not refer to the interpretation through *lakṣaṇā* in his commentary on the relevant passages in the *Chāndogya* Upaniṣad where the *mahāvākya* occurs, he does speak of the primary meaning of the word "you" *(tvaṁśabdavācya)*, which he says refers to a limited self-understanding involving the sense of doership and enjoyership: "I am qualified to do these rites, I will do them and enjoy their results here and hereafter."[27] And he says this primary meaning of the word "you" ceases when one has been awakened by the sentence "you are That", which reveals the true nature of oneself, because of the contradiction *(virodha)* that is set up between the primary meaning and what is actually revealed by the sentence.[28] Here, the ingredients necessary for indication are in place, i.e., (a) the inapplicability of the primary meaning in the context and (b) a relation between the primary meaning and the actual referent of the word.[29] However it is in his explanation of the sentence *tat tvam asi* in the eighteenth chapter of the *Upadeśasāhasrī* that Śaṅkara specifically refers to the use of *lakṣaṇā*.

In this chapter of the *Upadeśasāhasrī* he explicitly tells that it is by *lakṣaṇā* that the meaning of the word "you" *(tvam)* in *tat tvam asi* can refer to the inner-Self, even though the word "you" primarily denotes the ego. He says:

> Words refer to where there is the reflection [i.e. they directly refer to the mind]. They can indicate *(lakṣayeyuḥ)* the inner-most Seeing, but they cannot directly denote it. [18.29]

What Śaṅkara says here is that the word "you" *(tvam)* directly refers only to the ego, which is the reflection of pure Awareness in the mind. Since this ego-reflection does not exist separately from the Pure Awareness, its "substratum", there can be a relation between the primary and secondary meanings of the word "you", whereby the word "you" can pass through the primary meaning, the notion of the ego, to indicate the final subject, the unlimited pure Awareness. Later, he poses a rhetorical question to show the necessity of accepting his model, in which the ego is a reflection of pure Awareness, for it is only in this way that a medium exists through which words are able to indicate the Pure Awareness:

> If the word "you" is to finally mean the Overseer, how can you explain the relation between the ego and the Overseer, whereby the word "you" can indicate It? [18.79]

The *lakṣaṇā* referred to here would once again be *jahadajahallakṣaṇā*, where one aspect is retained, i.e., the essence of the ego as Pure Awareness, while one aspect is abandoned, i.e., the finitude of the ego-entity itself. Apart from these references to the use of indication in arriving at the final meaning of the word *"tvam"* in *tat tvam asi*, Śaṅkara's overall interpretation of this sentence necessitates that the liberating understanding is brought about through the use of *lakṣaṇā*. We will discuss his interpretation more fully in the following chapter when we see how Śaṅkara and Sureśvara explain this *mahāvākya*.

Another reference to the use of *lakṣaṇā* occurs in the commentary to the *Kena* Upaniṣad. The verse previous to the one where Śaṅkara makes the reference says:

> By whom it is not known, by him it is known. By whom it is known, he does not know it. It is unknown to those who know, and known to those who do not know. [2.3]

This verse says that Brahman cannot be objectified, and so Brahman cannot be an object of knowledge in the way that we know any sense object in the world. Those who would know Brahman in this way, as an object, a "thing", do not know. They know, if they do not know it as a "thing". But how then, Śaṅkara asks, does Brahman become known? He says that the answer is given in the first words of the next verse:

> It is known in each and every state of consciousness *(pratibodha)*. [2.4]

Concerning this, Śaṅkara comments:

> Cognitions are referred to here by the word *"bodha"*. That to whom all cognitions are objects is the Self who knows, i.e., reveals, all cognitions; and as it is by nature just the power of Awareness, it is indicated *(lakṣyate)* by the cognitions themselves, as the common factor in those cognitions. There is no other door to the knowledge of the Self.[30]

Thus we can see some notable uses of *lakṣaṇā* in Śaṅkara's works. And this is fitting, because when the Upaniṣad says that "words do not reach" the Absolute, it would amount to a denial that the Upaniṣads

-which are only in the form of words - can succeed as the means of knowledge *(pramāṇa)* about the Absolute. The only conclusion, if the Upaniṣads are to be a true *pramāṇa,* is that they can reveal the nature of Brahman through words, when words are used in their secondary or implied sense to indicate Brahman. I believe that all the major Upaniṣadic statements, those which reveal in a "positive" fashion, as well as those which negate, such as *"neti neti"*, are ultimately to be understood through *lakṣaṇā.*[31] There is more than one technique *(prakriyā)* in the Upaniṣads to reveal the acosmic *(niṣprapañca)* Brahman: there is the discussion of Brahman as the cause of the world *(kāraṇa-kārya-prakriyā);* there is the analysis of the three states of experience, waking, dream and deep sleep *(avasthātraya-prakriyā);* and there is the analysis of the "five sheaths" *(pañcakośa-prakriyā),* as we see in the *Taittirīya* Upaniṣad. Yet there is a single fundamental method in the Upaniṣads, and it consists in negation coupled with the use of *lakṣaṇā:* to negate the unreal and point to the real.

(2) Immediate and mediate knowledge of Brahman and the question of experience

This leads us to another important issue which has to do with the "knowledge" of Brahman. We will divide this topic into two. The first question we will take up is whether Śaṅkara holds that the Upaniṣadic words are themselves able to produce the direct and immediate *(aparokṣa)* knowledge of Brahman, or whether they can give us only an indirect *(parokṣa)* knowledge of Brahman. The second question has to do with the character of this liberating knowledge. What is the content of this knowledge? And what role does a special, spiritual "experience" *(anubhava)* play in Śaṅkara's understanding of liberation?

Many writers state that the Upaniṣads produce only an indirect, or theoretical, knowledge of Brahman. The indirect knowledge has to be made direct by meditative practices culminating in a meditative absorption or enstasis, frequently called *nirvikalpa samādhi,* in which experience the knowledge that was formerly received indirectly from the Upaniṣads is transformed into an immediate and self-certifying knowledge. A similar view to the one described here was already in existence in Śaṅkara's time, as we can see in the *Brahmasiddhi* of Maṇḍanamiśra.[32] The question is whether Śaṅkara himself holds the view that the *śruti* can give only an indirect knowledge. Some scholars evidently believe so, although some are a little ambiguous on the subject. For instance, Richard De Smet writes:

> The sentences of the *Śruti*, if they could be rightly understood at once, would suffice to awaken us to the truth they unequivocally express.[33]
>
> *Brahmajñāna* is immediate; it is produced as soon as the exact meaning of the 'great sayings' *(mahāvākyāni)* of the *Śruti* is thoroughly grasped.[34]

However, after highlighting the importance of the role of *lakṣaṇā*, De Smet remarks that implication can only give an indirect knowledge, for it can: "only start the process of reflection, meditation, recollection, concentration, to which the illumination of *sākṣātkāra* (direct realisation) is promised as an end."[35]

Some scholars are not only ambiguous, but are curiously misleading. T.M.P. Mahadevan has said on more than one occasion that the knowledge that one derives from the *śruti* is mediate *(parokṣa)*. This is also the view of M. Hiriyanna.[36] Yet both scholars are aware of an established tradition in Advaita that maintains that the *śruti* can give immediate *(aparokṣa)* knowledge of Brahman. For example, in his Introduction to the revised edition of Sureśvara's *Naiṣkarmyasiddhi*, Hiriyanna says: "But the latter [i.e. the followers of Śaṅkara] are of opinion that the true nature of *Brahman* is knowable *directly* [his emphasis] from the Upaniṣads."[37] In a technical context, such as when they are referring to the views of Sureśvara, a direct follower of Śaṅkara, both Mahadevan and Hiriyanna acknowledge this tradition; but in their own popular writings they present only one view: that the words of the Upaniṣads give an indirect knowledge of Brahman.

Maṇḍanamiśra was of the opinion that the Upaniṣadic knowledge is necessarily indirect, and his teaching on the subject was fused into the Śāṅkara school of Advaita by the great, but somewhat syncretistic scholar, Vācaspatimiśra, through his influential commentary on the *Brahmasūtrabhāṣya* of Śaṅkara, *Bhāmatī*. But this view of Maṇḍana and

Vācaspati does not accord with that of Śaṅkara and his immediate followers. For Saṅkara, the statements of the Upaniṣads that reveal the nature of Brahman, and reveal that the individual soul is essentially Brahman Itself, have the capacity to directly liberate the hearer, provided the hearer is sufficiently qualified, in a spiritual sense, to be able to sift the meaning of the words and grasp their true import as they are heard. It can easily be shown that this is the view of Śaṅkara. Towards the end of the *Brahmasūtra,* while discussing the *sūtra* that refers to the utility of repeated instruction, he makes provision for those who are able to be enlightened from even a single hearing of the *mahāvākya, tat tvam asi.* He says:

> Repetition would be useless to one who is able to experience that the Self is Brahman on being told just once: "you are That". But repetition is certainly of use to him who is unable to do so.[38]

A little later, he says:

> Those whose minds are acute, for whom the meaning of the words is not obstructed by either ignorance, doubt, or misunderstanding, are able to experience the meaning of the statement *"tat tvam asi"* even when it is uttered once.[39]

Although such instantaneous enlightenment would be the exception, since Śaṅkara says all obstructions must to be removed beforehand, the possibility nonetheless exists in exceptional cases. But that is enough to substantiate the point that according to Śaṅkara the immediate and liberating knowledge can arise from the words of the Upaniṣads when their meaning has been correctly grasped. He unambiguously says this in the eighteenth chapter of the *Upadeśasāhasrī:*

> There is no doubt that the true knowledge about one's own Self can arise: on account of [the hearer] being free from obstacles and because oneself is of the very nature of Awareness. [18.104]

Further,

> The true knowledge of the inner-Self from the sentences "you are Being Itself" etc. would be very clear, like it would be from the sentence "you are the tenth man". [18.192]

Śaṅkara's teaching in this regard is consistent with his understanding that the *śruti* is to be interpreted though indication *(lakṣaṇā)*. For although *lakṣaṇā* is sometimes translated as "indirect indication", it is indirect only in so far as it is not the literal meaning of the word, but there need be nothing "indirect" about the meaning received by the hearer. The content of a statement where *lakṣaṇā* is used is meant to be immediately apprehended, just as in the case of any meaningful utterance. Whether the indication is by way of *jahallakṣaṇā*, as in "the village is on the Ganges"; or *ajahallakṣaṇā*, as in "protect the curd from the crows"; or, as is generally the case in Advaita, by *jahadajahallakṣaṇā (bhāgatyāgalakṣaṇā)*, such as "this is that Devadatta" or "you are the tenth man", a sentence whose meaning is revealed by indication is meant to generate an immediate apprehension in the mind of the hearer.

The possibility that words produce immediate knowledge of the inner-Self rests upon an important philosophical precondition. If the words of the *śruti* refer to something remote *(parokṣa)* from the hearer there is no possibility that those words can generate an immediate knowledge about that thing. When someone hears the description of a hereto unknown place, the hearer can never have the direct experience of the speaker, because the speaker's words refer to something outside the experience of the hearer. However if the situation is such that words refer to something immediate *(aparokṣa)* to the hearer, though that immediacy is unknown to the hearer, as in the example of the "tenth man",[40] then the condition exists for words to produce immediate knowledge in the hearer. This precondition is fulfilled, according to Advaita, in the understanding that the Self is Awareness that is self-revealing *(svayaṁprakāśa)*.

The teaching that the Self is Awareness that is inherently self-revealing, or self-luminous, can be found, for example, in the *Bṛhadāraṇyaka* Upaniṣad, where Yājñavalkya teaches Uṣasta who seeks to know about the nature of the Brahman that is: "direct and immediate *(sākṣād aparokṣād brahma),* the Self that is within all" (BU 3.4.2; also see 4.3.9). In keeping with these teachings in the Upaniṣads, the proposition that Awareness is self-revealing is an important philosophical position for Śaṅkara, for it underpins the logic of much of his hermeneutics of the *śruti*. For example, he writes in the *Brahmasūtrabhāṣya:*

> Whatever is perceived, is perceived by the Light that is Brahman, but Brahman is not perceived by another light, as Its nature is self-luminous.[41]
>
> The Self is...self-established. For the Self does not become self-proved by depending upon a means of knowledge *(pramāṇa).* The various means of knowledge, such as perception, are used to make known to the Self previously non-established objects of knowledge, for nobody accepts that things like space and so forth are self-established and do not stand in need of a means of knowledge. But the Self, as the foundation of the operation of the means of knowledge, is established prior to the operation of those means of knowledge.[42]

In his commentary on the *Bṛhadāraṇyaka,* he writes:

> By the word "Self" (Ātman) is meant the Light, which is distinct from the aggregate of the body, the sense organs and their component parts, which reveals the body and the sense organs analogous to such external lights as the sun, but is not itself revealed by anything else.[43]
>
> What is meant by self-luminosity is that the Self is pure Awareness by nature.[44]

Instances could be multiplied, and indeed Śaṅkara makes repeated reference to the self-luminosity of the Self as pure Awareness throughout his commentary on the *Jyotirbrāhmaṇa* (4.3) in the *Bṛhadāraṇyaka* Upaniṣad, and frequently in the *Upadeśasāhasrī* as well.[45] Paul Hacker, who was rather favourably impressed by this teaching about the self's self-luminous nature, has made some significant remarks about the concept of the self-luminosity of the self.[46]

According to Śaṅkara, since the Self is self-luminous, i.e., it is self-revealing Awareness, its existence is not established by a means of proof that would itself depend upon the existence of such a Self. As Hacker has accurately stated the matter: "...that which makes a thing possible, or is the basis of it, cannot possibly itself be made possible by the thing which it makes possible."[47] Therefore, while all objects in the world require to be revealed by an appropriate means of knowledge, the existence of the Self is self-evident. And this is so, because the Self is Awareness by nature, and Awareness, while revealing its objects, also reveals itself. So for Śaṅkara, the Upaniṣads are not just a means of knowledge about the existence of the absolute Self, nor are they mere "road maps" showing the way towards a distant location, but they can directly point out the true nature of Awareness, through negation coupled with indication. Their words, when the import is correctly grasped, remove the mistaken understanding concerning the finite nature of Awareness. In the eyes of Śaṅkara, the Upaniṣads are truly a means of direct knowledge.

As mentioned, the understanding of Awareness as Self-luminous underpins much of Śaṅkara's hermeneutics of the *śruti.* For if the true Self is remote *(parokṣa)* from experience, then words could not reveal it, and the use of *lakṣaṇā,* as a way of directly indicating the Self, would be of no use. It seems that Śaṅkara's elder contemporary, Maṇḍanamiśra, did not interpret the *śruti* through *lakṣaṇā,* and there would have been no need for him to do so since he believed that words could provide only indirect knowledge.[48] The teaching that the Awareness-Self is self-luminous is important; both for its own sake, as a philosophical perspective of the nature of Awareness, as well as for understanding Śaṅkara's teaching concerning the possibility and the nature of Self-knowledge. It is important too for clarifying the question of "experience" *(anubhava)* in Śaṅkara's Advaita.

The question arises that if the true Self, the absolutely simple pure Awareness, is self-luminous and therefore already given in experience, in what sense can we speak of having an "experience" of the Self? The verb "experience" is transitive, but how can the pure Awareness be experienced in an objective fashion? Śaṅkara's understanding of the experience *(anubhava)* of the Self is in keeping with his fundamental position that the Self, as pure Awareness, is self-luminous. He says that the nature of Brahman and Ātman is Experience Itself *(anubhavātmaka, anubhavātman).*[49] Just as Śaṅkara's disciple Hastāmalaka, in his poetic composition *Hastāmalakīya,* uses the refrain that the Self is: "eternal Awareness by its very nature" *(nityopalabdhisvarūpa),* so does Śaṅkara use this same expression to refer to the Self.[50] Such expressions as *anubhavātman* and *nityopalabdhisvarūpa* are significant and unambiguous. Śaṅkara is saying that the Self, as pure Awareness, is not an experience, but is Experience, for its very nature is *anubhava.* It is the Awareness in the Light of Which all experiences are objectively revealed.

If the fundamental Self is Experience Itself, in what sense can we have an *experience of* this pure Awareness-Self? How can Awareness be experienced, if it is That by Which ordinary experience is possible? How can Awareness be experienced at all, if it is the very content of the experiencer, if it is the final Subject? Śaṅkara is very much aware of the problem of experience and objectification, as we can see from this passage of his commentary on *Brahmasūtra* 1.1.4:

> Brahman does not come within the sphere of acts through being an object of the action of knowing, for there is the denial that It is an object of the action of knowing in the passage: "It is other than the known and above [different from] the unknown" (KeU 1.4), as well as in: "Through what can one know That, through Which, one knows all this?" (BU 2.4.14). So too there is also the denial of Brahman being an object of a meditative action, for having first presented Brahman as not an object, in the passage: "That which is not uttered by speech, That by Which speech is uttered" (KeU 1.5), it is said: "Know That to be Brahman; it is not what people meditate upon as 'this'." (KeU 1.5).
>
> If it is objected that since Brahman is not an object it cannot possibly be revealed through the scripture, we say that is not so. For the scripture aims at the removal of differences that are superimposed by Ignorance. It is not that the scripture seeks to present Brahman as an object, as a "this". How does the scripture present It? The scripture,

> in presenting Brahman as the inner-Self, as not an object, removes the difference of the known, the knower, the act of knowledge etc. which are superimposed through Ignorance.[51]

Clearly, if there is to be an "experience" of Brahman, it must be different to the way in which we experience any sense object, and it must be different too from the way that we experience mental objects, i.e., thoughts etc. But Śaṅkara does not speak of a "mystical" realisation of Brahman in some unusual state of consciousness, analogous to the Yogic *nirvikalpa samādhi.* In his genuine works he nowhere says that Brahman realisation depends upon the cultivation of the meditative "state" called *nirvikalpa samādhi.*[52] And indeed on one occasion he specifically denies that yogic concentration *(cittavṛttinirodha)* is a means to liberation.[53] Surely, if it was his belief that liberation results from yogic concentration culminating in *nirvikalpa samādhi,* as many Vedāntins do believe, he would have devoted some space in his works to expounding such a view?

But if Śaṅkara does not speak of *nirvikalpa samādhi* type experience, does he speak of experience at all? And if so, in what way? Concerning the question of "experience" in Advaita, Arvind Sharma has sought to provide a wider scope for spiritual experience in contrast to Anantanand Rambachan who sees the *śruti* as generating the knowledge of Brahman without there being any need for some special experience apart from the liberating meaning that arises from the words of *śruti,* when rightly understood.[54] I do not wish to deny the possibility of extra-ordinary states of mind loosely called "mystical" experiences, such as we can see, for example, in the lives of Rāmakṛṣṇa and Ramaṇa Maharṣi. We should note, however, that the type of experiences that Rāmakṛṣṇa and Ramaṇa underwent do not seem to have that much in common. Also, I wish to suggest that the repeated characterisation of Rāmakṛṣṇa's experiences as *"nirvikalpa samādhi"* seems to be more of a convenient label to refer to his particular states of noetic absorption than it is a factual description of *asaṁprajñāta samādhi,* better known as *nirvikalpa samādhi,* as presented in the Yoga and the Tantra-Yoga traditions where these terms are most prevalent. I do not seek to call into question the validity of an insight that can be gained though deep meditative absorption, or states where there is absorption in some kind of intuitive awareness, such as we can see in the case of Rāmakṛṣṇa; but there is a danger that in accepting the description of the experiences of Rāmakṛṣṇa and others, as they are portrayed and coloured by their pious biographers, as constituting yogic *nirvikalpa samādhi*, which is then presented as the paradigm of how spiritual experience ought to be, an imagination is created that spiritual experience must be of such and such a type, and that very imagination itself becomes a significant impediment to understanding the type of simple intuition, or discriminative insight, about which Śaṅkara speaks.

From what we have seen in the preceding paragraphs concerning Śaṅkara's understanding of the self-luminosity and immediacy *(aparokṣatva)* of pure Awareness, and his understanding of the Self as Experience Itself *(anubhavātman)*, there is no doubt that when Śaṅkara speaks of the knowledge of the Self he refers to an intuitive knowledge, or direct insight, about the already existing fact of the Self as pure Awareness. He does not put forward the view that the experience of pure Awareness must be produced; a view we find, for example, in the Tantric tradition, with its model of the *chakras* and the ascent of the *kuṇḍalinī*. Rambachan has correctly highlighted the centrality of the *śruti* in Śaṅkara's thought and his analysis is fundamentally accurate, though he is perhaps too wary of the word "experience", for Śaṅkara does use that word. Let us now see, as far as possible, how Śaṅkara uses the word "experience" *(anubhava)*, and what is the nature of that experience.

In the course of his commentary upon *Brahmasūtra* 1.1.2, in a passage that is frequently cited, Śaṅkara writes:

> The *śruti* etc. [i.e. as supported by inference] are not the only means of knowledge in the inquiry into Brahman as they are in the inquiry into religious duty (dharma). But the *śruti* etc., as well as experience *(anubhava)* etc. are, in accordance with their possibilities, the means of knowledge about Brahman, and that is because the knowledge of Brahman culminates in experience and refers to an already existing entity.[55]

Although there are a number of elements in this passage that remain somewhat vague, there can be no question that Śaṅkara explicitly says that the knowledge of Brahman "culminates", literally "ends", in experience *(anubhava).* Elsewhere, in speaking of the scope of reason, he legitimises the use of reasoning that is in keeping with the tenor of the *śruti,* and he says that such reasoning can be accepted, as it is "a help to *anubhava" (anubhavāṅgatvena).*[56] Again, in 3.3.32, he speaks about the connection between knowledge and experience:

> Since knowledge [of the Supreme Self] produces an immediately felt result, it is not logically possible for there to be a doubt concerning the lack of a result. In the case of the results of action, like heaven etc., which are not met with in experience, there can be a doubt as to whether that result will occur or not, but the result of knowledge is present to experience, for there is the statement of the *śruti:* "The Brahman that is direct and immediate" (BU 3.4.1), and there is the statement "you are That" (CU 6.8.7) which teaches [that Brahman] is something already accomplished. This sentence "you are That" cannot be interpreted to mean you will become That, after you are dead. And the *śruti:* "Seeing this [Self] to be That [Brahman], the sage Vāmadeva knew: 'I was Manu, and the Sun' " (BU 1.4.10) shows that the result of knowledge, i.e., the Self being everything, takes place at the very time of right understanding.[57]

There are a number of statements in the *Brahmasūtrabhāṣya* which speak of the result of knowledge as "present to experience" *(anubhavārūḍha),* and as something that is "directly felt" *(pratyakṣīkṛta).*[58]

What sort of experience is Śaṅkara referring to? To answer this question we need to keep in mind some important points mentioned above. Firstly, Śaṅkara is committed to the understanding that the Self is self-luminous, for it is by nature pure Awareness *(svayaṁjyotiṣṭvaṁ nāma caitanyātmasvabhāvatā).*[59] Secondly, in accord with this view of the self-luminosity of the Self as Awareness, Śaṅkara has characterised the Self as: "Experience Itself" *(anubhavātman).* We should therefore expect that the experience about which Śaṅkara speaks is the "intuition", "insight", or even "recognition" of oneself *as* pure Awareness. It cannot be a new experience, of producing something that did not previously exist, nor can it be an experience involving the objectification of Awareness. It is, rather, the "experience" of oneself *as* Awareness, without limitation. For that is what one is, and so finds oneself to be, when there is the apprehension of one's own fundamental Awareness-nature, together with the apprehension of the "seeming", or the apparent nature *(mithyātva),* of all limiting adjuncts *(upādhis):* those that pertain to the individual body-mind *(tvam),* as well as to the Lordship of Brahman *(tat).*

This is borne out from what he says. In the *Brahmasūtrabhāṣya* 4.1.2 we have the following significant passage:

> [referring to the meaning of *"tat tvam asi"*, Śaṅkara says] The sentence "you are That" *(tat tvam asi)* tells that what is meant by the word "you" is by nature identical to what is meant by the word "That". ...The meaning of the word "That", which goes by the name of "Brahman", which is free from all the attributes of phenomenal existence and which is of the nature of Experience Itself, is well known to those who are proficient in the Upaniṣads. So too, the meaning of the word "you" is the inner-Self, the hearer, who is considered to be the inner-Self as [being identical to] the body and so forth until it is finally determined to be Awareness. In the case of those people to whom the meaning of these two words remain obstructed by ignorance, doubt, or misconception, the sentence *"tat tvam asi"* cannot produce the correct cognition of its meaning, for the knowledge of the sentence has to be preceded by the knowledge of the individual words. And so, for such people, the repetition of the scripture and reasoning is necessary, as its purpose is to discern what the words truly mean. ....
> [objection] What you have said makes sense if anyone could have the understanding of which you speak, but the understanding of oneself as sorrowful etc. is very strong. Hence no one understands oneself to be without sorrow etc.
> [reply] That is not so, because it is logically possible that the presumption of being sorrowful and so forth is a false

> presumption, just like the presumption that one is the body etc. For it is directly evident that when the body is being cut or burnt the false presumption is seen: "I am being cut" and "I am being burnt". So too, when sons or friends etc., who are more external [to oneself than the body], are suffering, the superimposition is seen that: "I myself am suffering". The presumption of being sorrowful etc. is also like that, for sorrow etc. are perceived as something "outward" with respect to Awareness, just like the body etc. And furthermore, sorrow etc. do not persist during deep sleep etc., whereas scripture declares that Awareness persists even during deep sleep, as in the statement: "That It does not see in that state is because, though seeing then, It does not see" (BU 4.3.23) etc. Therefore, this is the experience of the Self: "I am solely of the nature of Awareness that is entirely free from all sorrow."[60]

Here, two things are to be noted. Firstly, while Śaṅkara generally uses the word "experience" *(anubhava)* in this passage (of which only part has been quoted) according to the common understanding of what we normally mean by "experience", he also uses the word *"pratipatti"* ("understanding") as an alternative to the word *anubhava.* Since these two words are used almost interchangeably in his comments on this *sūtra,* we must restrict the somewhat vague meaning of *anubhava* in keeping with the more specific meaning of *pratipatti,* and we must also interpret the word *pratipatti* so that it accords with the sense of "immediacy" implicit in the word *anubhava.* Therefore the *anubhava* that is spoken about here must be a "direct knowledge", a "direct awareness", a "direct or immediate understanding". Secondly, in the final sentence of the quotation Śaṅkara plainly tells us what he means by the "experience of the Self" *(ātmānubhava).* It is the experience, i.e., the direct awareness, or immediate understanding, that: "I am solely of the nature of Awareness that is entirely free from all sorrow".[61] In his independent work, *Upadeśasāhasrī,* we can see how Śaṅkara frequently extols upon his own, inherent nature, as Awareness.

(3) Liberation, Jīvanmukti and Prārabdhakarma

We have seen that the insight, intuition, or the immediate understanding called "Self-knowledge" can arise directly from the Upaniṣad statements, provided the hearer is able to grasp the true import of those statements. Though Śaṅkara makes allowance for rare, already perfected beings, such as the *ṛṣi* Vāmadeva, who could gain Self-knowledge even while in the womb and without needing to undergo instruction, his works show a persistent emphasis on the importance of receiving traditional instruction, as we can see from his frequent compounding of the two words "scripture" *(śāstra)* and "teacher" *(ācārya)*.[62] If the student is not of the highest calibre, and there are obstacles to the rise of knowledge from hearing the principal *śruti* teachings, a situation which presumably would be the more usual, then the teacher is advised to engage the student in repeated hearing *(śravaṇa)* of the texts, to continue in the discernment of their import *(manana)*, and to repeatedly contemplate upon the truth they reveal *(nididhyāsana)* until there is immediate knowledge:

> Hearing *(śravaṇa)* etc., when repeated, culminate in immediate knowledge *(darśana)* and thus have a tangible purpose, just as threshing and so on which culminate in producing the grain of rice etc. Furthermore, the words *"upāsana"* and *"nididhyāsana"* refer implicitly to an action that involves the quality of repetition.[63]

In his commentary upon the well-known passage in the *Bṛhadāraṇyaka* Upaniṣad where the words *śravaṇa* etc. occur ["The Self, my dear, is to be made immediately evident, it must be heard *(śrotavya)*, reflected about *(mantavya)* and contemplated upon *(nididhyāsitavya)"]*, Śaṅkara says that immediate knowledge arises from all three means in combination, but "not by hearing alone" *(na...śravaṇamātreṇa)*. Since Śaṅkara has explicitly stated in his commentary on *Brahmasūtra* 4.1.2 that immediate knowledge *can* arise from hearing itself in the case of those rare seekers who have no obstructions, we should understand that he is referring in his *Bṛhadāraṇyaka* commentary to what is perhaps the more usual situation, where the seeker should combine and repeat all of the three, *śravaṇa, manana and nididhyāsana*, as long as necessary.[64]

Since the Self is inherently Brahman, the means to liberation have a negative function in so far as they remove the obstacles *(pratibandha)* to the knowledge of the Self that is then discovered to have never really been bound.[65] Śaṅkara refers on a number of occasions to liberation as the destruction of obstacles.[66] These "obstacles" consist of "ignorance, doubt, or misconception" about what is revealed; though even the untimely intervention of past karma can create an obstacle. Śaṅkara says:

> Knowledge arises in this very life provided the means *(sādhana)* for knowledge, once they have been commenced, are not obstructed by some other result of past deeds that just then arises. When such an obstruction happens, then [knowledge arises] in a later life. ...And when the *śruti* says that Vāmadeva realised the state of being Brahman even while in his mother's womb (BU 1.4.10), it just shows that knowledge arises in a later birth through the means stored up from a previous birth.[67]

It is well-known that Advaita upholds that liberation is compatible with continuing to remain with the body; in other words, to be "liberated while still living" *(jīvanmukti).* However before discussing further Śaṅkara's idea of the "liberated person" *(jīvanmukta),* it may be worthwhile to present some instances from Śaṅkara's works where he articulates his understanding of the *jīvanmukta.* The first passage speaks of the knower of Brahman as having two ways of self-understanding: as seeing everything as the Self, from the standpoint of seeing that everything is an *upādhi* to Awareness, and also from the standpoint of Awareness itself. He says:

> The person who knows, i.e., this person who is a knower of Brahman, has these characteristics: [in seeing himself as] having everything as his limiting adjunct *(upādhi),* i.e., that everything is the Self, he becomes all. But [in seeing himself as] without any adjunct, he is without name, without interior or exterior, whole, solely of the nature of Awareness, unborn, without old age, deathless, free from

fear, motionless, characterised as "not this, not this", neither gross, nor subtle.[68]

We call him a knower of Brahman who always knows that the Self is beyond the phenomenal condition of hunger etc. and has no connection to sin.[69]

> The person who knows that the Self is the invariable Seeing and is intrinsically without agentship. and who has also given up the idea that he is a knower of Brahman, such a person is a knower of the Self and no one else. [US 12.13]
>
> A person would be a knower of the Self when the self-referring cognitions of "I" and "mine" no longer have any meaning. [US 14.29]
>
> A man is liberated if, completely removing the ideas of "I" and "mine", he has a firm understanding of the "state" which is comparable to space, which is free from the body, and which has been declared [by us] according to the well-studied scripture and by reasoning. [US 15.54]
>
> The person whose knowledge about the Self - a knowledge which negates the cognition that the body is the Self - [is firm], like [the previous] cognition that the body is the Self, he is liberated even without wishing it. [US 4.5]

Knowledge about the truth of the Self is only the cessation of identifying the Self with what is extraneous [i.e. the body-mind complex]. An identification does not need to be directly established with regard to the Self, because the

> identification is already present. This identification with the Self is constant for everyone but it seems to be related to something else. Therefore, apart from the cessation of the false appearance of being related to something else, no identification with the Self need be accomplished. When the identification with other things is gone, the natural identification with one's own Self becomes unobstructed and it is thereby said that "the Self is known".[70]
>
> In connection with the subject matter of injunctions, some thing, such as *agnihotra* etc., still remains to be performed at a time other than when there is the knowledge of the meaning of the statement [describing it].... But that is not the case here, in the matter of the higher knowledge, where the thing in question comes to completion at the same time as there is the knowledge of the meaning of the statement, because there is nothing [more that needs to be done] apart from remaining merely in the knowledge of the meaning that is revealed by the words themselves.[71]

If this last passage, from the commentary on the *Muṇḍaka* Upaniṣad, is read in isolation, one could perhaps believe that the knowledge referred to is merely verbal and conceptual, but such a conclusion is ruled out by statements in the *bhāṣya* on the preceding passage (1.1.5).[72] And we can clearly see that the knowledge that is spoken of is not merely verbal when we read this quotation in relation to the others cited above. The first six quotations show liberation as an existential insight about the deepest aspect of one's Being, as pure Awareness. The seventh quotation tells that liberation is not an "attainment" of something new, but the discovery of what already exists, upon the negation of superimposition. The eighth quotation says that there is nothing to be done: "apart from remaining merely in the knowledge of the meaning that is revealed by the words themselves." This quotation again centres the liberating insight in the context of the sacred word, but what is spoken of here is not merely remaining in the knowledge of the words, but remaining in the existential knowledge of the *meaning* of the words.

As the Self is without change, it can only be metaphorically said to be bound or liberated. If the question is asked as to who, then, is bound or freed, the answer must be that the ideas of bondage and liberation pertain to the psychological self, the ego or "I"-notion, which is Awareness as reflected in the mind. The Self can be said to undergo bondage and suffering by way of the ignorance belonging to the superimposed "I"-notion, and the Self can be said to be liberated by way of the knowledge that takes place for the superimposed "I"-notion.

Certain qualifications are required as the prerequisite for this knowledge. Śaṅkara specifies a fourfold qualification that entails having the capacity to discern between what is lasting and what is merely ephemeral; developing dispassion towards ephemeral goals; cultivating a life centred around sense-control, tranquillity of mind and the renunciation of worldly pursuits; and having the desire for spiritual liberation. Formally, they are presented as: (1) the capacity to discriminate between what is lasting and what is impermanent; (2) dispassion toward the enjoyment of the fruits of one's actions *(karmaphala)* in this world, or in another world; (3) the cultivation of tranquillity of mind, sense-control, renunciation, forbearance, trust, and concentration of the mind; (4) the desire to be free.[73] He states that Brahman can be inquired into and known when these qualifications are present[74] and he is insistent that an aspirant for this knowledge should possess a high degree of dispassion toward the attractions of the world.[75]

While Śaṅkara's theoretical audience consists of the three higher classes, Brāhmaṇas, Kṣatriyas and Vaiśyas, all of whom are entitled to study the Veda, he particularly has in mind throughout his works the community of Brāhmaṇas, whose life is especially defined by the duties of the four stages of life *(āśrama,* i.e., student, householder, forest-dweller and renunciate). In the course of discussion the question arises whether members of these classes, who for some reason are outside any of the four recognised stages of life, can still be qualified for the knowledge of Brahman. Śaṅkara says they can, because there is the instance of a person like Raikva (CU 4.1f.) who had the knowledge of Brahman but who was not known to be associated with any *āśrama;* and we also hear, he says, of the woman Gārgī (BU 3.6.1; 3.8.1f.) who was a knower of Brahman.[76] Śaṅkara goes on to enunciate the general principle that the mere absence of any prohibition to the contrary is sufficient to qualify a seeker to undertake hearing the texts etc. in pursuit of knowledge.[77]

In the case of Śūdras, however, the situation is different. Śaṅkara argues that there is a specific prohibition against their studying the Veda, because they are excluded from investiture with the sacred thread *(upanayana)* which is the prerequisite for entry into Vedic study.[78] He does acknowledge that some Śūdras have indeed acquired the knowledge of Brahman due to their past mental impressions, but he says that though Śūdras can listen to the Itihāsa and the Purāṇa literature, they are not entitled to acquire knowledge directly through the Veda.[79] In a similar way to Śaṅkara, Rāmānuja too interprets the statements of the *Brahmasūtras* as prohibiting Śūdras from Vedic study.[80] These *ācāryas* reflect the circumstances of their own times, and they ought not be condemned as discriminatory from the vantage point of our times when the principle of political equality, stemming from the European Enlightenment, is now widely accepted as a moral right; though we can see that it still remains restricted in many ways in the West, such as in the current prohibition against women priests by some of the major Christian Churches.

We should bear in mind that equality, whether in Śaṅkara's time, or now, is subject to restriction, though in each age we define the restrictions differently, based upon our current moral presuppositions. Nevertheless, if Śaṅkara had wished to argue the opposite, radical view, that Śūdras ought to be entitled to Vedic study, it would not have been impossible for someone of his ability to mount a substantial argument in favour of that position, for in the extensive literature of the *śruti* and *smṛti* there is always some passage that could be marshalled to support one's argument. For example, when Śaṅkara argues that *sannyāsa* could be adopted from any stage of life, he does so largely on the basis of a single Vedic text, from the *Jābāla* Upaniṣad, and in the course of the discussion he cites and restricts the scope of other Vedic texts that could be used to support the opposite view from the one he favours. So although in those times Śūdras were to be at least theoretically debarred from studying the Veda, they could acquire liberation from the various *smṛti* texts, which are based ultimately upon the Vedic revelation.

The liberated person *(jīvanmukta)* continues to live in the world, having a physical body that suffers the same fate, old age, sickness and death, as the bodies of other people.[81] However the liberated person knows the true unembodied nature of the Self, and as a result of that knowledge there is no longer the ego-driven identification with the body-mind, so that Śaṅkara can speak of the liberated person, in a paradoxical way, as "bodiless".[82] Among the various passages that Śaṅkara sees as referring to the state of liberation while living *(jīvanmukti)*, one of the most important is the passage in the *Bṛhadāraṇyaka*, which says:

> Just as the lifeless slough of a snake is cast off and lies on an ant hill, so does this body lie. Then the liberated person is bodiless, immortal, the supreme Self, Brahman, the Light. [BU 4.4.7]

Śaṅkara says that just as a living snake discards its old skin as something no longer itself, the liberated person discards the false presumption of being the body. Previously he was embodied, and therefore mortal; but now he has ceased to identify with the body, he is the Self of all, his essence is bodiless, and thereby he is immortal.[83]

What is the reason the *jīvanmukta* is said to be free from subsequent karma and rebirth? And regarding the state of *jīvanmukti* itself, why does the body remain alive; why does release from the body not occur simultaneously with the rise of knowledge? Also, is it possible that the liberated person might revert to the previous condition of error? Śaṅkara answers the first two questions in terms of the different operations of karma. His explanation is that if the effects of the various good and bad deeds done in a previous life, or in the present life before the rise of knowledge, have not yet begun to operate, then they are all destroyed by the knowledge of the true nature of the Self. So too, any actions done by the liberated person after the rise of knowledge *(āgāmikarma)* do not create new karma to be later experienced. The reason why all this is so, Śaṅkara says, is that the experience of the effects of past actions, as well as the creation of new actions, requires agency, someone who believes "I do". But agency *(kartṛtva)* is a notion belonging to the ego, and it has been sublated by the cognition that the Self is truly actionless:

> The knower of Brahman understands: "I am Brahman, whose nature is without doership or enjoyership in all the

> three periods of time [past, present and future], the very opposite of the doership and enjoyership previously held to be true. Even prior to this I was neither an agent nor an enjoyer, I am not so now, nor will I be so at a future time." It is only in this way that liberation is logically possible.[84]

What about the results of those past deeds that have already begun to operate *(prārabdha* karma) by producing the current birth in which enlightenment takes place? To account for the situation that knowledge cannot negate the type of karma that has begun to produce its results, for we see that the liberated person remains alive and encounters a variety of pleasant and painful experiences, Śaṅkara often employs the analogy of the arrow which must continue on its course when it has left the bow, or the analogy of the potter's wheel which continues to spin for some time under its own momentum once it has been set in motion.[85] In the following passage Śaṅkara raises the question about the continuance of the *prārabdha* karma:

> [objection] The understanding that the Self is not an agent destroys, by its intrinsic power, the results of actions; but how can this knowledge destroy some kinds of karma while it leaves others intact? When seeds equally come into contact with fire we cannot accept that some have their power of germination destroyed while others do not.
> [reply] The origination of knowledge is not logically possible without relying on the aggregate of karma that has begun to produce its results. When that is depended upon, since there is no obstruction to its momentum in the intervening period, we must wait for the momentum to come to its own end, as in the case of the potter's wheel. Further, the knowledge that the Self is not an agent exterminates the results of actions by sublating wrong knowledge *(mithyājñāna)*. But even when that wrong knowledge is sublated, it persists for some time owing to the mental impressions that it left behind, like the knowledge of a double moon. Moreover, it is not a matter

> for dispute here as to whether or not the knower of Brahman retains the body for some time, for when one person knows in his own heart that he has the knowledge of Brahman, as well as retains a body, how can someone else deny it?[86]

Śaṅkara's explanation is that complete knowledge *(samyagjñāna)* "burns up" the seeds of the karma that has not yet begun to produce its result. Since this karma has wrong knowledge *(mithyājñāna)* as its support, it is no longer able to "sprout" once that support has been removed. But knowledge cannot "burn up" what already exists, and the experience of duality, like the experience of two moons (which may remain for a while due to habituation, even after the ocular problem is rectified), continues until the *prārabdha* karma that produced this birth has been experienced.[87] The liberated person does not generate any new karma, because of the absence of agentship, but merely experiences with equanimity the remaining *prārabdha* karma. Such a person, being free in this life, does not, after the death of the body, take up a new body. In the words of the Upaniṣad: "being free, he is freed" *(vimuktaś ca vimucyate* KaU 2.2.1).

In regard to the third question raised above, about the possibility that a liberated person might revert to the previous condition of error, which may then lead to wrong actions, Śaṅkara says that the liberated person will not behave contrary to the knowledge of the truth, because it is the false presumption of identity with the body that leads a person into various activities, but this identity is absent for the liberated person.[88] While Śaṅkara does not accept that a liberated person can have false notions *(viparītapratyaya)* which are based upon ignorance of his nature and superimposition etc., he does accept the possibility that memories - which may well resemble false notions - can arise from the mental impressions of false notions which were antecedent to knowledge of the truth. These memories can suddenly engender the type of error that belongs to false notions themselves, as even a person who knows the directions of the compass can suddenly have a momentary confusion about the direction.[89] Thus Śaṅkara does not accept that false notions can be present subsequent to the rise of knowledge, but he does allow that memories from past experiences prior to knowledge could still cause a sudden, momentary, confusion.[90]

(4) Sannyāsa and Videhamukti

What style of life would the liberated person follow? In Śaṅkara's opinion, if he is a householder he would renounce the domestic life to become a wandering ascetic. Renunciation *(sannyāsa)* is not something the liberated person has to undertake, like a person has to carry out the performance of an obligatory ritual, but rather Śaṅkara thinks that renunciation would automatically follow from the mere absence of involvement with action, such as the performance of the Vedic rites.[91] The reason the knower of Brahman takes to the way of life of a renouncer is because he has no desire for anything in this world, or in the world of the ancestors *(pitṛloka)*, or in the world of the gods *(devaloka)*. The means to attain the three worlds, i.e., this world, the world of the departed ancestors and the world of the gods, are progeny and wealth. A man can achieve security in this world through producing male offspring, and by means of wealth he is able to perform the rites to obtain the world of the ancestors. He can even obtain the world of the gods if he combines the performance of the rites with certain types of meditation. The knower of Brahman has no desire for anything in the three worlds, and so sees no purpose in acquiring the means, i.e., progeny and wealth, to achieve those worlds. The key Upaniṣad passage that conveys such an idea is:

> The ancient sages, it is said, did not desire children [as they thought]: "what will we do with progeny, when for us this Self is this world [the desired result]". [BU 4.4.22]

According to Śaṅkara, this passage from the *Bṛhadāraṇyaka* Upaniṣad (as well as the passage at 3.5.1) reveals that when a person knows the true nature of the Self and is without desire as a consequence of seeing nothing separate from the Self, the person has nothing to achieve through the performance of rites and should, therefore, relinquish the life of the world and become a wandering ascetic.[92]

Śaṅkara says that the Upaniṣad itself provides an illustration of renunciation after knowing the Self, for the sage Yājñavalkya renounced the world: "through the strength of his Self-knowledge."[93] Śaṅkara, moreover, considers that the example of Yājñavalkya indicates that the *śruti* wishes to enjoin renunciation as a part of the knowledge of Brahman.[94] This contradicts what we said at the beginning of this section

("Renunciation is not something the liberated person has to undertake..."), but at this place in his commentary Śaṅkara is emphatic. He interprets the present tense indicative verb in the passage: "desiring only this world [the Self], the mendicants go forth *(pravrajanti)* from their homes" [BU 4.4.22] as having an injunctive meaning: "they ought to go forth" *(pravrajeyuḥ)* and he says that the above sentence does constitute an injunction upon the knower of Brahman to renounce.[95]

According to Śaṅkara, *sannyāsa* serves to "mature Self-knowledge which is the means of liberation."[96] In his commentary upon the following passage of the *Bṛhadāraṇyaka* Upaniṣad: "the intelligent seeker of Brahman, having known the Self, should bring about the fullness of understanding" [BU 4.4.21], Śaṅkara says that this "fullness of understanding" relates to what the student has been taught by the teacher and the scripture and the means to that fullness of understanding are renunciation, tranquillity, self-control, withdrawal of the senses, fortitude and concentration of the mind.[97] Thus Śaṅkara considers *sannyāsa* to be a part of Self-knowledge, in that it provides the opportunity to be solely grounded in the Self, due to the cessation with the preoccupation of other things.[98]

Śaṅkara also advises a person to adopt the life of *sannyāsa* if that person is dispassionate toward the things of the world and is a seeker after Self-knowledge. He again refers to the passage: "desiring only this world [the Self], the mendicants go forth from their homes" [BU 4.4.22] which he evidently understands as a general injunction about renunciation, whether one already knows Brahman, or is seeking to know Brahman *(vividiṣu)*.[99] Judging from his commentary on the *Bṛhadāraṇyaka*, there was evidently an ongoing debate in his time about whether a person, (a) ought to remain a householder for life; or (b) should proceed successively through all the stages of life: student, householder, forest-dweller and renouncer; or (c) could renounce the world without passing through the stages of householder and forest-dweller. Śaṅkara upholds the last view.[100] Against the first position, he cites texts that recognise the existence of stages of life other than that of a householder. Against the second, he says that a person need not undergo each of the four stages of life in succession, because it is possible to become a renouncer from the student life itself:

> The statement: "one can renounce from the student life itself" [*Jābāla* 4][101] etc. is reasonable, when the seeker after liberation is dispassionate toward the things of the world, even if he is without knowledge.[102]

In the *Upadeśasāhasrī* Śaṅkara advises that a student should have, among other important qualifications and virtues, the qualification of already having renounced *(sannyāsin).*[103] However in the same text he also mentions a celibate student *(brahmacārin)* seeking instruction from a teacher.[104] These were presumably his ideal situations, though he must have acknowledged some flexibility in the matter since the Upaniṣads refer to householders approaching sages in order to know Brahman, such as the wealthy Śaunaka in the *Muṇḍaka* Upaniṣad. We have seen that according to Śaṅkara only the first three classes in society, the Brāhmaṇa, Kṣatriya and Vaiśya, are eligible to study the Veda.[105] But even among the three classes, Śaṅkara considers that the Brāhmaṇa alone has the right to renounce. That is so, says Śaṅkara, because only the word "Brāhmaṇa" is mentioned in the text: "knowing this very Self, the Brāhmaṇas renounce the desire for sons, wealth and worlds, and lead a mendicant's life" [BU 3.5.1].[106] We shall see in the following chapter that his view on this matter did not go unchallenged.

Śaṅkara further specifies that the renouncer, whether he is seeking the knowledge of Brahman, or whether he already knows the truth, should become a wandering ascetic known as a *paramahaṁsa (paramahaṁsapārivrājya).*[107] In the *Mahābhārata*, as well as in some of the later Upaniṣads known as *Sannyāsa* Upaniṣads, renouncers are classified into four groups: *kuṭīcaka, bahūdaka, haṁsa* and *paramahaṁsa,* with each latter group considered to be superior in status to the preceding group.[108] According to a passage in the *Jābāla* Upaniṣad, a text to which Śaṅkara frequently refers on the subject of renunciation,[109] the renouncer:

> wears a discoloured [ochre?] cloth, has a shaven head, has no possessions, is pure, without enmity, resorts to begging, and becomes fit to become Brahman.[110]

The *Jābāla* Upaniṣad mentions other characteristics of the *paramahaṁsa* mendicants: they have no emblems, they have discarded the triple bamboo staff, the water pot, the sling [which is used to carry personal possessions, or the water pot] the alms bowl, the cloth for purifying water [which is tied to the staff], the tuft of hair, and the sacred thread.[111] Śaṅkara too says that the *paramahaṁsa* does not possess: "the sacred thread, the triple staff, water pot etc."[112] and he cites the passage from the *Jābāla* Upaniṣad, "...has a shaven head, has no possessions... ." From the above we can see that the *paramahaṁsa* mendicant does not bear the emblems of ascetics who belong to the stage of life of *sannyāsa (āśrama sannyāsa),* such as the *kuṭīcaka* and the *bahūdaka.*[113] Śaṅkara says there are other types of renunciation where emblems such as the sacred thread etc. are enjoined.[114] The *paramahaṁsa* is evidently "beyond the stages of life" *(atyāśramin)*[115] and has no emblems denoting a stage of life. Does that mean that the *paramahaṁsa* is without any outwardly distinguishing marks whatsoever? Śaṅkara cites a passage from the *Mahābhārata* which says that the "knower of the truth wears no signs"[116]; but along with that passage he also cites the above mentioned *Jābāla* text: "wears a discoloured (ochre) cloth, has a shaven head, has no possessions" etc. From this we can deduce that while the *paramahaṁsa* renouncer does not have the sacred thread, the top-knot, the triple staff etc., he does have a shaven head and the ochre cloth, if he wears clothes at all.[117]

Patrick Olivelle has remarked: "It is unclear whether Saṃkara advocated total antinomianism in the case of such [enlightened] renouncers". Olivelle goes on to indicate that he believes this to be the case when he says the enlightened renouncer: "...can wear what he pleases. He can act as he pleases. He can violate the norms of moral conduct and the rules of rational behaviour."[118] Though such behaviour is theoretically possible for the liberated person, as such a person knows the Self to be intrinsically unattached *(asaṅga)* and thereby unaffected or "untouched" by anything, Śaṅkara denies that the liberated person would behave in an antinomian manner. He says:

> Just because the person who has complete understanding is not an object of [scriptural] injunction, it does not follow that he can do as he likes. For in all cases it is only one's false presumption [of being the body] that impels one to act, and for the person who has complete understanding that false presumption is absent.[119]

Śaṅkara's disciple, Sureśvara, has strongly argued against the opinion that the enlightened person would break the conventions of moral conduct.[120] Olivelle subsequently modified his view, and in a more recent work, *The Āśrama System*, he says:

> Even though Śaṃkara undoubtedly considered at least some form of renunciation to be beyond the modes of life comprehended by the *āśramas*, he nowhere asserts that such renouncers are not bound by conventional morality or that theirs was a totally antinomian state... .[121]

In the *Bhagavadgītā*, Śaṅkara upholds the same view about *sannyāsa* as in his commentaries upon the Upaniṣads, namely that those who already know the truth should adopt the way of life of *paramahaṁsasannyāsa*, and this life is also to be recommended for those who seek to know the truth and who have no interest in the means or ends in the three worlds.[122] The text of the *Bhagavadgītā*, however, does not share the same enthusiasm for *sannyāsa* as Śaṅkara, and the trend of some of the verses in the *Gītā* compels Śaṅkara to acknowledge the possibility that a knower of Brahman may be a householder, or in some other stage of life, because of the force of *prārabdha karma*. In 3.20 there is the well known line: "For Janaka and others reached perfection just through action." Śaṅkara comments that supposing Janaka and others had the knowledge of the truth, they continued to perform action on account of their past *karma*, and they did so for the welfare of the world. However, Śaṅkara also provides an alternative explanation that Janaka and the others did not yet know the truth, and so performed action as a means to purify the mind.[123]

In some other verses Śaṅkara is more forthright in accepting that enlightened people are not invariably *paramahaṁsa* renunciates. In his commentary to 4. 20 and 23, Śaṅkara accepts that an enlightened person may continue to perform the activities associated with his stage of life. His acceptance, however, is made with some reluctance, because in both places he adds the caveat that renunciation of all actions would have taken place if nothing stood to prevent it. He says in his introduction to verse twenty:

> The person who, under the influence of his *prārabdha karma,* comes to have the correct understanding of the Self at a later time in life, certainly abandons rites together with their accessories as he does not see a purpose in rites and actions. But if for some reason he is unable to abandon all actions, and he continues to be engaged in action like before, it is for the sake of the welfare of the world, as he is without attachment to actions or to their results since he does not have any purpose of his own. He does not do anything, his action amounts to non-action, because it has been consumed by the fire of knowledge.[124]

In this commentary upon verses such as these, which contain such unambiguous expressions as: "even though engaged in action, he does not do anything at all" (4.20), Śaṅkara is forced to allow for a *jñānī* who, due to some circumstance, happens to be other than a *paramahaṁsa* renouncer.[125]

What happens to the *jñānī* when the *prārabdha karma* reaches its end? In the *Bṛhadāraṇyaka,* it is said:

> [Ārtabhāga asked Yājñavalkya]: "Yājñavalkya, when this [liberated] person dies, do his organs depart from him or not?" "No", said Yājñavalkya, "they resolve here itself. The body swells, becomes bloated, and in that condition lies dead." [BU. 3.2.11]

Further on, Yājñavalkya says:

> But the man who has no desire [does not transmigrate]. He who is without desire, who is free from desire, who has attained his desire, whose desire is the Self: his organs do not depart. Being Brahman, he is merged in Brahman. [BU 4.4.6]

In his commentary upon these passages Śaṅkara says that the organs, i.e., the organs that make up the subtle body, and the mental impressions which impel the subtle body to take another physical body, are merged in the Self, in Brahman, like waves in the ocean.[126] Why does the enlightened person cease to transmigrate? Śaṅkara says that desire lies at the root of transmigration.[127] The knower of Brahman has no more desires because there is nothing apart from the Self, so there is nothing "other" to desire. Therefore the knowledge of non-duality is the reason for the absence of desire; and when there is no desire there is no effort to secure something for oneself by means of rites or some other form of activity. Such a person merely experiences the results of *prārabdha* karma, and when that is over, his organs "do not depart." What happens to the enlightened person after the body dies? Nothing happens; there is no going anywhere, for there is no place to go, since only Brahman exists, and the very idea of reaching somewhere presupposes a traveller and the conventions of space and time. Just as when a pot breaks the space does not go anywhere, although the pot-space could be metaphorically spoken of as "merging" into the total space, similarly the enlightened person, being Brahman, does not go anywhere, but can be metaphorically said to "merge" in Brahman.

Rāmānuja and others have argued that the type of liberation described above would be tantamount to self-destruction. Rāmānuja says:

> If the seeker of liberation concludes that liberation is the destruction of the "I", he would keep away at the mere hint of the commencement of talk to do with liberation.
>
> "Even when I have been destroyed, some Consciousness other than me will remain."
> No one will strive to attain that![128]

But the Advaitin does not see it that way. Rāmānuja's argument rests on the conviction that the ego is the Self, whereas according to the Advaitin the ego, or psychological self, the "I"-notion, is the combination (known as *cidābhāsa)* of pure Awareness and the limiting adjunct of the mind. The existence of the ego depends upon the presence of the limiting adjunct (it is therefore *aupādhika)* and the Advaitin does not consider that the destruction of a limiting adjunct *(upādhi)* is equivalent to destruction of the Self. The Advaitin would argue that Rāmānuja's statement: "some

Consciousness other than me will remain" is wrong, because it asserts a difference between "me" and Consciousness, whereas according to the Advaitin the "me" is not a reality in its own right, for in the final analysis, the "I" turns out to be pure Consciousness itself.

We have seen in the previous chapter that the concept of *upādhi* is central to Śaṅkara's teaching of non-duality. In liberation following upon the death of the physical body *(videhamukti)*, the limiting adjunct that is the subtle body - the mind, the sense organs and the vital breath - dissolves when the physical body dies. But the pure Awareness-Self remains as before, unaltered by the presence or absence of the body. Śaṅkara says that:

> An enlightened person, after his death, does not undergo a change of condition - something different than when he was living. But he is said to be "merged in Brahman" just due to his not being connected to another body.[129]

Thus the true Self remains unaltered, whether associated with a body or not, just as space is the same whether it is associated with limiting adjuncts, pots and so forth, or not. Liberation is not the non-existence of the Self, for according to the Upaniṣads that just does not occur: "there is no loss of the Seer's Seeing, because it is imperishable" [BU 4.3.23], "There is no loss of the Knower's Awareness, because it is imperishable" [BU 4.3.30]. *Videhamukti*, then, means the absence of having particular experience due to the removal of the limiting adjuncts of name-and-form.

---

1 R.V. De Smet, *The Theological Method of Śaṃkara,* op.cit., p.245.

2 BGBh 13.v.12, p.203, line 10f., (tr) p.531. Also, TUBh 2.1, p.285, line 15, (tr) p.297. KeUB 1.3, p.20, line 8, (tr) p.45. US 18.30.

3 Also BU 3.9.26; 4.2.4; 4.4.22; 4.5.15.

4 BUBh 2.3.6, p. 755f., line 26f., (tr) p.239.

5 KeUBh 2.1, p.25, line 5.f., (tr) p.58.

6 BSBh 3.2.22, p.654, line 2f., (tr) p.625.

7 Ibid., p.656, line 10f., (tr) p.627.

8 Also, cf. verse portion, intro. v.17; ch.11, vv.12, 14; ch.14, vv.11, 48; ch. 17. v.71; ch.18, vv.19, 21.

9 Karl. H. Potter, "Introduction to the Philosophy of Advaita Vedānta" in Karl. H. Potter (ed.), *Encyclopedia of Indian Philosophies (vol. 111): Advaita Vedānta up to Śaṃkara and His Pupils.* Delhi: Motilal Banarsidass, 1981, p.8.

10 Ibid. p.60. "It is not Śaṃkara's contention that Brahman cannot be indicated by words -what he is saying is that Brahman cannot be directly designated by any word. However, It can be indirectly designated for example, by the word 'I'."

11 R.V. De Smet, *The Theological Method of Śaṃkara,* op.cit., p.289.

12 A. Rambachan, *Accomplishing the Accomplished,* op.cit., p.75f.

13 S. Mayeda, *A Thousand Teachings. The Upadeśasāhasrī of Śaṅkara.* Translated with Introduction and Notes. Tokyo: University of Tokyo Press, 1979, p.53f.

14 In Śaṅkara's commentary upon this whole passage he mentions seven times that the statement *"satyaṁ jñānam anantaṁ brahma"* is a definition of Brahman. TUBh 2.1, p.282, line 10 and 15, (tr) p.289f.; p.283, lines 1 and 4, (tr) p.291; p.284, lines 8 and 10, (tr) p. 294; p.285, line 18f., (tr) p.298.

15 TUBh 2.1, p.283, line 7f., and the preceeding para., (tr) p. 291.

16 GK 2.6; 4.31. Cf. the discussion of this point in chapters one and two.

17 TUBh 2.1, p.283, line 8f., (tr) p.291.

18 Ibid., p. 283, line 14f., (tr) 292.

19 Ibid., 284, line 13f., (tr), p.295.

20 As Hacker has pointed out, in Śaṅkara's thought Awareness is the most important term, not Being. Thus here, it is *jñāna* that is characterised as both *satya* and *ananta.* While Hacker is correct in noting that Awareness has primary significance rather than Being (cf. for example, "Being and Spirit in Vedānta" in W. Halbfass (ed.), *Philology and Confrontation,* op.cit., p.194.), I think that in his example from *Kaṭha* 2.3.12-13 he has somewhat overstated the case, and there are some occasions where Śaṅkara does refer to Brahman as Being *(sanmātra).*

21 TUBh 2.1, op.cit., p.285, line 13f., (tr) p.297.

---

22 Ibid., p.285, line 14, (tr) p.297.

23 Ibid., p.285, line 17f., (tr) p.297f.

24 Cf. Michael Comans, "The Essential Definition of Brahman. Taittirīya Upaniṣad 2.1.1.", *The Voice of Śaṅkara. A Quarterly Journal of Advaita-Vedānta.* (Madras) Vol. 11, no.3, 1986 contd. no.4, 1987.

25 TUBh 2.1, op.cit., p.285, line 19f., (tr) p.298.

26 KeUBh 2.1, p.25, line 5.f., (tr) p.58. Cf. *supra,* note no. 5.

27 CUBh 6.16.3, p.539, line 16f. (tr) p.498f.

28 Ibid.

29 K. Kunjunni Raja, *Indian Theories of Meaning.* Madras: The Adyar Library and Research Centre, 1977, p.231f.

30 KeUBh 2.4, p.27, line 6f., (tr) p.63.

31 In the course of explaining how *tattvamasi* reveals its meaning through *lakṣaṇā,* Śaṅkara says: "Thus they [the words *tat* and *tvam* through their juxtaposition] mutually convey the meaning of the sentence: 'not this, not this'." US 18. 198.

32 Cf. Michael Comans, "Śaṅkara and the Prasaṅkhyānavāda". *Journal of Indian Philosophy,* 24, 1996, pp.49-71.

33 R.V. De Smet, *The Theological Method of Śaṃkara,* op.cit., p.119.

34 Ibid., p.123.

35 Ibid., p.292, 343.

36 Cited in A. Rambachan, *Accomplishing the Accomplished*, op.cit., p.4, 8. Mahadevan and Hiriyanna can be found to have made a number of statements similar to those cited here.

37 Cf. *The Naiṣkarmyasiddhi of Sureśvarācārya with the commentary of Jñānottama*. Edited by G.A. Jacob, Revised Edition by M. Hiriyanna. Poona: Bhandarkar Oriental Research Institute, 1980, p.xxvi. That T.M.P. Mahadevan was also well aware of this tradition is evident in the introduction to his edition and translation of the *The Saṁbandha-Vārtika of Sureśvarācārya* [Madras: University of Madras, 1972.], as well as from his work: *The Philosophy of Advaita: with special reference to Bhāratītīrtha-Vidyāranya*. London: Compton Russell, 1977.

38 BSBh 4.1.2, p.829, line 1f., (tr) p.815.

39 Ibid., p.830, line 5f., (tr) p.817.

40 The story of the tenth man is used as an example to show that direct knowledge can arise from words. The story is that ten pilgrims were crossing a river on the way to their destination. After fording the river they stopped to regroup and each looked to see that the others had crossed safely. They each counted, but only arrived at the number nine. They then began to despair, for they did not know who was absent, but they knew that someone was missing. A bystander watched this spectacle with growing amusement and after a short time went up to the group and said, "the tenth man exists". They shouted, "Where is he?". "I will show you", the bystander said. The bystander lined them up and then asked one person to count the group. He reached the number nine and stopped. The bystander pointed to him and said: "and you are the tenth!". Immediately the fellow understood that he

had forgotten to count himself and that he was indeed the tenth man.

41 BSBh 1.3.22, p.242, line 9, (tr) p.201.

42 BSBh 2.3.7, p.508, line 3f., (tr) p.455. (the above translation relies on Thibaut in part).

43 BUBh 4.3.6, p.864, line 14f., (tr) p.421.

44 BUBh 4.3.23 (intro.), p.896, line 6f. *(svayaṁjyotiṣṭvaṁ nāma caitanyātmasvabhāvatā),* (tr) p.467.

45 BUBh 4.3.7, p.891, line 2, *viviktena svena ātmajyotiṣā svapnātmikāṁ dhīvṛttim avabhāsayan-avatiṣṭhate yasmāt tasmāt svayañjyotissvabhāva eva asau.* (tr) p.430-31. Also, cf. 4.3.9, p.879, line 15f., (tr) p.443. 4.3.10, p.880, line 10f., (tr) p.444. 4.3.21, p.891, line 23f., *ayam ātmā svayaṁ caitanyajyotissvabhāvaḥ sarvaṁ svena caitanyajyotiṣā-avabhāsayati* (tr) p.461. 4.3.22, p.895, line 22f., (tr) p.467. Cf. *Upadeśasāhasrī:* "On account of the intervention [of space and time] the ordinary visual seeing belonging to the non-self is mediate. Brahman is considered to be immediately evident because Seeing is the very nature of the Self." [17.40]; "Just as there is no requirement of another lamp to light up a lamp, similarly, no other awareness is required [to reveal the Self] because Awareness is the very nature of the Self." [17.41].

46 Hacker's remarks on this topic are instructive and worth noting at length. In his article "Śaṅkara's Conception of Man" (cf. W. Halbfass (ed), *Philology and Confrontation,* op.cit., p.177f.), he says, p.182:

"Buddhist philosophy taught that each consciousness-instant *(saṃvid),* like a lamp, illuminates itself and its object. From this doctrine the Prābhākaras had taken over the view that knowledge as such is luminous. But since they, unlike the Buddhists, acknowledged the existence of an abiding self as the substratum or agent of knowledge, they modified the theory. Knowledge, they explained, illuminates or manifests not only itself and its object but also the self which is the knower. Śaṅkara, however, found that it is neither the Inner Sense [as held by Sāṅkhya] nor the act of cognition which is self-luminous, but the self itself. ...To express this doctrine of the self-luminosity of the self, Śaṅkara had recourse to a term he found in an Upaniṣad: *svayaṃjyotis* (Bṛh.4, 3, 9). His choice of this term implicitly brings out his conviction that his doctrine was nothing but what was taught by the Veda." In his last article on Vedānta, "Cit and Nous, or the Concept of Spirit in Vedāntism and in Neoplatonism", Ibid., p.211f., he makes the following remark about the self-luminosity of the Self; a remark which an Advaitin would endorse (p.214): "Whatever names we may give to the principle that makes both mental and sensuous acts or events possible, whether we call it consciousness or spirit or thought or knowledge, it is absurd to assume that this principle should need an act of knowledge in order to attain that status which we call 'to be known' or 'to be manifest'. It is absurd because that which makes a thing possible, or is the basis of it, cannot possibly itself be made possible by the thing which it makes possible."

47 Ibid., p.214.

48 Kuppuswami Sastri, in the Introduction to his edition of the *Brahmasiddhi (Brahmasiddhi by Acharya Maṇḍanamiśra with Commentary by Saṅkhapāṇi.* Delhi: Sri Satguru Publications, 1984) mentions on p. xlv that: "In this context, it is also pointed out in the *Saṁkṣepaśārīraka* [1. v.252] that Maṇḍana's interpretation of the *Niṣedhavākhyas* obviates the need for having recourse to *lakṣanā* (secondary significative force) in the explanation of the meaning of Advaita texts." I think that Paul Hacker has underestimated the differences between the thought of

Maṇḍana and Śaṅkara when he says: "the few and rather insignificant divergencies between his thought and that of Śaṅkara are scarcely sufficient to account for the rivalry". Cf. "Relations of Early Advaitins to Vaiṣṇavism" in W. Halbfass (ed), *Philology and Confrontation*, op.cit., p.38.

49 BSBh 4.1.2, p.829, line 14, (tr) p.816. US 18.104, 205.

50 BSBh 2.3.40, p.550, line 9, *nityopalabdhisvarūpatvāt*, (tr) p.503, "for it is eternal consciousness by its very nature". A similar expression is found in 3.3.54, p.768, line 4, (tr) p.743.

51 BSBh 1.1.4, p.78f., line 6f., (tr) p.30f.

52 Michael Comans, "The Question of the Importance of *Samādhi* in Modern and Classical Advaita Vedānta". *Philosophy East and West*, vol.43, no.1, p.19-38. The *Vivekacūḍāmaṇi* highlights the importance of *samādhi*, as do a number of other, later Advaita works. With regard to the *Vivekacūḍāmaṇi*, there are a number of reasons why this is not a genuine work of Ādi Śaṅkara. In ascending order of importance these are as follows. (a) The style of the verses of the *Vivekacūḍāmaṇi* is highly poetic in contrast to the vigorous but not especially graceful style of the verses in the *Upadeśasāhasrī*, a work universally accepted as the composition of Ādi Śaṅkara. Although it may be argued that Śaṅkara's style could have changed, and that Śaṅkara's hymns are very poetic compositions, this does not constitute sufficient proof, since the hymns themselves are not universally accepted as the compositions of Ādi Śaṅkara. (b) The fact that there are very few commentaries on the *Vivekacūḍāmaṇi*, and no old commentaries by well known Advaita authors, would tend to indicate that the *Vivekacūḍāmaṇi* is not the composition of Ādi Śaṅkara and is, in fact, not a very old work. (c) Some aspects of the teaching of the *Vivekacūḍāmaṇi* are foreign to other works of Śaṅkara or are contradictory to them. The series of verses in the

---

Vivekacūḍāmaṇi extolling the importance of yogic-type *nirvikalpa samādhi* (eg. vv.341-42, 353-57, 360-63) sit at variance with the minimal importance Śaṅkara gives to *samādhi* practices in his other works. The statements belittling the importance of hearing the Upaniṣads (cf. v.364) would contradict his teachings in his commentary upon *Brahmasūtra* 4.1.2 and the whole theme of the lengthy eighteenth chapter of the *Upadeśasāhasrī*. Thus the *Vivekacūḍāmaṇi*, for all its merit as a manual explaining Vedānta, is not likely to be a composition of Ādi Śaṅkara and is more than likely to be a composition of some later Śaṅkarācārya, perhaps connected to the Śriṅgeri *pīṭham*. One of the Śriṅgeri Śaṅkarācāryas, Abhinava Nṛsiṁha Bhāratī 1 (who adorned the *pīṭham* from 1599-1622) founded a branch *maṭha* in Śivagaṅga and placed his disciple Śaṅkara Bhāratī, who took *sannyāsa* in 1615 and was himself an eminent scholar, in charge of this *maṭha* (cf. K.R. Venkataraman, *The Throne of Transcendental Wisdom: Śrī Śaṁkarācārya's Śāradā Pīṭha in Śriṅgeri*, Sringeri: Sri Sharada Trust, 3rd Ed., 1990, p.77). The concluding verse of the *Vivekacūḍāmaṇi* (v.580) contains the phrase *"eṣā śaṅkarabhāratī vijayate"* which is generally understood to mean that the "voice of Śaṅkara is victorious", referring to the teaching of Śaṅkara. However the word *"śaṅkarabhāratī"* could be a *double entendre (śleṣa)* referring also to the name of the author. Thus the author of the *Vivekacūḍāmaṇi* could well be the seventeenth century *sannyāsin*, Śaṅkara Bhāratī.

53 BUBh 1.4.7, p.663, line 7f., (tr) p.91. I may take this opportunity to remark that Paul Hacker's hypothesis concerning Śaṅkara's yogic background is highly speculative and unconvincing ("Śaṅkara the Yogin and Śaṅkara the Advaitin: Some Observations", in W. Halbfass (ed), *Philology and Confrontation*, op.cit., p.101f.). Concerning Śaṅkara's supposed authorship of the *Yogasūtrabhāṣyavivaraṇa*, see the three articles by T.S. Rukmani: "The Problem of the Authorship of the

---

Yogasūtrabhāṣyavivaraṇam", *Journal of Indian Philosophy*, vol.20, no.4, 1992; "Śaṅkara's views on *Yoga* in the *Brahmasūtrabhāṣya* in the light of the Authorship of the *Yogasūtrabhāṣya-vivaraṇa*", *Journal of Indian Philosophy*, vol.21, no.4, 1993; "The *Yogasūtrabhāṣyavivaraṇa* is not a Work of Śaṅkarācārya the Author of the *Brahmasūtrabhāṣya*", *Journal of Indian Philosophy*, vol. 26, no. 3, 1998.

54 Feature Review by Arvind Sharma of the book by Anantanand Rambachan, *Accomplishing the Accomplished: the Vedas as a Source of Valid Knowledge in Śaṅkara. Philosophy East and West*, volume 43, no.4, 1993. "A Response to Professor Arvind Sharma", *Philosophy East and West*, volume 44, no.4, 1994. "A Reply to Anantanand Rambachan", *Philosophy East and West*, volume 45, no.1, 1995.

55 BSBh 1.1.2, p. 51f., line 5f., (tr) p.15f.

56 BSBh 2.1.6, p.361, line 1f., (tr) p.314. Also cf. the reference to this passage in: "The Concept of Experience in the Encounter Between India and the West" in Wilhelm Halbfass, *India and Europe: An Essay in Understanding*. Albany: State University of New York Press, 1988, p.389.

57 BSBh 3.3.32, p.735, line 6, (tr) p.705.

58 In addition to 3.3.32, also, cf. 3.4.15, p.788, line 4f., (tr) p.769.

59 BUBh 4.3.23 (intro.), p.896, line 6f., (tr) p.467.

60 BSBh 4.1.2, p.829f., line 8f., (tr) p.816f.

61 Ibid, p.831, line 1f., *(tasmāt sarvaduḥkhavinirmukta-ekacaitanyātmako'ham ityeṣa ātmānubhavaḥ).*

62 Concerning the *ṛṣi* Vāmadeva, cf. BSBh 3.4.51, p.822, line 5, (tr) p.809. Also the discussion in BUBh 1.4.2, p. 648, line 18f., (tr) p.67f. The importance of the *śāstra* and the *ācārya* was touched upon in the previous chapter. It may be worthwhile to repeat the footnote from that earlier reference: the compound *śāstrācāryopadeśa* occurs seven times in his commentary on the *Bhagavadgītā* alone, along with variations such as *vedāntācāryopadeśa* . BG 2. 21, p.20, line 12; 2. 63, p.36, line 12; 8. 8, p.128, line 16; 13. 30, p.215, line 23; 13. 34, p.217, line 19; 18. 16, p.263, line 19; 18. 17, p.264, line 4; 18. 50, p.281, line 7; 18. 55, p.284, line 9. (Francis X. D'SA (ed.), *Word-Index to Śaṅkara's Gītābhāṣya.* Pune: Institute for the Study of Religion, 1985). (For other references, cf. BUBh, 2.1.20, p.744, line 23; 2.4.2, p.767, line 5; 2.5.15, p.776, line 12. ChUBh, 6.15.2, p.537, line 12; 8.1.6, p.571, line 2. KaUBh 1.5.12, p.96, line 1. MUBh 2.2.7, p.162, line 22. US, 17.51-52 and prose portion ch. 1 and 2).

63 BSBh 4.1.1, p.826, line 8f., (tr) p.813.

64 BUBh 2.4.5, p.760, line 20f., (tr) p.247. Also, KeUBh 2.1, p.25, line 14, "The disciple, told thus by the teacher, sat alone with his mind concentrated and investigated the meaning of the traditional teaching as told by the teacher, and having determined the meaning with the help of reasoning, and after making it a matter of his own experience, he approached the teacher and said...", (tr) p.59.

65 BUBh 2.5.15, p.775, line 13f., "Even before the knowledge of Brahman....a person has always been Brahman [but thought that he] was not Brahman due to ignorance; while being everything, [he thought that he] was limited. But once that ignorance has been removed by this knowledge, the knower of Brahman, who was always Brahman, 'became' Brahman; and though he was

already everything, he 'became' all.", (tr) p.273. Also, BUBh 1.4.10, p.669, line 12f., (tr) p.102; 3.3.1, p.799, line 20f., (tr) p.313; 4.4.6, p.919, line 5f., (tr) p.502f. US 15.49f.

66 BSBh 1.1.4, p.75, line 7, *mokṣapratibandhanivṛttimātram eva ātmajñānasya phalam,* (tr) p.29. See also BSBh 3.4.51.

67 BSBh 3.4.51, p.821, line 7f., (tr) p.808, and p.822, line 5f., (tr) p.809.

68 BUBh 2.5.15, p.775, line 23f., (tr) p.273.

69 BUBh 4.4.6, p.917, line 9f., (tr) p.500. Also, BUBh 4.4.8, p.923, line 1f., (tr) p.509. BSBh 4.1.15, p.851, line 2f., (tr) p.840.

70 BUBh 4.4.20, p.928, line 14f., (tr) p.518.

71 MUBh 1.1.6, p.145, line 5f., (tr) p.88.

72 Ibid 1.1.5, p.144f, line 26f., (tr) p.88, "even after the mastery of the assemblage of words, the realisation of the Immutable is not possible without some other effort consisting of approaching the teacher and so on, as well as detachment."

73 BSBh 1.1.1, p.36, line 3, (tr) p.9. Also, US (prose) 1. 2, 4, 5, 44. US 16. 72, 74; 17. 22, 23, 53, 86.

74 BSBh 1.1.1, p.37, line 1, (tr) p.9.

75 BUBh 1.3.7, p.632, line 13f., (tr) p.43; 1.4.1, p.646, line 13f., (tr) p.65; 1.5.2, p.693, line 7f., (tr) p.141; 1.6.1, p.713, line 19f., (tr) p.172. KaUBh. 2.1.1, p.86, line 6f., (tr) p.171. MUBh 1.2.12, p.152, line 11f., (tr) p.109.

76 BSBh 3.4.36, p.810, line 3f., (tr) p.793.

77 BSBh 3.4.38, p.810, line 14, *pratiṣedhābhāvamātreṇa api,* (tr) p.794.

78 BSBh 1.3.34, p.276, line 1f., (tr) p.230.

79 BSBh 1.3.38, p.181, line 2f., (tr) p.234.

80 Rāmānuja puts forward a very similar set of arguments to those of Śaṅkara. Cf. R.D. Karmarkar (ed. and tr.), *Śrībhāṣya of Rāmānuja,* (Three Parts), Poona: University of Poona Sanskrit and Prakrit Series Volume 1, 1959-64. Part 11, (1.3.33-39) p.454ff.

81 BUBh 1.4.7, p.664, line 16f., (tr) p.93. BSBh 4.1.15, p.850, line 3f., (tr) p.839f.

82 BSBh 1.1.4, p.97, line 2f, (tr) p.42. BUBh 4.4.7, p.921, line 14f., (tr) p.506. CUBh 8.12.1, p.595, line 17f., (tr) p.647..

83 BUBh 4.4.7, p.921, line 10f., (tr) p.506.

84 BSBh 4.1.13, p.847f., line 10f., (tr) p.837. Also, BSBh 3.3.30, p.729, line 11f., (tr) p.698. BUBh 4.4.22, p.936, line 3f., (tr) p.529.

85 BSBh 3.3.32, p.734, line 14, (tr) p.704; 4.1.15, p.850, line 11, (tr) p.840. BUBh 1.4.10, p.677, line 27, (tr) p.116. CUBh 6.14.2, p.536, line 13f., (tr) p.490. BGBh 13.23, p.211, line 19f., (tr) p.551.

86 BSBh 4.1.15, p. 850f., line 8f., (tr) p.840.

---

87 BSBh 4.1.19, p.854, line 3f., (tr) p.846.

88 BSBh 2.3.48, p.560, line 3f., (tr) p.514.

89 BUBh 1.4.10, p.678, line 2f., (tr) p. 116.

90 Ānandagiri makes a distinction here between mediate or theoretical knowledge *(parokṣajñāna)* and immediate knowledge *(aparokṣajñāna)* and he says that the person who has these memories does not have direct knowledge but only indirect knowledge. Śaṅkara, however, makes no such distinction evident. Also, Śaṅkara does not say that the *jñānī* actually has false notions, he says he may have memories that resemble false notions: *viparītapratyayāvabhāsāḥ smṛtayaḥ.*

91 AUBh (intro.) p.325f., line 27f., (tr) p.10f.

92 BUBh 2.4.1, p.757, line 12f., (tr) p.242; 4.4.6, p.916f., line 24f., (tr) p.499f; 4.4.22, p.933, line 4f., and 18f., (tr) p.525, 526; 4.5.15, p.947f., line 24 and 27f., (tr) p.550.

93 BUBh 2.5.15, p.777, line 5f., (tr) p.275.

94 BUBh 2.4.1, p.757, line 6 and 25 (tr) p.241, 242f. Also, 4.5.1, p.939, line 17, (tr) p.535; 4.5.15, p.944. line 15f., (tr) p.544f.

95 BUBh 4.4.22, p.934, line 6f., and line 12f., (tr) p.527. Also, 4.5.15, p.947, line 24f., (tr) p.550.

96 BUBh.4.4.7, p.922, line 12f., (tr) p.508. BSBh 3.4.20, p.796, line 8f., (tr) p.778.

97 BUBh 4.4.21, p.928f., line 26f., (tr) p.519.

---

98 BSBh 3.4.20, p.795, line 4, (tr) p.776.

99 BU 4.4.22, cited in BUBh 4.5.15, p.948, line 2, (tr) p.551.

100 BUBh 4.5.15, 944f., line 24f., (tr) p.545f.

101 *Jābāla* Upaniṣad 4. *Nāradaparivrājaka* Upaniṣad 77.

102 BUBh 4.5.15, p.948, line 14f., (tr) p.551. Also BSBh 3.4.17, p.788f., line 17f., (tr) p.770. US 18.v.222.

103 US (prose) 1. 2.

104 US (prose) 2. 45.

105 BSBh 1.3.34, p. 275f., line 7f., (tr) p.230. Also, BUBh 4.4.22, p.931, line 9f., (tr) p.523.

106 BU 3.5.1. See BUBh, 1.4.15, p.684, line 12, (tr) p.125; 3.5.1, p.812, line 10f., (tr) p.334; 4.5.15, p.948, line 25, (tr) p.552. MUBh 1.2.12, p.152, line 20f., (tr) p.110.

107 US (prose) 1.2 (the reference here is to a seeker after liberation). BUBh 3.5.1, p.813, line 5f, (tr) p.335 (the reference here is to one who already knows Brahman); also, p.816, line 3, (tr) 340. CUBh 2.23.1, p.408, line 4f., (tr) p.154; 8.12.1, p.598, line 24f, (tr) p.655. BGBh 3.3, p.45, line 17, (tr) p.135.

108 P.V. Kane, *History of Dharmasastra*, Vol.2, part 2, p.938f. Poona: Bhandarkar Oriental Research Institute, 1930-1962.

109 BSBh 3.4.18, p. 791, line 2f, (tr) p.772; 3.4.20, p.796, line 3f., (tr) p.777. BUBh 3.5.1, p.813, line 10, (tr) p.335; 4.5.15,

p.948, line 15, (tr) p.551. CUBh 2.23.1, p.408, line 7, (tr) p.154f.

110 *Jābāla* Upaniṣad 5, in J. L. Sastri (ed.), *Upaniṣatsaṅgrahaḥ*, Delhi: Motilal Banarsidass, 1980, p.146. Cited in BSBh 3.4.20, p.796, line 9f., (tr) p.778. BUBh 3.5.1, p.813, line 10, (tr) p.335. CUBh 2.23.1, p.408, line 7., (tr) p.154f. (adapted).

111 *Jābāla* Upaniṣad 6, Sastri, op.cit, p. 146.

112 CUBh 2.23.1, p.408, line 6, (tr) p.154.

113 The *Bhikṣu* Upaniṣad, one of the *Sannyāsa* Upaniṣads, mentions that the *Bahūdaka* is a *tridaṇḍī* etc. Cf. Kane, op.cit., p.939.

114 BUBh 3.5.1, p.815, line 4f., (tr) p.338f.

115 CUBh 2.23.1, p.408, line 7, (tr) p.155. Here, Śaṅkara does not speak of the *paramahaṁsa* as "beyond the stages of life", but he cites the *Śvetāśvatara* Upaniṣad 6.21, which speaks of the *atyāśramin*.

116 *Mahābhārata* 14.46.51, cited in BUBh 3.5.1, p.813, line 9f., (tr) p.335. CUBh 2.23.1, p.804, line 9, (tr) p.155.

117 From this evidence I do not know whether the *paramahaṁsa* keeps the single staff or not.

118 Patrick Olivelle, *Renunciation in Hinduism: a Medieval Debate*, Publications of the De Nobili Research Library, vol. XIII-IX, 1986-87; in the first vol., p.55.

119 BSBh 2.3.48, p.560, line 3f., (tr) p.514. BUBh 3.5.1, p.817, line 2f., (tr) p.341. NS 4. vv.62, 63, 64. Regarding the *sannyāsin* who is still a seeker cf. US 18.229.

120 NS 4. 62, 63, 64.

121 Patrick Olivelle, *The Āśrama System: The History and Hermeneutics of a Religious Tradition.* New York: Oxford University Press, 1993, p.277.

122 Śaṅkara refers to the *paramahaṁsaparivrājaka* a number of times in his commentary upon the Gītā, cf. BGBh 3.3, p.45, line 17, (tr) p.135; 13.31, p.216, line 23, (tr) p.564; 18.12, p.262, line 1, (tr) p.674; 18.53, p.283, line 5, (tr) p.727; 18.66, p.293, line 2, (tr) p.752.

123 BGBh 3.20, p.52, line 21f., (tr) p.153f.

124 BGBh 4.20, p.70, line 18f., (tr) p.199f.

125 He also mentions the possibility in BUBh 4.4.6, p.916, line 11., (tr) p.499.

126 BUBh 3.2.11, p.795, line 1f., (tr) p.306.

127 BUBh 4.4.6, p.916, line 10f., (tr) p.499.

128 R.D. Karmarkar (ed. and tr.), *Śrībhāṣya of Rāmānuja,* op.cit., Part One, p.63.

129 BUBh 4.4.6, p.917, line 23f., (tr) p.501.

CHAPTER SEVEN

Sureśvara

There has been an ongoing debate among scholars about whether Sureśvara is the same person as Maṇḍanamiśra, the renowned Mīmāṁsaka and author of the important Advaita work, *Brahmasiddhi*. Some of the legendary accounts of the life of Śaṅkara *(Śaṅkaravijayas)* mention that Śaṅkara defeated Maṇḍana in debate and the latter then became a *sannyāsin* follower of Śaṅkara having the name of Sureśvara.[1] However some other legendary accounts say that the opponent whom Śaṅkara debated was the scholar Viśvarūpa who then became the *sannyāsin* Sureśvara.[2] Among all these legendary biographies, Mādhava's *Śaṅkaradigvijaya* (c.1650-1798) has become the most popular. It draws heavily upon the material from earlier accounts, and it mentions both names. The popular tradition is that Maṇḍanamiśra became the disciple Sureśvara. M. Hiriyanna and S. Kuppuswami Sastri have argued against the identity of Maṇḍana and Sureśvara, while R. Balasubramanian has defended the tradition of identity on a number of occasions.[3]

The question of the identity of Sureśvara, before he became a disciple of Śaṅkara, is immaterial to the present study which confines itself to the writings of Sureśvara. But merely to express an opinion, it seems unlikely that Sureśvara is the same person as Maṇḍana, in spite of some similarities between them, such as the common argument, to be mentioned below, that perception cannot prove duality to be real. Perhaps the identification of the great Maṇḍanamiśra with Sureśvara was a deliberate contrivance on the part of some of the authors of the legendary biographies of Śaṅkara, for it served the purpose of subsuming a rival tradition into Śaṅkara's tradition. It is well known that in his *Brahmasiddhi* Maṇḍana advocates a combination of knowledge and ritual *(jñānakarmasamucchaya)* and he also says that this combination leads more quickly to liberation than the pursuit of knowledge alone, without the continued performance of rites.[4] This necessarily implies that Maṇḍana considers the life of a householder to be more spiritually efficacious than the life of *sannyāsa,* where rituals are abandoned. If Maṇḍana repudiates his beliefs and becomes a follower of Saṅkara, this would have the effect of making Śaṅkara's position - giving primacy to knowledge alone without the requirement to perform rites, as well as to the lifestyle of the renouncer over that of the householder - the sole representative view for orthodox Advaita, which it now is.

Whatever the antecedents of Sureśvara, after Śaṅkara he is the most revered figure in the history of Advaita, and we will now turn to the exposition of some of his teachings.

Sureśvara prefaces his important non-commentarial work, the *Naiṣkarmyasiddhi,* with this statement:

> Since all living beings, from the god Brahmā down to a plant, instinctively desire to be rid of any type of suffering, the pursuit to remove suffering is something innate. Suffering is caused solely by the fact of having a body, and since embodiment is connected to the prior accumulation of merit and demerit *(dharma* and *adharma),* suffering does not cease. Merit and demerit do not come to an end, because they have their source in action which is either enjoined or forbidden. Action is based upon desire and aversion, while the latter are linked up with the superimposition that something is either attractive or unattractive. Superimposition has, for its cause, duality, which is established only so long as it is not investigated. And as all duality - which is something comparable to the silver [superimposed] upon a mother-of-pearl shell- has as its basis the sheer ignorance of the Self that is self-established and non-dual, duality does not get removed. Thus, it is the ignorance of the Self that alone is the cause of all misery.

> The happiness which neither comes nor goes, and which does not depend upon something, is the very nature of the Self. Ignorance of the Self conceals that happiness. Therefore the fulfilment of all human endeavours lies in the total eradication of ignorance. Since the removal of ignorance is brought about solely by the gain of one's own essential nature, through right knowledge, it is right knowledge that is to be acquired. Right knowledge comes only from the statements of the traditional texts of the Vedānta [Upaniṣads]. That is so because [the Self], about whom there is Self-ignorance that is the cause of all misery, is not within the scope of ordinary means of knowledge, such as perception etc. not derived from the traditional texts. Hence the undertaking of this treatise, which serves as a compendium of the essence of the entire Vedānta.

This eightfold chain of cause and effect, from suffering to ignorance, echoes a similar series found in the *Upadeśasāhasrī* of Śaṅkara.[5] We can see from such statements that Advaita teachers understand their tradition as bringing about the removal of suffering, which is presented in formal terms as putting an end to the cycle of birth and death, but which is also seen, more positively, as the gain of happiness that does not depend upon anything. Thus Advaita, in common with Buddhism and all other major Indian religio-philosophical traditions, sees its role in liberation of the spirit. It is not meant to be mere metaphysical speculation without a practical consequence for life, but it is intended to be a teaching that, when brought to fruition, confers supreme benefit upon a human being in this life itself.

Furthermore, the teaching of Śaṅkara, and what we have just seen of Sureśvara, avoids the orientation that this teaching is mere theory, something that has to be subsequently realised through the practice of a spiritual discipline. In their view, *saṁsāra* is shown to depend upon nothing but ignorance of the true nature of the Self as Brahman, and liberation, therefore, can only occur through knowledge, for knowledge alone has the capacity to remove ignorance. Concomitant with this knowledge, or direct apprehension concerning the true nature of the Self, is the negation of the notion that duality is real. This leads to the further negation of the superimposition that something is intrinsically attractive *(śobhana)* or unattractive *(aśobhana)*, upon which notions rest the remainder of the chain of misery. Liberation, therefore, ultimately means the removal of the ignorance of the true nature of the Self by knowledge, and this knowledge negates the notion that duality is real and it negates false notions arising out of superimposition.

Finally, Sureśvara makes the point that the true nature of the Self cannot be revealed by our usual means of knowledge, namely sense perception and inference, because these means of knowledge operate only in relation to sense objects, whereas the Self, the Subject, is by definition outside their scope. Sureśvara says that the words of the Upaniṣads are able, under suitable conditions, to put an end to ignorance by directly revealing the true nature of the Self. The way in which this can be done is the principal topic of Sureśvara's *Naiṣkarmyasiddhi.*

(1) Duality

In the introduction to the *Naiṣkarmyasiddhi*, cited above, Sureśvara uses a particular expression to characterise duality. He says duality is: "established only so long as it is not investigated" *(avicāritasiddha).* Just as Śaṅkara frequently uses a particular expression to describe the Self when he says that the Self is: "by nature always pure, awake and free *(nityaśuddhabuddhamuktasvabhāva),* this statement of Sureśvara that duality is "established only so long as it is not investigated" is a signature expression as it regularly occurs in his works.[6] What does he mean by this statement? Sureśvara does not deny the fact of the world as it appears to common sense. But he says that along with the appearance of the world there is the idea that the perceived duality is something real. He says that such an idea is wrong, for duality is established "only so long as it is not investigated".

We have already seen that Gauḍapāda infers the unreality of phenomena from the fact of their transitoriness:

> What does not exist at the beginning and at the end, likewise [does not exist] even in the present. The things that are appearing are equivalent to unreal things, [yet] they are

> looked upon as though they are real. [2.6, 4.31]

If impermanence is a mark of unreality, absence of change is the defining feature of the real. Such a definition is proposed by Śaṅkara, as we can see from his own statement:

> Something is real when, once it is ascertained to be in a certain condition, that condition is not found to alter. Conversely, if a thing is ascertained to be in a certain condition but that condition alters, that thing is said to be unreal. Therefore that which undergoes change [or modification, *vikāra]* is unreal.[7]

And such an understanding is equally accepted by Sureśvara, who says:

> Since this world, together with the ego, appears and disappears, like a pot, in relation to the Self whose nature is pure Awareness, the world must be akin to an unreal presentation.[8]

We have also seen that Gauḍapāda says:

> This plurality does not exist as identical to the Self, nor even does it somehow exist of its own accord. Those who know reality, know that nothing exists different [from the Self] or as identical [to the Self]. [2.34]

We have seen that this too is in accord with Śaṅkara's teaching, for Śaṅkara uses the expression *tattvānyatvābhyām anirvacanīya* "not determinable as a reality or as something else" to mean that name-and-form cannot be definitively ascertained as either identical to Brahman, the reality, nor as something other than Brahman.[9] Sureśvara articulates this same understanding. He says that duality is unreal because its ontological status is indeterminable, for the world cannot be shown to exist either as something separate from Awareness, or as identical to Awareness itself. He says:

> Something other than the Self [i.e. any object] cannot be shown to exist separately from the Self, nor as identical, i.e., as the Self itself.[10]
>
> Since this plurality does not come about of its own accord, nor does it come about by way of the Self who is pure Awareness, nor even by both, therefore non-duality is established through the sublation of duality.[11]
>
> Since neither ignorance nor its effect can be shown to exist as non-different or as different [from Brahman], therefore they would be established only so long as they are not investigated.[12]

According to Sureśvara, the objects of Awareness, beginning with the ego-sense and ending with the entire physical world, cannot be established as existing separately from Awareness, nor can they be shown to be identical to Awareness itself, for then they would not be perceived at all, just as Awareness is not an object of sense perception. Therefore the ontological status of the world - from the ego onwards - is strictly indeterminable, because objects cannot be shown to exist separately from Awareness, nor are they identical to Awareness. Sureśvara says that duality is thus shown to be unreal, i.e., it is only "seeming" or apparent *(mithyāsiddha)*.[13]

It is evident that in developing their teachings Advaitins rely on the revelation of the Upaniṣads and they also develop a line of reasoning presented in some of the notable passages of these texts. For instance, there is the famous *svayaṁjyotirbrāhmaṇa* portion of the *Bṛhadāraṇyaka* Upaniṣad that reveals the real nature of the Self to be self-luminous Awareness; and there is the well known *vācārambhaṇa* passage in the *Chāndogya* Upaniṣad which illustrates that a thing has no reality of its own independently of its material cause.[14] The followers of Advaita apply the revelation, and the reasoning, concerning the true nature of the Self and the *mithyātva* of the world to the phenomenology of everyday experience when they argue that the Self, as self-luminous Awareness, is invariable in all experience, and is therefore real *(satya),* while duality is indeterminable in relation to Awareness, and is therefore unreal *(mithyā).* Exemplifying this approach, which involves reflection upon the ordinary experience of Awareness in the light of revelation, Sureśvara says:

> The cognitions of the mind are established by depending upon the constant, self-established and unchanging Awareness. Physical objects, such as pots and so forth, are proved to exist through their dependence upon the cognitions.[15]
>
> These phenomena such as the mind etc. cannot be proved to exist without a means of knowledge, because they need Awareness in order to be manifest. But what does the Self, the Knower, depend upon?[16]
>
> Perception etc. are proved depending upon the Self that is Experience *(anubhava)* itself. Since Awareness is self-evident, what is required in order to prove its existence?[17]

The perceptible world is not self-evident; its existence is proved by the fact that it can be cognised. Something may well exist without being cognised, but the proof of existence depends upon its cognition *(vṛtti).* According to Advaita, cognition is not self-evident, because a mental state is an object of knowledge, and as such it too belongs to the sphere of the known. The proof of the existence of a cognition depends upon the Self, whose nature is Awareness or Experience Itself *(anubhava).* We can see in the last of the verses cited above that Sureśvara, like Śaṅkara, occasionally uses the word *anubhava* as a description of the very nature of the Ātman, or as a synonym for the Ātman.[18] He says that the proof of the existence of everything ultimately depends upon Awareness. What then does the proof of Awareness depend upon? Awareness is self-evident, because to prove the existence of Awareness one would need to depend upon a means of proof that would itself depend upon Awareness. So following the revelation of the Upaniṣads and the reasoning exhibited therein, and applying particular methods of reasoning, such as the distinction between subject and object, to one's everyday experience of Awareness, Advaitins conclude that the Self is essentially nothing but self-luminous Awareness that is invariable and therefore real *(satya)*, while all duality is *mithyā* since it cannot be established as identical to, or as other than, this pure Awareness.

Sureśvara also advances another argument with regard to duality, an argument reminiscent of Maṇḍana.[19] Sureśvara argues that perception does not reveal duality, i.e., perception does not show that something is actually different from something else. Perception simply reveals objects, but it does not perform the function, either simultaneously or subsequently, of revealing difference. The scope of perception is in the mere revelation of phenomena; the differentiation between objects is a mental act subsequent to perception. Thus difference is cognitive, but not perceptual. Sureśvara argues that difference is not given in perception because a means of knowledge just reveals an existing thing, like a table or a chair. The role of perception is simply to reveal things. But "difference" is not a "thing", it is not some object like a table or a chair, and so perception cannot reveal difference.[20]

To put this matter more technically, the idea of difference *(bheda)* depends upon distinguishing between things. To distinguish between A and B means to exclude A from B; and exclusion *(vyāvṛtti)* consists of the knowledge that A and B are mutually absent *(anyonyābhāva)* in each other.[21] When we say that A is different from B we mean that they are mutually absent in each other: A does not exist in B and vice versa. Thus difference depends upon the knowledge of absence *(abhāva)*, but absence is not given in perception, because perception deals only with existing things not with the absence of something. So difference does not fall within the scope of perception.

From the above discussion, as well as from previous chapters, we are able to see that Advaita does not deny the appearance of duality. What it

(2) The World

Sureśvara's views about the origin of the world do not show divergence from the teachings of Gauḍapāda. The fundamental contention of Gauḍapāda is that a real creation is not possible from the standpoint of the changeless *turīya*-Brahman. Sureśvara too says: "So, considering the real state of things, there never was, nor is, nor will there be [the creation of the world by Brahman]."[22] The "real state of things" refers, in the words of Sureśvara, to the fact that Brahman is "neither a cause nor an effect" *(akāryakāraṇa)*[23] :

> The *śruti* [i.e. KaU 2.18] which says: "nothing originates from this [Ātman], nor does this Ātman originate from anything", negates [the idea that the Ātman] is the cause etc.[24]

> It is not possible to speak of creation from the standpoint of the unconditioned Brahman, which is non-different from all, undergoes no change, is one, and is neither a cause nor an effect.[25]

Apart from a convergence of outlook from the ultimate perspective, we can also see that Sureśvara and Gauḍapāda share some principles of reasoning and have some expressions in common. For instance, Sureśvara says reasoning demonstrates that the real origination of the world from the changeless Brahman is not tenable:

> What does not exist *(asat)* cannot be considered to have any connection to birth. Nor can an existent thing, since it already exists. There is no alteration in the Immutable. Therefore birth is due to Ignorance.[26]

The last two sentences of the above quotation resemble Gauḍapāda's statement in kārikā 3.27:

> The birth of what exists *(sat)* is reasonable only through *māyā*, not in reality.

While the first sentence resembles kārikā 3.28:

> The birth of what does not exist *(asat)* is certainly not reasonable- whether it is through *māyā*, or in reality. The son of a barren woman is not born in reality, nor even through *māyā*.

Just as Gauḍapāda calls duality "merely *māyā*" in kārikā 1.17 *(māyāmātram idaṁ dvaitam)*, so does Sureśvara too refer to the world as "merely *māyā*" *(māyāmātram idaṁ sarvam)*.[27] He also uses the same expression as Gauḍapāda when he speaks of the "appearance of duality" *(dvayābhāsa)*.[28] Sureśvara cites with approval *Gauḍapādakārikā* 3.15, which says the various Upaniṣad statements that speak of the creation of the world are but a means or device *(upāya)* to lead to the understanding of the truth concerning the oneness of the Self and Brahman. Sureśvara says:

> This [talk of] creation is a device to bring people to awakening. Given the fact that the Self is immutable,. creation is in no way logically feasible.[29]

> This matter has also been spoken of by Gauḍapāda, who knows the conclusive teaching of the entire Veda, and I have dealt with it in the same way.[30]

He then quotes the *Gauḍapādakārikā:*

> Creation has been presented in different ways [in the Upaniṣads, by using such illustrations]

> of clay, iron, sparks etc. This is a means to lead to [the truth]. There is no difference whatsoever [between the *jīva* and the Ātman].[31] [GK 3.15]

In another place, but again in the context where Sureśvara says the Upaniṣad statements speaking of causality are a stepping stone to understand the Self that is "neither a cause nor an effect", he presents the following verse, which I cite here because it is perhaps the most frequently quoted verse in the entire writings of Sureśvara:

> Whichever way people can come to the clear knowledge of the inner-Self would be a good way here [in the Vedic tradition]. But that way is not fixed *(yayā yayā bhavet puṁsāṁ vyutpattiḥ pratyagātmani. sā saiva prakriyeha syāt sādhvī sā cānavasthitā).*[32]

This verse says that the reason the *śruti* gives discrepant accounts about the process of creation is because it does not have its final purport in revealing a real creation. Its final purport lies elsewhere: in generating the understanding that the true Self is none other than the unconditioned (or acosmic) Brahman that is neither a cause nor an effect. The teaching about creation is a means or device *(prakriyā)* by which the *śruti* proceeds, so as to lead us to this more subtle insight. Since that is its aim, the way itself need not be something fixed, which is why one Upaniṣad speaks about the creation of five elements, whereas another Upaniṣad speaks of the creation of only three elements.

Advaita is concerned with denying a real creation only from the level of the highest truth, while from the level of ordinary dealings, Advaita accepts the world just as it appears to common sense. From the "level" of the highest truth *(paramārtha),* the world is an unreal appearance, or illusory transformation *(vivarta),* of the unchanging Brahman. In fact, the *ajātivāda* associated with Gauḍapāda and the *vivartavāda* of later Advaita are not two different teachings; they are the same teaching at the ultimate, *paramārtha,* level, but from two different angles. When the focus is kept on the changeless Brahman, and as a consequence of that perspective the world is seen to be merely an unreal appearance, the teaching is "*ajātivāda*". When the focus shifts to the empirical fact of the world-appearance, and specifically onto the relation between the world-appearance and Brahman, the teaching is *vivartavāda*. Gauḍapāda, Śaṅkara and Sureśvara have all employed the analogy of the rope-snake to describe the "relation" between Brahman and the world, and this may help to clarify the point.[33] When the primary focus is upon the rope, the teaching would be *ajātivāda*, because the rope has undergone no change whatsoever to produce the snake-appearance. When, however, the snake-appearance is highlighted, and consideration is made about the relation between that appearance and the rope, there is *vivartavāda*, because the snake that is present right before the eyes has no real relation to the rope, it has only an apparent, or *mithyā* relation, since it is an illusory transformation of the rope. Thus the *ajātivāda* looks at the world from the standpoint of Brahman and finds the world to be "like a dream and a magic..."; while the *vivartavāda* looks at Brahman from the standpoint of the world and finds the relation illusory. Though Sureśvara has used the word *vivarta*,[34] it has not yet become the technical term in Advaita to express the teaching that creation is, ultimately, an apparent, or illusory, transformation of Brahman. Nevertheless, there can be no doubt that all three authors have understood the world, from the perspective of the highest truth *(paramārthataḥ)*, to be an apparent transformation of Brahman.

(3) Ignorance *(avidyā)*

We discussed the ambiguous nature of the word *avidyā* in chapter five, and at the end of that chapter we suggested that for Śaṅkara the word *avidyā* primarily signifies the mysteriously concealing, and ultimately unreal, primary stuff of the world called "unmanifest name-and-form" *(avyākṛtanāmarūpa)*. Unmanifest name-and-form has therefore three dimensions: its primary cosmological dimension as the constitutive material of the world; an epistemological dimension which can be seen when it is referred to by the word *avidyā* used in its primary meaning of (concealing) ignorance, "[it is] of the nature of ignorance" *(āvidyātmikā)*; and an ontological dimension when that primary stuff is found to be ontologically unreal *(tattvānyatvābhyām anirvacanīya)*. Later Advaita dropped the specific reference to unmanifest name-and-form and identified it as *avidyā*, so that the latter, essentially epistemological term, was used to cover the other two aspects. It is only when the word *avidyā* is acknowledged as having all these dimensions that we are able to account for its usage in various contexts. We may note that the word *avidyā* can be interpreted in two distinct senses: (a) in the epistemological sense of "what is opposed to knowledge" *(vidyāvirodha),* and also (b) in the ontological sense of "what does not exist" *(na vidyate-iti-avidyā).* So the term *avidyā* finally bears all these three meanings: its epistemological and ontological senses, as well as the idea that it is the "stuff" of the world, as a result of it taking on the meaning of unmanifest name-and-form.

When Sureśvara uses the word *avidyā* in its epistemological sense he means that ignorance is the absence of discriminative knowledge of the true nature of things.[35] The consequences of ignorance are error *(bhrānti),* superimposition *(adhyāsa),* sorrow etc. When *avidyā* is used in this sense, what is emphasised is that *avidyā* can be terminated by knowledge because ignorance is opposed to knowledge.[36] He says, for example:

> The absence of knowledge here [concerning the Self] is very precarious. For it has illumination [Awareness] as its very essence. It departs merely due to some cause, like a *badara* fruit balanced upon the tip of one's nose.[37]

Ignorance disappears when it is removed by the knowledge arising from the *śruti:*

> This is considered to be the particular definition concerning the nature of ignorance: it cannot withstand the blow that is dealt by the means of knowledge.[38]
>
> On the mere rise of right knowledge generated by sentences such as "you are That" etc., ignorance, along with its effects, was not, is not, and will not be.[39]

The word *avidyā*, however, does not always just mean the absence of knowledge. It is also regularly used to refer to a mysterious and "beginningless" *(anādi)*[40] "power" *(śakti)*, inexplicable and ultimately unreal,[41] and in this sense it can be referred to as *māyā* or as *avyakta* etc. For instance:

> This *avidyā*, though not really existing, appears as name-and-form etc. It is *māyā*.[42]

Traditional scholars cite the following verse to show that Sureśvara understands *avidyā* to be a primary, causal power *(mūlāvidyā)*, since his expression *maulī avidyā* can be seen as equivalent to the later, standard term, *mūlāvidyā:*

> ...The primary *avidyā (maulī avidyā)* continuously appears in the form of the manifest and unmanifest.[43]

In his references to *avidyā*, Sureśvara says that it is located in the Self, i.e., in Brahman,[44] that it conceals the nature of Brahman,[45] that it is present in the state of deep sleep,[46] is the sole *upādhi* in the state of deep sleep,[47] and that objects are a product of *avidyā*.[48] What we have given here is a bare presentation of Sureśvara's understanding of *avidyā* and a more comprehensive examination, covering the whole corpus of his writing, still remains to be carried out.

A final point to note is that causality can only be ascribed to Brahman by way of *avidyā:*

> Ignorance *(ajñāna)* is the material cause of this false appearance of duality. Brahman, with reference to that *ajñāna*, is spoken of as the cause.[49]

Sureśvara quite frequently refers to *avidyā* as the "material cause" *(upādāna)* of the world.[50] Brahman can be the cause of the world only when Brahman is considered as having the *upādhi* of Ignorance (he treats *avidyā* and *ajñāna* as synonyms).[51] Brahman, who is intrinsically "neither cause nor effect" *(akāraṇakārya),*[52] is apparently conditioned by *avidyā,* and as such is Īśvara, the Creator who manifests the cosmos through the *upādhi* of *avidyā:*

> Whatever exists, beginning with Īśvara and ending with physical objects, is manifested by *avidyā.* The *śruti* clearly tells that it is so: "understand that *prakṛti* is *māyā,* and that the Lord is the possessor of *māyā* (ŚvU 4.10).[53]
>
> Neither Īśvara, the unmanifested world, the vital-energy *(prāṇa),* Viraṭ, the elements, the senses and so forth, could possibly exist in the inner-Self without having *avidyā* as their support.[54]

Though there is no fundamental divergence between these teachings of Sureśvara and the teachings of Śaṅkara as expressed in the *Brahmasūtrabhāṣya,* we can see in the thought of Sureśvara the beginning of a trend that continues in later Advaita: a greater focus on the role of *avidyā* in manifesting the phenomenal world, leading to a more specific demarcation between *para* Brahman and Īśvara.

(4) Some differences between Sureśvara and Śaṅkara

Sureśvara refers to his teacher on a number of occasions. He tells us in the *Naiṣkarmyasiddhi* that he is composing this text at the request of his teacher.[55] There, and elsewhere, he calls him by the name of Śaṅkara[56] and respectfully refers to him as "highly revered" *(bhagavatpūjyapāda, bhagavatpāda).*[57] He also mentions that his teacher is from the South *(drāviḍa),*[58] and that he is an ascetic *(yati)* who leads a group of seekers of liberation.[59] He poetically compares Śaṅkara to the sun, and his students to its rays, and he says that the darkness of the whole country has been removed by the rays of his renowned students.[60]

There are occasions, though, when Sureśvara can be seen to diverge from Śaṅkara's interpretations. These instances occur in his commentaries *(vārttika/vārtika)* upon Śaṅkara's own commentaries on the *Taittirīya* and *Bṛhadāraṇyaka* Upaniṣads. A Vārtika takes the form of a consideration of another work with particular reference to what it says, leaves unsaid, or says wrongly *(ukta-anukta-duruktacintā)*.[61] Shoun Hino and K.P. Jog note these divergences in their translation of Sureśvara's *Bṛhadāraṇyakopaniṣad-bhāṣya-vārtika*. Many of the differences between Sureśvara and Śaṅkara are minor and we shall briefly mention a couple of them, reserving the most important till last.

In the *Taittirīyopaniṣadbhāṣyavārttika*, Sureśvara differs from Śaṅkara on four occasions.[62] To cite one example, it is said in *Taittirīya* Upaniṣad 3.1 that Bhṛgu practised *tapas* in order to know Brahman. But what is meant by the word *"tapas"?* Śaṅkara considers the word to mean the "concentration of the mind and the sense organs",[63] whereas Sureśvara suggests that *tapas* could instead refer to the discriminative method of reasoning by way of continuity and discontinuity *(anvayavyatireka)*, so as to discern the changeless Self from all that is impermanent.[64] This important method of reasoning will be discussed in detail later in the chapter.

In the *Bṛhadāraṇyakopaniṣadbhāṣyavārttika*, Sureśvara proposes a number of alternative interpretations to Śaṅkara.[65] One interesting instance, though only of minor importance, occurs in *Bṛhadāraṇyaka* Upaniṣad 4.3.1, when Yājñavalkya goes to meet Janaka. Śaṅkara understands part of the passage to read: *sa mene na vadiṣya iti* and interprets it as Yājñavalkya thinking: "I will not say anything to the king".[66] Sureśvara interprets the text differently, so as to read: "I will converse with him" *(sam enena vadiṣya iti)* and he also says that his interpretation is more satisfactory in view of the fact that there is no reason given why Yājñavalkya would not wish to speak with Janaka.[67]

There is, however, one instance of a real difference of opinion. This can be seen from Sureśvara's repeated assertion that renunciation *(sannyāsa)* legitimately pertains to all three social classes, Brāhmaṇas, Kṣatriyas and Vaiśyas, and not just to Brāhmaṇas alone. Śaṅkara states in his commentary on the *Bṛhadāraṇyaka* Upaniṣad that only Brāhmaṇas are entitled to *sannyāsa*, because the text only mentions the word

"Brāhmaṇa".[68] Sureśvara presents an alternative view that *sannyāsa* is open to all three classes, and whenever Śaṅkara states his view, Sureśvara controverts it:

> Since *sannyāsa* is seen in the *śruti* to pertain to all the three classes, the statement in the commentary that only the Brāhmaṇa is eligible for *sannyāsa* is contradicted by the *śruti*.[69]

According to a much quoted passage from the *Jābāla* Upaniṣad (4) a person can renounce from the stage of life of the celibate Vedic student *(brahmacārin),* and since all the three classes can be students of the Veda, they should also be equally eligible for *sannyāsa*.[70] Sureśvara says:

> The word itself [brāhmaṇa], unsupported by reasoning, is not adequate evidence. So the meaning you want is not proved on just the strength of the word "brāhmaṇa".[71]

> When *sannyāsa* is heard in the *śruti* for all three classes without distinction, the mention of the word "brāhmaṇa" would have the purpose of implying the others as well.[72]

> If it is accepted that knowledge puts an end to the eligibility concerning rites, then on what strength of reasoning is a restrictive rule made about the eligibility to renounce?[73]

Sureśvara, like Śaṅkara, accepts *sannyāsa* as part of the knowledge of Brahman, and he envisages *sannyāsa* as forming a preliminary step to the inquiry into the Vedānta.[74] However unlike Śaṅkara he does not appear to accept that the *śruti* actually enjoins renunciation.[75] Sureśvara's view is that the *śruti* informs us that *sannyāsa* is an aid to knowledge, and on account of dispassion toward the things of the world the seeker after liberation would take to *sannyāsa*, but Sureśvara does not think that the *śruti* actually enjoins *sannyāsa*.[76]

In his introduction to the *Naiṣkarmyasiddhi*, Sureśvara stated that "ignorance of the Self is the cause of all misery".[77] He went on to say that ignorance conceals the happiness which is the very nature of the Self and that is why the removal of this ignorance is the supreme purpose of life. He said that the removal of ignorance is through the knowledge of one's real nature; but such knowledge cannot be brought about by the operation of the usual means of knowledge, sense perception and inference, because these two means of knowledge are applicable only for the revelation of sense objects and they cannot reveal the true nature of the Self as the latter is not a sense object. Sureśvara says the Upaniṣad sentences alone constitute the valid means of knowledge in this matter. We shall now discuss in some detail, and with specific reference to chapters two and three of the *Naiṣkarmyasiddhi*, what Sureśvara envisages to be (a) the pre-conditions for this knowledge to arise from the Upaniṣad sentences and (b) the way in which these sentences can convey their liberating meaning.

(5) Anvayavyatireka

Sureśvara commences chapter two of the *Naiṣkarmyasiddhi* with a diagnosis as to the reason why the "great sentences" *(mahāvākya)* of the Upaniṣads, of which the most famous is "you are That" *(tat tvam asi)*, fail to produce liberating knowledge. He says:

> If a person who has been taught "you are That" *(tat tvam asi)* does not understand the meaning of the sentence, it is because he does not recognise the meaning of the word "you" *(tvam)*. So we will now tell the way to understand the meaning of *tvam*.[78]

By the word "you" *(tvam)* Sureśvara means, of course, the subject, the first person singular "I". He continues:

> A person who has not developed dispassion towards this world of birth and death will not desire its cessation. A person who has not stopped thirsting after things will not seek to be free.[79]
>
> A person who is not a seeker of freedom will not approach the feet of a spiritual teacher. Without association with a teacher one would not hear the sentence [of the *śruti*].[80]
>
> Without the sentence, there are neither words nor their meanings. Without words and their meanings, what can be the basis for reasoning on the principle of continuity and discontinuity *(anvayavyatireka)* ?[81]
>
> Without this reasoning on the principle of continuity and discontinuity there will be no knowledge of the meaning of the sentence. And without such knowledge, the removal of ignorance is not logically possible.[82]

The above verses reveal that among a chain of important factors - he mentions dispassion, the desire to be free *(mumukṣutā)* and association with a guru from whom one hears the *śruti* - it is reasoning based upon the principle of continuity and discontinuity *(anvayavyatireka)* that plays a crucial role in enabling a person to grasp the liberating meaning of the *śruti* sentence. This type of reasoning, relying upon the discrimination between what is continuous and what is discontinuous, is presented by Śaṅkara himself in the eighteenth chapter of his *Upadeśasāhasrī*.[83] Since Sureśvara is familiar with the *Upadeśasāhasrī* judging from the number of times he quotes it in his *Naiṣkarmyasiddhi*,[84] as well as in his other works,[85] it is clear that this method of reasoning is not Sureśvara's innovation, though it figures more prominently in his writings than in those of Śaṅkara.[86]

What exactly is this reasoning based upon continuity and discontinuity? Continuity *(anvaya)* refers to the continuing presence of something, while discontinuity *(vyatireka)* refers to the absence of something. Reasoning through finding continuity and discontinuity has three applications, of which the third appears to be unique to Advaita.[87] Firstly, *anvayavyatireka* is used to ascertain a relation of cause and effect between two things by showing that one depends upon the other:

> When X occurs, Y occurs *(anvaya)*
> When X does not occur, Y does not occur *(vyatireka)*[88]

For example, when the clay exists, the pot exists. In the absence of the former there is the absence of the latter, therefore clay is the cause (in this context, the material cause) of the pot. Secondly, *anvayavyatireka* is employed to establish the necessary condition for a valid inference, namely positive and negative concomitance in a statement and its contraposition[89]:

> When X occurs, Y occurs *(anvaya)*
> When Y is absent, X is absent *(vyatireka)*[90]

In addition to using it in the above two ways, i.e., to demonstrate a causal relation between two things *(kāryakāraṇasaṁbandha)*, or to infer the existence of one thing from the existence of something else *(vyāpyavyāpakasaṁbandha)*, Advaitins employ this reasoning to establish the independent existence of a thing. In this third way, *anvayavyatireka* is used specifically to establish a relation of persisting and non-persisting between two things *(anuvṛttavyāvṛttasaṁbandha)*:

> When X occurs, Y occurs *(anvaya)*.
> When X occurs, Y is absent *(vyatireka)*[91]

Śaṅkara and Sureśvara use *anvayavyatireka* to show that one term is independent of the other (X is independent of Y).[92] This is how Sureśvara understands *anvayavyatireka* reasoning in the present context when he says:

> The continuous presence of Awareness is observed everywhere among the effects of Ignorance. Discontinuity is well known through the negation of the effect.[93]

Therefore, according to both Śaṅkara and Sureśvara, the continued presence of one thing is juxtaposed with the absence of something else in order to show that the former exists independently of the latter.

Sureśvara mentions two types of *anvayavyatireka* reasoning.[94] The first is based upon the logical distinction between the subject, the seer *(dṛk)*, and the object seen *(dṛśya)*. The second is based on the continued presence of the "witness" *(sākṣin)* in contrast with the discontinuity of what is witnessed. The first method aims to arrive at the "pure subject" by successively discarding whatever can be objectified, for what can be objectified cannot be identical to the subject. The second method reveals that Awareness is invariable by showing the non-deviation *(avyabhicāra)* of Awareness in spite of the deviation of other factors. For example, the non-deviation of Awareness as against the changeability of cognitions, and the non-deviation of Awareness throughout the three variable states, waking, dream and dreamless sleep. This second type of *anvayavyatireka* reasoning is also known as "*vyabhicāra* (deviation) and *avyabhicāra* (non-deviation)" and these two terms clearly indicate the procedure involved in this reasoning.[95] Both types of *anvayavyatireka* have essentially the same purpose: to negate adventitious factors and conditions from the "I", in order to reveal the true meaning of the word "I" as the absolute "subject", as pure Awareness, the invariable among the variable.

Much of the second chapter of the *Naiṣkarmyasiddhi* involves the application of this reasoning to ascertain the real meaning of "I". Sureśvara proceeds by way of negating the physical body, then also the subtle body which comprises the senses, the life-energy *(prāṇa)*, the mind and the ego. He presents a number of reasons to negate the idea that the physical body is the true Self. Firstly, he says that the physical body is not the Self because the body is a product of digested food, and no discriminating person would look upon food as the Self. Then he presents the two types of *anvayavyatireka* reasoning, (a) the body is not the Self because the body is an object of Awareness, and (b) all objects of Awareness are variable and are therefore not the invariable Self. A few of these verses, together with their prose introductions, arguing that the body is not the Self because the body is a product of food, are given below, so that the reader can see Sureśvara's vivid treatment of the topic:

> Just as it is understood that faeces is not the Self since it is the product of food, likewise, the physical body and the senses are a product of food. Why are they not seen [as not the Self]?[96]

It is well known [that food] is not the Self before [it is eaten] and at the end [when it is excreted], so what is the obstacle [to seeing that food is not the Self] during the intervening period?

> Before, [food] is certainly not the Self, once eaten it becomes the Self due to ignorance. Therefore a person of discrimination ought to look upon the body like it is a garland or an ointment.[97]

This teaching - that everything from the mind to the physical body is not the Self - is fully in accord with the *śruti.* This is said in the next verse:

> Just as the one seed is threefold, as chaff, grain and bran, similarly food exists in three ways, as mind, flesh and excretion.[98]

He is referring here to the *Chāndogya* Upaniṣad 6.5.1: "Food, when eaten, becomes divided in three ways. The grossest constituent turns into faeces. The medium constituent becomes flesh. The most subtle constituent becomes mind."

The second reason why the body is not the Self directly utilises the *anvayavyatireka* method of reasoning. He says:

> The wise should know that the body is not the Self because (a) just as a pot is an object of Awareness by means of the sense organs, the

> body is an object of Awareness by means of those same sense organs, and (b) because the body does not persist in dream.[99]

The second reason that is given here, "because the body does not persist in dream" is not asserting that the body somehow ceases to exist when we dream (or sleep), but it says that during dream we have no experience of the continuation of our waking body, whereas Awareness does persist. That must be so, since dream objects stand revealed to the dreamer.

Sureśvara says reasoning should also distinguish the subtle body from the Self. While the subtle body consists of seventeen factors,[100] Sureśvara concentrates his attention upon the most important of these, the mind, and he determines through the *anvayavyatireka* mode of reasoning that cognitive states cannot be the pure Self:

> "I" and "mine", effort and desire, are not attributes of the Self, because (a) they are objectively experienced, like the attribute of being thin, and (b) because they are transient, like clothes.[101]

The reasoning based upon the distinction between subject and object is frequently used in Advaita, and it figures prominently in Śaṅkara's introduction *(Adhyāsabhāṣya)* to the *Brahmasūtra*, which we shall see in detail in the following chapter.

There is the danger that this type of rational reflection, based on the principle of the distinction between subject and object, might come to rest merely at the ego, resulting in subjectivism, but Sureśvara pays considerable attention to the problem of discriminating out the objective factors from the very notion of the ego, or "I"-thought, so as to leave the Self as the residual Awareness that reveals the ego-entity itself. In order to do this, Sureśvara presents a number of arguments that rely on the two types of *anvayavyatireka* just mentioned; namely that (a) whatever is seen is not identical to the Seer, and (b) whatever is variable cannot be the persisting Self. In the following verse he presents an argument that shows the application of the first type of reasoning:

> A thing is the quality of the location where it is perceived, it is not the quality of the one who sees it. For what is identical to the seer cannot become an object of perception, like the Awareness of the seer.[102]

Sureśvara argues that as the "I"-thought, or ego, is something perceived, it cannot be an attribute of the perceiver. The ego is therefore strictly an attribute of the mind, not of the Seer, the pure Awareness. He presents a series of verses to negate the notion that the "I"-thought is the essential Self. In the next verse he utilises the second type of *anvayavyatireka* reasoning, and in the two verses that follow it he again employs the first type:

> If the "I" is an attribute of the Self, it would continue in liberation and in deep sleep. Since it does not continue, the "I" must belong to something else [i.e. to the mind].[103]

> Since the "I" is known through the means of knowledge [such as mental perception and inference] its relation to the Seeing is like that of a pot etc. [i.e. an object].[104]

> Nowhere can the same entity be simultaneously the Seer and the seen. Nor can the Seer be seen by that which is seen [by the Seer]. Nor can the Seeing observe the Seer [as they are identical].[105]

Sureśvara has argued that whatever is an object of Awareness, or is found to be variable, cannot be identified with the Self. The process of negation began with the physical body, extended up to the mind and included the "I"-thought as a particular property of the mind. Negation, however, is not an end in itself. In the case of the rope-snake it is not sufficient merely to negate the apparent snake, the real basis of that appearance must also be pointed out. Similarly, Sureśvara negates the body-mind as the Self only with a view to reveal the Self as the unnegated substratum. He argues that it is a matter of one's own introspective experience that cognitions are transient and that there is an invariable witness *(sākṣin)* of those cognitions.[106] We will now highlight some of his discussion about the "witness" Consciousness *(sākṣin)*.

He says it is evident that the mind changes, because it knows things sequentially. The mind is engaged in thinking about some matter, then it becomes involved in thinking about something else, and so on, and thus it is evident that the mind undergoes change. He says:

> The mind can be associated with something, like pleasure, a pot, etc. When it knows one thing, it does not know something else at the same time. Therefore the mind undergoes modification.[107]

He says that the Self, as the witness of the mind, is changeless, because the Self reveals "at one stroke", and without undergoing any alteration, whatever cognition is present in the mind:

> The one, eternal Self, which sees without any sequence, constantly pervades, as it were, by its Awareness, the cognitions that disappear in a moment and take on the various forms of sound and so forth.[108]

> Whether in memory, dream, or waking, there is no cognition of the mind that remains unpervaded by Awareness. Therefore the self-luminous Seeing is ever free from modification.[109]

And arguing on the basis of the distinction between subject and object as applied to one's ordinary experience of Awareness, he says that the Awareness-Self, as the residual principle of knowing, must be inherently free from the known, i.e., it must be intrinsically unaffected by what it reveals. Therefore by its very nature it is unattached *(asaṅga)*, or in the language of Gauḍapāda "untouched" *(aspṛṣṭa)* by what it reveals. Sureśvara expresses this point in the following two verses:

> If the Self is miserable, who would be the witness of the one who is miserable? It is not correct to say that the one who is miserable is the witness. Nor is it right to say that the witness is miserable.[110]

The one who is miserable cannot be the witness-Consciousness, because unhappiness is something known and therefore cannot be identical to the knower. So too the witness-Consciousness cannot be miserable, because the subject cannot become its own object, and if the witness-Consciousness is miserable the unhappiness could never become known. Sureśvara then says:

> In order to explain the previous verse, the following is said:
> One does not become miserable without undergoing a change. How can the one who undergoes the change be the witness? Therefore I am free from change, the witness of the thousand modifications of the mind![111]

The question arises whether *anvayavyatireka* reasoning renders the *śruti* superfluous. The Upaniṣads would not be required if we can arrive at the Self as the invariable and unaffected knower by reasoning upon our own experience using the method of *anvayavyatireka*. Sureśvara himself raises this pertinent objection:

> The followers of Sāṅkhya raise an objection. They say that ignorance means erroneous knowledge *(mithyājñāna)* and it consists in holding fast to the idea of Self in what is not the Self, namely the physical body, the sense organs, the mind and the intellect etc. As a result of such ignorance, the Self is associated with various miseries. Since that ignorance is

> removed just by the *anvayavyatireka* reasoning, the sentence *"tat tvam asi"* etc. would have no scope.[112]

He answers this objection in the following verse:

> This discriminative knowledge contains the idea of difference. In the witness there is no difference. The idea of difference is the effect of ignorance. Statements [like *"tat tvam asi"]* remove [ignorance by revealing the Self] as pure Awareness.[113]

What Sureśvara says is that reasoning by means of *anvayavyatireka* is a necessary preparatory step, but it is not sufficient in itself for the knowledge of reality. This is because discrimination between the Self and the "not-Self" gives rise to the radical dualism of Self and Other. By reasoning on the basis of the distinction between subject and object we can distinguish the Self as the invariable witness; the subject over and against the world, the body and the mind, all of which are witnessed. Reasoning can proceed thus far, but it terminates in a duality of seer and seen, where the latter is as real as the former. So while we can arrive at the knowledge of the Self as the witness-Consciousness through such reasoning, that knowledge is not yet *advaita,* it is not non-duality. This is presumably why Sureśvara says in his *Sambandhavārtika:* "The witness is in relation to the witnessed. The Self is not inherently a witness."[114] For there is something more to be understood about the Self, namely that it is intrinsically not limited *(ananta).* The Self has yet to be liberated from its false notion of limitation, from its sense of finitude, from its felt boundaries. Sureśvara says: "In the witness there is no difference" and he says that the idea of difference, as something real, is "the effect of ignorance". He envisages that the identification statements of the *śruti,* of which the most famous is *tattvamasi,* can remove this ignorance and thereby convey a non-relational knowledge of the Self as Absolute and non-dual.

We have seen Sureśvara say in the introductory statement to his *Naiṣkarmyasiddhi* that neither perception nor inference can remove the ignorance of the true nature of the Self, because these means of knowledge reveal sense objects, and the nature of the subject lies therefore outside their scope. However the identification statements of the *śruti*, such as *"tat tvam asi"*, do have the capacity to generate the immediately liberating knowledge of the subject, if the seeker is sufficiently prepared, i.e., if the seeker has done the discrimination of the Self from the "not-Self" by means of *anvayavyatireka*, or can do so at the moment of hearing the sentence. If the person is not so well-prepared, the *anvayavyatireka* reasoning must be done subsequent to hearing the sentence, so that the person will come, at some later time, to understand what was originally revealed at the time of hearing the sentence. Whether this type of discriminative reasoning known as *anvayavyatireka* is done before, at the time of, or after hearing the identification statements, *anvayavyatireka* forms the necessary precondition for the rise of knowledge. But it is the revelation of the *śruti* that provides the content of the liberating knowledge, and so once again we see the centrality of the *śruti* for the traditional follower of Advaita.

(6) How Śaṅkara and Sureśvara interpret the sentence "tat tvam asi"

Śaṅkara

In the third chapter of the *Naiṣkarmyasiddhi*, Sureśvara explains how *śruti* statements such as *"tat tvam asi"* are able to reveal, through words, something that lies outside the scope of ordinary language. We will see Sureśvara's explanation of this statement in the light of Śaṅkara's own treatment of it in the *Upadeśasāhasrī*, a text that Sureśvara himself has closely followed.

The difficulty that Śaṅkara must address is how liberation can take place through language. We have discussed this problem in chapter six and we will just highlight the main issues here. The ordinary function of language is to describe sense objects: words denote nouns (Devadatta), adjectives (Devadatta is bald), actions (Devadatta cooks) and relations (Devadatta owns a cow). But if language primarily refers to things, how can language reveal the true nature of the subject who is, by definition, not a sense object? Perhaps all that the Upaniṣads can do is tell us some ultimate reality exists; but they cannot directly enlighten us about it, because the Upaniṣads are in the form of words, and words are impotent to reveal something that is not a "thing", something that has not been first objectified by the senses. In Śaṅkara's discussion of the sentence *tattvamasi* in the eighteenth chapter of the *Upadeśasāhasrī* he tries to show how it is possible for the words of the *śruti*, limited though they are like other words, can yet directly reveal the true nature of the subject.

As a first step towards a solution to this problem Śaṅkara analyses the structure of the human person, and it is in this context that he introduces his conception of the ego as a "reflection" *(ābhāsa)* of pure Awareness in the mind. What Śaṅkara says is that the mind, which he conceives to be a subtle, material entity, exists in immediate proximity to pure Awareness. Awareness is reflected in this subtle material, and it is the reflection of Awareness in the mind that constitutes the individual "I", the ego. Śaṅkara provides the illustration of the reflection of a face in a mirror. According to this analogy, the face represents the Self, i.e., the pure Awareness, the mirror represents the mind, and the reflection of the face in the mirror is akin to the "reflection" of the Self in the mind. Such a reflection is the ego.

Śaṅkara says:

> Just as a mirror, which has the reflection of a face, takes the form of the face [so that we can say] "the reflection is the same as the face", similarly, the "mirror" of the cognitions has the reflection of Awareness and then [the word] "I" [can be used to refer to Brahman].[115]
>
> It is only in this way that the knowledge can arise that "I am Being Itself". There is no other way. Moreover the instruction "you are That" would be meaningless if there is no medium.[116]

What Śaṅkara says is that although the Self, the unconditioned I, the pure Awareness, is not an object of language, there is a way for words to reveal the Self and that is through the medium of the ego. The express sense of the word "you" *(tvam)* is the ego, the reflection of Awareness in the mind, but since the reflection is not something other than the original Awareness, the word "you" can indicate the non-objective Self if the hearer is prepared to negate the express sense and take the word in its implied sense *(lakṣaṇā)*. This is possible, since the ego, which is the object of the express sense of the word "you", is not apart from the inner Self, and thus the ego becomes the medium through which the meaning of the word "you" is able to indicate the inner-Awareness as the true Self. Śaṅkara says:

> Words refer to where there is the reflection [i.e. the mind]. Words can indicate *(lakṣayeyuḥ)* the inner-most Seeing, but there is no way they can directly express it.[117]
>
> If it is the case that the mind has the reflection of Awareness while the Self is Awareness itself, then the Veda is right when it reveals the Self through words such as Awareness *(jñāna)* [which directly refer to cognition but which can indicate the Self].[118]

In this way, Śaṅkara maintains that the words of the *śruti* can indeed reveal the nature of the subject; in that they first expressly refer to the ego and then, through the medium of the ego, they indicate the true Self that is the essence of the ego.

Having presented the way by which words can be made to indicate the Self, Śaṅkara proceeds to the analysis of the complete sentence. He says that the meaning of the word *tat* (That) and the meaning of the word *asi* (is) are already known to the hearer.[119] The word *tat* expresses Being Itself *(sat)* which was revealed earlier in the *Chāndogya* Upaniṣad (6.2.1) as the fundamental reality ("one only, non-dual") present prior to the origin of the world and from which the world of "name-and-form" *(nāmarūpa)* became manifest. The word *asi* (is) shows that the two words *tvam* (you) and *tat* (That) refer to a single entity.[120] *Tvam* and *tat* are thus to be mutually identified: *tvam* is identical to *tat* and *tat* is identical to *tvam*. But that does not mean the two words are initially presented as synonyms, for each word conveys its own meaning: the word *tvam* (you) literally refers to the ego, whereas the word *tat* (That) literally refers to Brahman, Being Itself. These two words, which have different primary meanings, are made explicitly co-referential by the verb *asi* (is), and it is their co-referentiality that becomes the key to unlocking the meaning of the sentence. Co-referentiality *(sāmānādhikaraṇya)* is an important grammatical term which describes the situation when words in a sentence are in the same grammatical case, and have a single referent, without being synonyms.[121] The principal feature of co-referentiality is that different words refer to one and the same entity. In the case of *"tat tvam asi"*, however, the co-referentiality of the two terms produces what seems to be an unintelligible meaning.[122] How can the primary meaning of *tvam*, the ego, be identified with *tat*, the Being itself that existed prior to the manifestation of the world? The co-referentiality of the two terms calls the intelligibility of the sentence into question. At this critical juncture a solution can be found by discarding the incompatible elements of the words *tat* and *tvam* while retaining whatever is common to the two terms. Thus the solution is possible through indication (or implication) *(lakṣaṇā)*, by abandoning the primary senses of the two words and accepting a common implied meaning; and the ability to do this requires that the hearer has first ascertained, through *anvayavyatireka*, that the true Self is pure Awareness and not the ego. Śaṅkara says:

> In the case of sentences such as *tat tvam asi* etc., the meaning of the sentence, namely that "I am ever free", does not become evident owing to a lack of discrimination concerning the meaning of the word "you" *(tvam)*. Therefore there is the mention of *anvayavyatireka* in order to discriminate the meaning of *tvam*, and for no other purpose. For when there is the discrimination of the word "you", the meaning of the sentence becomes evident, like a *vilva* fruit placed in the palm of one's hand.[123]

Śaṅkara explains how the sentence reveals a non-relational *(akhaṇḍārtha)* meaning, through the negation of the primary meaning of the two terms and the understanding of the implied meaning. He says:

> Since the word *tvaṁ* is in association [with the word *tat]* which expresses freedom from sorrow, the word *tvaṁ* comes to mean the one who is free from sorrow. So too, because of the association of the word *tat* [with the word *tvaṁ]* which expresses the inner-Self, the word *tat* [comes to mean the inner-Self].[124]

> The word *tat* means the inner-Self and *tvaṁ* has the meaning of the word *tat*. The two words remove [the notions that the inner-Self] is sorrowful and that [Brahman] is other than the inner-Self.[125]

> Since obstructions have been removed, and because one's nature is Experience *per se* [i.e. pure Awareness], the right knowledge about one's Self would certainly arise then, there is no doubt.[126]

To summarise. The words *tat* and *tvaṁ* express different meanings. The word *tat* refers to the self-existing absolute Being. The word *tvam* directly refers to the ego, i.e., the mind possessing the reflection of Awareness *(cidābhāsa)*. Since the *cidābhāsa* is not separate from its substratum, pure Awareness, the word *tvaṁ* can indicate the substratum if the hearer has clarified the understanding of *tvam* through *anvayavyatireka.* When the sentence is heard, the co-referentiality of the two words brings their literal meanings into opposition and the meaning of the sentence is rendered unintelligible. The juxtaposition of the terms shows that they qualify each other, the meaning of *tat* is qualified by the meaning of *tvam* and vice versa, and this juxtaposition provides the solution to their opposition and to the unintelligibility of the sentence if the hearer resorts to *lakṣaṇā:* for each term negates the contrary attribute, given in the express meaning, from the other term, so that the two words reveal by implication what is common to both; and thus the sentence reveals the undivided nature of the Self. Śaṅkara says:

> The basis of the word "I" is in the luminous, inner-Self. It is this substratum which is said [by the sentence] "you are Being Itself". The result is liberation.[127]

The sentence thus serves to liberate the ego from its sense of finitude by revealing that its basis and true Self is undivided *(akhaṇḍa)* Being-Awareness.

Sureśvara

Most of the third chapter of the *Naiṣkarmyasiddhi* is devoted to an analysis and explanation of the sentence *"tat tvam asi"*. We have seen that Śaṅkara has referred, though in a somewhat unsystematic manner, to co-referentiality *(sāmānādhikaraṇya)*, the juxtaposition of the two terms, and to the use of implication. Near the beginning of his chapter Sureśvara encapsulates in one verse these three points which he will later expand upon. He says:

> Co-referentiality *(sāmānādhikaraṇya)*, the relation of qualifier and qualified *(viśeṣaṇaviśeṣyatā)*, and the relation of indicated and indication *(lakṣya-lakṣaṇasambandha)*. These are the relations that exist between the words, their meanings, and the inner-Self.[128]

Thus there are three steps to understanding the sentence "you are That" *(tattvamasi)*. The first involves co-referentiality *(sāmānādhikaraṇya)*. Here, the second person singular of the verb to be *(asi)* shows that the words "you" *(tvam)* and "That *(tat)* are in grammatical apposition and refer to one and the same entity. The second step then follows, for as a result of their co-referentiality the meanings of the two words qualify one another *(viśeṣaṇaviśeṣyatā):* the meaning of *tvam* is the meaning of *tat*, and vice versa. But this brings the primary meanings of the words into opposition, for it is not intelligible to equate the meaning of *tvaṁ*, the finite *jīva*, with the meaning of *tat*, the infinite Brahman. This leads to the final stage; in order to make sense of the sentence the primary meanings of both terms are abandoned and a secondary meaning is understood. This third step necessitates the use of implication *(lakṣaṇā)*, where a relation of indication and what is to be indicated *(lakṣyalakṣaṇasambandha)* occurs between the ego "I" and the innermost Self, the pure Awareness. If this explanation is reasonably clear then we should be able to follow what Sureśvara says in the following verses:

> The word "that" *(tat)* reveals many things in the world, but without relinquishing its sense of remoteness. Remoteness belongs to the primary meaning of the word.[129]
>
> In the same way, the word "you" *(tvam)* expresses the meaning of mere immediacy, but without relinquishing its sense of referring to the suffering individual *(saṁsārin)*. For that [referring to the suffering individual] belongs to the primary meaning of the word.[130]

Since the primary meanings are contradictory, the meanings of remoteness and suffering cannot be the intended sense. This is said:

> The subject *[tvam]* of the sentence *[tat tvam asi]*, who possesses the specific quality [of suffering], does not enter into a relation with what is signified by the predicate *[tat]*.[131]
>
> The word "that" *[tat]* is the qualifier [i.e. the predicate] and "you" *[tvam]* is the qualified [i.e. the subject]. The relation of indicated

> and indication between the two words must take place through the inner Self.[132]
>
> Just as the snake can indicate the rope, so can the "I" indicate the innermost Self. One knows the meaning of the sentence just by the negation of the "I", because the innermost Self is the basis of the "I".[133]

This immediate apprehension of the non-relational meaning is only for the person who knows the method of *anvayavyatireka*. For:

> To the extent that a person moves toward the innermost Self by setting aside [identification with] the body etc., to that extent the meaning of *tat* is ready to enter into the meaning of *tvam*.[134]

The co-referentiality of the words brings their meanings into juxtaposition; but the sentence is unintelligible if we understand the words according to their primary meanings. The seemingly inescapable situation of contradiction and unintelligibility forces the hearer to seek a solution that will immediately resolve what is, in fact, the bafflement of a paradox. The search for a way out impels the hearer to grasp *lakṣaṇā* as the only alternative. The primary meanings must be abandoned, and a secondary, implied meaning common to both terms has to be sought. By doing so, the hearer directly apprehends the solution that the innermost Awareness is in fact the limitless Brahman. In this way, by revealing the true nature of the inner-Self, the sentence serves to release the inner-Self from its sense of finitude.[135] Such an understanding can occur if the hearer -who is endowed with qualities such as tranquillity *(śama)* etc.-is able to discriminate the non-Self from the Self by means of *anvayavyatireka*. In the absence of such discrimination, Sureśvara says the sentence would be like music to a deaf person.[136]

We can see that according to both Śaṅkara and Sureśvara the *mahāvākya* sentence *tattvamasi* reveals its meaning through indication *(lakṣaṇā)*.[137] The question arises as to what is the type of *lakṣaṇā* they use. I have discussed *lakṣaṇā* with reference to Śaṅkara in the preceding chapter and so I will confine my comments to Sureśvara. We saw in the previous chapter that *lakṣaṇā* is said to be of three types. (1) *Jahallakṣaṇā*, where the primary meaning is completely given up, as in the statement: "the village is on the Ganges". Here the unintelligible literal meaning "on the Ganges" is completely abandoned in favour of an implied meaning: "on the bank". (2) *Ajahallakṣaṇā*, where the primary meaning is not given up, but an additional meaning is implied, as in the statement "the white is running". Here the direct meaning of the word "white" is retained and a further meaning is added, as implied by the context in order to make the sentence intelligible. Thus the statement "the white is running" might contextually imply: "the white horse is running". (3) *Jahadajahallakṣaṇā* or *bhāgatyāgalakṣaṇā*, where a part of the primary meaning is retained and a part of it is given up. In the case of the sentence denoting a recognition: "this is that Devadatta", there is the negation of the incompatible aspects belonging to past time and place, i.e., "that", and present time and place, i.e., "this", so as to recognise the essential identity of the person as persisting throughout, for otherwise it is not logically possible that Devadatta of the past and the present could be identical.

In the *Naiṣkarmyasiddhi*, Sureśvara uses *lakṣaṇā* of the first and the third type, though he does not use the names by which they have become known in later Advaita literature. In the following verse it seems he uses *jahallakṣaṇā* :

> Just as the snake can indicate the rope, so can the "I" indicate the innermost Self. One knows the meaning of the sentence just by the negation of the "I", because the innermost Self is the basis of the "I".[138]

Here, the entire meaning of *"tvam"* is negated in favour of the implied meaning of its basis, the pure Awareness. However at other places his teaching would suggest *bhāgatyāgalakṣaṇā*, because the juxtaposition of the meaning *(viśeṣaṇaviśeṣyabhāva)* of the two terms serves to remove the limitations from the meaning of *tvam* and this is compatible with an interpretation by way of *bhāgatyāgalakṣaṇā*. Also, he frequently says that the Self is indicated "through the 'I'-thought" *(ahaṁvṛttyā)*.[139] The use of the instrumental case "through" suggests that the indication is by way of *bhāgatyāgalakṣaṇā*, for in the sense of "I" it is the objective ego aspect that is given up, while the non-object, pure Awareness aspect, the core-I, is what is indicated through the ego aspect. For example, he says:

> Due to some partial similarity, the Self is indicated by the "I"-thought, which is both a subject and an object. The Self is not directly denoted [by the "I"].[140]

Though the ego is the subject of transactional life, it is an object to the pure Awareness, so the ego is said to be both a subject and an object. Again:

> Immutable Awareness, that is innermost, is the inherent nature of the Self. It [the fact that the Self is Awareness and is innermost] is the cause for [the mind having respectively] cognisership and the sense of "I". Due to this reason, the Self is indicated through these two [cognisership and the "I"].[141]

The difference between the two approaches of *jahallakṣaṇā* and *bhāgatyāgalakṣaṇā* (or *jahadajahallakṣaṇā)* would seem to be quite subtle, for by *jahallakṣaṇā* there is the negation of the ego-entity in its entirety, and the indication refers to its substratum, the pure Awareness. According to *bhāgatyāgalakṣaṇā*, however, the "I"-sense is treated as a composite of two aspects, the ego aspect, as well as the pure Awareness aspect. The ego aspect is set aside and the indication refers to the non-objective, pure Awareness aspect of the "I"-sense. Śaṅkara taught that there are two aspects involved in the "I"-sense and this was further highlighted by Padmapāda, as we shall see. Later Advaitins, notably Vidyāraṇya in the *Pañcadaśī* and Sadānanda in the *Vedāntasāra*, have argued that the correct way of interpreting the sentence *"tat tvam asi"* is only by *bhāgatyāgalakṣaṇā (jahadajahallakṣaṇā)*, and this is also the way that is presented in some of the works ascribed, though erroneously, to Śaṅkara, such as the *Vivekacūḍāmaṇi.*[142] The explanation of the sentence by way of *bhāgatyāgalakṣaṇā* does seem to be the most satisfactory way of interpretation. Some of the later Advaita texts have also specified that the primary meaning *(vācyārtha)* of the word *tat* is Īśvara. This has the advantage of bringing the primary meaning of the two terms *tat* and *tvam* into sharper opposition, which then allows for resolution by way of *bhāgatyāgalakṣaṇā*, where both the *upādhis* of *jīvatva* and *Īśvaratva* are set aside in the implication of their common ground as undivided Awareness.

Whether Sureśvara explains *tattvamasi* by means of *jahallakṣaṇā* or *bhāgatyāgalakṣaṇā*, or by either at different places, there is no doubt that he interprets the sentence by way of *lakṣaṇā*. He employs *lakṣaṇā* in his other works as well; and in his *vārtika* on the *Bṛhadāraṇyaka* Upaniṣad he interprets the statement "not this, not this" *(neti neti)* by way of *lakṣaṇā.*[143] This only strengthens what we said in the previous chapter: there is fundamentally a single method in the classical Advaita of Śaṅkara and his immediate disciples, and it consists in the negation from the Self of all objectified aspects *(dṛśya)*, coupled with the use of *lakṣaṇā* to directly point out one's true nature. The purpose is to liberate the self from its sense of finitude by revealing that the innermost Self is actually the limitless Brahman. The use of *lakṣaṇā* must be acknowledged if words, which are relational by nature, are to function as the vehicle for generating a non-relational *(avākyārtha)* knowledge. According to Śaṅkara and Sureśvara, an immediate, non-relational, and liberating knowledge can arise out of understanding the implied meaning of the principal *śruti* sentences.[144] Other Advaitins, who did not use *lakṣaṇā* in their interpretation of the *śruti*, held that words could only produce mediate, theoretical knowledge, which necessitated further supplementation with yogic-type practices in order to transform into direct knowledge. Sureśvara takes issue with their position, a view that has, nonetheless, become dominant in later Advaita circles under the influence of the commentator Vācaspatimiśra (c. 850 CE).[145] It is to this discussion that we will now turn.

(7) Sureśvara on the Prasaṅkhyāna

Both Śaṅkara and Sureśvara present a refutation of *prasaṅkhyāna*, a rival doctrine in the Advaita tradition.[146] The teaching called *prasaṅkhyāna* was espoused by Maṇḍanamiśra, an Advaitin who is believed to have been an elder contemporary of Śaṅkara, and whose views diverged from those of Śaṅkara on a number of matters, especially concerning the combination of Upaniṣadic knowledge with the continued performance of rites. In his *Brahmasiddhi*, Maṇḍana puts forward the following view concerning the capacity of the *śruti* to generate liberating knowledge.

> Even when reality has been determined with certainty from a means of knowledge and the false appearances all cease, they nonetheless can still persist due to some special cause. For example, the error of seeing a double moon, or a confusion about direction, persists in people who have ascertained the truth about the moon or the direction from the speech of a competent person. In the same way, false appearances persist in a person who has understood the true nature of the Self from the traditional texts, which are free from doubt, because of the power of strong mental impressions accumulated through the repetition of beginningless wrong understanding. In order to remove those false appearances, something other [than just knowledge from the traditional text] is required. On the basis of ordinary experience what is required is the repetition of the seeing of reality, and as well as that there is the performance of rituals etc. which are known from the Veda. Repetition makes a mental impression firm, it obstructs earlier impressions and builds upon its own effect. Rituals etc. accomplish the same thing in some unseen manner, or as others say, by destroying the impurities which stand in the way of the highest good, since the purpose of the obligatory rituals is to remove sin.[147]

Maṇḍana says that the *śruti* is a true means of knowledge *(pramāṇa)*. It reveals to us the truth just as a competent authority can tell us the truth about which way is north or south if we are confused about the direction. When we have heard the truth from the *śruti* our mistaken notions cease, just as they do when we have found out the true direction. But in addition to this, Maṇḍana says that even when we come to know the truth from the *śruti*, and our erroneous knowledge therefore ceases, that erroneous knowledge nonetheless can still be seen to persist. This seems to be a contradiction, for why should error continue once the truth is known? This is because the knowledge gained from the *śruti* is merely theoretical. The false appearances "cease" only in so far as we have now learnt what the truth is, but they "persist" because our knowledge is still theoretical or conceptual.

Maṇḍana explains this point through the illustration of a person who, having found out what the true direction is, can still become bewildered again. Or a person who has been told that there is only a single moon and yet continues to see two moons! But why should error continue even when we have learnt the truth? Maṇḍana says it is because the previous, erroneous mental impressions, are stronger than the impression generated by the operation of the *pramāṇa*. The erroneous impressions have been strengthened by habitual repetition in the mind over a long period, and they naturally tend to overwhelm the new impression generated by hearing the truth, with the result that even when the truth is known, the error born of habit is seen to persist. What is the remedy for this? According to Maṇḍana, the remedy is to make the new impression generated by the *pramāṇa* stronger than the erroneous impressions. Just as the erroneous impressions became firmly embedded through habituation, so the knowledge of the truth must be repeatedly meditated upon to the extent that it can no longer be overwhelmed by erroneous impressions. It is a matter of common sense, Maṇḍana says, that when we repeat our knowledge of something the knowledge becomes firm in our minds. Maṇḍana further says that in addition to repeated meditation, commonly known as *prasaṅkhyāna*, the performance of the prescribed Vedic rituals generates a helpful effect and so they ought to be performed.

Later in the *Brahmasiddhi*, he says:

> Verbal knowledge is indirect *(parokṣa)*, while the appearance of the world is directly experienced *(pratyakṣarūpa)*. So since they do not mutually oppose each other, the

> appearance of the world is *not* something unrelated to the Self, it is *not* that it doesn't do anything and it *is* a bondage. ....When the nature of the Self is made directly evident to a person through meditation *(upāsana)* etc., then there is opposition [between the directly experienced appearance of the world and the immediate knowledge of the Self], so even if the appearance of the world continues to exist it is not related to the Self....it doesn't do anything and it is not a cause of fear. ....
> Moreover, verbal knowledge, depending upon a means of knowledge, lasts just an instant and there is opportunity for confusion once again. For we see that if a person does not continuously remember the means of knowledge, a rope can once again cause fear due to the error that it is a snake! But if [you say] that even in meditation, the person has just continually to repeat the verbal knowledge [obtained from the Upaniṣads], [we reply] what else is *upāsana* other than this?[148]

The important point to be noted from the above passage is that Maṇḍana explicitly states that verbal testimony can produce only an indirect knowledge. Verbal knowledge functions by way of understanding the meaning of sentences, and to understand the meaning of a sentence requires an understanding of the meaning of the individual inflected words in the sentence, as well as their interrelationship. Verbal knowledge is necessarily relational, it is infused throughout with duality, it is conceptual and produces only indirect knowledge.[149] This indirect knowledge acquired from the Upaniṣads cannot oppose our direct experience of duality, hence something additional is required to convert the indirect knowledge into a direct knowledge. Maṇḍana says that repeated meditation makes the indirect Upaniṣadic knowledge into direct knowledge; the latter can then stand in opposition to the appearance of duality and put an end to the idea that duality is real as well as to all the other errors conditional upon that idea. The second point to note here is that Maṇḍana specifies what he means by meditation: meditation is repeatedly going over the indirect knowledge gained from the Upaniṣads until that knowledge becomes immediate and vivid, like a perception. By meditation, Maṇḍana does not mean an explicit yogic discipline requiring total sense suspension, or concentration upon some imagined centres located within the body; he means the repetition of the indirect knowledge obtained from the Upaniṣads until it becomes immediate knowledge. So we should not overlook the centrality of the Upaniṣads to the world of the traditional Vedāntin, even in this matter of repeated meditation.

On a number of occasions in the *Naiṣkarmyasiddhi* Sureśvara outlines a teaching of *prasaṅkhyāna* that resembles the view of Maṇḍana described above. Sureśvara understands *prasaṅkhyāna* to involve the repetition of the *śruti* statements, such as "I am Brahman", as well as the repetition of the *anvayavyatireka* reasoning.[150] The essential characteristic of *prasaṅkhyāna* is that it is a mental activity involving repetition. Its purpose is to convert the necessarily mediate *(parokṣa)* knowledge gained from the *śruti* into an immediate experience of the truth.

Here he presents the view of an opponent which is very similar to that of Maṇḍana:

> Though the right knowledge is powerful, we find that it gets sublated by wrong knowledge arising from something other than a means of valid knowledge. Because even when someone has the highest knowledge, ideas of doership and enjoyership, desires and aversions etc.-which come from ignorance- still make their appearance. And there is no possibility of those occurring without right knowledge being negated, as they are opposed to right knowledge.[151]
>
> ....Others say that the knowledge "I am Brahman" produced from the Vedānta sentences does not apprehend the real nature of the Self, because such knowledge is relational. What then? When one repeats this knowledge continuously, like the flow of the Gaṅgā, another knowledge arises that is non-relational and is different [from the verbal knowledge]. And it is that knowledge alone which removes the entire darkness of ignorance, for there is the *śruti* statement: "the Brāhmaṇa, after knowing, should gain direct knowledge" (BU 4.4.21).[152]

The argument contained in these passages can be reduced to two points.[153] (a) The knowledge gained from the Upaniṣads is always mediate, because knowledge is always relational. So there cannot be an immediate apprehension of the truth through the medium of language. This is evident from the fact that even people who are said to understand the highest truth can be found to exhibit characteristics in common with ignorant persons, such as doership and enjoyership, desires and aversions. (b) Since this is so, the remedy lies in the repetition of the Upaniṣad sentences such as "I am Brahman", along with repeated use of *anvayavyatireka* reasoning. Such constant repetition will generate a new, non-verbal knowledge, that will have the capacity to remove ignorance.

Śaṅkara and Sureśvara oppose this teaching called *prasaṅkhyāna* because they maintain that the words of the *śruti* do have the capacity to produce liberating knowledge in the mind of a prepared seeker. Sureśvara replies to the first of the above passages in the following verse:

> Since ignorance has been sublated, it never sublates knowledge. The impressions left over by ignorance will certainly become an occasion to recollect the knowledge.[154]

Sureśvara refuses to accept that knowledge, once it has arisen and sublated ignorance, can be sublated by the return of ignorance. Any impressions of ignorance that may still arise, consisting of notions of doership and so forth, are negated when they arise since they become the occasion for the recollection of the knowledge of one's true nature. And at the end of the *Naiṣkarmyasiddhi*, Sureśvara dismisses the idea that the *jñānī* could behave in some sinful manner.[155]

In response to the second passage, Sureśvara says:

> The knowledge from the scripture, at one stroke, destroys ignorance which is the support of action and the factors of action. Therefore, there is no combination of these two [knowledge and rituals].[156]

Repetition of the verbal knowledge is a mental action, and such an action requires the notion of real agentship, as does the performance of rituals. But when knowledge destroys ignorance - upon which rest the erroneous notions of the reality of agentship etc. - why should one perform those ritual activities that presuppose the reality of agentship?

Sureśvara's other arguments against the *prasaṅkhyāna* are basically of two types. Firstly, he says that the teaching of *prasaṅkhyāna* fails to appreciate a very important fact, namely that the Self is, by its very nature, self-luminous and thereby self-evident. If the Self is always immediately evident *(aparokṣa)* to experience, how can you argue that it can be known only mediately *(parokṣa)* ? He says:

> Though a thing is mediate, it appears as if immediate and as if the Self on account of the witness-Self. So how can there be the idea that the Self is mediate?[157]

The second set of arguments revolve around the point that the *śruti* is a means of knowledge whereas meditation is not a means of knowledge. If a means of knowledge fails to generate knowledge, mere repetition of the means of knowledge will not produce knowledge. At best, he says, it will increase one's power of concentration.[158] Moreover, the *śruti* statements will relinquish their self-validity and will be reduced to the position of mere auxiliary statements *(arthavāda)* that are for the purpose of inculcating meditation:

> If [you say that] experience takes place from [a combination of] merely hearing the scripture as well as from performing the enjoined action [i.e. *prasaṅkhyāna]*, then [we say] that if reality is not ascertained [from the *śruti* itself] the *śruti* would be just informative, as is seen in the case of auxiliary statements.[159]

Sureśvara, however, is prepared to make room for the teaching of *prasaṅkhyāna*, on his own terms, as he points out with a touch of humour:

> If you cannot live without *prasaṅkhyāna*, we will provide a place for it within listening *(śravaṇa)* etc. How?
>
> > Let the method of repetition in the *prasaṅkhyāna* be applied to one's hearing the *śruti*. A person understands upon correctly hearing what was heard a little, or half-heard.[160]

The essential disagreement is that the follower of *prasaṅkhyāna* believes that the *śruti* just provides informative statements about Brahman. Brahman has then to be realised by repeating the meaning of the sentences such as "I am Brahman" and continuing to reason about the Self and the not-Self. Thus the follower of *prasaṅkhyāna* lives under the expectation that the manifestation of the real nature of the Self depends upon generating some type of experience through repeated acts of reasoning and meditation. Śaṅkara and Sureśvara oppose this teaching, because it sets up a false dichotomy between theory and practice, with hearing the *śruti* falling within the ambit of the former; whereas they both maintain that the words of the *śruti* have the capacity to produce liberating knowledge when their meaning is correctly understood. Śaṅkara and his followers treat repetition as having the essentially negative function of removing obstructions to seeing what is directly revealed by the *śruti;* whereas the followers of *prasaṅkhyāna* have the opposite view, that the theoretical knowledge from the *śruti* has to be turned into a direct knowledge through the practice of repetition. Thus Śaṅkara and Sureśvara differ from the *prasaṅkhyānavādins*, like Maṇḍana and also Vācaspatimiśra, about the role that the *śruti* plays in liberation and, as a result of this, they further differ about just how the practices of rational reflection *(manana)* and contemplation *(nididhyāsana)* fit into the context of liberation. This last point is further developed by Padmapāda, as we will see in the following chapter.

1 According to Jonathan Bader, three texts name the opponent of Śaṅkara in the debate as Maṇḍana: the influential *Śaṅkaravijaya* of Anantānandagiri, the *Śaṅkaravijayavilāsa* of Cidvilāsa, and the *Śaṅkarābhyudaya* of Tirumala Dīkṣita. (Mādhava's *Śaṅkaradigvijaya* (c.1650-1798), drawing upon diverse sources, mentions both the names, Maṇḍana and Viśvarūpa). Cf. Jonathan Bader, *Conquest of the Four Quarters: Traditional Accounts of the Life of Śaṅkara.* Unpublished Ph.D. Thesis, The Australian National University, 1991, p.51, 60.

2 Ibid., p.51, 60. Four texts refer to Viśvarūpa: the *Śaṅkaravijaya* of Vyāsācala, the *Śaṅkarācāryacarita* of Govindanātha, the *Śaṅkarābhyudaya* of Rājacūḍāmaṇi Dīkṣita, and the *Guruvaṁśakāvya* of Lakṣmanaśāstrī. S. Śrīrāma Śāstrī, in the Sanskrit introduction to his edition of the *Pañcapādikā,* equates Sureśvara in his *pūrvāśrama* with Viśvarūpa, who composed the commentary *Bālakriḍā* on the *Yājñavalkyasmṛti,* but he does not identify him with Maṇḍana. Cf. S. Śrīrāma Śāstrī (ed.), *Pañcapādikā of Padmapāda with two Commentaries and the Pañcapādikāvivaraṇam of Prakāśātman with two Commentaries,* Madras Govt. Oriental Series CLV, 1958, p.15f. Patrick Olivelle, however, questions the identification of Viśvarūpa with Sureśvara. Cf. Patrick Olivelle, *The Āśrama System: The History and Hermeneutics of a Religious Tradition,* op.cit., p.199 and n.54.

3 See the introduction by S. Kuppuswami Sastri to his edition of the *Brahmasiddhi.* S. Kuppuswami Sastri, *Brahmasiddhi by Acharya Maṇḍanamiśra With Commentary by Saṅkhapāṇi.* Delhi: Sri Satguru Publications, 1984 [first published 1937] p.1 ff. For the opposing view see R. Balasubramanian, "Identity of Maṇḍanamiśra", *Journal of the American Oriental Society,* vol.

82, Oct-Dec. 1962. His arguments are largely restated in his book, *A Study of the Brahmasiddhi of Maṇḍana Miśra.* Varanasi: Chaukhamba Amarabharati Prakasan, 1983. His views have been criticised by Allen Thrasher in his work, *The Advaita Vedānta of Brahma-Siddhi.* Delhi: Motilal Banarsidass, 1993, p.156, n.37. J. Bader, in his *Conquest of the Four Quarters,* op.cit., p.60, n.34, makes the interesting observation that the important *Śaṅkaravijaya* of Vyāsācala (5.37ff.), and the *Guruvaṁśakāvya.* of Lakṣmanaśāstrī (2.47ff.), refer to an attendant and disciple of Kumārila named Maṇḍana who is quickly won over by Śaṅkara just prior to Śaṅkara meeting Viśvarūpa.

4 S. Kuppuswami Sastri, *Brahmasiddhi by Acharya Maṇḍanamiśra*, op.cit., p.36, line 18ff.

5 US (verse portion) 1. 3-5.

6 The term *avicāritasiddha,* or a variation of it such as *avicāritaprasiddha,* or the more frequently used term *avicāritasaṁsiddhi,* are characteristic expressions of Sureśvara that occur regularly in the NS and the BUBhV. For example: NS 1.1 *(sambandhokti);* 2.97 (samb.); 2.112 (samb.); 3.66 *(vicāraṁ na sahate)*; 3.113 (samb.). BUBhV 1.4.332, 1329; 2.3.192, 224; 2.4.422; 3.4.131; 3.8.31; 4.3.352, 382.

7 TUBh 2.1, p.283, line 8f., (tr) p.291.

8 NS 2. 95.

9 Cf. Chapter five, (4) "Nāmarūpa".

10 NS 2.45.

11 NS 2.112.

---

12 BUBhV (vol.1) 1.4.332, p.333. Also, BUBhV (vol.1) 1.4.340, p.334; also verse 985, p.415. 2.3.186, p.664. 2.4.229, p.694.

13 NS 2.44, 45 (samb).

14 CU 6.1.4ff. BU 4.3.1ff.

15 NS 2.115.

16 NS 2. 99.

17 BUBhV (vol.1) 189, p.47. T.M.P. Mahadevan [Ed. and tr.], *The Saṁbandha-Vārtika of Sureśvarācārya*. Madras: University of Madras, 1972 [second edition], 189b-190a, p.97. Also BUBhV (vol.1) 190, p.48; 1002, p.181; 1058, p.189. TUBhV 2.611, 614.

18 For example, in the *Sambandhavārttika* cf. BUBhV (vol.1) 151, 189, 190, 1001, 1002, 1058. Also TUBhV 2. 614 (also found with slight alteration in BUBhV 1.4.873).

19 R. Balasubramanian, *Advaita Vedānta*. Madras: Centre for Advanced Study in Philosophy, University of Madras, 1976, p.146ff. Also R. Balasubramanian, *A Study of the Brahmasiddhi of Maṇḍana Miśra*, op.cit., cf. ch. V.

20 BUBhV (vol.1) 919-922, p.169f. Mahadevan, op.cit., 920-923, p.492f. Also BUBhV 2.1, 594, 595, p.638.

21 R. Balasubramanian, *The Taittirīyopaniṣad-Bhāṣya-Vārtika of Sureśvara*, Madras: University of Madras, 1984 (revised ed.), p.169-70. Also R. Balasubramanian, *A Study of the Brahmasiddhi of Maṇḍana Miśra*, op.cit., ch. V. Also, BUBhV

(vol.1) 922, p.170. Mahadevan, op.cit., 923, p.493. Also, BUBhV (vol.1) 2.1, 594, p.638.

22 TUBhV 2.144.

23 Sureśvara uses the expression *akāryakāraṇa* fairly frequently, eg. TUBhV 2. 140. BUBhV(vol.1) 2.4, 206, p.692; 347, p.707. BUBhV(vol.2) 3.8, 123, p.859; 4.2.88, p.905.

24 BUBhV (vol.1) 2.4. 244, p.696. The statement that "nothing originates from this [Ātman]" etc. is modelled upon KaU 2.18. Also cf. BUBhV (vol.1) 1.4.403, p.343.

25 TUBhV 2.140.

26 BUBhV (vol.1) 1.4.626, p.371. This verse is repeated at 2.1.384, p.617. Ānandagiri says: "The non-existent is not born, because it is non-existent, like a man's horn. Nor even is the existent born, because it exists, like the Self. Nor is there no origination, because it is seen that there is. Therefore origination is an imaginative construction by the mind *(kalpita).*"

27 BUBhV (vol.1) 2.1.266, p.605.

28 TUBhV 3.68. GK 3.29-30; 4.61-62.

29 BUBhV (vol.1) 2.1.385, p.617.

30 BUBhV (vol.1) 2.1.386, p.617. Sureśvara also refers to Gauḍapāda in BUBhV (vol.2) 4.4.886 p.1227, and verses 887, 888 cite GK 2.38 and 3.46 respectively. However this reference occurs in the context of developing the argument of a *pūrvapakṣin.* He also refers to Gauḍapāda in NS 4.44, and verses 41, 42 cite GK 1.11 and 15 respectively.

---

31 BUBhV (vol.1) 2.1.387, p.617. Also cf. BUBhV (vol.1) 1.2.27, p.206: "Cause and so forth are presented to establish the Self that is of the nature [mentioned in the previous verse as: 'unborn, one, self-existent, the inner-Self, seeing nothing as other']. Those who know [the tradition, i.e., Gauḍapāda] have briefly stated: 'it is a means to lead one to understand'."

32 BUBhV (vol.1) 1.4.402, p.342.

33 GK 2.17, 18. Śaṅkara, eg. BUBh 3.5.1, p.811, line 6, (tr) p.333. Sureśvara, eg. BUBhV (vol.2) 4.3.321, p.946.

34 BUBhV (vol.2) 3.8.130, p.859.

35 BUBhV (vol.1) 1.4.381, p.340.

36 NS 2. 52 (samb); 3. 112 (samb).

37 NS 3. 110. Also, BUBhV (vol.1) 1.4 .860, p.399, which is repeated in TUBhV 2. 603.

38 BUBhV (vol.1) *Sambandha,* 181, p.46. Mahadevan, op.cit., 181b-182a, p.94.

39 BUBhV (vol.1) *Sambandha,* 183, p.47. Mahadevan, 183b-184a, p.95.

40 He refers to *avidyā* as *anādi* in BUBhV (vol 2) 4.3. v.1409, p.1075.

41 From the standpoint of Brahman itself *(paramārthatah),* there is no *avidyā.* BUBhV *sambandha,* vv.176, 184, pp.45, 47; Mahadevan, op.cit, v.176b-177a, p.90; v.184b-185a, p.95.

42 BUBhV (vol.1) 1.2, v.135, p.221.

43 BUBhV (vol.1) 1.2, v.136, p.221. Pandit T. Śrīnivāsa Śāstrī, formerly of Deccan College, in a personal communication referred to the expression *maulī avidyā* from this verse to show that Sureśvara accepts a primary power often called *avidyā*. This verse is also cited as evidence by S. Śrīrāma Śāstrī in the introduction to his edition of the *Pañcapādikā*. S. Śrīrāma Śāstrī (ed.), *Pañcapādikā of Padmapāda with two Commentaries*, op.cit., p.53.

44 NS 3.1 (samb).

45 NS 3. vv.7-8.

46 NS 3.58 (samb).

47 Cf. for example, BUBhV (vol.2) 4.3.979, p.1026.

48 NS 3.1 (samb), *anātmanaścājñānaprasūtatvāt*. For Sureśvara, *avidyā* and *ajñāna* are synonyms, cf. BUBhV (vol.1) *sambandha*. 1088-1089, p.194. Mahadevan, op.cit, vv.1089b-1090a, 1090b-1091a, p.582.

49 BUBhV (vol.1) 1.4.371, p.338. Also, TUBhV 2.371, 408, 417 (this latter verse exhibits a resemblance to GK 2.12.).

50 NS 3.15 (samb). BUBhV (vol.1) *sambandha*. 1006, p.182. Mahadevan, op.cit., 1007b-1008a, p.539. BUBhV (vol.1) 1.4.371, p.338; (vol.2) 4.3.338, p.948. With reference to the beginninglessness of *avidyā* cf., for example, BUBhV(vol.1) 2.1, v.223, p.600; (vol.2) 3.9, v.160, p.883; 4.3, v.348, p.949.

---

51 BUBhV (vol.1) 1.2.128, p.220; 1.4.487, p.354; verse 1382, p.463; 2.3.7, p.644; 2.5.8, p.721; (vol.2) 3.9.157, p.883.

52 See n.23 above.

53 BUBhV (vol.1) 1.4.382, p.340.

54 BUBhV (vol.1) 1.4.487, p.354.

55 NS 1.3.

56 NS 4. 74. BUBhV (vol.2) 6.5.25, p.1370.

57 NS 4.19, 43 (samb.). BUBhV (vol.1.) 1.4.1124, p.432.

58 NS 4.44.

59 TUBhV 3.91.

60 BUBhV (vol.2) 6.5.25, p.1370.

61 This definition, from the *Kāvyamīmāṁsā,* is cited in the Introduction to Shoun Hino and K.P. Jog, *Sureśvara's Vārtika on Aśva and Aśvamedha Brāhmaṇa.* Delhi: Motilal Banarsidass, 1990, p.xvi, xviii.

62 TUBhV 2. 541. 3.19, 38, 40.

63 TUBh 3.1, p.314, line 10f., (tr) p.373.

64 TUBhV 3.19. Also the introduction by R. Balasubramanian to his edition, p.14.

65 Eg. BUBhV (vol.1) 1.2.146. p.223. 1.5.16, verses 279-281, p.552; 1.5.17, verses 284, 288, p.552f.; (vol.2) 3.5.1, verse 89, p.819; 4.3.1, verses 12-14, p.909. The last four instances (1.5.16.etc.) are identified by R. Balasubramanian in his article, "Identity of Maṇḍanamiśra", op.cit., p.526f.

66 BUBh 4.3.1, p.861, line 10f., (tr) p.416.

67 BUBhV (vol.2) 4.3. 12-14, p.909.

68 BUBh 1.4.15, p.684, line 12, (tr) p.125; 3.5.1, p.812, line 10f., (tr) p.334; 4.5.15, p.948, line 25, (tr) p.552.

69 BUBhV (vol.1) 1.4.1651, p.494.

70 Cf. Kane, *History of Dharmaśāstra,* op.cit., vol.11, part 11, p.943.

71 BUBhV (vol.1) 1.4.1652, p.495.

72 BUBhV (vol.2) 3.5.89, p.819.

73 BUBhV (vol.2) 3.5.90, p.819.

74 NS 1.52 (samb.); 3.4 (samb.). Also, BUBhV (vol.1) *(sambandha),* 130, p.37; 214, p.52; 219, p.53; 225, 226, p.55. 2.4.27, 28, p.674; 35, p.675. (vol.2) 3.5. 141, 142, p.825; 4.5. 5, p.1280.

75 Cf. Chapter six, (4) Sannyāsa and Videhamukti.

76 BUBhV (vol.1) 2.4. 6-7, p.672. Also cf. S. Hino, *Sureśvara's Vārtika on Yājñavalkya-Maitreyī Dialogue.* Delhi: Motilal

Banarsidass, 1982, p.79, "Sureśvara does not admit of any injunction either for urging renunciation or for prescribing renunciation as a means to the knowledge of the Brahman."

77 NS 1.v.1 (samb.)

78 NS 2.1. Also, cf. US 18.90 where Śaṅkara makes a similar point.

79 NS 2.6.

80 NS 2.7.

81 NS 2.8.

82 NS 2.9.

83 US 18.96, 191.

84

NS	**US**
4.v.20 is identical to:	18.v.78 (first line)
4.v.21.	18.v.90 (first line)
4.v.22.	18.v.96.
4.v.23	18.v.97.
4.v.24.	18.v.99.
4.v.25.	18.v.101

4.v.26	6.v.1
4.v.27.	6.v.3.
4.v.28.	6.v.2.
4.v.29.	6.v.4.
4.v.30.	15.v.16.
4.v.31.	18.v.190.
4.v.32.	18.v.191.
4.v.33.	18.v.192.
4.v.34.	18.v.174.
4.v.35.	18.v.175.
4.v.43.	17.v.26.
4.v.65.	18.v.231.
4.v.66.	18.v.232.

There are other verses of Sureśvara in the NS which show resemblances to verses in the US. For example, NS 1.58 has a resemblance to US 2.1; NS 2.63 resembles US 5.2-3; NS 2.76 resembles US 16.9; NS 2.86 resembles US 18.68; NS 3.10 resembles US 18.171; NS 3.80 resembles US 18.173.

85 For example, BUBhV *(sambandha)* 206=US 18.190; 207=US 18.191; 208=US 18.192. BUBhV (vol.1) 2.4.112=US 18.191.

(This verse, US 18.191, has also been cited in the NS 4.32 and in the *sambandhavārttika* 207). BUBhV (vol.1) 1.4.639 resembles US 9.1. BUBhV (vol.1) 2.4.111 closely resembles US 18.190. BUBhV (vol.2) 3.6.13 resembles US 9.1. BUBhV (vol.2) 4.3.436 closely resembles US 5.2.

Incidentally, there are frequent instances of cross-quotation in Sureśvara's works. For example, below are some instances of cross-quotations between the BUBhV and the TUBhV:

BUBhV	TUBhV
1.4, v.857 is identical to:	2.v.600
v.858	v.601
v.859	v.602
v.860	v.603
v.861	v.604
v.862	v.605 (similar)
v.863	v.607 (similar)
v.864	v.608
v.866	v.606 (similarity)
v.868	v.609
v.869	v.610
v.870	v.611

v.871	v.612
v.872	v.613
v.873	v.614 (similar)
v.874	v.619
v.875	v.620 (similar)
v.876	v.621
v.877	v.622
v.878	v.623 (similar)
v.879	v.624 (similar)
v.880	v.625 (similar)
v.881	v.626
v.883	v.629 (similar)
v.884	v.630 (near identity
v.888	v.716
v.889	v.717 (near identity
v.890	v.672
v.891	v.673
v.892	v.615 (similar)

v.893	v.616 (similar)
v.895	v.617 (similar)
v.896	v.618 (similar)
v.1058	3.v.20 (similar)

Instances of cross-quotations between the BUBhV and the NS:

BUBhV	**NS**
(sambandha) v.211 identical to:	3.v.64
v.212	3.v.65 (similar)
v.213	3.67 (near identity)
1.4, v.1451	4.v.57
v.1452	4.v.58
v.1455	4.v.59
3.5, v.185	3.v.3
v.186	3.v.9
4.3, v.396	2.v.77

86 Apart from many references to *anvayavyatireka* in the NS, it is also referred to in his other works, for example: TUBhV 2. vv 335, 656, 714, 715. 3. vv 8, 9, 11, 19, 30. Also, BUBhV 1.4.

vv 64, 1060, 1345, 1386, 1387. 2.1. vv 167, 170, 173. 2.4. vv 107, 114. 3.5. vv 179, 181.

87 I would like to thank Swami Paramārthānanda, of Chennai (Madras), who provided me with additional clarification on this important topic of *anvayavyatireka.*

88 *yatsattve, yatsattvam. yadabhāve, yadabhāvaḥ. tasmāt tat tasya kāraṇam.*

89 W. Halbfass, *Tradition and Reflection.* New York: State University of New York Press, 1991, p.169.

90 *yatra dhūmaḥ, tatra vahniḥ. yatra vahnyabhāvaḥ, tatra dhūmābhāvaḥ.* There is therefore the necessary *vyāpyavyāpakasaṁbandha* to infer the presence of fire from the presence of the smoke.

91 *jāgradavasthāyām ātmanaḥ sattve, sthūlaśarīrasattvam (anvaya). svapnāvasthāyām ātmanaḥ sattve, sthūlaśarīrāsattvam (vyatireka). Tasmād ātmā anuvṛttaḥ, sthūlaśarīraṁ vyāvṛttam.*

92 Cf. US 18. 96, 97.

93 BUBhV (vol.1) 2.1. 170, p.595.

94 NS 3. 54 (samb.).

95 Cf. NS 2. 78 (with samb.). 3. 14. BUBhV 1.4. 305, p.329. 2.1. 235, p.602; and verse 296, p.608. 2.4. 266, p.698. (vol.2.) 4.3. 193, p.930; also verse 198, p.931; and verse 221, p.934. Also, cf. Halbfass, *Tradition and Reflection,* op.cit., p.173ff.

96 NS 2.11.

97 NS 2.12 (with samb.).

98 NS 2.15 (with samb.).

99 NS 2.19.

100 Cf. Chapter five, (2) Jīva. Sureśvara refers to seventeen factors in BUBhV1.3. 258.

101 NS 2.22.

102 NS 2. 25.

103 NS 2. 32.

104 NS 2. 37 (half verse).

105 NS 2. 39.

106 NS 2. 78 (samb.); 59 (samb. and verse).

107 NS 2. 81. Also, cf. 2. 70, 87.

108 NS 2. 69. Also, cf. 2.82.

109 NS 2. 83.

110 NS 2. 76.

111 NS 2. 77 (samb. and verse). This verse also occurs in BUBhV 4.3.396. Cf. also NS 2. 108, 109, 110.

112 NS 3. 6 (samb.)

---

113 NS 3. 6.

114 BUBh.1086, p.194. Mahadevan, op.cit., 1087b, p.581.

115 US 18. 109.

116 US 18. 110.

117 US 18. 29.

118 US 18. 50.

119 US 18. 195.

120 US 18. 196.

121 In Kaiyyaṭa's commentary upon the *Mahābhāṣya (Pāṇini-Sūtra* 1.2.42) *sāmānādhikaraṇya* is defined in this way: *"bhinnapravṛttinimittaprayuktasya anekasya śabdasya ekasmin arthe vṛttiḥ sāmānādhikaraṇyam ucyate."*

122 I have simplified Śaṅkara's account here, for he says *tattvamasi* as like the sentence: "the horse is black". But this sentence does not create the unintelligibility that is necessary in order to resort to *lakṣaṇā*. The commentators Ānandagiri and Rāmatīrtha both point out that the purport of this illustration is only to show the co-referentiality *(sāmānādhikaraṇya)* of the two words in referring to a single entity [i.e. it does not go to the next step of showing the unintelligibility of the primary meaning of the terms that are co-referential]. Cf. also G. Cardona, "On reasoning from Anvaya and Vyatireka in Early Advaita", in D. Malvania and N.J. Shah (ed), *Studies in Indian Philosophy.* A Memorial Volume in Honour of Pandit Suklaji Sanghvi. Ahmedabad: L.D. Institute of

Indology, 1981, p.88. Also cf. Michael Comans, "Śaṅkara and the Prasaṅkhyānavāda", *Journal of Indian Philosophy,* vol.24, 1996, pp.49-71.

123 US 18. 181, 182 , 183 (first *pāda).*

124 US 18. 171.

125 US 18. 197.

126 US 18. 104.

127 US 18. 101.

128 NS 3. 3. This verse is also found in BUBhV 3.5.185.

129 NS 3. 23.

130 NS 3. 24.

131 NS 3. 25.

132 NS 3. 27.

133 NS 3. 27.

134 NS 3. 28.

135 NS 3. 78 (samb) "The non-duality, that was previously unknown in respect of the inner-Self signified by the word *tvam,* is revealed by the meaning of the word *tat.*"

136 NS 4. 21.

---

137 For example, NS 3. 102; 4. 25 (samb.), 4. 39. Sureśvara says in NS 2. 56, that the inner-Self can also be directly revealed by words. However this is more of a "bold assertion" *(prauḍvāda)* on his part and it does not form a part of the main teaching.

138 NS 3. 27. His examples in 3.97 seem to suggest *jahallakṣaṇā.*

139 NS 1. 93; 2. 55; 3. 43, 97, 100, 102. Also 4.39.

140 NS 3. 102.

141 NS 3. 11.

142 With regard to the *Vivekacūḍāmaṇi,* see the discussion in note 52 of chapter six. Regarding the *Pañcadaśī* cf. 7.74, 75.

143 Sureśvara has also referred to the use of *lakṣaṇā* in his other works, for example, TUBhV 2. 95, 97, 98. BUBhV (Sambandha V.) 704; Mahadevan, op.cit., 705. BUBhV 2.3 215, 229 and verses 253, 254. In those four verses from BUBhV 2.3, he says that *"neti neti"* also functions by way of *lakṣanā.* In BUBhV 2.3.215 he says:

> The negation [in *neti neti]* does not have its purpose in what is to be negated, for its sole purpose is to indicate *(lakṣaṇā)* [the Self]. Since Brahman is not established by other means of knowledge, the only result would be a void [if there was no resort to *lakṣaṇā].*

Śaṅkara too suggests the use of *lakṣaṇā* with regard to understanding *neti neti,* in US 18. 198.

144 In NS 4. 33-35, Sureśvara cites US 18.192, 174 and 175 which refer to the famous "tenth man" story. Sureśvara also refers to the

"tenth man" story in BUBhV 1.4. 600-603. The story of the tenth man is used as an example to show that knowledge can immediately arise from words. For the story, cf. chapter six, note 40.

145 H. Nakamura mentions in his *A History of Early Vedānta Philosophy*, op.cit., p.68, note 1, that Paul Hacker proposed the date of Vācaspati as c. 970.

146 Śaṅkara refutes this doctrine in the eighteenth chapter of his *Upadeśasāhasrī*. He presents the *prasaṅkhyānavāda* as a *pūrvapakṣa* in US 18. 9-18 and his response, with some digressions, forms the content of the rest of the chapter. Cf. Michael Comans, "Śaṅkara and the Prasaṅkhyānavāda", *Journal of Indian Philosophy*, 24., 1996, pp.49-71.

147 *Brahmasiddhi*, op.cit., p.35, line 1ff.

148 *Brahmasiddhi*, ibid, p. 134, line 3ff.

149 Ibid., p. 33, line 15ff. The view expressed here, while not Maṇḍana's acknowledged *siddhānta*, is in accord with his position.

150 NS 3. 90 (samb.), 124 (samb.). BUBhV (Sambandha V) 803, 818.

151 NS 1. 38 (samb.).

152 NS 1. 67 (samb.).

153 The *prasaṅkhyāna pūrvapakṣa* in the BUBhV (Sambandha V.) 761-789, can be reduced to the ideas presented in these passages. As can the *pūrvapakṣa* in the TUBhV 2. 639-647.

154 NS 1 38. Two learned translators of the NS, Professor S.S. Raghavachar (1965) and Professor R. Balasubramanian (1988) respectively translate *tadvāsanā* in the third *pāda* as: "The impressions left by enlightenment" and "The impressions left over by knowledge". I feel it is better to interpret the pronoun *tad* in the compound as referring to ignorance, i.e., "the impressions left over by ignorance". The commentator Jñānottama provides this as an alternative explanation. It also fits in with what Śaṅkara has said in the BUBh 1.4.10, p.678, line 2ff., (tr) p.116. Cf. Chapter six, towards the end of section (3) Liberation, *Jīvanmukti* and *Prārabdhakarma*.

155 NS 4. 62-69.

156 NS 1. 67.

157 BUBhV (Sambandha V) 792. Mahadevan, op.cit, 793, p.422.

158 NS 3 90. Also BUBhV (Sambandha V) 857.

159 BUBhV (Sambandha V) 844. Mahadevan, op.cit., 845, p.451. Also, BUBhV (Sambandha V) 809, 841.

160 NS 3. 125.

CHAPTER EIGHT

Padmapāda

In this chapter we will see, in some detail, the issues Padmapāda raises in his commentary upon Śaṅkara's important introduction to the *Brahmasūtra*, the *Adhyāsabhāṣya*. Towards the end of the chapter we will also discuss Padmapāda's understanding of *śruti* and its role in liberation.

(1) Why talk of superimposition *(adhyāsa)?*

Śaṅkara introduces his commentary upon the *Brahmasūtra* with an important essay, generally referred to as the *Adhyāsabhāṣya* (the "treatise concerning superimposition"). In this essay Śaṅkara presents the important concept of superimposition *(adhyāsa)* between the Self and the "not-Self". He begins by saying that such a type of superimposition does indeed exist, even though it may seem at the outset to be unfeasible, in so far as the mutual superimposition of subject (Self) and object ("not-Self") is a logical impossibility since they are so fundamentally distinct. He goes on to define superimposition, and argues in favour of its actual occurrence, before proceeding to show its ramifications in everyday life. He concludes by saying that the study of the Upaniṣads is undertaken to gain the knowledge of the oneness of the Self, so as to put an end to this superimposition. By his placing such an arresting and important essay at the beginning of his major work, the commentary upon the *Brahmasūtra*, it is evident that Śaṅkara considers the mutual superimposition of Self and "not-Self" to lie at the core of human bondage. For Śaṅkara, it is the "fundamental problem" to which the sorrows of life can ultimately be traced.

Śaṅkara commences his treatise on superimposition with this statement:

> Once it has been established that it is logically impossible to mutually identify the object and the subject - the respective spheres of the concept of "you" [i.e. "this"] and "I" - as they have opposing natures like light and darkness, it is all the more impossible that their attributes should be identified. For this reason it should be impossible for there to be the superimposition of the object, namely what falls within the sphere of the concept of "you" [i.e. "this"], and the superimposition of the attributes of the object, onto the subject, who is within the sphere of the concept of "I" and is of the nature of pure Awareness; and the converse of that, namely the superimposition of the subject and its attributes onto the object. Nonetheless, because of not discriminating between these two which are entirely distinct in both nature and attributes, people do superimpose the nature and the attributes of the one onto the other, and as a result of thus coupling together the real and the unreal, there occurs the natural, everyday expression such as "I am this" and "this is mine". Such expression has erroneous knowledge as its basis.[1]

And he concludes by saying:

> The study of the Upaniṣads is commenced to attain the knowledge of the oneness of the Self, so as to remove this superimposition, the cause of all misfortune.[2]

Padmapāda begins his lengthy exposition upon the *Adhyāsabhāṣya* with an objection about the necessity of even raising the topic of superimposition. The objector says that it is the customary practice for an author to first specify the subject matter *(viṣaya)* and to point out the benefit *(prayojana)* that will result from studying the work. The objector says that Śaṅkara has pointed out both at the conclusion of his essay: the subject matter is shown in the statement "to attain the knowledge of the oneness of the Self", and the benefit is also shown when he says "so as to remove this superimposition, the cause of all misfortune". The objector argues that as the above sentence gives both the subject matter and the benefit, this sentence would form a sufficient introduction, and therefore there is no need for the entire essay on superimposition.[3] Padmapāda replies that the discussion of superimposition is necessary. He says that the first *sūtra* in the *Brahmasūtra* ("Then, therefore, the desire to know Brahman") speaks of knowledge, so it is the *knowledge* of Brahman which gives the benefit of removing what is undesirable. Padmapāda says that what is undesirable is the very ego itself, with its sense of doership and enjoyership. If doership and enjoyership are real, they could not be removed by knowledge, because knowledge can only remove ignorance. If, however, they are themselves a product of ignorance, then it is logically correct to say that knowledge removes them. So when the author of the *Brahmasūtra* speaks of the *knowledge* of Brahman, we must draw the necessary implication that the misfortunes centred on the ego-notion are due to ignorance, and that is what Śaṅkara makes explicit in his discussion of superimposition.[4]

Padmapāda further argues that it has to be accepted, as a necessary implication, that the above mentioned undesirable things are due to ignorance. He says:

> The purport of this treatise [the *Brahmasūtra]* is that the Vedānta [the Upaniṣads] culminates in showing that the ultimate nature of the Self - who is under the apprehension of being a suffering, mortal, entity - is solely and simply immutable Awareness, which is complete happiness, and is identical to Being. That purport is contradicted by the appearance, which is accepted as perceptual and seems to be without negation, namely that "I am a doer", "I am happy", "I am unhappy". So, *[the Brahmasūtra]* would be meaningless, just like the statement about the "old bull" etc.,[5] as long as this contradiction is not removed by demonstrating that the idea that the Self is opposite in nature to Brahman is a creation of ignorance. Therefore, to remove that contradiction, it has to be shown that the idea that the Self is other than Brahman is a play of ignorance.[6]

The Vedānta teaching and our experience seem to contradict each other. This contradiction can be removed if it is shown that our idea of being other than Brahman is due to ignorance. Padmapāda does not say that there is a contradiction between two means of knowledge, the Upaniṣads and perception. When he says that the experiences "I am happy", "I am unhappy" etc. are "accepted as perceptual" and "seem to be without negation", he does not grant these ideas the status of valid perceptual knowledge. They are a perceptual appearance, but they are not valid perceptual knowledge, and so there is no contradiction between two means of knowledge.[7]

(2) Though superimposition is not logically possible, it nonetheless occurs

Padmapāda soon commences his discussion of the text of the *Adhyāsabhāṣya*. He refers to part of the first sentence, "Once it has been established that it is logically impossible to mutually identify the object and the subject as they have opposing natures like light and darkness", and asks what is meant by having "opposing natures" whereby one cannot become the other.[8] He says that the opposition in this context means "the absence of mutual identification" *(parasparānātmatālakṣaṇa)*. The illustration of light and darkness is just intended to point out the fundamental distinction between subject and object. When they stand so diametrically opposed to each other, it follows that there can be no intermingling between them *(itaretarasambheda)*.

Why are subject and object so distinct that there can be no intermingling? Padmapāda says that the subject cannot, of its own accord, become an object, because the subject is solely and simply Awareness by nature, and there is no possibility that Awareness can have any objective properties.[9] Nor can the subject become an object because of some other reason, i.e., under the influence of some object, because Awareness does not undergo transformation and it is by nature unattached. Neither can the object, of its own accord, become the subject, because if it did it would cease to be an object. Nor can the object become the subject due to some other reason, i.e., under the influence of the subject, for he says, referring here to the *Yogasūtra*, that Awareness does not enter into contact with the object.[10] Therefore the subject cannot become an object, nor the reverse.

Padmapāda then comments on the next sentence of the *bhāṣya* ("For this reason it should be impossible for there to be the superimposition of the object, namely what falls within the sphere of the concept of "you" [i.e. "this"], and the superimposition of the attributes of the object, onto the subject, who is within the sphere of the concept of "I" and is of the nature of pure Awareness; and the converse of that, namely the superimposition of the subject and its attributes onto the object."). At this point Padmapāda provides an important clarification of the concept of the ego or "I". In the *Upadeśasāhasrī* Śaṅkara has explained the ego in the same manner as Padmapāda is about to do, and so has Sureśvara in his *Naiṣkarmyasiddhi,* but Padmapāda highlights this particular point; it forms a distinctive feature of his analysis of the Self, and we will see that he often refers to it.[11] What he says is that the "I"-cognition, or "I"-sense, *(asmatpratyaya),* i.e., the ego, consists of two "portions": a "not-this" portion *(anidamaṁśa)* which cannot be objectified, and a "this portion" *(idamaṁśa)* which is objectively experienced. He says:

> In the "I"-cognition there is a non-objectified portion which is simply Awareness. In that Awareness there is, by definition, on account of being revealed by the power of that Awareness, the appearance - like an intermingling - of an objectified aspect, i.e., the identification with being a man etc. That appearance, a seeming intermingling, is what is meant by superimposition.[12]

Padmapāda says "by definition" *(lakṣaṇataḥ),* because the ideas that "I am a man", "I am so and so" etc. do not seem to be objects at all; such self-reflexivity seems to be an intrinsic part of the subject, but they are nonetheless objects "by definition" because they are objectively revealed by the power of Awareness.[13]

Padmapāda then comments upon the expression in the *bhāṣya* that superimposition "should be impossible" *(mithyā-iti bhavituṁ yuktam)* and he explains that the word *"mithyā"* has two distinct meanings. It can mean denial *(apahnava)* and also inexpressibility *(anirvacanīyatā),* and here it is used in the sense of denial.[14] He says that Śaṅkara so far has conveyed that the subject and the object are so diametrically opposed that there can be no connection between them, and therefore their mutual superimposition cannot logically occur.

The term *mithyājñāna*

Although the mutual superimposition of subject and object is a logical impossibility Śaṅkara says that our experience demonstrates that such superimposition does in fact happen ("Nonetheless...there occurs the natural, everyday expression such as "I am this" and "this is mine". Such expression has erroneous knowledge as its basis *(mithyājñānanimitta)").* Padmapāda's explanation of this compound, *mithyājñānanimitta,* is of considerable interest for it has proved to be highly influential in later Advaita. The term *mithyājñāna* occurs frequently in Śaṅkara's commentary on the *Brahmasūtra;*[15] and judging from these usages of the term, Padmapāda might justifiably be accused of engaging in some highly creative commentating in his interpretation of the term in the present context. Whereas *"mithyājñāna"* would normally mean "wrong understanding" *(mithyā-jñāna),* or error *(bhrānti),* Padmapāda interprets it as *mithyā-ajñāna.* He says that *mithyā* means inexpressibility *(anirvacanīyatā),* which is the second of the two meanings of the term as mentioned above. The word *"ajñāna"* does not mean simply an absence of knowledge, but he says it refers to "the power of ignorance *(avidyāśakti)* which is insentient by nature *(jaḍātmikā)* and stands opposed to knowledge."[16] This *mithyā-ajñāna* is the *nimitta,* by which Padmapāda means the material cause *(upādāna),* of the everyday expressions involving "I" and "mine" *(lokavyavahāra).* What Padmapāda says here is that the term *mithyājñāna,* at least in its present context, is not an epistemological term meaning erroneous understanding, but it is an ontological term. The expression means that ordinary dealings *(vyavahāra)* have some sort of "power" as their material cause, and this power, the *avidyāśakti,* is inexpressible: it is *mithyā,* because it cannot be stated as indubitably real *(sat),* nor is it entirely unreal, i.e, fictitious *(asat),* not can it be both simultaneously real and unreal *(sadasat).*

Though Padmapāda's explanation of the compound *mithyājñānanimitta* does seem in the present context to be an unwarranted metaphysical interpretation of what is actually a straightforward expression, his overall understanding is nonetheless in accord with the tenor of Śaṅkara's teaching as we have discussed it under the topic of *avidyā* in chapter five. Therefore when Padmapāda refers to *mithyā-ajñāna* as the material cause of the world I do not feel that he is introducing a foreign concept into Śaṅkara's teaching. We may note, however, that he has explicitly defined *ajñāna* as "insentient" *(jaḍa)*, and though this idea may well be implicit in Śaṅkara's understanding of the nature of unmanifest name-and-form, Śaṅkara has not used this term. Padmapāda's introduction of the term *jaḍa*, which will hereafter be regularly included in the definition of *avidyā* by later Advaitins, serves to radically demarcate *ajñāna* (or *avidyā)* from Brahman, though in so doing it also contributes to the concept of *avidyā* as some sort of quasi-entity in its own right, as almost a second thing to Brahman.

Since Padmapāda has understood *mithyājñānanimitta* to mean that all worldly dealings have an inexpressible power called *avidyā* as their material cause, he has to reconcile this with the statement in the *bhāṣya* that superimposition is something beginningless *(naisargika)*.[17] How can superimposition be beginningless and yet have *avidyā* as its material cause? In discussing this, Padmapāda further elaborates upon the nature of the *avidyāśakti*. He says: "we have to accept that this *avidyāśakti* in things external and internal [i.e. external as well as mental] accompanies the very nature of the Self.[18] Otherwise there is no logical possibility for the appearance of unreal *(mithyā)* things."[19] What he says is that we have to accept that this *avidyāśakti* exists in order to account for the fact that unreal things appear. Padmapāda is here arguing by postulation *(arthāpatti)* from the effect to the cause. The power called *avidyā* must somehow exist, because we see that unreal things exist - from the ego appearing in Awareness, to silver appearing in a shell - and all these things cannot appear without a cause, so a causal potency, referred to by the term *avidyā*, has to be admitted.[20] From the statement that *avidyā* "accompanies the very nature of the Self" the Vivaraṇa tradition understands that the Ātman is the locus *(āśraya)* of *avidyā*.[21]

Padmapāda continues to discuss the *avidyāśakti* and he says:

> The *avidyā* present in inert objects does not obstruct the objects from appearing as they really are, because the non-apprehension of inert objects is just due to a deficiency in a means of knowledge. For we see the true nature [of the shell] both before and after the appearance of silver, even

> though *avidyā* is all the while present [in the shell]. So in the case of inert objects *avidyā* is solely the cause for them to appear as something else.[22]

What he says here is that the *avidyāśakti*, which is present in all matter, does not obstruct material things from appearing, what it does is cause things to appear as other than what they are. The *Vivaraṇa* interprets this passage to mean that the inert things *(anātman)* are not the object *(viṣaya)* of *avidyā*. *Avidyā* does not obstruct things from appearing, because things are inert, and there is no point in concealing things that are themselves inert by nature.[23] Therefore the Ātman must be the object of *avidyā*. Padmapāda himself says this in the next sentence:

> However as the inner-Self is self-revealing, since it is of the very nature of Awareness, there can be no other reason [apart from *avidyā*] for the Brahman-nature of the Self not to appear. So the non-appearance of that Brahman-nature is solely due to the obstruction brought about by the power of *avidyā* which is associated in a beginningless way with the inner-Self. Therefore the power of *avidyā* obstructs the inner-Awareness from appearing as Brahman, and it becomes the cause for the manifestation of what is other than Brahman, namely the "I" [ego] etc.[24]

Here Padmapāda explicitly says that the Ātman is the object of the *avidyāśakti*. The Self is self-revealing, so its nature as Brahman should be plainly evident. But if that is not the case, then there must be some factor to account for the obstruction of that Brahman-nature, and so we must postulate that the Brahman-nature of Awareness is concealed by the *avidyāśakti*. Thus Brahman-Ātman is both the locus of *avidyā* and the object of *avidyā*. This is also the view of Sureśvara, and it would seem to be the position of Śaṅkara as well.[25]

Padmapāda concludes this discussion by saying:

> And in deep sleep etc. the power of *avidyā* remains as a mere impression *(saṁskāra)* of the projection *(vikṣepa)* consisting of the "I" etc., and [at the time of waking] the

> power of *avidyā* again arises. So even though the everyday expression involving "I" and "mine", i.e., the identification with being a man and so forth, is without beginning, it is said to have inexpressible ignorance as its material cause, it is not adventitious. Therefore the beginninglessness [of the superimposition] does not contradict it having a cause.[26]

Padmapāda says that the *avidyāśakti* both conceals the real nature of the Self and projects the "non-Self", i.e., the ego etc. He explicitly mentioned that *avidyā* is the cause of the manifestation of the ego etc. when he said, in the quotation preceding the one above: "the power of *avidyā*...becomes the cause for the manifestation of what is other than Brahman, namely the "I" [ego] etc." In summary, these passages make the following points: (a) we have to postulate the presence of an *avidyāśakti,* for otherwise we cannot account for the appearance of the *mithyā* world; (b) the *avidyāśakti* has the Self as its locus, and it also conceals the real nature of the Self (i.e. it has the Self as its object), for otherwise the Brahman-nature of Awareness would be self-evident[27]; (c) the *avidyāśakti* projects the "non-Self" beginning with the ego; and (d) the *avidyāśakti* remains in deep sleep in the form of an impression *(saṁskāra)* of the ego which is again projected in the waking state.

How does this statement about *avidyā* answer the question that he himself had posed earlier: how can superimposition, which is experienced in such expressions as "I am this" and "this is mine", be understood as beginningless when it has *avidyā* as its material cause? It has to be said that Padmapāda's style is sometimes lacking in perspicuity. While the style is fluent, there are notable occasions when he gives the impression that he has deliberately restrained himself from saying anything further, even though he has more to say. He presumably thinks himself sufficiently understood by his informed audience, so he does not elaborate the point, though various topics could well do with greater explanation. His answer, as far as we can gather, is that superimposition can be said to be beginningless in so far as its material cause, the *avidyāśakti,* is beginningless. But superimposition can be said to have a beginning when it is seen as a specific effect of the *avidyāśakti.*[28]

(3) The definition of superimposition *(adhyāsa)*.

Superimposition means that something [A] appears in something else [B] though the former does not actually exist in the latter *(atadrūpe tadrūpāvabhāsa)*.[29] Padmapāda specifies that the "I", or ego, is the first superimposition[30] and he says:

> When the "I" [ego] is a superimposition, everything that goes along with it would also be a superimposition. When someone in a dream is anointed as a king, or when a king is conjured up out of a great magic, all the paraphernalia of royalty do not thereby become real. In the same way, the everyday dealings, beginning the ego, and consisting of actions, their instruments and their results, are superimposed on the Self whose nature is ever pure, ever aware and ever free.[31]

Padmapāda then goes on to say that the remaining portion of the *Adhyāsabhāṣya* is intended to prove superimposition. He subdivides the remaining portion into three topics. He says that Śaṅkara firstly defines superimposition, he then shows that superimposition is possible, and lastly demonstrates the way in which superimposition actually exists.[32]

Before presenting the definition, Padmapāda answers a few preliminary objections. An objector says that if it can be demonstrated that superimposition actually exists, what is the need of the definition and the attempt to show that its occurrence is possible? Padmapāda replies that when a person has the erroneous identification of "I" and "mine" in the physical body and the senses etc., merely to tell him that the fact of being a cogniser involves superimposition is not sufficient to prove to such a person that cognisership is an actual instance of superimposition. Why would it be insufficient? Padmapāda says a person does not experience cognisership as actually involving superimposition in the way the person can experience silver appearing on a shell as a case of superimposition. When something is sublated, like the appearance of silver on the shell, it can then be easily known to be a superimposition, but cognisership is not found to be sublated. Therefore superimposition has firstly to be defined, and then it can be said that whatever is applicable to the definition constitutes superimposition.[33]

Well, the objector says, it should be sufficient to define superimposition and demonstrate that it actually exists. What is the need of showing its possibility? The objector further explains that if a thing is not found to exist though the application of a means of knowledge like perception and inference etc., then we can legitimately doubt whether it does in fact exist or not, and in such a case it is relevant to demonstrate the possibility of its existence. Padmapāda replies that is true, but the situation here is different. For there can also be the case where an object is actually seen, and no defect is discovered in the means of knowledge that reveals it, nonetheless the existence of the object is considered an impossibility because its existence contradicts the evidence of "common sense." In such a situation, we have to show that what is seen is also possible. The existence of superimposition can be doubted, even though it is seen in experience, and so the possibility of its occurrence has also to be shown.[34]

Taking up the matter of the formal definition of superimposition, Śaṅkara says that superimposition is: "the appearance [of something] previously seen [which is now being seen] somewhere else, and this appearance is similar to memory" *(smṛtirūpaḥ paratra pūrvadṛṣṭāvabhāsaḥ).*[35] Padmapāda says that the expression "similar to memory" means that the appearance only resembles memory, but it is not the same as memory, because memory is always about something not present, whereas in the case of superimposition the thing superimposed is immediately evident, like the silver that is seen appearing on the shell. Its similarity to memory is because the appearance is of something which had been seen before, because the superimposition of silver on the shell could not happen if a person had never previously experienced silver.[36]

Following this,[37] Padmapāda enters into a debate about superimposition, mostly with the Prābhākara school of Mīmāṁsā.[38] He then returns to the discussion of the definition of superimposition. A definition should indicate the essential characteristic of the thing in question so as to distinguish that thing from everything else.[39] A definition should not suffer from the fault of under applicability *(avyāpti),* where the definition fails to cover all the relevant instances. An objection is raised that the above definition of superimposition suffers from under applicability because it does not extend to such things as dream events and feelings of sorrow, both of which the Advaitin would class as superimposition. In dream and sorrow there is no sense contact with anything. So because in dream there is no sense contact, dream cannot be a case of the appearance of something, somewhere else *(paratra parāvabhāsa).* The objector says that dream is caused solely by the revival of past impressions: it is only a memory.[40]

Padmapāda wishes to show that dream is also a case of superimposition. He replies that dream cannot be classed as memory because the dream object, unlike the remembered object, is immediately evident. Padmapāda then tries to show how dream satisfies the definition of superimposition. He says that a superimposition is always caused by a combination of three factors.[41] These are: (a) a sense organ, (b) some defect in the sense organ which obstructs its normal functioning and helps to revive (c) a particular mental impression. In dream, the mind - which is here accepted as a sense organ - is overcome by the defect of sleep, and with the assistance of a particular mental impression which arose due to some unknown factor, it generates a cognition whose content is unreal *(mithyā,* i.e., inexpressible as *sat* or as *asat).*[42] These three conditions: the sense organ *(indriya),* a defect *(doṣa)* in the sense organ, and the arising of a mental impression *(saṁskāra),* are the cause of dream superimposition as well as of other cases of superimposition such as silver appearing on shell.

Furthermore, the characteristic feature of superimposition is that something appears as something else *(paratra parāvabhāsa)* eg., the shell appears to be silver. Padmapāda says that dream is a superimposition because it too partakes of the characteristic feature of superimposition, i.e., something appears as something else. He says that in dream, when the mind produces the cognition which has an unreal content, what happens is that: "the power of *avidyā (avidyāśakti)* - that is located in the immediately evident Awareness *(aparokṣacaitanya)* which is conditioned by the mind - appears to transform *(vivartate)* into the content of the cognition."[43] Therefore in dream the power of *avidyā* appears to transform into the dream object. This satisfies the defining feature of superimposition because something, the *avidyāśakti,* is appearing as something else, the dream object. This is the first occasion where Padmapāda has used the term "appears to transform" *(vivartate/ vivarta);* a term that became, in later Advaita, the standard technical expression to denote illusory transformation.[44]

At this point an interesting objection is raised which allows Padmapāda to say something further about the nature of Awareness. The objector asks how dream objects can be within Awareness when they are experienced during dream as external to Awareness, similar to how waking objects are experienced in the waking state. Padmapāda gives the following answer. He says that waking is similar to dream in so far as even in the waking state the immediacy *(aparokṣatā)* pertaining to the experienced sense object cannot be separated from the immediacy of the inner-Awareness that reveals the sense object, because the immediacy is identical.[45] So we have to accept, Padmapāda says, that like in dream, even in the waking state a sense object is enveloped by the immediately evident inner-Awareness, for otherwise there is no logical possibility that an inert object could be revealed. Therefore, in both dream and waking, the object is not outside of Awareness, though in both cases the object appears to be outside Awareness. When we awaken from dream we know that the object was not outside Awareness. Padmapāda says that just as in dream:

> even in waking, [the appearance of the object as separate from Awareness] is a display of *māyā*, because the whole world has Awareness as its sole substratum. And since Awareness is without parts, there is no difference of place [as inside and outside]. Awareness *(tat)* has distinctions imposed upon it just due to the diversity of the world, and Awareness thereby appears as if it is divided, as though there is an outside and an inside.[46]

In this discussion Padmapāda is not trying to equate the waking and dream states; he is attempting to show that objects are not outside of Awareness. He argues that the objects in the waking state are in Awareness, because in the perception of a sense object the immediacy of the object cannot be distinguished from the immediacy of the Awareness revealing the object, for there is a single continuum of immediacy. If it were not so, there is no way an inert sense object could become manifest. So in waking, as in dream, the object is not separate from Awareness. The supposition that objects are outside Awareness is a "display of *māyā*". Whereas in fact, from the standpoint of Awareness itself, there is neither inside nor outside, such divisions are superimposed by the objects, the names-and-forms, in Awareness that is a single, uniform, Experience.

Following this discussion, which began with the objection that dream does not fit the definition of superimposition, Padmapāda again returns to the discussion of the definition. In the course of further comment he says that if the definition was just presented as: "the appearance, similar to memory, [of something] previously seen *(smṛtirūpaḥ pūrvadṛṣṭāvabhāsa)"*, but the definition did not include the phrase: "[which is now being seen] somewhere else *(paratra)"*, then the definition would extend to the illogical teaching of the Mādhyamika who accept that superimposition can occur without a substratum.[47] This remark initiates some discussion with regard to Buddhism. The Buddhist wishes to know why it is untenable to accept superimposition without a substratum, and he asks about such occurrences as *keśoṇḍraka*, the appearance of a dark mass that is seen when one shuts one's eyes. Such things as these are appearances without a substratum. Padmapāda replies that even the *keśoṇḍraka* has a substratum, namely particles of light. For without light nothing would be seen at all. The objector next says that superimposition and its substratum could have a relation of mutual dependence. For example, in the case of the unreal appearance of silver on a shell, the cognition could have the silver as its substratum while the silver could have the cognition as its substratum, just as the seed and the sprout are dependent upon each other. Padmapāda replies that the example is inappropriate, because the sprout arises from a seed but the seed did not arise from that very same sprout but from some other sprout. So the example of seed and sprout is not an example of mutual dependence and it just leads to an infinite regress.[48]

Furthermore, negation always has a positive limit. Even when we know that the thing appearing as a snake is not a snake, we do not rest content with this negative knowledge, but we seek to discover what the thing actually is, and we are only content when we come to know that it is a stick or the like. Thus a negation has to end in a positive substratum.[49] Padmapāda then speaks of the unnegated substratum. He says that when the *keśoṇḍraka* etc. are negated, only the association that the *keśoṇḍraka* etc. have with Awareness is negated, but the Awareness of the *keśoṇḍraka* etc. is not negated. Thus negation has Awareness as its ultimate limit. He says: "because mere Awareness is not negated, and because it is not seen to have any intrinsic distinguishing characteristics, the negation of everything has the immutable, immediately evident and uniform Awareness as its limit."[50]

Another objector now comes forward. He says that an expression such as "I am a man" etc. is just a metaphorical usage, it is not an instance of superimposition. The objector argues that if the Self is not inherently separate from the body there is no way that we can prove the Self to be separate. The Self is either shown to be separate by perception or it cannot be proved to be separate. So those who accept a Self distinct from the body must admit that this distinction is perceptual. When we identify the Self with the body it is only a metaphorical identification, because we already know by perception that they are not identical.[51] In reply, Padmapāda says it is true that the "I" refers to an experiencer distinct from the body, but because this is not clearly understood, we do superimpose the attributes of the body onto the Self. Conversely if the "I" should manifest itself as entirely distinct from the body there would be no controversy about this point and the wish to inquire into the matter would not even arise. Since there is the need to investigate the matter, the Self is not perceptually distinct from the body.

The objector then says that even though the "I" is perceptually distinct from the body, we only come to know this after investigating the matter with the help of reason. Padmapāda replies that it is not the case that the "I" is perceptually distinct prior to reasoning. Just because the expression "I am a man" may be found to be figurative after reasoning, it does not mean that it is figurative *before* the investigation through reason. So before the reasoning takes place statements such as "I am a man" etc. are certainly just a case of superimposition.[52] Padmapāda says that the application of reason, such as distinguishing between subject and object, is not sufficient to ensure that subsequent statements of "I am a man" etc. will always remain metaphorical. He explains that even though the "I" inherently refers to the Self, the "I" also refers to the body etc. on account of the beginningless ignorance which obstructs the "I" from referring solely to the Self.[53] So the fact that the "I" refers to the Self does not preclude the fact that the "I" also seems to refer to the body. Even after we clarify through reasoning what the "I" actually refers to, it is still not sufficient to impede the "I" from continuing to refer to the body etc. Thus while reasoning shows that the "I" refers solely to the subject, our long established behaviour overwhelms this reasoning and our expressions such as "I am a man" etc. are not metaphors, even after the investigation by reasoning.[54]

(4) The possibility of superimposition

Śaṅkara now undertakes to show that superimposition is feasible by introducing the following discussion:

> [objection]: How can the superimposition of the object and its properties occur on the inner Self who is not an object? For everyone superimposes one object onto another object that is perceptually evident. But you say that the inner Self, being outside the scope of the concept of "this", is not an object!
> [reply]: We do not say that the Self is entirely a non-object, because it is the object of the "I"-cognition.[55]

This portion of Śaṅkara's commentary presents a difficulty, for what does Śaṅkara mean when he writes that the Self is the "object of the "I"-cognition *(asmatpratyaya)"?* Padmapāda says that the "I"-cognition means the ego, the "I" *(ahaṅkāra).*[56] He again makes the point that the "I" consists of two aspects: a "this" portion and a "not-this" portion, and he says that such a truth is a matter for verification by one's own introspection:

> Let the learned critics look closely at the "I" with great care and attention, like an examiner of coins, without concealing their own experience; and let them say whether the "I" has the above mentioned characteristics or not.[57]

How does this statement about the nature of the ego answer the objection that the locus of superimposition must be an object, and since the Self is not an object, there is no possibility that the Self can be the locus of superimposition? Most people believe that the "I" is the actual Self. The followers of Advaita, however, say that the nature of the "I" requires to be further investigated. Padmapāda says here that the "I", or ego *(ahaṅkāra),* is a combination of two factors: the Self, or pure Awareness, and the mind. Pure Awareness and mind blend to form the thought or the expression of "I". In the "I"-sense, the "not-this" aspect is the pure Awareness, the absolute Self, the core I. The "this" aspect is the mind. Both these, Awareness and mind - the "not-this" and the "this" - combine in the sense of "I".

The ego is thus a combination of pure Awareness and mind. Padmapāda says that because pure Awareness and mind are mingled together, the mind is thereby able to manifest the "not-this" pure Awareness, like a mirror is able to manifest a reflection. In so far as the mind manifests the "not-this" pure Awareness, the pure Awareness is *figuratively* said to be an object.[58] Padmapāda says:

> Though [the Self] is uniform Awareness and is not an object since it is of the nature of "not-this", still, in the "I" the Self becomes available for everyday dealings and so it is figuratively spoken of as an object of the "I"-cognition.[59]

The commentators also give the analogy of a mirror.[60] Though sunlight is present everywhere in the sky, a mirror - while itself is revealed by the sunlight - is able to manifest that light in a special way, whereas an opaque object like the earth cannot manifest the light. The Awareness-Self is compared to the sunlight and the mind is analogous to the mirror: the Awareness reveals the mind and the latter is also able to manifest the Awareness. The example of the mirror and the reflection is just to assist the understanding that something (A) that is revealed by something (B) can also function to reveal that thing (B). Padmapāda will return to this topic later; meanwhile a number of other matters intervene.

Awareness and Experience

After Padmapāda's examination of the nature of the ego, a discussion takes place with the Mīmāṁsakas, principally the followers of Prabhākara, concerning the relation of the Self to Awareness. Prabhākara's view can be briefly stated as follows. In any knowledge such as "I know this pot" there are always three components. There is the knowing subject, the "I" *(pramātā);* the object of knowledge, the "pot" *(prameya);* and the experience of "knowing" *(pramiti).* The experience of knowing arises out of the operation of an appropriate means of knowledge, and once the experience of knowing has arisen, it is self-evident. As the experience of knowing occurs it reveals the sense object and it also simultaneously reveals the knowing subject "I" as the locus of the experience of knowing. This experience of "knowing" is analogous to a light which reveals the object to the non-object Self and in the process reveals the latter also.

Prabhākara's view amounts to saying that the experience of "knowing" is self-revealing Awareness, and the Self is the insentient substratum that becomes revealed in the act of knowing. Padmapāda argues that the above explanation is untenable, for it is not the case that there is an insentient Self who is revealed as the substratum once the self-revealing experience of knowing occurs. Padmapāda says that the Self is none other than self-revealing Awareness, and there is no way to prove that the experience of knowing is something other than the very nature of the Self.[61] Padmapāda argues that if the self-revealing experience of knowing arises from a means of knowledge, as the followers of Prabhākara say, then there should be some distinguishing characteristic in each experience of knowing to separate one experience from another. The experience of knowing yellow should be different from the experience of knowing blue. Padmapāda says that distinctions are the properties of the objects, not of the Experience, i.e., the Awareness. Apart from the distinctions caused by the objects, there is no distinction in the experience of knowing.[62]

But suppose, as the Buddhists say, that Awareness does have distinctions due to the fact that Awareness arises and perishes. Previously we had the experience of something yellow, now there is the experience of something blue. The fact that we are now aware of something blue and no longer aware of something yellow leads to the supposition that the Awareness of yellow has perished while an Awareness of blue has arisen.[63] Padmapāda says in response to this objection that it cannot be proved that Awareness *intrinsically* alters, that it arises and perishes. He says it can be proved that the preceding Awareness [A] has perished once it can be shown that a succeeding Awareness [B] arises, but in order to show that the succeeding Awareness arises it must first be shown that the preceding Awareness [A] has perished. So because the proof of destruction depends upon arising, and the proof of arising depends upon destruction, neither the destruction nor the arising of Awareness can be proved.[64]

Nor is it reasonable to say that Awareness does have innate distinctions, but these distinctions are not evident because of the great similarity between each discrete Awareness. Padmapāda repeats his assertion that it cannot be proved that Awareness contains innate distinctions. Nor is it correct, he says, to infer that Awareness has innate distinctions on the analogy of how a lamp flame produces the semblance of being a single flame when it is actually composed of many similar flames that continually flicker. Padmapāda briefly dismisses such a view with the remark that one's own experience and also reason contradict it.[65] The commentators explain the point by saying that our experience is that Awareness is identical to itself through different periods of time. They explain that the opponents view contradicts reason, because if difference is innate to Awareness, then when Awareness manifests itself it should also make its innate difference manifest.[66] Padmapāda concludes the discussion, saying:

> Therefore, the Self has Awareness as its very nature, and when the Self is "limited" by the various objects of knowledge, the Self is called "experience" *(anubhava).* Words such as "Self" *(ātman)* etc. are used when the Self is spoken of without reference to limiting adjuncts.[67]

The nature of the ahaṅkāra

The follower of Prabhākara now accepts that the Self is self-revealing Awareness, but he continues to maintain that the Self means the ego, "I" *(ahaṅkāra).* Padmapāda responds by saying that if the "I" is the Self, why is the "I" not present during sleep? The idea is that the Self is invariable, so if the "I" is the Self it should be continuously present. The follower of Prabhākara replies that the "I" is present in sleep as the experiencer, but since there is nothing to experience in sleep it is not clearly evident then as the experiencer. Padmapāda repeats that if the ego "I" is the Self, pure Awareness, then the "I" should always be evident, but that is not so, for upon waking there is no recollection that the "I" was present in sleep.[68]

The opponent says that if it is the case that the "I" is not the essential Self, what is the nature of the "I" and what is its source? Padmapāda says that the teaching of Śaṅkara presents the correct and traditional understanding:

> We should accept the teaching of the revered commentator [Śaṅkara], the very best among those who know Brahman, who assumed a physical body to promote the true knowledge, solely to benefit the world.[69]

With this introduction, Padmapāda proceeds to discuss the origin and the nature of the "I" *(ahaṅkāra)*. He firstly speaks of the material and the efficient cause of the "I". He says:

> Beginningless ignorance *(avidyā)* is referred to in diverse ways in the *śruti*, the *smṛti*, *itihāsa* and the *purāṇas*: as *nāmarūpa*, *avyākṛta*, *avidyā*, *māyā*, *prakṛti*, *agrahaṇa*, *avyakta*, *tamas*, *kāraṇa*, *laya*, *śakti*, *mahāsupti*, *nidrā*, *akṣara* and *ākāśa*. This beginningless ignorance obstructs Awareness from appearing as the nature of Brahman, which is what it really is, and it brings about the individuation of Awareness in so far as it serves as the wall for the painting consisting of the impressions of error, actions and past knowledge. During sleep it conceals the luminosity [of Awareness] and remains in the form of mere impressions *(saṁskāra)* of the projection [of the ego etc.]. The "I" *(ahaṅkāra)* is a particular transformation *(pariṇāmaviśeṣa)* of the beginningless *avidyā*, that transformation taking place under the control of the supreme Lord *(parameśvara)*.[70]

So according to Padmapāda, the material cause of the "I" is *avidyā* while *Īśvara* is the efficient cause. What is the nature of the "I"? He continues:

> The "I" is the location of both the power of thought and the power of activity. It is the sole basis of the sense of doership and enjoyership, it acquires its luminosity through

> its association with the immutable Awareness. It is [thus] self-revealing and immediately evident.[71]

He then points out that due to the mutual superimposition between Awareness and the "I", the former seems to become an enjoyer:

> The essential Self, i.e., the "not-this" portion which is the immutable Awareness, on account of intermingling with the "I", becomes the well-known enjoyer, something entirely *mithyā*.[72]

Why is the "I" not present during sleep? Padmapāda answers: "How can the "I" remain during sleep when *avidyā* is without any of its transformations?" He continues:

> The followers of Vedānta designate the "I" - the particular transformation [of *avidyā]* which they distinguish by discrimination from the "not-this" Awareness-Self - as the "internal-organ" *(antaḥkaraṇa),* the "mind" *(manas),* the "intellect" *(buddhi)* and as the "possessor of the "I"-cognition" *(ahampratyayin).* They call the "I" by these terms with reference to its particular power of thought. They call it as the "life-energy" *(prāṇa)* due to its power of vibration.[73]

The idea is that in the sense of "I" *(ahaṅkāra)* there is a fusion of pure Awareness and mind *(antaḥkaraṇa).* The "not-this" aspect *(anidamaṁśa)* in the "I" is the pure Awareness-Self. The "this", or objective aspect *(idamaṁśa/ yuṣmadartha),* is the mind proper, i.e., the "this" aspect consists of the self-reflexive "I"-thought, as well as the various cognitions that are associated with the "I"-thought.

Padmapāda concludes with the following illustration:

> So, the Self erroneously *(mithyā)* acquires the sense of "I" due to the influence of the internal-organ [mind]. It is analogous to how a pure crystal becomes red on account of a limiting adjunct.[74]

He then further explains the nature of the ego using this analogy of the crystal and the imposition of redness upon it:

> Just as in the crystal there is the influence of the limiting adjunct, so too in the Awareness-Self there is the influence of the "I". Then, because both become intermingled, there is, as it were, a knot, and that is why the "I" *(ahaṅkāra)* is referred to as a knot *(granthi)*.[75]

There is some dissimilarity between the illustration of the crystal and its limiting adjunct, such as a red flower, and the Self and the "I". Since the crystal is inert it does not reveal the redness; it is the exterior light that illumines the crystal that also reveals the red colour. In the case of the Self and the "I", however, the latter is directly revealed by the luminous Self without the intervention of any type of cognitive activity.[76] So the Self reveals the "I" directly, and then it reveals everything else, i.e., mental states and the perception of the world, through the "I".

Padmapāda then says:

> So, [in the "I"] the "this" portion is spoken of by definition, but not according to ordinary dealings *(vyavahārataḥ)*.[77]

There is a "this" portion *(idamaṁśa)* in the "I" by definition, because upon inquiry it is found to be objectively revealed by Awareness. However in everyday dealings, when we normally use the word "I", the distinction that there is a "this" portion in the "I" is not particularly evident. That is why he says that the "this" portion is "by definition, but not according to ordinary dealings." Padmapāda goes on to say that what happens in everyday life is that the "not-this" Awareness-Self has erroneously acquired the "I" because of the influence of the mind. And thus having the "I" as its "self", so to speak, the Self transacts in everyday life through the functioning of the "I". And according to everyday transactions, it is the body, senses and the sense objects that become known as "this".[78] The idea in this cryptic statement is that through the superimposition of the mind, the Self seems to acquire the "I", and the non-object Self thereby becomes the transactional subject

"I", following which the body, the senses and the rest of the world become the transactional objects to that transactional subject.

In response to those who say that there is no object-portion *(idamaṁśa)* in the "I", Padmapāda says that though the "I" does, by definition, have an object-portion, in transactional life this is not so evident. However intelligent people do not think it extraordinary that there is an object-portion in the "I".[79] He concludes by referring to what he had said earlier:

> That is why it was said that those who ascertain what the "I" is by observing it very carefully, like an examiner of coins, find that the "I" is intermingled with the form of "this".[80]

The meaning of the illustrations used in the discussion of superimposition

Padmapāda employs the illustration of the red colour and the crystal to indicate how there can be the superimposition of the ego on the Self. Apart from this example, there are also other illustrations such as the reflection of a face in a mirror, or in clear water. These different illustrations help to highlight particular aspects of the teaching. Padmapāda says that the illustration of the reflection of a face in a mirror is meant to show that the "not-this" aspect of the "I" is not something other than Brahman, but it is Brahman itself, like a reflection is not something other than the original.[81] He says that the reflection of the face is identical to the face, whereas the differences between the face and the reflection, such as the physical separation of the face from the reflected image and the fact that the face and its reflection are opposite to one another, are *mithyā*.[82]

An objector comes forward to dispute the appropriateness of the illustration. He asks: how can you assert that the reflection and the face are identical? For we can see that in the case of silver appearing on a shell, the silver presents itself as identical to real silver even though it is something *mithyā*. Padmapāda says that the two cases are different. The silver is *mithyā* because it is found to be sublated by the knowledge "this is not silver", but the reflection is not sublated, therefore it is not *mithyā*.[83] Once again we can see that Padmapāda considers sublation *(bādhā)* to be the criterion for determining *mithyātva.* Well, says the objector, let us take the sentence "you are That" *(tat tvam asi).* In this sentence there is the sublation of the meaning of the word "you" *(tvam),* because liberation would be impossible if there was no sublation of the *saṁsārin,* the one who is under the spell of transmigratory existence. Padmapāda replies that the sentence *"tat tvam asi"* teaches that the individual soul *(jīva),* who stands in the position of the reflection, is Brahman that stands in the position of the original. If the sentence is intended to sublate the meaning of the word "you", then instead of saying "you are That" it would say "you are not", like when silver is sublated on the shell we say "there is no silver".[84] Padmapāda is saying here that the co-referentiality *(sāmānādhikaraṇya)* of the words *"tat"* and *"tvam"* are meant to reveal identity *(ekatva)* rather than sublation *(apavāda).*[85]

The teaching later known as *"pratibimbavāda"* is presented here in the example of the reflection of a face in a mirror, or of a moon in clear water. Padmapāda says that the entire group of examples is: "intended to remove the idea that what has been established by the *śruti,* by reasoning and by experience, is impossible; and it is meant to be concordant with one's understanding, but it is not meant to directly establish the reality itself [i.e. the nature of Brahman]".[86] In other words, all these illustrations are just means *(upāya/prakriyā)* to assist our understanding; they are not intended to be taken as literal truth and then argued about, as increasingly happened in later Advaita.[87] In fact the so-called "doctrine of reflection" *(pratibimbavāda)* which became associated with the name of Padmapāda needs to be understood more carefully. Padmapāda refers to the *jīva* as a reflection, and he says the sentence *"tat tvam asi"* teaches the identity of the *jīva,* who is in the position of the reflection, with Brahman that is in the position of the original. But Padmapāda also makes it clear what exactly he means by reflection when he says: "the 'not-this' aspect of the 'I' is not something other than Brahman, but it is Brahman itself, like a reflection is not something other than the original."[88] So when he says that the *jīva* is a reflection, and that the reflection is identical with the original, we must bear in mind that he is using the word *jīva* quite loosely, for what he precisely means is that the "not-this" Awareness is identical to the original. Therefore he is not really saying that the *jīva* is identical to the original, which is how he is generally interpreted; what he says is that in the sentence *"tat tvam asi"* there is the identification of the *anidamaṁśa* -the pure Awareness- with Brahman. So when Padmapāda says that the co-referentiality in *"tat tvam asi"* is used in the sense of identity *(ekatva)* and not sublation, he is not in fundamental disagreement with Śaṅkara or Sureśvara, because Padmapāda has already discriminated the "this" portion *(idamaṁśa)* from the *anidamaṁśa*, and once that is done it is only logical that the sentence should reveal the identity of the *anidamaṁśa* with Brahman.

Perception

We have seen that the "I" is a blend of pure Awareness *(anidamaṁśa)* and mind *(idamaṁśa)*. All the everyday dealings of life are possible only subsequent to the superimposition of the mind and the pure Self. Padmapāda now speaks about the process of ordinary perception, subsequent to that superimposition. Padmapāda's account of perception is difficult as it is particularly compressed. We shall explain what he says, as far as possible, and then note a couple of points about what Śaṅkara has said on the matter. In describing the process of perception, Padmapāda begins by saying (1): "the 'this' portion of the 'I', whose nature has been presented [as a blend of *idamaṁśa* and *anidamaṁśa]*, undergoes a particular activity known as a 'cognition'."[89] The "this" portion of the "I" is the internal-organ *(antaḥkaraṇa)*, which for the sake of simplicity we shall refer to as "mind". What he says is that the mind undergoes a particular operation called knowledge or cognition *(jñāna)*. Padmapāda next says: "since cognition is transitive, it is oriented towards an object, and it produces a particular condition in its locus, for an activity causes a change to that in which it inheres." The idea is that cognition is always of something or the other, and when cognition of the object occurs it generates a change in the mind as the latter is the locus of the cognition. The change in the mind that is referred to is the generation of the cognising subject, for the occurrence of the cognition itself generates the mental condition of being the cogniser, and so when the cognition occurs it brings about a change in the mind that results in the establishment of a "relation between the cogniser and the cognised".

(2) Padmapāda then says that once the mind is connected to the object through the cogniser-cognised relation the mind particularises *(avacchedaka)* the pure Awareness. By "particularising Awareness" it would seem that Padmapāda means that Awareness becomes conditioned

by the mind in the form of the cogniser and in the form of the cognition, for the condition of being the cogniser and the activity called cognition are both processes belonging to the mind which is a very subtle form of matter *(nāmarūpa)*. So Awareness becomes conditioned in the form of the cogniser and in the form of the cognition.

(3) Once the cognition takes place, the object is then enveloped by the cognition. Padmapāda says, in a particularly cryptic statement:

> because [the object, eg. pot] is itself an apparent transformation *(vivarta)* of Awareness, the object reveals an immediacy identical to the immediacy particularised by the particular condition of being the cogniser, such a condition being itself the outcome of the cognition.[90]

What Padmapāda is saying is that perception is characterised by its *immediacy*. The fact of immediacy is because neither the cognising subject nor the cognised object are outside Awareness. When the cogniser and the cognised are joined by means of the cognition, the subject and the object are at one in their immediacy, because there is a single Awareness underlying both the epistemological subject and the object. What happens in a perception is that the act of cognition generates a condition in the mind called cognisership, and Awareness becomes particularised by that mental condition and becomes the cogniser. The cognition provides the link between the mind and the object outside the mind. Though the object is external to the mind, nothing is external to Awareness. So once the link between the mind and the object is established, the object stands revealed in an immediacy of Awareness that is identical with the immediacy of Awareness by which the cogniser is revealed. The subject and the object are at one in their immediacy, and it is this sheer immediacy that characterises perception. Even though Awareness is equally present everywhere, all objects are not revealed to the cogniser simultaneously. That is because the cogniser can know an object only when a relation is established between the cogniser and the object by way of a cognition.[91] Thus in all knowledge of the world there is a cogniser, an object external to the cogniser, and their inter-relation through a relevant cognition.

Padmapāda does not specify that the cognition actually "goes out" from the mind, though he does imply this when he says that a cognition, being transitive, is oriented towards its object, and he also says that the object is "enveloped" *(āviṣṭa)* by the cognitive activity. Śaṅkara also does not specifically say that the cognition "goes out", but he does say that the cognition: (a) pervades the sense object, and that (b) the cognition takes on the form of the object.[92] So it would seem that Śaṅkara too indicates that the cognition "goes out" through the senses. It is clear that Śaṅkara and Padmapāda say that perception involves the correspondence between the mind and the sense object, and this correspondence is accomplished because the cognition pervades the object and assumes the form of the object.

Conclusion of the topic dealing with the possibility of superimposition

Padmapāda has ranged over a variety of issues since he commented upon the statement: "We do not say that the Self is entirely a non-object, because it is the object of the I-cognition." After pursuing a lengthy debate with followers of Buddhism, he again returns to this statement in order to conclude his discussion of this portion of the *bhāṣya* dealing with the objection to the possibility of superimposition. Śaṅkara had raised the objection that the superimposition of objects and their attributes on the inner-Self is impossible, because all cases of superimposition involve superimposing one thing onto some other thing that is a perceptible object. If the inner-Self is not an object, how can something be superimposed on it? In reply, Śaṅkara said that the inner-Self is not entirely a non-object, "because it is the object of the 'I'-cognition" *(asmatpratyayaviṣayatvāt).* Padmapāda now says:

> The "knot" that is the "I" *(ahaṅkāra)* is what is referred to by the word "I" *(asmat-śabda),* and that "I" is a cognition *(pratyaya).* It is comparable to a mirror for a reflection. Since [the "I"] is mixed with the "not-this" Awareness, it becomes the cause for the manifestation of the "not-this" Awareness. So [Awareness] becomes, as it were, an object of the "I", and thus the essential "not-this" Awareness-Self

> is metaphorically spoken of as an object of the "I"-cognition.[93]

Just as a mirror is revealed by light and also reveals light, the "I" is revealed by Awareness and also manifests Awareness, so the pure Awareness can be figuratively spoken of as an object of the "I".

Though this discussion has given us a valuable account of the nature of the ego as consisting of the blending of the mind *(idamaṁśa)* and pure Awareness *(anidamaṁśa),* it nonetheless begs the question about the very possibility of the occurrence of superimposition. For this explanation presupposes the superimposition of the mind on the Self, but the question is how can such a superimposition occur? It is only subsequent to the superimposition of the mind on the Self that the Self becomes manifest in the "I"-cognition and thereby further superimposition becomes possible, such as "I am a man", "I am a father", "I am lame" etc. Therefore Śaṅkara's answer: "because the inner-Self is the object of the 'I'-cognition" is only suitable in accounting for superimposition subsequent to the superimposition of the mind and the Self, but it does not account for the superimposition of the mind. However, Śaṅkara puts forward another answer. He says:

> And it is well known that the inner-Self is immediately evident *(aparokṣa).* There is no fixed rule that an object can be superimposed only upon an object that is present to the senses. Boys superimpose a surface as well as impurity etc. on space, even though space is not a sense object. So there is no contradiction concerning the superimposition of the not-Self on the inner-Self.[94]

Śaṅkara says there is no requirement that something has to be a sense object in order for it to be the locus of superimposition. It is sufficient if the locus is immediately evident. The inner-Self is not a sense object, but it is immediately evident, and so it can be the locus of superimposition. Padmapāda says:

> The inner-Self is self-evident, it is the final limit of anyone's rejecting or accepting, it can be neither rejected

> nor accepted [attained], it is able to be [the locus] of superimposition because it is immediately evident just through its inherent greatness.[95]

Śaṅkara's second answer does not presuppose the superimposition that has to be established, and so it should form the principal answer to the question.[96]

In concluding the section on the possibility of superimposition, Padmapāda comments on the following sentence of the *bhāṣya:*

> Learned people consider that the superimposition, so defined, is "ignorance" *(avidyā).* And they call the ascertainment of the real nature of a thing, by the discrimination of what is superimposed, as "knowledge".[97]

Padmapāda raises this objection: if superimposition means "ignorance" *(avidyā),* then would it not have been better if Śaṅkara had used the word *avidyā* throughout his introductory essay? It is surely a more straightforward procedure to consistently use the word *avidyā* rather than to commence with the word *adhyāsa* and then change to using the word *avidyā* halfway through the same piece of writing. Padmapāda replies that the word *avidyā* primarily refers to the concealment of something, and if *avidyā* alone was used then only concealment would be referred to. But not only is there concealment of the real, there is also the presentation of something other that what really is. Śaṅkara refers to this erroneous presentation by the word *adhyāsa.* Then he refers to the erroneous presentation, the *adhyāsa,* as *avidyā,* to show that the *adhyāsa* can be removed just by knowledge, since it is grounded in concealment.[98] Here, Padmapāda again makes the point that *avidyā* both conceals the real and presents something other than what is.

(5) The existence of superimposition

Padmapāda says that in the concluding section of the *Adhyāsabhāṣya* Śaṅkara demonstrates the actual existence of superimposition. Śaṅkara introduces this topic by saying:

> All epistemological activities, whether of a worldly or a Vedic nature, take place presupposing this mutual superimposition of the Self and the not-Self which has been called *avidyā*. And so do all the scriptures, whether they deal with injunctions and prohibitions, or with liberation.[99]

Śaṅkara raises the following question: how can it be said that all the means of valid knowledge *(pramāṇa)*, as well as the contents of all the scriptures, refer to a person who is subject to erroneous superimposition? In reply, Śaṅkara says that epistemological operations cannot occur without a cogniser, and cognisership is not possible without the identification of "I" and "mine" with regard to the body and the senses. Śaṅkara further explains:

> Ordinary dealings such as perception etc. are impossible without using the senses. The senses cannot function without a location [the body]. And no one acts through a body which is without the superimposed sense of Self. And without all of the above, the Self, who by nature is unattached, cannot logically become a cogniser. And [it was said that] epistemological operations do not occur without a cogniser. Therefore, all the means of valid knowledge, as well as the scriptures, only refer to the one who is subject to erroneous superimposition.[100]

Padmapāda does not go into much additional detail here. He says that the Self does not undergo transformation, and so any type of transformation, such as the feeling of desire etc., cannot occur without the "I" which is intermingled with the mind that undergoes transformations. Therefore, he says: "the inherently unattached and unchanging [Self] cannot logically become the cogniser without the erroneous superimposition taking place."[101] He goes on to say that even though all the epistemological operations of the means of knowledge are only subsequent to this superimposition, it does not mean that the operations of the various means of knowledge are thereby invalidated. Superimposition is something common to all the means of knowledge, it affects neither their validity or invalidity. All the means of knowledge are found to be inherently valid because the knowledge they produce is not sublated.[102] Padmapāda says it is a fact that all epistemological activity requires superimposition, and it is equally a fact that epistemological operations are valid so long as they are not found to be falsified.

Towards the end of the *Adhyāsabhāṣya* Śaṅkara briefly defines superimposition once again. He says: "superimposition means the cognition of a thing [A] in something [B] where it [A] does not actually exist *(atasmin tadbuddhiḥ)*."[103] This second definition brings out the essential feature of superimposition more clearly than the formal definition given earlier. Having briefly presented the meaning of superimposition, Śaṅkara proceeds to illustrate its actual occurrence on the basis of one's own experience. He says:

> For example, a person superimposes external attributes on himself if, when his son or wife etc. are either injured or fine in health, he thinks: "I am injured" or "I am fine". So too a person superimposes the attributes of the physical body on himself when he thinks: "I am fat", "I am thin", "I am fair", "I am standing", "I am going", "I am jumping". So too a person superimposes the attributes of the senses when he thinks: "I am dumb", "I am one-eyed", "I am impotent", "I am deaf", "I am blind". Likewise, a person superimposes the attributes of the mind such as desire, intention, doubt, determination etc. In the same way, one superimposes the mind on the inner-Self, the witness of all the activities of the mind, and conversely, one superimposes the inner-Self, the witness of everything, on the mind etc.[104]

We shall see Padmapāda's comments on the above passage in some detail. He notes that when Śaṅkara says that a person superimposes external conditions, the physical body and its attributes, the attributes of the senses and the attributes of the mind, "on himself" *(ātmani)*, what Śaṅkara is referring to by the word *ātman* is not the pure Self, but the "I", or ego, i.e., the Self that is intermingled with the mind.[105] In the series of superimpositions that Śaṅkara has portrayed, the first superimposition to occur is the one mentioned last, i.e., the mutual superimposition between the Self, the "not-this" pure Awareness, and the mind. It is this superimposition that produces the "I" (ego) who is a blend of pure Awareness and mind. All subsequent superimposition involves the "I": "I am fat", "I am blind", "I desire" and so on. It is this "I" that becomes the basis for all *saṁsāra*, as Padmapāda vividly portrays:

> By the word *"sva"* [in the phrase "the witness of all the activities of the mind" *aśeṣasvapracārasākṣiṇi]* what is spoken of is the "knot" consisting of the "I" *(ahaṅkāragranthi)* which forms the principal pillar of the dance-hall of *saṁsāra*.[106] The activities of the mind consist of various types of transformations such as desire, intention, the sense of doership etc. It is on account of these transformations that a living being keeps going around, helplessly, like one whose head is on fire, [in various bodies] from Brahmā down to an immobile object.[107]

Padmapāda next refers to Śaṅkara's use of the words "witness" *(sākṣin)* and "inner-Self" *(pratyagātman)*. In the first sentence he refers to the meaning of the word *sākṣin*, and in the next to the word *pratyagātman:*

> The essential Awareness *(citidhātu)*, free from either rejecting or accepting [anything] as it is unattached and without change, reveals that entire activity directly *(sākṣāt)*, i.e., without anything intervening. And the essential Awareness is called "inner" *(pratyak)* since it is observed that it seems to go in the reverse direction with respect of the body etc. which becomes external as "this". And it is the Self *(ātman)* because it is literally the essential nature *(svarūpa)*.[108]

Padmapāda then says that Śaṅkara is specific in referring to the mutual superimposition between Self and mind ("one superimposes the mind on the inner-Self....and conversely, one superimposes the inner-Self, the witness of everything, on the mind etc.") because what happens in the case of a superimposition is that only the superimposed object is seen and the locus remains unknown. When silver is superimposed on shell the latter is not revealed. So if there is only the superimposition of the mind etc. on the Self then the Self would not be revealed, but that is not the case because the Self is always directly evident. So too, if there is only the superimposition of Awareness on the mind etc. then the whole world from the mind onwards would not be revealed. Since it is in accord with experience that both Awareness and mind are manifest, Śaṅkara says that there must be a mutual superimposition.[109]

A final point. If the primary superimposition is between the Self and the mind, and all subsequent superimposition presupposes this primary superimposition in so far as all other superimposition involves the mind, then why does Śaṅkara indicate that the pure Awareness itself is superimposed in all subsequent superimposition? Śaṅkara has said (supra): "and conversely, one superimposes the inner-Self, the witness of everything, on the mind etc." The use of the word "etc." indicates that the superimposition of pure Awareness occurs in all cases of superimposition. Padmapāda replies that it is true that the primary superimposition is between the Self and the mind and that all subsequent superimposition involves the mind. However in all the subsequent cases of superimposition the mind does nothing more than make a thing capable of being objectively revealed by Awareness. So in all cases of superimposition - whether directly, as between Awareness and mind, or indirectly as when Awareness and mind are superimposed on the senses and the body etc. - the light of Awareness is invariably present. Therefore the Self, the witness of everything, is superimposed on the mind and on the senses etc.[110]

(6) The *śruti* and its role in liberation

At the conclusion of the *Adhyāsabhāṣya* Śaṅkara presents the result of the inquiry into Brahman:

> Thus there is this beginningless and endless, natural flow of superimposition; it is in the form of wrong notions, it is the source of the sense of doership and enjoyership and it is directly evident to everyone. All the Vedānta [i.e. Upaniṣads] are begun [i.e. their study is undertaken] to

> attain the knowledge of the oneness of the Self so as to remove this superimposition, the cause of all misfortune.[111]

Padmapāda points out that when it is said that the Upaniṣads are studied to put an end to an endless superimposition, what is implied is that the Upaniṣads alone are the cause for its removal, otherwise it would be endless.[112]

Padmapāda then raises an objection, the answer to which helps clarify our understanding of the role of the Upaniṣads in generating the liberating knowledge:

> [objection] Superimposition, the cause of misfortune, is beginningless, so how can it be ended? Let me explain. There is the superimposition merely of a class characteristic "man" etc. Even when the "I"-cognition [ego] is distinguished from that superimposition by reasoning, the superimposition will continue as before since it is beginningless.[113]

The idea is that superimposition, in the form of a mere general identification "I am so and so", is beginningless. And because it is beginningless, mere discriminative reasoning is insufficient to remove it. Padmapāda replies to this objection:

> No, because what is required is another knowledge, one that arises from the sentence such as "you are That" etc. and apprehends the nature of Brahman. For that knowledge accurately reveals Brahman, and as it arises it removes the beginningless *avidyā* which (a) brings on the condition of being an individual soul by concealing the fact that Awareness is Brahman, and (b) is the cause of the projection of the "I" etc. Then, once the cause is removed, it is appropriate that its effect, i.e., the "I", the sense of enjoyership in the individual soul, ceases along with all its retinue. But the "I"-cognition is beginningless, for it exists in the company of the entire aggregate of the body

> and senses which are themselves beginningless, and as there is no opposition [between the "I"-cognition and the body-sense complex] the [superimposition] does not cease merely by discriminating one's essential nature.[114]

Padmapāda says, similar to what Sureśvara too has said,[115] that the "I"-cognition is a part of the superimposition itself, so it is not opposed to superimposition, and therefore merely discriminating out the "I" from the body and the senses etc. is not sufficient to remove superimposition. The knowledge generated by the Upaniṣads, however, is a different type of knowledge, for it reveals Brahman. The *Vivaraṇa* points out here that *saṁsāra* is not caused by a lack of discrimination of oneself as distinct from the body etc., but it is caused by not knowing oneself to be Brahman.[116] So it is ignorance of oneself as Brahman that is the cause of *saṁsāra* and such ignorance is removed only by the knowledge from the Upaniṣads.

Padmapāda will again return to this topic. Meanwhile he replies to two objections concerning the sentence in the *Adhyāsabhāṣya* referred to above, where it was said that the study of the Upaniṣads is undertaken: "to attain the knowledge of the oneness of the Self so as to remove this superimposition, the cause of all misfortune." The first objection asks why the removal of superimposition, the cause of all misfortune, is mentioned separately from the attainment of "the knowledge of the oneness of the Self". Surely the removal of superimposition is part and parcel of the knowledge of the Self, so why mention it separately? Padmapāda replies that the removal of superimposition is mentioned separately because the subject matter of the Upaniṣads is only to reveal the real nature of oneself as Brahman. The removal of superimposition is the "by-product" of this knowledge and that is why it is mentioned separately.[117] He says that when sentences such as "you are That" reveal Brahman, the negation of ignorance happens as the necessary by-product of the rise of knowledge, like when one side of a set of scales is raised the other side is automatically lowered, or like how the knowledge that "this is shell" automatically removes the false notion of silver. His point here is that the words of the Upaniṣads have their scope just in revealing Brahman, not in the removal of ignorance, and that is why the removal of ignorance is mentioned separately. But when Brahman is revealed, the removal of ignorance along with its effect, superimposition, takes place as the invariable by-product of the knowledge.[118]

The second objection concerns the use of the word "attain" in the sentence "to attain the knowledge of the oneness of the Self" *(ātmaikatvavidyāpratipattaye).* This seemingly pedantic query leads into an important discussion. The objection is that it should be sufficient to say that the Upaniṣads are studied "for the knowledge of the oneness of the Self", and there is no need to use the word "attain". Padmapāda agrees that the word "attain" would normally be redundant, but he says there is a reason for its use here. He explains:

> In the present context [the knowledge of the oneness of the Self from the Upaniṣads], even though the knowledge has arisen, it is not firm, because the subject matter is overpowered by the thought that it is something improbable, and by habitual ways of contrary thinking. Just like in the world, a person may decide that something cannot possibly exist at a particular place and time, but if somehow by fate that thing is actually perceived, even though the person sees it himself he is not convinced until he shows it to be possible by using supporting logic. Hence even right knowledge, if it is not certain about its subject matter, seems to be unattained. So the knowledge takes the help of supporting logic in order to establish itself. That is why the logicians say that logic assists the various means of knowledge.
> [objection] What do you mean by "supporting logic" *(tarka)?*
> [reply] Reasoning *(yukti).*
> [objection] This is just a synonym. Tell me its nature.
> [reply] It is a cognition which determines the possibility or the impossibility of the means of knowledge [eg. whether a means of knowledge possesses intrinsic validity or not], and of the relation between the word and its meaning [eg. whether there is a literal meaning or a secondary meaning], and of the subject matter [eg. whether there is difference or non-difference between *jīva* and Brahman].

> [objection] If [the Vedānta] reveals its meaning by relying on logic it would relinquish its independence and would thereby cease to be a means of valid knowledge.
> [reply] No it would not, because it gives definite knowledge of its subject matter just through its inherent greatness.
> [objection)] What then is the use of logic?
> [reply] When there is a doubt about the possibility of what is taught, and as a result the benefit of experience does not arise, the utility of logic lies in removing the obstruction to the experience by showing the possibility of what is taught. So, in regard to the sentence "you are That", the individual soul - the one expressed by the word "you" - does not see the possibility of being Brahman, which is the meaning of the word "That", and the individual soul thinks itself to be of an opposite nature; and even though the knowledge has arisen, the individual soul is not certain until it sees the possibility that it is Brahman by removing the contradiction by logic. Even though knowledge arose from the sentence prior to using logic, the knowledge seems as though it has not been attained.[119]

A significant point to be noted from this quotation is that Padmapāda repeatedly says that the liberating knowledge arises from the sentence. This teaching is held in common by Śaṅkara and Sureśvara, and by Toṭaka as well.[120] They all agree that immediate knowledge *(aparokṣajñāna)* can take place from hearing the Upaniṣadic teaching. Padmapāda is particularly explicit about this, for not only can immediate knowledge arise from the sentence, but he says three times that the knowledge *has arisen (vidyā uditāpi; samutpanne'pi jñāne; vidyā uditāpi vākyāt)* though it may not be firmly established. Padmapāda's view is that the liberating knowledge directly arises from hearing the sentence, but it may be obstructed in the production of its result, i.e., liberation, because of the feeling of a lack of certainty about the knowledge *(asambhāvanā),* and also by the pattern of habitual contrary thinking *(viparītabhāvanā).* Padmapāda is saying that when the words of the Upaniṣads reveal the knowledge, liberation does not thereafter need to be *gained,* but rather the obstructions to the reception of that liberating meaning have to be *removed.* There may not seem much difference between speaking of "gaining" liberation and "removing" the obstructions to liberation, because if the knowledge from the sentence stands obstructed then liberation is as good as unattained. Nevertheless, there is a considerable psychological difference between the two positions, because the first sees the *śruti* as a mere "road map" to the goal of liberation, whereas the second looks upon *śruti* as directly able to deliver the liberating knowledge. According to Padmapāda the liberating knowledge has arisen, and only the obstructions have to be removed for its full flowering. This teaching of these early Advaita *ācāryas*, which is centred around the liberating capacity of the Upaniṣadic word, gradually lost ground over the centuries to the cultivation of *samādhi*- oriented yogic practices, though such a tendency can be seen in Advaita even from the time of Maṇḍanamiśra.

In the above quotation Padmapāda advocates reasoning as the means to remove the thought that the Upaniṣads teach something improbable. This reasoning can consist of investigating such matters as whether a means of knowledge is inherently valid or whether it has to be validated extrinsically, and whether language can reveal the nature of Brahman given that Brahman is not an object of words. The investigation of such matters helps one to see the possibility of the *śruti* as the means of knowledge about Brahman. Apart from improbability, Padmapāda also mentioned "habitual contrary thinking" *(viparītabhāvanā)*, but he has not dealt with that issue here.[121] Therefore, the word "attain" in the *Adhyāsabhāṣya* is not inappropriate, because it refers to the firmness of the knowledge.

At this point we will introduce a discussion from later in the *Pañcapādikā* as it pertains to a matter just raised, namely how can the *śruti* reveal Brahman if Brahman is not an object of words? The objection is put in this way: the Advaitin wishes to deny that Brahman is the object of an action, and in so doing he denies that Brahman is an object of even the act of knowing. But to deny that Brahman can be an object of knowledge would be to deny that Brahman could be known through the Upaniṣads. The task before Padmapāda is to show how the Upaniṣads can reveal Brahman while he upholds the position that Brahman is not an object of words. Padmapāda replies to the objection, in a particularly compressed passage, where he says:

> The *śāstra* is the means of knowledge for Brahman in a way that is analogous to the worldly sentence "this is that [Devadatta]" etc. To explain. The sentence "this is that Devadatta" reveals non-difference through the falsification of the different adjuncts of place and time. In a similar way, the one who is expressed by the word "you" [in the sentence "you are That"] thinks that he is the "I" [ego], and from the sentence "you are That" he comes to understand his oneness with what is expressed by the word "That". It is analogous to the sentence "this is that Devadatta", [for what happens is] the "not-this" Awareness is conditioned by the world consisting of the known, the knower and the act of knowing; these [differences] themselves being caused by the limiting adjunct of the "this" portion, i.e., the "I". The one expressed by the word "you" is shown to be the result of the means of knowledge, i.e., to be the "not-this" Awareness, through the implied falsification of that world consisting of the known, the knower and the act of knowing which are caused by the limiting adjunct of the "this" portion, i.e., the "I".[122]

Padmapāda says that just as the essential Devadatta is recognised through the falsification of the different limiting adjuncts of place and time, so too the person referred to by the word "you" is revealed to be the non-object Awareness through the falsification of the duality of knower, known and the act of knowing, which is caused by the limiting adjunct of the mind. The knowledge of one's real nature takes place simultaneously with the falsification of the differences brought about by the limiting adjunct. He says that the falsification is "implied" because the statement of identity like "this is that Devadatta" or "you are That" cannot be understood without the negation of erroneous differences. Padmapāda continues:

> When those conditioning aspects are destroyed [i.e. when the differences of knower etc. are falsified], at that very time he [the hearer] abandons even the result of the means of knowledge, and becomes free from distinctions. So even

> though the four beginning with the cogniser disappear simultaneously, the fruit of the experience, which is conditioned by these four, depends upon the sentence. That is why those who know the Veda teach that liberation *(nirvāṇa)* is solely the domain of the Veda.[123]

Padmapāda says that the sentence, operating as a means of knowledge, has produced its result *(pramāṇaphala)* which is the specific cognition "I am Brahman (i.e. "I am the unconditioned 'not-this' Awareness"). Once the operation of the means of knowledge is over, the result of the means of knowledge, the specific cognition "I am Brahman", also disappears along with the falsification of the knower, the known and the act of knowing. So the sentence produces the liberating cognition "I am Brahman", but while that particular cognition also disappears, it leaves behind the immediate understanding of one's real, limitless nature. And the Upaniṣad sentence is required for the occurrence of that cognition. So the Upaniṣads reveal Brahman, but not how other means of knowledge such as perception reveal their objects, for the Upaniṣads reveal the Self as Brahman by way of the falsification of limiting adjuncts.[124]

Padmapāda again takes up the issue raised earlier, that mere discrimination is insufficient for liberation, unlike the knowledge arising out of the Upaniṣads. The objector argues that if mere discrimination is insufficient, so too the knowledge of the Self as Brahman that arises from the *śruti* would also be unable to remove the superimposition, for in both cases the knot that is the "I" *(ahaṅkāragranthi)* continues unaltered, and superimpositions such as "I am a man" etc. are still seen to persist.[125] Padmapāda replies:

> That may be so here [in the mere discrimination of the "I" from the body etc.], because ignorance has not been removed. But here [in the knowledge of being Brahman], as the knowledge that the Self is Brahman arises it removes the defect of ignorance. How can it fail to remove that flow [of superimposition] beginning from the knot of the enjoyer when ignorance is the cause? For the understanding by the individual soul that the Self is

> Brahman does not arise without sublating the ignorance about that.[126]

The point about the removal of ignorance *(avidyā)* leads to the final topic that we will but briefly discuss, which is about the liberated person *(jīvanmukta)*. How intelligible is it to speak of "liberation while living" once *avidyā* is removed, because ordinary relations *(vyavahāra)* entail superimposition, and superimposition is the outcome of *avidyā?* The topic is raised in this way:

> [objection] If ignorance *(agrahaṇa)* is removed by the knowledge of Brahman, the consequence would be the disappearance, at that very time, of the knot consisting of the "I", since the "I" is caused by ignorance.
> [reply] No, because it is possible for ignorance to persist even on account of an impression *(saṁskāra)*, like how fear persists. To explain. Even when fear has ceased because of right knowledge, it persists on account of its impression, and becomes the cause of trembling etc. So too ignorance also persists on account of its impression and becomes the cause of the knot consisting of the "I". So there is nothing incongruous.[127]

Padmapāda says that *avidyā* is removed by the knowledge of Brahman; he does not say that a trace *(leśa)* of *avidyā* remains.[128] What remains is only the impression of *avidyā*. And just as the impression of past fear is sufficient to cause the persistence of trembling and sweating, or just as the scent of a flower lingers even after the flower is removed, so the liberated person continues to live on account of the impression of *avidyā*, but not because of the persistence of *avidyā*.

---

1 BSBh *(Adhyāsabhāṣya)* p.4f., line 1f, (tr) p.1.

2 Ibid., p.25ff., line 4, (tr) p.6.

3 PP p.9, (MRI) p.23ff., (tr) p.2.

4 PP p.10f., (MRI) p.25f., (tr) p.2.

5 The "old bull" is an example of a nonsense verse. "An old bull with a blanket and sandals stood at the door singing *madrakā* songs. A Brahman lady wanting a son, asks him: 'O king, what is the price of garlic in the land of Rumā?'." Cf. tr. p.4, n.5. (MRI) p.30, cf. the commentary, *Tattvadīpana.*

6 PP p.12f, (MRI) p.29f., (tr.) p.3f.

7 Śaṅkara also makes this point in US 18. 215-217.

8 PP p.19f., (MRI) p.34f., (tr.) p.6.

9 PP p.21, (MRI) p.39, (tr.) p.7.

10 Cf. (tr.) p.7, n.14. 4.22 of the *Yogasūtra.* Padmapāda's expression resembles the words in the *sūtra: "citer apratisaṅkramāyāḥ...."* This expression is also found in the *Brahmasiddhi,* Kuppuswami Sastri (ed.), op.cit., p.4, line 3.

11 Cf. US 5. 5 and 6. 5-6. NS 2.46. PP p.70f., (MRI) p.128, (tr.) p.46. Also, PP p.86, (MRI) p.152f., (tr.) p.56.

12 PP p.22, (MRI) p.41, (tr.) p.7.

13 Cf. *Vivaraṇa,* p.60, (MRI) p.41.

14 PP p.23, (MRI) p.42, (tr.) p.8.

15 According to the *Word Index to the Brahma-Sūtra Bhāṣya of Śaṅkara* (Univ. of Madras, Part One, 1971, Part Two, 1973), the compound *mithyājñānanimitta* occurs, apart from the above usage, on three other occasions (BSBh 1.1.4, p.94, line 8, (tr.) p.40; 1.2.8, p.167, line 17, (tr.) p.118; 4.2.8, p.862, line 7, (tr.) 857). In addition, there are other similar expressions eg. *mithyājñānakalpita* (BSBh 1.2.8, p.168, line 4, (tr.) p.118; 1.4.10, p.309, line 1, (tr.) p.263) and *mithyājñānakṛta* (BSBh 1.3.19, p.236, line, 5, (tr.) p.193) and also *mithyājñānavijṛmbhita* (BSBh 2.1.14, p.376, line 4, (tr.) p.329; 2.1.22, p.395, line 2 (tr.) p.349). The term *mithyājñāna* occurs uncompounded with other expressions on eleven occasions (BSBh 1.1.2, p.53, line 3, (tr.) p.16; 1.1.4, p.90, line 3, (tr.) p.38; and p.95, line 4, (tr.) p.40; 1.3.28, p.254, line 5, (tr.) p.211; 2.1.9, p.365, lines 6 and 12, (tr.) p.319; 2.1.14, p.376, line 7, (tr.) p.329; 2.3.30, p.540, line 13, (tr.) p.491; 4.1.13, p.847, line 8, (tr.) p.837; 4.1.15 p.851, line 1, (tr.) p.840; 4.1.19, p.854, line 9, (tr.) 846).

In most of the above instances it is unclear whether *mithyājñāna* refers to a *bhāvarūpājñāna* or simply means "wrong understanding". On most occasions the term could be understood either way, depending upon the presuppositions with which one approaches the text. There are a couple of instances, however, where Śaṅkara unambiguously uses the expression to mean merely a "wrong understanding". For example, BSBh p.1.1.4, p.95, line 4, when he says *śarīrātmābhimānalakṣaṇaṁ mithyājñānam*. Also, cf. BSBh 1.1.2, p.53, line 3; 1.3.28, p.254, line 5.

16 PP p.26, (MRI) p.46, (tr.) p.10.

17 Padmapāda too qualifies *avidyā* by both the terms *anādi* and *anirvacanīya*, cf. PP p.66, (MRI) p. 122. Also (MRI) Fourth Varṇaka, p.506, *mithyaivānirvacanīyānādyavidyāvilasita*.

18 PP p.27, (MRI) p.50f., (tr.) p.11. The term *"tat"* in *tatsvarūpasattāmātrānubandhinī* is glossed by the *Vivaraṇa*, PP p.89, as *ātmatattva*. This would be correct because Padmapāda had previously said, PP p.23, *naisargika=pratyak-caitanyasattāmātrānubandhī*.

19 PP p.27, (MRI) p.53, (tr.) p.11.

20 *Vivaraṇa* p.64f, (MRI) p.46, *nanu katham mithyājñānam adhyāsasya upādhānam? tasmin sati adhyāsasya udayāt, asati ca anudayād iti brūmaḥ*.

21 *Vivaraṇa* p.89, (MRI) p.53.

22 PP p.28, (MRI) p.56f., (tr.) p.11.

23 *Vivaraṇa* p.96, (MRI) p.56.

24 PP p.29, (MRI) p.60f., (tr.) p.12.

25 NS 3. v.1 (samb.). Śaṅkara, in BUBh 1.4.10, p.669, line 25 to p.670 line 6, (tr) p.102f. Here, Śaṅkara argues by postulation based on *śruti (śrutārthāpatti)* that Brahman is the object of *avidyā*. And when he says that, "there is no other sentient entity apart from Brahman who is the author of *avidyā* or subject to error" he indicates by postulation that Brahman must also be the locus of *avidyā*.

26 PP p.30, (MRI) p.62f., (tr.) p.12.

27 He refers to postulation based on *śruti (śrutārthāpatti)* to prove the "existence" of *avidyā* in PP p.73f., (MRI) p.135f., (tr.) p.47f. Again cf. PP p.81, (MRI) p.150, (tr.) p.54.

28 Cf. *Vivaraṇa* p.74, (MRI) p.49f. The explanation of the *Vivaraṇa* is repeated in the commentary *Prabodhapariśodhinī* of Ātmasvarūpa, PP p.30, "*avidyākāryatvaṁ prasādya, avidyārūpeṇa anāderapi kāryavyaktirūpeṇa sāditvam aviruddham.*"

29 PP p.23, (MRI) p.42, (tr.) p.8.

30 PP p.31, (MRI) p.67, (tr.) p.13. The *Vivaraṇa,* p.112 (MRI) p.67, makes the amendment that the very first *adhyāsa* is that of *ajñāna* on *caitanya.* Ātmasvarūpa, p.31, observes that the *ajñānādhyāsa* in the *ātmā* is *anādi* and the ego is the first *kāryādhyāsa.*

31 PP p.32, (MRI) p.68f., (tr.) p.13f.

32 PP p.32f., (MRI) p.69f., (tr.) p.14. Padmapāda says that the portion of the *bhāṣya* from "*ko'yam adhyāso nāma*" up to "*kathaṁ punar avidyāvadviṣayāṇi*" is meant to present the definition of *adhyāsa* and show its possibility. The portion from "*kathaṁ punar avidyāvadviṣayāṇi*" onwards is meant to demonstrate the actual existence of *adhyāsa.*

33 PP p.33f., (MRI) p.70f. (the reading should be *pṛthak na kartavyaḥ),* (tr.) p.14f.

34 PP p.34f., (MRI) p.72f., (tr.) p.15f.

35 BSBh p.10f., line 1. (tr.) p.2.

36 PP p.40f., (MRI) p.75f., (tr.) p.17f.

37 At this point Padmapāda says: "this definition is also applicable to the manifestation [i.e. to the knowledge] which has that thing [the silver] as its object." PP p.41, (MRI) p.78, (tr.) p.18. Padmapāda is referring to what is known as *viṣayādhyāsa* (or

arthādhyāsa). He says that the definition of *adhyāsa* as "the manifestation, similar to memory, of something which was seen before and is now seen somewhere else", is applicable to both the manifested object, the silver, and to the cognition that manifests the object. In our everyday dealings *(vyavahāra)* a distinction is made between the sense object and the cognition of the sense object, eg. the table and our cognition of the table. The table *(viṣaya)* and our cognition of the table *(viṣayākāravṛtti)* are considered to be distinct. Similarly, even in the case of *adhyāsa,* the Advaitin makes a distinction between the *prātibhāsikaviṣaya,* the perceptual object silver which appears on the shell, and its cognition. Thus a distinction is maintained between the *rajata* and the *rajatajñāna.* So just as in *vyavahāra* there is a distinction between the object and its cognition, a similar distinction is upheld even in a *prātibhāsika* situation. This means that in such cases as silver appearing on shell, the Advaitin accepts the existence of a *prātibhāsika* silver as distinct from the *prātibhāsika* cognition of silver.

38 In the course of this discussion Padmapāda briefly makes a point that is worth noting. He says that in the case of silver appearing on shell: "the cognition that has something unreal *(mithyā)* as its object is called an unreal cognition. The knowledge (cognition) is not itself unreal, because it is not negated." PP p.52, (MRI) p.95, (tr.) p.28f. Here, as elsewhere (eg. PP p.55, (MRI) p.104, (tr.) p.32) Padmapāda says that sublation *(bādhā)* is the criterion for unreality *(mithyātva).* The silver appearing on the shell is unreal (i.e. inexpressible, *nirupākhya,* as either *sat* or *asat* - for this is what the word *mithyā* means) because the silver is negated. The cognition, or knowledge, is not unreal because it is not negated. The *object* of knowledge is unreal but the *knowledge* of the object is not unreal because the knowledge is not negated. Here, we find the teaching that knowledge is inherently valid *(svataḥ prāmāṇya).*

39 Cf. The *Tarkadīpikā* of Annanbhaṭṭa, "A definition presents the specific property *(asādhāraṇadharma)* which is co-extensive with what is to be defined *(lakṣyatāvacchedakasamaniyatatvam).* Y.V. Athalye, *Tarka-Saṁgraha of Annambhaṭṭa, with the author's own Dīpikā and Govardhana's Nyāya-Bodhinī.* Poona: Bhandarkar Oriental Research Institute, 1974, p.4.

40 PP p.55, (MRI) p.109, (tr.) 33f.

41 Padmapāda first referred to these earlier, cf. PP p.51f., (MRI) p.94f., (tr.) p.28.

42 PP p.56, (MRI) p.110, (tr.) p.35.

43 PP p.56, (MRI) p.110, (tr.) 35.

44 Padmapāda uses the term *vivarta* or *vivartate* on four other occasions. (1) PP p.115, (MRI) p.201, (2) (MRI) p.532 (5th Varṇaka), (3) (MRI) p.561 (6th Varṇaka), and (4) (MRI) p.562. (We have also come across one occasion when Sureśvara used the expression *jagad vivartate,* BUBhV vol.2, 3.8.130). However at this time the word *vivarta* does not seem to have become the special technical term to denote an apparent transformation. This can be seen in Padmapāda's use of the word, because in the present context he speaks of the *avidyāśaktir ālambanatayā vivartate.* The author of the *Vivaraṇa,* Prakāśātman *(circa* 1000 AD), amends Padmapāda's statement. Prakāśātman said that it is only the Awareness that appears to transform, through its *avidyāśakti,* into the dream objects *(caitanyam eva svāvidyayā vivartate).* PP *(Vivaraṇa)* p.180f., (MRI) p.111. Prakāśātman later on presents a definition of *vivarta* and of *pariṇāma.* (MRI) p.532. He says *vivarta* is when: "one thing, without deviating from its real nature, comes to appear in various unreal forms which are of an opposite nature to the original" *(ekasya tattvād apracyutasya pūrvaviparītāsatyānekarūpāvabhāso vivartaḥ).* A.J.

Alston, closely following Paul Hacker's work *Vivarta* (Wiesbaden, 1953), points out that this definition is modelled upon the definition of *vivarta* given in the *Vākyapadīya Vṛtti (ekasya tattvād apracyutasya bhedānukāreṇa-asatyavibhaktānyarūpopagrāhitā vivartaḥ).* A.J. Alston, *Early Post-Śaṃkara Advaita,* Ph.D. thesis, Banares Hindu University, 1963, p.417. Prakāśātman's definition of *pariṇāma* is: "one thing comes to assume another, real form, by abandoning its prior condition *(ekasya pūrvarūpaparityāgena satyarūpāntarāpattiḥ pariṇāmaḥ).* Therefore by the time of Prakāśātman the word *vivarta* is clearly used as a technical term to describe an illusory transformation. We have argued throughout this book that none of the authors discussed accept that Brahman undergoes any real transformation. All authors, though they may not have used the term *vivarta,* or may not have used it in its later specialised meaning, are alert to avoid the consequence of impermanence should Brahman undergo the slightest real change. In fact, the whole discussion of *māyā* is introduced in Advaita only to account for the possibility of the appearance of the world given that Brahman is ultimately untransformed.

45 PP p.57, (MRI) p.112 where the reading of PP seems preferable, (tr.) p.35.

46 PP p.58, (MRI) p.113f. (tr.) p.36.

47 PP p.62, (MRI) p.118, (tr.) p.40. It is sometimes wondered whether Advaitins have correctly understood the Mādhyamika teaching. Certainly, the *śūnyavāda* does not say that nothing exists; *śūnyavāda* teaches the relativity of everything. It may be that Advaitins have not fully understood the *śūnyavāda,* but Padmapāda's objection is not based upon a misunderstanding. Padmapāda just asks the question *in what* does everything appear? Any unreal appearance must have a final, unnegated substrate, which is something the Mādhyamika denies.

48 PP p.63, (MRI) p.118f., (tr.) p.40.

49 PP p.64, (MRI) p.120, (tr.) p.40f.

50 PP p.65 f., (MRI) p.120f., (tr.) p.41f. Stephen Phillips in his article, "Padmapāda's illusion argument", *Philosophy East and West*. Vol.37, no.1, 1987, finds no reason why the pure Awareness should be unsublatable. His argument is vitiated to some extent by the supposition he brings to his reading of Advaita, i.e., he shares the common view that Advaita is speaking of some "mystical experience". What Advaita is saying may indeed appear mystical, but when properly understood, Advaita (or at least the Advaita of Śaṅkara and his disciples, Sureśvara, Padmapāda, Toṭaka and Hastāmalaka) is speaking about the nature of everyday Consciousness (which it distinguishes from "thought") and it attempts to liberate the seeker from the misunderstanding about the finite nature of that ordinary Consciousness. It is not talking about the existence of a "super-Consciousness" as something existing apart from ordinary Consciousness itself. Also, note the comments of Wilhelm Halbfass: "Padmapāda's argumentation, which is based on a phenomenology of immediacy and deals with the nature of experiencing as such, is obviously different from any mystical reliance on extraordinary experiences. As a matter of fact, Padmapāda never refers to such special experiences." W. Halbfass, "The Concept of Experience in the Encounter Between India and the West" in, *India and Europe: An Essay in Understanding*. Albany: State University of New York Press, 1988, p.391. The topic of "experience" was discussed in some detail in chapter six.

51 PP p.76f., (MRI) p.146f., (tr.) p.50f.

52 PP p.78f., (MRI) p.148, (tr.) p.52. The discussion is somewhat unclear at this point and Padmapāda's reply has had to be reconstructed with the help of the commentaries.

53 PP p.79f. *(tathā hi ...)*, (MRI) p.149, (tr.) p.53, cf. n.110. Śaṅkara also says: "O how unfathomable, impenetrable and wondrous is this *māyā!* For all living beings, though in truth identical with the supreme reality, when they are taught this they fail to grasp 'I am the supreme Self' and they take themselves to be the non-Self, the aggregate consisting of the body and the senses etc., even though that aggregate is something seen by the Self, like a pot etc.; and even without being told they say 'I am the son of so and so'." KaUBh 1.3.12, p.82, line 24f., (tr.) p.162f.

54 PP ibid.

55 BSBh p.16f., line 2f., (tr.) p.3.

56 The *Vivaraṇa* p.230, and the commentary of Ātmasvarūpa (p.85) who follows the *Vivaraṇa* , say that the word *ahaṅkāra* means the internal-organ *(antaḥkaraṇa)*.

57 PP p.86, (MRI) p.152f., (tr.) p.56.

58 PP p.133f., (MRI) p.237f., (tr.) p.100.

59 PP p.113f., (MRI) p.195, (tr.) p.80.

60 *Vivaraṇa* p.230, (MRI) p.152, *Prabodhapariśodhinī* p.85.

61 PP p.91, (MRI) p.162f., (tr.) p.59f. *ātmaiva citiprakāśa āpadyate, na tadatiriktatathāvidhaphalasadbhāve pramāṇam asti.* The *Vivaraṇa*, p.254, (MRI) p.163, says *sthāyyātmaivānubhavaḥ.* The *Prabodhapariśodhinī*, p.92, says *ātmaivānubhavaḥ.*

62 PP p.92, (MRI) p.163f., (tr.) p.60.

63 PP p.92, (MRI) p.164, (tr.) p.61. The *Vivaraṇa* , p.254, (MRI) p.164 says, *nanu nīlasaṁvitsthitikāle pītasaṁvido'bhāvāt sthitivināśau dṛṣṭau dharmibhedaṁ kalpayataḥ iti codyam udbhāvya pariharati.*

64 PP p.92, (MRI) p.164, (tr.) p.61.

65 PP p.93, (MRI) p.164f., (tr.) p.61.

66 *Vivaraṇa* p.256, (MRI) p.165 with the *Tattvadīpana*, line 15f, *Prabodhapariśodhinī*, p.93.

67 PP p.93, (MRI) p.165, (tr.) 62.

68 PP p.94f., (MRI) p.165f., (tr.) p.62f. I have omitted the following discussion about sleep for according to the commentators (*Vivaraṇa* p.266, (MRI) p.172, *Prabodhapariśodhinī* p.96) it does not present the *siddhānta* but is just showing that the opponent's position is not tenable from the opponent's own standpoint.

69 PP p.97, (MRI) p.172, (tr.) p.66.

70 PP p.98f., (MRI) p.173f., (tr.) p.66f.

71 PP p.99, (MRI) p.174, (tr.) p.68.

72 Ibid. The word *mithyā* should be understood in its full meaning of "inexpressible as truly real or as entirely fictitious" *(sadasadbhyām anirvācyam).*

73 PP p.100, (MRI) p.176f., (tr.) p.68f. Padmapāda says that the "I" *(ahaṅkāra)* - which essentially refers to the mind itself - is the

"location of both the power of thought and the power of activity". With reference to the power of activity it is called as *prāṇa*. This presents a certain difficulty, for in sleep the *prāṇa* continues to function whereas the "I" is not manifest at that time. So how can the *prāṇa* and the *ahaṅkāra* be the same? The author of the *Vivaraṇa* is aware of this difficulty and he offers three explanations to get around the problem. His primary explanation is to qualify Padmapāda's statement by saying: "*prāṇa* is not meant to be understood as just the *ahaṅkāra*, but what is said is just that the *ahaṅkāra* has the power of action in that the *ahaṅkāra* is the cause for the *prāṇa* - which has a separate existence - to operate in its fivefold way. For it is seen that the function of the *prāṇa* depends upon the mind." Alternatively, he says that as the mind has parts it can be supposed that just one part, i.e., the power of thought, disappears in sleep. PP *Vivaraṇa*, p.269, (MRI) p.174, line 10f.

74 PP p.100, (MRI) p.178, (tr.) p.69.

75 PP p.102, (MRI) p.180, (tr.) p.70.

76 PP p.102, (MRI) p.180f., (tr.) 70f.

77 PP p.102, (MRI) p.181, (tr.) p.71.

78 PP p.102, (MRI) p.181, (tr.) p.71.

79 PP p.103, (MRI) p.181f., (tr.) 71f.

80 PP p.104, (MRI) p.182, (tr.) p.72.

81 Śaṅkara also uses the illustration of a face and its reflection in the US 18. vv.37, 38 and especially 43. Śaṅkara and Padmapāda are each using the example in very different ways. Śaṅkara uses the example to show that just as the reflected image is unreal, so too the ego, the reflection of the Ātman in the mind, is unreal.

Padmapāda is using the illustration to show that the *anidamaṁśa* in the "I" is Brahman itself, like how a reflection is identical to the original *(ahaṅkartur anidamaṁśo bimbād iva pratibimbaṁ na brahmaṇo vastvantaram.* PP p.104, (MRI) p.182). So Śaṅkara employs the illustration of the reflection to show the unreality of the ego, whereas Padmapāda uses it, not to show the unreality of the ego, but to show that the essence of the ego, the *anidamaṁśa,* is real and none other than Brahman, like how a reflection of a face is identical to the original face. Thus they are both using the same example to say different things, but not contradictory things. Padmapāda's interpretation of the illustration should not be pressed too far, because the *anidamaṁśa* is not really a reflection and so his use of the illustration is fairly loose. Padmapāda is *not* saying that the *jīva* is real and identical to Brahman, which is the way in which he is generally interpreted. He is saying that the *anidamaṁśa* aspect of the *jīva* is real and identical to Brahman.

82 PP p.104, (MRI) p.182, (tr.) p.72.

83 PP p.107, (MRI) p.185, (tr.) p.74. In defending the view that the reflection is not *mithyā,* Padmapāda is contradicting Śaṅkara in US 18. vv.37, 43, where Śaṅkara argues that the reflection is unreal. It ought be remembered, however, as mentioned above in note 81, that Śaṅkara and Padmapāda are using the illustration differently, and that has put Padmapāda at variance with Śaṅkara over the interpretation of the status of the reflection in the illustration. There is no contradiction in their final teachings.

84 PP p.108, (MRI) p.185, (tr.) p.74.

85 In the BSBh 3.3.9, Śaṅkara discusses four possible meanings of co-referentiality. These are (1) *adhyāsa,* here he refers to the metaphorical *adhyāsa* as in the superimposition of the deities on the forms of the images, (2) sublation as in *yad rajataṁ sā*

śuktiḥ, (3) identity as in *so'yaṁ devadattaḥ*, (4) specification *(viśeṣaṇa)* as in *nīlam utpalam*.

86 PP p.113, (MRI) p.195, (tr.) p.79.

87 As, for instance, in the *Vivaraṇa* where the *pratibimba* viewpoint is defended, p.189f., (MRI) p.189f.

88 PP p.104, (MRI) p.182, (tr.) p.72. *ahaṅkartur anidamaṁśo bimbād iva pratibimbaṁ na brahmaṇo vastvantaram.*

89 PP p.114f., (MRI) p.199f., (tr.) p.80f.

90 PP p.115f., (MRI) p.200f., (tr.) p.81.

91 PP p.117, (MRI) p.203, (tr.) p.83.

92 US 14. 3-4; 18. 155-157. In the TUBh 2.1.1, p.284f., line 25f., (tr.) p.296, Śaṅkara says that the mind transforms into the shape of the sense objects.

93 PP p.133f., (MRI) p.237f., (tr.) p.100.

94 BSBh p.17f., line 2f., (tr.) p.3.

95 PP p.136, (MRI) p.241, (tr.) p.103f.

96 Cf. *Vivaraṇa* p.342, (MRI) p.238. *savikalpake adhiṣṭhāne savikalpādhyāsa iti vadataḥ asmatpratyayaviṣayatvāt iti parihāra uktaḥ. idanīṁ nirvikalpake'pi savikalpādhyāsa sambhavati ityāha*...These remarks of the *Vivaraṇa* are repeated in the *Prabodhapariśodhinī*, p.135.

97 BSBh p.19, line 2f., (tr.) p.3f.

98 PP p.138, (MRI) p.244, (tr.) p.105.

99 BSBh p.20, line 1f., (tr.) p.4.

100 BSBh p.20f., line 4f., (tr.) p.4.

101 PP p.143f., (MRI) p.251, (tr.) p.109.

102 PP p.144 *bādhānupalabdheḥ prāmāṇyam,* (MRI) p.252, (tr.) 110.

103 BSBh p.24, line 2, (tr.) p.5.

104 BSBh p.24f., line 2f., (tr.) p.5f.

105 PP p.154f. *asmadarthaś ca- ahampratyayisambhinna eva- anidaṁcidaṁśo viṣayaḥ, na punaḥ śuddha eva...* (MRI) p.263, (tr.) p.120.

106 The tenth chapter in the *Pañcadaśī, Nāṭakadīpa,* could conceivably have taken its inspiration from this sentence of the *Pañcapādikā.*

107 PP p.156, (MRI) p.264, (tr.) 121.

108 PP p.156f., (MRI) p.264, (tr.) p.121.

109 PP p.157, (MRI) p.267, (tr.) p.122.

110 PP p.158f., (MRI) p.267f., (tr.) p.122f.

111 BSBh p.25f., line 3f., (tr.) p.6.

112 PP p.160f., (MRI) p.268, (tr.) p.124.

113 PP p.162, (MRI) p.269, (tr.) p.126.

114 PP p.162f., (MRI) p.269f., (tr.) p.126f. The phrase *brahmaṇo- avacchidya* has been translated as "accurately reveals Brahman". Venkataramiah also translates "revealing the real nature of

Brahman" (tr.) p.126. Dr R. Krishnamurti Śāstrī of Madras explained the phrase as: *brahma saṁyag bodhayitvā* and said that the word *brahmaṇaḥ* is a *karmaṇi ṣaṣṭhī.*

115 Cf. The section discussing *anvayavyatireka* in the preceding chapter.

116 *Vivaraṇa* p.377, (MRI) p.270, *na ca vyatirekānavabodhanimittaḥ saṁsāraḥ kintu brahmānavabodhanimittaḥ.*

117 PP p.165, (MRI) p.272, (tr.) p.128f. *yadyevaṁ brahmātmàvagatināntarīyakam anarthahetor avidyāyāḥ prahāṇam....tena pṛthaṅ nirdiśyate.* PP p.169, (MRI) p.279, (tr.) p.132. *tad evam aśābdam avidyāvilayaṁ manvānaḥ śrutinyāyakovido bhagavān bhāṣyakāro viṣayāt pṛthag nirdiśati -asyānarthahetoḥ prahāṇāya iti.*

118 PP p.166f., (MRI) p.276f., (tr.) p.129f.

119 PP p.170 f., (MRI) p.280f., (tr.) 133f.

120 Cf. Michael Comans (tr), *Extracting the Essence of the Śruti: The Śrutisārasamuddharaṇam of Toṭakācārya.* Delhi: Motilal Banarsidass, 1996.

121 The *Vivaraṇa* tries to include it by saying that *tarka* means purity of mind, p.408, (MRI) p.286, (tr.) p.134, note 257.

122 (MRI) 9th Varṇaka, p.636f., (tr.) p.307f.

123 (MRI) p.638, (tr.) p.308.

124 This whole discussion centres on the passage in the BSBh 1.1.4, p.79, line 1f., (tr) p.31: "[objection] If Brahman is not an object, there is no logical possibility that the *śāstra* can reveal Brahman. [reply] No, because the *śāstra* aims at removing the differences

superimposed through ignorance. The *śāstra* does not seek to present Brahman as an object referable by a 'this'. How then does it teach Brahman? The *śāstra* reveals Brahman as the inner-Self, as not an object, by way of removing the difference of cognised, cogniser, cognition etc. which is superimposed by ignorance."

125 PP p.173, (MRI) p.289, (tr.) p.135f.

126 PP p.173, (MRI) p.289, (tr.) p.136.

127 PP p.174, (MRI) p.290, (tr.) p.136f.

128 The *Vivaraṇa*, p.415, (MRI) p.291, brings in *avidyāleśa* as an alternative explanation.

Postscript on Method

By way of conclusion I wish to summarise my views about the method of traditional Advaita. Firstly, it is impossible to understand the authors discussed here without recognising their profound commitment to the *śruti* as revelation. Though the word *śruti* refers to the Veda as a whole, it is the portion of the *śruti* known as Upaniṣads that constitutes the special focus of the Advaita tradition. The followers of Advaita consider that the Upaniṣads are the means of knowledge *(pramāṇa)* capable of revealing the metaphysical reality called Brahman. That reality is not an object of the senses, so it cannot be known through perception. Neither can it be known by inference, since inference depends upon the data of perception. Traditional Advaita is therefore centred upon the revealing words of the *śruti.*

Secondly, it is clearly the view of Śaṅkara and those disciples whom we have discussed, Sureśvara and Padmapāda, that the Upaniṣads do more than merely point out the existence of that metaphysical reality. The Upaniṣads also offer ways by which we can know that reality. The Upaniṣads employ various ways, or stratagems *(prakriyā),* to communicate it. Notable among these are the utilisation of cause and effect *(kāraṇa-kārya-prakriyā);* the analysis of the three states of experience: waking, dream and dreamless sleep *(avasthātraya-prakriyā);* and the analysis of the five "sheaths" *(pañcakośa-prakriyā).* The Upaniṣads frequently employ teachings that rely upon the relation of the First Cause, which is always both the efficient and the material cause, to its effects, in order to reveal That which is, ultimately, neither a cause nor an effect. They also refer to the three states of experience, to waking, dream and dreamless sleep, as a way of revealing That which underlies the three states but is never "touched" by those states or by the attributes belonging to those states. In the *Taittirīya* Upaniṣad there is the presentation of the five "sheaths" to discern the innermost Self as

Brahman. Thus the Upaniṣads employ various techniques. But the fundamental method of the Upaniṣads and of classical Advaita, I believe, is just one. It consists of the negation of superimposition together with the use of the implied meaning *(lakṣaṇā)* of certain significant words that can point to the nature of the reality that is not the object of the direct meaning of any word. Thus the basic method of the Upaniṣads, as understood by Śaṅkara and his disciples, can be seen to consist in negation coupled with the use of *lakṣaṇā.*

Thirdly, not only do the Upaniṣads teach the existence of the fundamental metaphysical reality, and also present various ways for its realisation, but in the eyes of Śaṅkara and his disciples the Upaniṣads can *directly* reveal the nature of that reality itself, through the implied meaning of certain words. To these Advaitins the Upaniṣads are more than "maps" revealing the existence of the goal and describing how to reach it; they can directly take the seeker to the goal, since there is no actual distance between the seeker and the sought, the true Self. Therefore the Upaniṣads are more than manuals of instruction; they are themselves capable of directly revealing the truth provided the seeker is sufficiently ready. And they can do this through the method of implication that is used along with negation. Since the *śruti* itself has this liberating capacity, meditative practices for Śaṅkara and his followers are more concerned with contemplating the *meaning* of what is revealed through the words of the Upaniṣads, and integrating that meaning into one's own existential self-understanding, than about the cultivation of yogic practices involving suppression of the mind leading to *nirvikalpasaṁādhi.* Contemplation, or assimilation *(nididhyāsana),* is about being rather than doing, for doing presupposes the agentship of the *jīva* whereas the Advaita contemplation does not of necessity involve such practices as control of the mind. Advaita contemplation involves the negation of superimpositions by knowledge, so as to see oneself as intrinsically free from all superimposed *upādhis.* In the centuries after Śaṅkara, *samādhi*-orientated practices were increasingly fostered onto Śaṅkara's Advaita when Maṇḍana's view about the role of the *śruti* and the need for its supplementation by other *sādhana* was incorporated into Śāṅkara Advaita by Vācaspati, who in turn linked that view to yogic *samādhi,* and taught that the *śruti* necessarily presents mediate *(parokṣa)* knowledge which must then be made immediate through disciplines such as the suppression of the mind leading to *samādhi.*

This *śruti-* centred method of Advaita, as we can see in the case of Śaṅkara and his disciples, requires a link between a pupil *(śiṣya)* and a guru, where the pupil hears the traditional teachings explained by the guru who should be learned in the scriptures *(śrotriya)* as well as established in the knowledge of Brahman *(brahmaniṣṭha).* At various places Śaṅkara speaks of the qualities required of the pupil, and in the *Upadeśasāhasrī* he also refers at length to the qualities required of the teacher of *Brahmavidyā.* The association between *śiṣya* and *ācārya* rests at the very heart of Indian spiritual life, and for Śaṅkara too the tradition of a received and, in turn, transmitted wisdom *(sampradāya)* occupies a central place in his outlook. We can see this played out in the legendary biographies of Śaṅkara, for all the *Śaṅkaravijayas* contain the episode of Śaṅkara meeting his guru Govindapāda, and by doing so he is shown to be connected to an illustrious lineage that extends back through Gauḍapāda to the seers Śuka and Vyāsa.[1] So the importance of traditional instruction, of hearing the teaching from a qualified teacher *(sampradāyavit),* is not to be overlooked, for it forms an integral part of the method of traditional Advaita. Consequently, one's own independent reading of the texts, without having received any instruction from a teacher who represents the *sampradāya,* does not form a part of the traditional Advaita method which is intended, after all, for the purpose of liberation.

A final point. With regard to the process of the negation of superimposition, I do not believe the *śruti* negates fictitious superimpositions. It is not the case that the *śruti,* as part of its technique *(prakriyā),* sets up imaginary superimpositions in order to negate them. Rather, the Upaniṣads negate superimpositions that empirically exist. Thus I do not believe that Īśvara is set up as some sort of fictitious entity merely to serve the higher purpose of negation. In the Upaniṣads Brahman is declared to be the efficient as well as the material cause of the objectively existing world. When Brahman is spoken of in the context of the causality of the world, it is Brahman as Īśvara that is referred to. The negation of *Īśvaratva* in Brahman is concomitant with the negation - or to be more precise the ascertainment of the *mithyātva* - of the relation of the effect to its material cause. For when the effect, the world, is found to be *mithyā,* the material and efficient causality of Brahman too is discovered to be *mithyā*. But even then, at this level of ultimate truth *(paramārthataḥ)*, it is less than accurate to say "Īśvara is negated". Rather, it is the Īśvara-ness of Brahman, the aspect of "rulership" etc. that are relational to the creatorship of a real world, that ultimately "disappears" *(apagata)*, leaving the unconditioned Awareness-Being, the *para* Brahman, appearing as, or being only apparently transformed *(vivarta)* into, the universe.

Thus in statements about superimposition and negation we should not down play the *Īśvaratva* aspect of the *para* Brahman and mistakenly believe that Īśvara is just a fiction posited for the purpose of negation. To do so ignore the undeniable existence of the *vyavahāra* world *(mithyā* though it proves to be upon inquiry). Thus the understanding of Advaita requires the correct appreciation of the domains of *vyavahāra* and *paramārtha*, and the making of a proper demarcation between each, while yet being able to appreciate, though perhaps not rationally explain, the seeming paradox of two simultaneous "levels", or perspectives, of truth. According to the tradition we have discussed, the liberated person continues to transact in the empirical world that is the manifestation of Īśvara, at the same time having the immediate knowledge that the untransformed, and thereby acosmic *(niṣprapañca)*, *para* Brahman, is the highest truth.

---

1 J. Bader, *Conquest of the Four Quarters: Traditional Accounts of the Life of Śaṅkara*, op.cit., p.51, 57.

Select Bibliography

1. SANSKRIT TEXTS AND TRANSLATIONS

(a) Gauḍapāda

The Āgamaśāstra of Gauḍapāda. Bhattacharya, Vidhushekhara (ed. and tr.). Delhi: Motilal Banarsidass, 1989 (reprint).

Gauḍapāda-Kārikā. Karmarkar, R.D. (ed. and tr.). Poona: Bhandarkar Oriental Research Institute, 1973.

Svayamprakāśānanda Sarasvatī. *Mitākṣarā: a gloss on Śrī Gauḍapāda Ācharya's Māndūkya Kārikas.* Benares: Chowkhambā Sanskrit Book Depot (Haridās Sanskrit Series No. 1), 1910.

(b) Śaṅkara

texts

Bṛhadāraṇyakopaniṣad with commentary of Śaṅkara, the subcommentary of Ānandagiri and the ṭippaṇī of Viṣṇudevānanda Giri. Two vols. Rishikesh: Kailās Āśram (n.d.)

Brahmasūtra-Śāṅkarabhāṣyam. Edited by J.L. Shastri. Delhi: Motilal Banarsidass, 1980..

Māṇḍūkyopaniṣad with the commentary of Śaṅkara, the subcommentary of Ānandagiri and the ṭippaṇī of Viṣṇudevānanda Giri. Rishikesh: Kailās Āśram (n.d.)

Shrī Shankarāchārya's Upadeshasāhasrī with the gloss Padayojanikā by Shrī Rāmatīrtha. Edited by D.V. Gokhale. Bombay: The Gujarati Printing Press, 1917.

Shri Shankarabhagavatpada's Upadeshasahasri with the Tika of Shri Anandagiri Acharya. Edited by S. Subramanyasastri. Varanasi: Mahesh Research Institute, 1978.

Upaniṣadbhāṣyam Vol. 1 Edited by S. Subrahmanyashastri. Varanasi: Mahesh Research Institute, 1979.

Upaniṣadbhāṣyam Vol. 11 Edited by S. Subrahmanyashastri. Varanasi: Mahesh Research Institute, 1982.

Upaniṣadbhāṣyam Vol. 111 Edited by S. Subrahmanyashastri. Varanasi: Mahesh Research Institute, 1986.

Works of Śaṅkarācārya in Original Sanskrit, vol. 1. *Ten Principal Upaniṣads with Śāṅkarabhāṣya.* Delhi: Motilal Banarsidass, 1978.

Works of Śaṅkarācārya in Original Sanskrit, vol.11. *Bhagavadgītā with Śāṅkarabhāṣya.* Delhi: Motilal Banarsidass, 1978.

translations

Bhagavadgītā With the Commentary of Śaṅkarācārya. Translated by Swami Gambhirananda. Calcutta: Advaita Ashrama, 1984.

The Bṛhadāraṇyaka Upaniṣad with the commentary of Śaṅkarācārya. Translated by Swami Mādhavānanda. Calcutta: Advaita Ashrama, (5th Ed.) 1975.

Brahma-sūtra-bhāṣya of Śrī Śaṅkarācārya. Translated by Swami Gambhirananda. Calcutta: Advaita Ashrama, 1977.

Chāndogya Upaniṣad With the Commentary of Śrī Śaṅkarācārya. Translated by Swami Gambhirananda. Calcutta: Advaita Ashrama (n.d.).

Eight Upaniṣads With the Commentary of Śaṅkarācārya. Two Vols. Translated by Swami Gambhirananda. Calcutta: Advaita Ashrama, 1977.

"That Thou Art" Chapter XVIII of The Thousand Teachings (Upadeśasāhasrī) of Śrī Śaṃkara. Translated by A.J. Alston. 3rd. ed. London: Shanti Sadan, 1982.

A Thousand Teachings. The Upadeśasāhasrī of Śaṅkara. Translated with Introduction and Notes by S. Mayeda. Tokyo: University of Tokyo Press, 1979.

Upadeśasāhasrī of Srī Sankarāchārya: A Thousand Teachings in two parts-prose and poetry. Translated by Swami Jagadānanda. 7th. ed. Madras: Sri Ramakrishna Math, 1984.

Vedānta-Sūtras with the commentary by Śaṅkarācārya. Translated by George Thibaut. Two Vols. (Sacred Books of the East vols. 34 and 38) Delhi: Motilal Banarsidass, 1980 [reprint of OUP 1890].

(c) Sureśvara

Bṛhadāraṇyakopaniṣad Bhāṣyavārtikam with the commentary of Ānandagiri. Vol. I. Edited by S. Subrahmanya Shastri. Varanasi: Mahesh Research Institute, 1982.

Bṛhadāraṇyakopaniṣad Bhāṣyavārtikam with the commentary of Ānandagiri. Vol. II. Edited by S. Subrahmanya Shastri. Varanasi: Mahesh Research Institute, 1990.

Nyāyakalpalatikā: a commentary on the Bṛhadāraṇyakopaniṣad-bhāṣya-vārttika by Vidyāsāgara Ānandapūrṇa Munīndra. Two Vols Edited by V. Subrahmanya Sastri. Tirupati: Kendrīya Sanskrit Vidyāpīṭa, 1975.

The Naiṣkarmyasiddhi of Sureśvarācārya with the commentary of Jñānottama. Edited by G.A. Jacob. Revised Edition by M. Hiriyanna. Poona: Bhandarkar Oriental Research Institute, 1980.

The Naiṣkarmyasiddhi of Sureśvara. Edited and translated by R. Balasubramanian Madras: Radhakrishnan Institute for Advanced Study in Philosophy, University of Madras, 1988.

Naishkarmya-Siddhi of Sri Sureśvarācārya with the commentary Kleśāpahāriṇī by Śrī Saccidānandendra Sarasvatī. Holenarsipur: Adhyatma Prakasha Karyalaya, 1968.

Naiṣkarmyasiddhi of Śrī Sureśvarācārya. Translated by S.S. Raghavachar. Mysore: Univ. of Mysore, 1965.

The Saṁbandha-Vārtika of Sureśvarācārya. Edited and translated by T.M.P. Mahadevan. Madras: University of Madras, 1972 [second edition].

Sureśvara's Taittirīyopaniṣad-Bhāṣyavārtikam. Translated by J.M. van Boetzelaer. Leiden: E.J. Brill, 1971.

Sureśvara's Vārtika on Yājñavalkya-Maitreyī Dialogue. Translated by Shoun Hino. Delhi: Motilal Banarsidass, 1982.

Sureśvara's Vārtika on Madhu Brāhmaṇa. Translated by K.P. Jog and Shoun Hino. Delhi: Motilal Banarsidass, 1988.

Sureśvara's Vārtika on Aśva and Aśvamedha Brāhmaṇa. Translated by Shoun Hino and K.P. Jog. Delhi: Motilal Banarsidass, 1990.

Sureśvara's Vārtika on Udgītha Brāhmaṇa. Translated by K P. Jog and Shoun Hino. Delhi: Motilal Banarsidass, 1991.

Sureśvara's Vārtika on Puruṣavidha Brāhmaṇa. Translated by K.P. Jog and Shoun Hino. Delhi: Motilal Banarsidass, 1993.

Sureśvara's Vārtika on Saptānna Brāhmaṇa. Translated by Shoun Hino and K.P. Jog. Delhi: Motilal Banarsidass, 1995.

Sureśvara's Vārtika on Śiśu and Mūrtāmūrta Brāhmaṇa. Translated by K.P. Jog and Shoun Hino. Delhi: Motilal Banarsidass, 1996.

The Taittirīyopaniṣad-Bhāṣya-Vārtika of Sureśvara. Edited and translated by R. Balasubramanian. Madras: Radhakrishnan Institute for Advanced Study in Philosophy, University of Madras, 1984 [revised ed.].

(d) Padmapāda

Pañcapādikā of Śrī Padmapādācārya with the commentaries Prabodhapariśodhinī of Ātmasvarūpa and Tārtparyārthadyotinī of Vijñānātman and Pañcapādikāvivaraṇa of Śrī Prakāśātman with Tātparyadīpikā of Citsukhācārya and Bhāvaprakāśikā of Nṛsimhāśramin. Edited by S. Srirāma Śāstrī and S.R. Krishnamurthi Śāstrī. Vol.1 comprising 1 and 2 Varṇakas. Tirupati: Kendriya Sanskrit Vidyapeetha, 1985 [reprint of first two Varṇakas from the Madras Government Oriental Series CLV, 1958.].

Srī Padmapādācārya's Pañcapādikā with the commentaries Vivaraṇa by Śrī Prakāśātmamuni, Tattvadīpana by Śrī Akhaṇḍānandamuni and Ṛjuvivaraṇa by Śrī Viṣṇubhaṭṭopādhyāya. Edited by S. Subrahmanyaśāstrī. Varanasi: Mahesh Research Institute, 1992.

The Pañcapādikā of Padmapāda. Translated by D. Venkataramiah. Baroda: (Gaekwad's Oriental Series No. CVII) Oriental Institute, 1948.

2. SECONDARY SOURCES

Alston, A.J. *Early Post-Śaṃkara Advaita* [unpublished Ph.D thesis] Benares: Benares Hindu University, 1963.

Alston, A.J. "Śaṃkara in East and West Today" [unpublished article, forthcoming in a Feliciation volume for Richard de Smet S.J., ed. by Bradley Malkovsky].

Bader, J. *Meditation in Śaṅkara's Vedānta.* New Delhi: Aditya Prakashan, 1990.

·Bader, J. *Conquest of the Four Quarters: Traditional Accounts of the Life of Śaṅkara.* Unpublished Ph.D Thesis. The Australian National University, 1991.

Balasubramanian, R. *Advaita Vedānta.* Madras: Centre for Advanced Study in Philosophy, University of Madras, 1976.

Balasubramanian, R. *A Study of the Brahmasiddhi of Maṇḍana Miśra.* Varanasi: Chaukhamba Amarabharati Prakasan, 1983.

Balasubramanian, R (ed.). *The Tradition of Advaita: Essays in Honour of Bhāṣyabhāvajña V.R. Kalyānasundara Śāstrī.* Delhi: Munshiram Manoharlal, 1994.

Basham, A.L. (ed.) *A Cultural History of India.* Oxford: Oxford University Press, 1975.

Bhattacharya, Vidhushekhara. "The Gauḍapāda-Kārikā on the Māṇḍūkya Upaniṣad", *Proceedings of the Second Oriental Conference, Calcutta, Jan. 28-Feb.1, 1922.* Calcutta: Calcutta University Press, 1922.

Cardona, G. "On reasoning from Anvaya and Vyatireka in Early Advaita", in D. Malvania and N.J. Shah (ed), *Studies in Indian Philosophy. A Memorial Volume in Honour of Pandit Suklaji Sanghvi.* Ahmedabad: L.D. Institute of Indology, 1981.

Chatterjee, A.K. *The Yogācāra Idealism.* Delhi: Motilal Banarsidass, 1975.

Clooney, Francis X. *Theology after Vedānta.* Delhi: Sri Satguru Publications, 1993.

Comans, Michael. "The Essential Definition of Brahman. Taittirīya Upaniṣad 2.1.1.", *The Voice of Śaṅkara. A Quarterly Journal of Advaita-Vedānta.* (Madras) Vol. 11, no.3, 1986 y no.4, 1987.

Comans, Michael. *Advaitāmoda by Vāsudevaśāstrī Abhyankar: A Study of Advaita and Viśiṣṭādvaita.* Delhi: Sri Satguru Publications, 1988.

Comans, Michael. "Jñānasvarūpa is Ātmasvarūpa: Advaitins Respond to Rāmānuja's Critique" , *Journal of Indian Philosophy,* vol. 17, no. 2, 1989.

Comans, Michael. "The Self in Deep Sleep according to Advaita and Viśiṣṭādvaita", *Journal of Indian Philosophy,* vol. 18, no.1, 1990.

Comans, Michael. "The Question of the Importance of *Samādhi* in Modern and Classical Advaita Vedānta", *Philosophy East and West,* vol 43, no.1, 1993.

Comans, Michael. "Śaṅkara and the Prasaṅkhyānavāda", *Journal of Indian Philosophy,* vol. 24, 1996.

Comans, Michael. *Extracting the Essence of the Śruti: The Śrutisārasamuddharaṇa of Toṭakācārya.* Delhi: Motilal Banarsidass, 1996.

Comans, Michael. "Later Vedānta", in B. Carr and I. Mahalingam (ed.), *Companion Encyclopedia of Asian Philosophy,* London: Routledge, 1997.

Conio, C. *The Philosophy of the Māṇḍūkya Kārikā.* Varanasi: Bharatiya Vidya Prakashan, 1971.

Conze, Edward (tr). *The Perfection of Wisdom in Eight Thousand Lines and Its Verse Summary.* Berkeley: The Four Seasons Foundation, 1973.

Conze, Edward. *Buddhist Thought in India.* London: Allen and Unwin, 1983.

Copleston, F.C. *Aquinas.* Middlesex: Penguin Books, 1970.

Cross, Stephen. *Continuities and Contrasts: Four Concepts of Mahayana Buddhism - Pratitya-samutpada, Sunyata, Paratantra-svabhava, Alaya-vijnana.* (Honours) Thesis. The University of Sydney. 1996.

Dasgupta, S.N. *A History of Indian Philosophy.* Vol 1, Delhi: Motilal Banarsidass, 1975 [reprint from Cambridge Univ. Press, 1922].

D'Sa, Francis X (Ed.). *Word Index to Śaṅkara's Gītābhāṣya.* Pune: Institute for the Study of Religion, 1985.

Datta, D.M. *The Six Ways of Knowing.* Calcutta: University of Calcutta, 1972 [2nd Ed.1960].

De Smet, R.V. *The Theological Method of Śaṃkara.* Rome: Pontifical Gregorian University. Unpublished Dissertation, 1953.

De Smet, R V. "The Logical Structure of "Tattvamasi" According to Suresvara's Naiṣkarmya Siddhi", *The Indian Philosophical Quarterly,* vol. 33, no.4, Jan. 1961.

De Smet, R V. "Śaṅkara's Non-Dualism (Advaita-Vāda)" in *Religious Hinduism,* by Jesuit Scholars. Allahabad: St Paul Society, 1968. And subsequently, De Smet, R. and Neuner J. (eds.), *Religious Hinduism* (fourth revised edition). Bombay: St Pauls, 1997.

De Smet, R V. "Śaṅkara and Aquinas on Creation", *Indian Philosophical Annual.* University of Madras, vol. 6, 1970.

De Smet, R V. "Towards an Indian View of the Person" in Margaret Chatterjee (ed.), *Contemporary Indian Philosophy,* series 11. London: Allen and Unwin, 1974.

Deussen, Paul. *The Philosophy of the Upanishads.* New York: Dover, 1966.

Deutsch, Eliot. *Advaita Vedānta: A Philosophical Reconstruction.* Honolulu: University Press of Hawaii, 1973 [reprint of 1969].

Devaraja, N.K. *An Introduction to Śaṅkara's Theory of Knowledge.* Delhi: Motilal Banarsidass, 1972 [2nd Ed.].

The Diamond Jubilee Souvenir of the Advaita Sabha Kumbakonam (Advaitasabhā ṣaṣṭhyabdapūrti ratnotsava śubhanibandhaḥ). Kumbakonam, 1956.

Eliade, M. *Yoga: Immortality and Freedom.* Princeton: Princeton Univ. Press (Bollingen Series LVI), 1973.

Eliade, M. (ed) *Encyclopedia of Religion,* Macmillan and Free Press, 1987.

Feuerstein, Georg. *The Philosophy of Classical Yoga.* New York: St. Martin's Press, 1980.

Fort, Andrew. O. *The Self and Its States.* Delhi: Motilal Banarsidass, 1990.

Fort, Andrew. O. "Knowing Brahman while Embodied: Śaṅkara on Jīvanmukti", *Journal of Indian Philosophy,* vol.19, no. 4, 1991.

Fort, Andrew. O., and Mumme, Patricia, Y. (ed.). *Living Liberation in Hindu Thought.* Albany: State University of New York Press, 1996.

Fort, Andrew. O. *Jīvanmukti in Transformation: Embodied Liberation in Advaita and Neo-Vedānta.* State Univ. of New York Press, 1998.

Gangolli, D.B. *Sri Satchidanandendra Saraswati Swamiji.* Holenarsipur: Adhyatma Prakasha Karyalaya, 1997.

Goeller, Richard. "Aristotle's View of Substance", *Mananam: a Journal of Vedānta.* Vol. IV, No.3, 1981.

Gokhale, V.V. "The Vedānta-Philosophy Described by Bhavya in his *Madhyamakahṛdaya.*" *Indo-Iranian Journal,* vol.2, no.3, 1958.

Gokhale, V.V. "Masters of Buddhism Adore the Brahman through Non-Adoration". *Indo-Iranian Journal,* vol.5, no.4, 1962 .

Gonda, J. *Change and Continuity in Indian Religion.* Delhi: Munshiram Manoharlal, 1985 [first published 1965].

Gough, A.E. *The Philosophy of the Upanishads and Ancient Indian Metaphysics.* London: Kegan Paul, Trench, Trubner and Co., 1891.

Hacker, Paul. "Eigentumlichkeiten der Lehre und Terminologie Śaṅkaras: Avidyā, Nāmarūpa, Māyā, Īśvara", in L. Schmithausen (ed), *Kleine Schriften,* Weisbaden: Franz Steiner, 1978.

Halbfass, W. *India and Europe.* Albany: State University of New York Press, 1988.

Halbfass, W. *Tradition and Reflection.* Albany: State University of New York Press, 1991.

Halbfass, W. (ed.). *Philology and Confrontation: Paul Hacker on Traditional and Modern Vedānta.* Albany: State University of New York Press, 1995.

Huntington, C.W. *The Emptiness of Emptiness.* Honolulu: University of Hawaii Press, 1989.

Inada, Kenneth K. *Nāgārjuna: Mūlamadhyamakakārikā.* Tokyo: The Hokuseido Press, 1970.

Ingalls, Daniel H.H. "Śaṃkara on the Question: Whose is avidyā?, *Philosophy East and West*, 3, 1953.

Ingalls, Daniel H.H. "Śaṃkara's Arguments Against the Buddhists", *Philosophy East and West*, 3, 1954.

Ingalls, Daniel H.H. "The Study of Śaṃkarācārya", *Annals of the Bhandarkar Oriental Research Institute*, 33 1952.

Isayeva, Natalia. *Shankara and Indian Philosophy*. Delhi: Sri Satguru Publications, 1993.

Jha, Ganganatha. *Pūrva-Mīmāṁsā in its Sources*, Varanasi: The Banaras Hindu University, 1964.

Kane, P.V. *History of Dharmasastra*, Poona: Bhandarkar Oriental Research Institute, 1930-62.

King, R. *Early Advaita Vedānta and Buddhism: The Mahāyāna Context of the Gauḍapādīya-kārikā*. Albany: State Univ. of New York Press, 1995.

King, R. "Early Advaita Vedānta: The Date and Authorship of the Gauḍapādīyakārikā", *Indo-Iranian Journal* 38, 1995.

Krishna Warrier, A.G. *God in Advaita*. Simla: Indian Institute of Advanced Study, 1977.

Krishnaswamy Iyer, K.A. *Vedanta or The Science of Reality*. Bangalore: Adhyatma Prakasha Karyalaya, 1991 [Third Ed. First Ed. 1930].

Kunjunni Raja, K. *Indian Theories of Meaning*. Madras: The Adyar Library and Research Centre, 1977 [reprint of Ist Ed. 1963].

Lamotte, E. *History of Indian Buddhism - from the origins to the Śaka Era*. Translated from the French by Sara Webb-Boin. Louvain: Peeters Press, 1988 (original French Edition, 1958).

Lindtner, C. *Nagarjuniana: Studies in the Writings and Philosophy of Nāgārjuna.* Delhi: Motilal Banarsidass, 1990 [reprint].

Lindtner, C. "Remarks on the Gauḍapādīya-Kārikās", *Indo-Iranian Journal* 28, 1985.

Lott, Eric. *Vedantic Approaches to God.* London: Macmillan, 1980.

Mahadevan, T.M.P. *Gauḍapāda: A Study in Early Advaita.* Madras: University of Madras, 1960 [3rd edition].

Mahadevan, T.M.P. (ed), *Preceptors of Advaita.* Secunderabad: Sri Kanci Kamakoti Sankara Mandir, 1968.

Mahadevan, T.M.P, (Ed.). *Word Index to the Brahma-Sūtra-Bhāṣya of Śaṅkara.* Two Vols. Madras: Centre of Advanced Study in Philosophy, Univ. of Madras. 1971-1973.

Mainkar, T.G. *The Making of the Vedānta.* Delhi: Ajanta Publications, 1980.

Malkani, G.R.; Das, R.; Murti, .T.R.V. *Ajñāna.* London, Luzac ų Co., 1933 (Calcutta Oriental Series, 26).

Malkovsky, Bradley. "The Personhood of Śaṁkara's *Para Brahman*", *The Journal of Religion*, Volume 77, Number 4, October 1997.

Markandeya Sastri, C. *Sureśvara's Contribution to Advaita,* Vemur: Sundari Samskrita Vidyalaya, n.d.

Matilal, B.K. "Gauḍapāda" in M. Eliade (ed), *Encyclopedia of Religion,* Macmillan and Free Press, 1987.

Mayeda, S. "The Advaita Theory of Perception", *Wiener Zeitschrift fur die Kunde Sudasiens,* XXII-X111 1968-69.

Mayeda, S. "On the Author of the Māṇḍūkya Upaniṣad and the Gauḍapādīyabhāṣya", *The Adyar Library Bulletin,* Dr V. Raghavan Felicitation Volume, Vols. XXXI-XXXII, 1967-68.

Mayeda, S. "Śaṃkara and Sureśvara: their Exegetical Method to Interpret the Great Sentence '*tat tvam asi*'", *The Adyar Library Bulletin,* vol. 44-45, 1980-81.

Murti, T.R.V. *The Central Philosophy of Buddhism.* London: Allen and Unwin 1974 [reprint].

Murty, K.S. *Revelation and Reason in Advaita Vedānta.* New York: Columbia University Press, 1959.

Nagao, Gadjin. *The Foundational Standpoint of Mādhyamika Philosophy.* Translated by John P. Keenan. Delhi: Sri Satguru Publications, 1990 [reprint].

Nagao, Gadjin M. *Mādhyamika and Yogācāra.* Edited and translated by L.S. Kawamura. Delhi: Sri Satguru Publications, 1991 [reprint].

Nakamura, Hajime. "The Vijñānavāda Theory as Presented in the Fourth Chapter of the Māṇḍūkyakārikā". V. Raghavan (ed), *Proceedings of the First International Sanskrit Conference, March 26-31, 1972.* Delhi: Ministry of Education and Social Welfare, 1981, Vol.4.

Nakamura, Hijime. *A History of Early Vedānta Philosophy.* Delhi: Motilal Bannasidass, 1983.

Nakamura, Hijime. *Indian Buddhism: A Survey with Bibliographical Notes.* Delhi: Motilal Banarsidass, 1989 [reprint].

Olivelle, Patrick. *Renunciation in Hinduism: a Medieval Debate,* Publications of the De Nobili Research Library, vol. XIII-IX, 1986-87.

Olivelle, Patrick. *The Āśrama System.* New York: Oxford University Press, 1993.

Otto, Rudolf. *Mysticism East and West.* New York: Living Age Books, 1957.

Pande, Govind Chandra. *Life and Thought of Śaṅkarācārya.* Delhi: Motilal Banarsidass, 1994.

Pandey, S.L. *Pre-Śaṁkara Advaita Philosophy.* Allahabad: Darshan Peeth, 1974.

Pappu, S.S. Rama Rao (Ed.). *Perspectives on Vedānta: Essays in Honor of Professor P.T. Raju.* Leiden: E.J. Brill, 1988.

Phillips, Stephen. "Padmapāda's illusion argument", *Philosophy East and West.* Vol.37, no.1, 1987.

Potter, Karl. H. *Encyclopedia of Indian Philosophies (vol. 111): Advaita Vedānta up to Śaṃkara and His Pupils.* Delhi: Motilal Banarsidass, 1981 [reprint Princeton, 1981].

Rambachan, Anantanand. *Accomplishing the Accomplished: The Vedas as a Source of Valid Knowledge in Śaṅkara.* Hawaii: University of Hawaii Press: Monographs of the Society for Asian and Comparative Philosophy, no. 10. 1991.

Robinson, Richard H. *Early Mādhyamika in India and China.* Delhi: Motilal Banarsidass, 1978.

Ruegg, David. S. *The Literature of the Madhyamaka School of Philosophy in India.* A History of Indian Literature vol. VII. Wiesbaden: Otto Harrassowitz, 1981.

Rukmani, T.S. "The Problem of the Authorship of the *Yogasūtrabhāṣyavivaraṇam*", *Journal of Indian Philosophy,* vol.20, no.4, 1992.

Rukmani, T.S. "Śaṅkara's views on *Yoga* in the *Brahmasūtrabhāṣya* in the light of the Authorship of the *Yogasūtrabhāṣya-vivaraṇa*", *Journal of Indian Philosophy*, vol.21, no.4, 1993.

Rukmani, T.S. "The *Yogasūtrabhāṣyavivaraṇa* is not a Work of Śaṅkarācārya the Author of the *Brahmasūtrabhāṣya*", *Journal of Indian Philosophy*, vol. 26, no. 3, 1998.

Saksena, S.K. *Nature of Consciousness in Hindu Philosophy*. Delhi: Motilal Banarsidass, 1971 [2nd Ed.].

Sangharakshita, Bhikshu. "Buddhism", in A.L. Basham (ed.) *A Cultural History of India*. Oxford: Oxford University Press, 1975.

Sarasvati, Satchidanandendra. *Mūlāvidyā Nirāsaḥ; athavā Śrī Śaṅkara Hṛdayam*. Holenarśipur: Adhyatma Prakasa Karyalaya, 1929. Translated by A.J. Alston under the title: *The Heart of Śaṃkara*. London: Shanti Sadan, 1993.

Sarasvati, Satchidanandendra. *Vedānta-prakriyā-pratyabhijñā*. Holenarsipur: Adhyatma Prakasa Karyalaya, 1964. Translated from the Sanskrit by A.J. Alston under the title: *The Method of the Vedanta*. London and New York: Kegan Paul International, 1989.

Sarasvati, Satchidanandendra. *Misconceptions about Śaṅkara*. Holenarsipur: Adhyatma Prakasa Karyalaya, 1973.

Schmithausen, Lambert. *Ālayavijñāna -On the Origin and the Early Development of a Central Concept of Yogācāra Philosophy* (Two vols.). Tokyo: The International Institute for Buddhist Studies, (Studia Philologica Buddhica Monograph Series 1Va) 1987.

Shastri, D.N. *The Philosophy of Nyāya-Vaiśeṣika and its Conflict with The Buddhist Digṅāga School*. Varanasi: Bharatiya Vidya Prakashan, 1976.

Sprung, Mervyn (ed.) *The Problem of Two Truths in Buddhism and Vedānta.* Holland: D. Reidel, 1973.

Sprung, Mervyn. *Lucid Exposition of the Middle Way.* London: Routledge and Kegan Paul, 1979.

Stanley, R. *A Translation of the Vijñaptimātratāsiddhi of Vasubandhu: including Vasubandhu's Viṃśatikā (and vṛtti) and Triṃśika and Sthiramati's Triṃśikabhāṣya.* Unpublished Honours Thesis, Australian National University, 1983.

Stanley, R. *A Study of the Madhyāntavibhāga-bhāṣya-ṭīkā,* unpublished Ph.D. thesis, Australian National University, 1988.

Stcherbatsky, Th. *The Central Conception of Buddhism and the Meaning of the word "Dharma".* First published 1923 by the Royal Asiatic Society. Reprinted, Delhi: Motilal Banarsidass, 1970.

Suzuki, D.T (tr). *The Lankavatara Sutra: A Mahayana Text.* London: Routledge, 1932.

Suzuki, D.T. *Studies in the Lankavatara Sutra.* London: Routledge and Kegan Paul, 1957 (reprint).

Taber, John. *Transformative Philosophy: A Study of Śaṅkara, Fichte, and Heidegger.* Delhi: Sri Satguru Publications, 1992 (reprint from Hawaii University Press, 1983).

Thrasher, Allen.W. "Maṇḍana Miśra's Theory of Vikalpa", *Wiener Zeitschrift fur die Kunde Sudasiens,* XXII, 1978.

Thrasher, Allen. W. *The Advaita Vedānta of Brahma-siddhi.* Delhi: Motilal Banarsidass, 1993.

Vaidya, P.L. (ed.). *Madhyamakaśāstra of Nāgārjuna with the commentary Prasannapadā by Candrakīrti.* Buddhist Sanskrit Texts no.

10. Darbhanga: The Mithila Institute of Post-Graduate Studies and Research, 1960.

Vaidya, P.L. (ed.). *Aṣṭasāhasrikā Prajñāpāramitā.* Buddhist Sanskrit Texts No. 4. Darbhanga: The Mithila Institute, 1960.

Vaidya, P.L. (ed.). *Saddharmalaṅkāvatārasūtram.* Buddhist Sanskrit Texts no. 3. Dharbanga: The Mithila Institute, 1963.

Vetter, Tilmann. "Māṇḍūkya-Upaniṣad-Bhāṣya und Gauḍapādīya-Kārikā-Bhāṣya", *Studien Zur Lehre Und Entwicklung Śaṅkaras.* Vienna: Publications of the De Nobili Research Library, vol. VI, 1979.

Warder, A.K. *Indian Buddhism.* Delhi: Motilal Banarsidass, (2nd revised edition) 1980.

Warder, A.K. "Dharmas and Data", *Journal of Indian Philosophy,* vol.1, 1971.

Werner, Karel (ed.). *Love Divine: Studies in* Bhakti *and Devotional Mysticism.* Durham Indological Series No. 3. Surrey: Curzon Press, 1993.

Williams, P. *Mahāyāna Buddhism: The Doctrinal Foundations.* London: Routledge, 1989.

Wood, T.E. *The Māṇḍūkya Upaniṣad and the Āgama Śāstra: an Investigation into the Meaning of the Vedānta.* Delhi: Motilal Banarsidass, 1992 [reprint Hawaii 1990].

Index